W9-DDU-946

The Costa Rican Catholic Church,
Social Justice, and the Rights of Workers,
1979–1996

Editions SR/Éditions SR

Editions SR/Éditions SR is a general series of books in the study of religion, encompassing the fields of study of the constituent societies of the Canadian Corporation for Studies in Religion/Corporation canadienne des sciences religieuses. These societies are: Canadian Society of Biblical Studies/Société canadienne des études bibliques; Canadian Society of Church Historic Studies/Association canadienne des études patristiques; Canadian Society for Study of Religion/Société canadienne pour l'étude de la religion.

General Editor: *Theodore de Bruyn*

EDITIONS SR
VOLUME 30

The Costa Rican Catholic Church, Social Justice, and the Rights of Workers, 1979–1996

Dana Sawchuk

Published for the Canadian Corporation for Studies in Religion/
Corporation Canadienne des Sciences Religieuses
by Wilfrid Laurier University Press
2004

This book has been published with the help of a grant from the Canadian Federation for the Humanities and Social Sciences, through the Aid to Scholarly Publications Programme, using funds provided by the Social Sciences and Humanities Research Council of Canada. We acknowledge the financial support of the Government of Canada through the Book Publishing Industry Development Program for our publishing activities. We acknowledge the Government of Ontario through the Ontario Media Development Corporation's Ontario Book Initiative.

Library and Archives Canada Cataloguing in Publication

Sawchuk, Dana M. (Dana Marie), 1968–
    The Costa Rican Catholic Church, social justice, and the rights of workers, 1979–1996 / Dana Sawchuk.

(Editions SR ; v. 30)
Co-published by the Canadian Corporation for Studies in Religion / Corporation canadienne des sciences religieuses.

Includes bibliographical references and index.
ISBN 0-88920-445-4

    1. Church and labour—Costa Rica—History—20th century. 2. Labour movement—Costa Rica—History—20th century. 3. Social justice—Costa Rica—History—20th century. I. Canadian Corporation for Studies in Religion. II Title. III. Series

BX1436.2.S28 2004   261.8'5   C2004-904220-3

Cover design by Leslie Macredie. Photograph of the front of La Basilica de Nuestra Señora de Los Angeles, Cartago, Costa Rica, courtesy Unicorn Multimedia. The front cover photograph with children depicts living conditions on a Costa Rican banana plantation and is used courtesy of Nick Shaw/Banana Link.

Text design by P.J. Woodland.

Every reasonable effort has been made to acquire permission for copyright material used in this text, and to acknowledge all such indebtedness accurately. Any errors and omissions called to the publisher's attention will be corrected in future printings.

Printed in Canada

Order from:
Wilfrid Laurier University Press
Wilfrid Laurier University
Waterloo, Ontario, Canada N2L 3C5
www.wlupress.wlu.ca

To David,
and in memory of Dex Michael Di Meo

Contents

Abbreviations

ASBANA	Asociación de Bananeros Nacionales [National Banana Association]
ASEPROLA	Asociación Servicios de Promoción Laboral [Association for Labour Promotion Services]
BANDECO	Banana Development Corporation
CCSS	Caja Costarricense de Seguro Social [Costa Rican Social Security Bureau]
CEBs	comunidades eclesiales de base [base ecclesial communities]
CECODERS	Centro Coordinador de Evangelización y Realidad Social [Coordinating Centre for Evangelization and Social Reality]
CECOR	Conferencia Episcopal de Costa Rica [Costa Rican Episcopal Conference]
CELAM	Consejo Episcopal Latinoamericano [Latin American Episcopal Council]
CIDA	Canadian International Development Agency
CIMA	Consejo Intermagisterial Asociado [Associated Inter-Magisterial Council]
CONEL	Comisión Nacional Episcopal de Laicos [National Episcopal Commission of Laity]
CPT	Consejo Permanente de los Trabajadores [Permanent Workers' Council]
CUT	Confederación Unitaria de Trabajadores [Unitary Workers' Confederation]
DEI	Departamento Ecuménico de Investigaciones [Ecumenical Research Department]
ESJ23	Escuela Social Juan XXIII [John XXIII Social School]
FOLSA	Frente de Organizaciones Laborales del Sector Agropecuario [Front of Labour Organizations of the Agricultural Sector]
FOSSS	Frente de Organizaciones Sindicales del Sector Salud [Front of Health Sector Union Organizations]
FSLN	Frente Sandinista de Liberación Nacional [Sandinista National Liberation Front]
GDP	Gross Domestic Product
GNP	Gross National Product

HdT	Hermandades de Trabajo [Brotherhood of Workers]
ICFTU	International Confederation of Free Trade Unions
IFIM	Instituto de Formación Integral Mixto [Co-ed Institute for Integrated Training]
ILO	International Labour Organization
IMF	International Monetary Fund
ITAC	Instituto Teológico de América Central [Central American Theological Institute]
ITCO	Instituto de Tierras y Colonización [Lands and Colonization Institute]
JOC	Juventud Católica Obrera [Young Catholic Workers]
LEO	Liga Espiritual Obrera [Workers' Spiritual League]
PINDECO	Piñas de Costa Rica [Pineapples of Costa Rica]
PLN	Partido Liberación Nacional [National Liberation Party]
PRN	Partido Rescate Nacional [National Recovery Party]
PUN	Partido Unión Nacional [National Union Party]
PUSC	Partido Unidad Social Cristiana [Social Christian Unity Party]
SEDAC	Secretariado Episcopal de América Central y Panamá [Episcopal Secretariat of Central America and Panama]
USAID	United States Agency for International Development

Acknowledgments

M any people in many places generously lent me their time, assistance, and support while I was writing this book. At the outset, I must thank the residents of Finca 11 and Finca 6 in Río Frío, Sarapiquí, Costa Rica. It was they who, long before I had the idea to undertake a formal investigation of the Costa Rican Catholic Church, introduced me to their beautiful country with warmth and hospitality.

The success of my eventual research in Costa Rica was guaranteed by the collegial support and friendship of several Costa Rican scholars, and especially Rosa María Pochet, J. Amando Robles, and Erick Solera. They encouraged me with their genuine enthusiasm and enlightened me with their insightful comments on my project. For their continued friendship and hospitality during all my trips to Costa Rica, I must also thank Rosmery Durán Cosio, *mi segunda mamá* Anneth Quiros, and the Quesada Arias family. Many of my best memories of Costa Rica are associated with these dear friends.

The friendly and knowledgeable staff members at several Costa Rican institutions, libraries, and archives were also always willing to help *la machita* from Canada with any number of tasks—especially photocopying! I am particularly grateful to those people associated with the Instituto de Investigaciones Sociales at the Universidad de Costa Rica, the Archivo Curia Metropolitana, *Eco Católico*, the Conferencia Episcopal de Costa Rica, the Biblioteca Nacional Miguel Obregón, and the libraries at the Universidad de Costa Rica and the Universidad Nacional de Costa Rica.

Of course, there would be no book at all if it were not for the co-operation of the Catholic Church agents I interviewed. Without exception, they were forthright with their comments and generous with their time. In particular, many of them went out of their way to help me attain the information, contacts, and even lodging I sought. Deserving of special mention in this regard are Hernán Hermosilla and Gustavo Blanco of the Asociación Servicios de Promoción Laboral, Padre Eduardo Ramírez in Limón, Padre Claudio Solano of the Escuela Social Juan XXIII, Padre Jesús Doncel in Río Frío, and Mario Solis of the Centro Coordinador de Evangelización y Realidad Social.

In Canada, the publication of this book was made possible with the help of a grant from the Canadian Federation for the Humanities and Social Sciences, through the Aid to Scholarly Publications Programme (ASPP), using funds provided by the Social Sciences and Humanities

Research Council of Canada (SSHRC). I wish to further acknowledge the financial assistance received from the Wilfrid Laurier University (WLU) Research Office, through a grant partly funded by WLU operating funds, and partly by the SSHRC Institutional Grant awarded to WLU. I was also fortunate to receive previous financial assistance from the Social Sciences and Humanities Research Council of Canada in the form of a doctoral fellowship and from the University of Toronto in the form of various travel grants and fellowships.

It was also at the University of Toronto where I met many individuals whose friendship has so enriched my life and academic odyssey: Michele Murray, Annette Nierobisz, Jane Barter Moulaison, Phil Harland, Kristen Sweder, Catherine Caufield, and Arthur McCalla. They are good friends and inspiring scholars all, and many of them have helped to make the University's Centre for the Study of Religion a most vibrant academic community. During the course of this project, I also received much advice and assistance from several faculty members at the centre—most notably from Marsha Hewitt, Roger O'Toole, David Raby, and C. Thomas McIntire.

During the final stages of this project, Theodore de Bruyn, of the Canadian Corporation for Studies in Religion (CCSR), W.E. Hewitt, of the University of Western Ontario, and the anonymous readers who reviewed the manuscript on behalf of the ASPP and the CCSR made several valuable suggestions that have improved the resulting book. My colleagues in the Department of Sociology and Anthropology at WLU were also a welcome source of friendship and advice during this time. Nicole Henderson, of the Department of Political Science, served as a discerning proofreader. I must further thank the efficient and pleasant staff at Wilfrid Laurier University Press and especially Carroll Klein, whose wise counsel and extra effort were most appreciated and admired. The responsibility for any errors or omissions contained within the present work rests, nonetheless, entirely with me.

In addition, I must acknowledge the love and support of my immediate and extended families. In particular, I need to thank my parents, Kate and Don. Over the years, they have provided me with unequivocal emotional sustenance and generous financial assistance. They have been consistently kind and patient, and they have had an unfailing faith in me. I will never be able to thank them enough.

Finally, my debt to my husband, David Bryce, is immeasurable. It is no coincidence that my last years writing this book were such happy ones. This had less to do with the book itself and more with the fact that those years were also the first ones of our marriage. For much of that time, he kept flowers on my desk, food in my belly, and a smile on my face. For such unselfish love, support, and patience I will always be grateful.

Preface

In 1993, I spent a year working in the public schools of a banana plantation in Costa Rica. At that time, I had just defended a master's thesis on the Latin American Church—but had never been to Latin America. By that time, I could translate Church documents from Spanish to English—but could barely converse in the language. And so, in part to remedy some of the deficiencies in my practical education and in part to collaborate personally in a movement for social justice, I idealistically joined a volunteer program and headed off to Costa Rica. My assignment was to teach English and environmental education in Río Frío, a cluster of plantation settlements carved out of the rainforest a couple of hours north of San José.

Based on what I had heard and read about the country, I was somewhat relieved that it was actually *Costa Rica* to which I was travelling. Costa Rica, as many had told me, was a peaceful and tranquil oasis in Latin America. I was not likely to be abducted, as development workers had been in Colombia; I was not going to witness the extreme and widespread poverty of a Nicaragua or an El Salvador.

Indeed, my very first trip into Río Frío seemed to reinforce my preconceptions. As I bounced along in the bus (certainly noticing the *río* but failing to understand how anything in these steamy lowlands could earn the adjective *frío*), I was greeted by a series of brightly coloured billboards. As I passed each new settlement, I read a message that was some variation of "Welcome to Farm 6: We are *solidaristas*, producing and exporting as we work in peace and harmony." At that time, I did not know who or what *solidaristas* were, and I suppose I was a bit suspicious about the cheerful Dole company logos with their rays of sunshine bursting forth beside the slogans. Overall, however, I was naively reassured by those signs and their declarations.

Soon after, I witnessed the difficult living conditions the *solidaristas* (members of a certain labour organization) often endured on the plantations: the planes flying overhead and dropping yellow clouds of pesticides that floated far beyond their intended targets, the crime, the prostitution, the diseases among workers. Many of my students were the children of plantation workers and, as I got to know them and their families, I saw at first hand the poverty and exploitation that are part of agribusiness and a banana-oriented economy. This was clearly another Costa Rica: another side to the presumably pacific and prosperous nation that many refer to as the "Central American Switzerland."

When I came back to Canada and was talking to people about where I had been, I found that it was quite difficult to divest them of the same myths about Costa Rica's stability and affluence. When I returned to university and doctoral work, moreover, I found that few North American scholars were interested in analyzing Costa Rica. This included those fascinated by the subject of religion and politics; with few exceptions, they too had ignored the country. A sizeable gap in the literature on the Latin American Church had thereby developed, presumably because scholars viewed Costa Rica as lacking significant socio-economic hardship, or as having very little in the way of progressive Church programming and activism.

My doctoral studies and, eventually, this book grew out of such experiences and my desire to dispel these misconceptions. Subsequent research trips—days spent in archives in the capital city instead of schools on the plantation, hours passed in conversation with priests and labour activists instead of students and parents—confirmed that there is more to the Costa Rican story than many people suspect. What follows, therefore, is an account written to reveal how and why many of the myths about Costa Rica are quite false. An account of Church and state, priests and politics, and bishops and banana workers, it is written with the hope that those who are working to bring true peace and prosperity to the nation will one day succeed in their quest.

Introduction 1

The question is not whether the Church is
involved in politics, but how it is involved.
—Scott Mainwaring, *The Catholic Church and Politics in Brazil, 1916–1985*

Since the 1960s, scholars have been fascinated by the relationship between the Roman Catholic Church and politics in Latin America. The emergence of liberation theology, the conversion of certain national Churches and many individual members of the clergy to the "option for the poor," and the participation of thousands of Church members in the continent's political struggles have provided the basis for a small mountain of books and articles on the Latin American Church.[1] Not surprisingly, given the unprecedented participation of Catholics in the Nicaraguan Revolution and the embroilment of Salvadoran and Guatemalan Catholics in their respective nations' civil wars, focus on the Catholic Church in the particular region of Central America has also been intense.

The Catholic Church in Costa Rica, however, has been largely overlooked by scholars, many of whom judge the country to be free from political turmoil and progressive pastoral innovation. In this book I seek both to challenge these widespread perceptions of Costa Rica and to help fill the gap in existing scholarship. More precisely, I analyze the Costa Rican Catholic Church's varying positions on social justice and the rights of workers during the period from 1979 to 1996. Against the background of Costa Rican socio-economic history and the Catholic Church's social teaching tradition, I study the words and actions of key Costa Rican Church figures and institutions as they attempt to minister to workers and their families.

The logical starting point—since neither Costa Rica nor its Church can be considered in isolation—appears to be to place my study within the context of the large body of research on Latin American Catholicism. I therefore begin by highlighting some of the books, themes, and regions that have received the most recent attention and by discussing how the existing literature on Costa Rica fits into this broader field of study.

Studies of the Church and Politics in Latin America

J. Lloyd Mecham's *Church and State in Latin America* stands at the head of a long line of studies on religion and politics in the region.[2] An oft-cited classic originally published in 1934 and revised in 1966, Mecham's book provided later scholars with a wealth of detail on formal Church-state relations in Latin America. Although in the revised edition Mecham did discuss the colonial period, his main concern was to describe the constitutional issues and party politics affecting the Church's legal status in various nations from independence to the mid-1960s. Importantly, Mecham also observed that, after the Second World War, some of the Churches in Latin America were beginning to flirt with movements for social reform; his recognition that the Catholic Church could not be identified solely with conservative political interests foreshadowed the research of many scholars soon to follow.

Of the early works that treated the progressive factions in the Latin American Church more thoroughly, Ivan Vallier's *Catholicism, Social Control, and Modernization in Latin America* is the most influential.[3] In this 1970 book and in a related article,[4] Vallier presented an evolutionary scale of ideal types of Church influence on society and evaluated the extent to which each type would impede or facilitate the secular forces toward economic modernization and "national change." He characterized Church initiatives such as co-operatives, literacy courses, and agrarian reform projects as indicative of the "social development" strategy for influencing society. Although Vallier acknowledged that the social development ideology and activities could contribute to the process of modernization, he felt that the "cultural-pastoral" Church type would be the most supportive of modernizing trends. Vallier saw this type of Church as providing a socio-ethical framework from which "autonomous" laity could emerge to foster social change as Christian citizens. While many contemporary scholars criticize Vallier's assumptions,[5] his work remains important as one of the first attempts to assess in theoretical terms the relationship between the Latin American Church and modernization.

Vallier's concern with modernization, however, meant that his survey of Catholic progressives was somewhat restricted. Although Vallier acknowledged the existence of revolutionary figures and movements within the Catholic Church, he was primarily interested in groups seeking the reform and development of the capitalist order, not its overthrow. In contrast, Vallier's contemporary Frederick Turner, while sharing the former's interest in modernization, also paid close attention to the radical Catholic left in Latin America.[6] At about the same time, Emanuel de Kadt published *Catholic Radicals in Brazil*.[7] In it, de Kadt discussed Church-related initiatives of the "social development" type, as well as more confrontational actions against the existing socio-economic order. Both Turner and de Kadt thus showed the ways in which the actions and ideologies of the Catholic progressives in Latin America could span the range from reformist to revolutionary.

Yet de Kadt's work was noteworthy for another reason. *Catholic Radicals in Brazil* was one of the earliest examples of a book-length treatment of the Catholic Church in a specific country. In fact, from the time that it was published in 1970 to this day, much of the important historical data collection and theoretical innovation in the field has been done by scholars who examine the Church in one or two countries in particular. Significantly, and with some notable exceptions (e.g., Daniel Levine on Venezuela and Colombia and Brian Smith on Chile),[8] much of this work has also focused on Brazil.[9] Some analysts of the Brazilian Church, such as Thomas Bruneau,[10] concentrate mainly on the institutional dynamics of progressive Catholicism. Others, including Madeleine Adriance and Scott Mainwaring,[11] favour an approach that considers institutional constraints and strategies on the one hand, but also the viewpoints and activism of believers at the grassroots on the other. Adriance's more recent work, W.E. Hewitt's empirical study, and Manuel Vásquez's micro/macro analysis (that combines a case study with the world systems paradigm) focus specifically on the composition and religious and political orientations of Brazilian *comunidades eclesiales de base* (CEBs, base ecclesial communities).[12]

This concentration on CEBs in Brazil is part of a larger trend, evident among Latin Americanists in the last fifteen years, toward the study of what is referred to as the "popular church." In general, scholars are focusing less on Church elites and official pronouncements and more on the interaction of religion and politics in the lives of ordinary men and women. Levine, for one, has played a key role in the theoretical elaboration of the concept of "the popular" and has produced one of the most detailed explorations of popular voices in Latin American Catholicism to date.[13]

Some of the most valuable material on the popular church, however, comes from scholars concentrating on Central America. Phillip Berryman, for instance, has provided a rich historical overview of the popular churches' political involvement in countries such as Nicaragua, El Salvador, and Guatemala.[14] There also exists a large collection of more interpretative single-country studies on the popular church in Central American conflicts.[15] The widespread participation of Catholics in the region's revolutionary struggles, and their definition of this participation as a specifically Christian duty, has made the link between religion and politics in these countries indisputable—and studying it irresistible.

Studies of the Pre-1979 Church in Costa Rica

The contemporary Costa Rican Catholic Church, as I have noted, has not been studied nearly as much as the Church in Costa Rica's neighbours to the north. Instead, many of the existing studies on the Costa Rican Church deal with the pre-Vatican II era. Interestingly, several of these are detailed accounts of the important figures and events in sixteenth- to nineteenth-century Church history, written by a man who himself was to become the most important figure in the Costa Rican Church in the first half of the twentieth century, Víctor Sanabria Martínez.[16] Sanabria was named archbishop of San José in 1940 and used his position to support reformist social legislation in Costa Rica: the Social Security Law (1941), the Social Guarantees (1943), and the Labour Code (1943). With President Rafael Angel Calderón Guardia (who, like Sanabria, had been heavily influenced by European social Christian philosophy and papal social teachings) and Communist Party leader Manuel Mora, Sanabria was part of the famous 1943 "unlikely alliance" that promoted the legislation at the base of Costa Rica's welfare state. In line with his commitment to these social reforms, Sanabria also created a series of Catholic workers' organizations and unions.

Much has been written on Monseñor Sanabria, from largely biographical accounts to more scholarly treatments of his thought and work. Some authors concentrate on outlining the outstanding contributions Sanabria made to the Costa Rican Church and to the *patria*,[17] while others provide a more subtle interpretation of Sanabria's actions in the 1940s. Miguel Picado, for example, argues that, although Sanabria was a visionary genuinely inspired by Christian principles to act on behalf of the poor, practical considerations also factored into Sanabria's actions as he tried to protect and increase the institutional power of the Church in a society undergoing rapid political and economic changes.[18] In the end, Picado sees Sanabria as a skilled institutional leader whose prophetic voice has not been echoed in the Costa Rican archbishopric since his death in 1952.

Certainly, Sanabria's immediate successors in the archbishop's role have been widely criticized for their conservatism and silence in the face of Costa Rica's social problems. Javier Solís, for example, argues that Monseñor Rubén Odio Herrera (1952–59) and particularly Monseñor Carlos Humberto Rodríguez Quirós (1960–79) were traitors to Sanabria's legacy.[19] In fact, some scholars refer to the time from Sanabria's death in 1952 to Rodríguez's stroke in 1978 as "the long period of silence."[20] They frequently refer to the influential study by José Miguel Rodríguez, which found that, of 325 official Church documents issued between 1953 and 1970, only 18.76 percent commented on social and political matters, with the majority of these focusing on the threat of communism. Williams also notes that between 1970 and 1978 careful socio-economic analysis was equally absent from official pronouncements.[21] While many of their counterparts outside Costa Rica were striving to put into action the conclusions of Vatican II and of the 1968 Medellín conference of Latin American bishops, the Costa Rican bishops were by and large unaffected by the currents of transformation in the Catholic Church.

Regardless—and scholars have not neglected this fact—during this period of official silence there were several attempts at ecclesial renovation and social change involving individuals and groups at lower levels of the Church.[22] As a priest, Javier Solís, for example, tried in the late 1960s to reorient the Catholic weekly *Eco Católico* to a more critical and leftist stance on socio-economic issues and Church structure. He was also a leader, in the early to mid-1970s, of the Grupo Ecuménico Exodo, an ecumenical social justice group that participated in the Christians for Socialism movement and was heavily influenced by the teachings of liberation theology and the conference at Medellín. However, faced with repeated resistance from the hierarchy, these initiatives all suffered. Solís's actions at one point even earned him a disciplinary transfer out of his parish; he later left the priesthood. Other priests who broke with the official Church's conservatism (by participating in a controversial May Day demonstration, for example) were also subjected to the authoritarian actions of the hierarchy. Finally, after the religious congregations in charge of the Instituto Teológico de América Central (ITAC, Central American Theological Institute) began to educate both religious and secular seminarians in the social sciences and in the progressive spirit of Vatican II and Medellín, the bishops withdrew the secular seminarians and sent them to the more conservative Seminario Central for their training. In general, during the 1960s and until the end of Rodriguez's archbishopric in 1979, the few progressive sectors that did exist in the Costa Rican Church were harassed and largely overshadowed by the conservative and authoritarian hierarchy.

The Scope and Theme of This Study

Both the Costa Rican Church and its context, however, began to change rather significantly in 1979. Monseñor Román Arrieta Villalobos, one of the very few bishops who had spoken on social issues during Rodriguez's tenure (he was a vocal supporter of an agrarian reform project in his diocese), was appointed archbishop of San José. Also during this year, the Costa Rican hierarchy collectively and definitively broke its lengthy silence by issuing a pastoral letter on social and economic problems entitled *Evangelización y realidad social de Costa Rica*.[23] This was a timely document, given the shocking situation in which the country was beginning to find itself. Costa Rica, long seen as one of Latin America's most stable and prosperous nations, had begun to feel the effects of a worsening economic and political crisis. Costa Ricans were also shocked and affected by the events next door in Nicaragua, where the Frente Sandinista de Liberación Nacional (FSLN) overthrew the dictator Anastasio Somoza Debayle—with the help of the Catholic Church. Slightly farther afield, the Latin American bishops held a general conference in Puebla, Mexico, and once again plunged the continent's Church leaders into a debate over the role of the

Church and its members in social change. In light of all these factors and given the importance that they held for the Costa Rican Church and its constituents, 1979 appears a logical point at which to begin this analysis.

To date, there exist few published studies that contain detailed information on the Church in Costa Rica after 1979. Of these, the most outstanding are *La Iglesia costarricense entre el pueblo y el estado* by Miguel Picado,[24] *Costa Rica: La Iglesia católica y el orden social* by Andrés Opazo,[25] and *The Catholic Church and Politics in Nicaragua and Costa Rica* by Phillip Williams.[26] All three books contain valuable information on the Costa Rican Church, and all three fit within the general parameters of the above-cited literature on the contemporary Latin American Church. Phillip Williams, for example, provides an analysis of the Church as an institution, showing how the Church's alliance with the established elites and the concern to preserve the Church's social influence in Costa Rica condition Church leaders' responses to social change. Miguel Picado provides a class analysis and analyzes how the conditions created by Costa Rica's welfare state are interconnected with the Church's political options and pastoral practices and how, in turn, this affects the Church's relationship with the country's popular movements. Andrés Opazo takes the most complex approach by paying careful attention to institution, class, and ideology. His work studies the Church's institutional structure and needs; he also looks at the mutually reinforcing relationship of Church and state in Costa Rica and discusses how this relationship frustrates a genuine Church commitment to the popular sectors. But Opazo also looks closely at the Church's religious discourse and discusses how this symbolic production is related to social and political actions. In general, Opazo's approach most closely resembles the one I adopt in this work. In fact, all three works provide important data and theoretical insights for the present study.

The works by Williams, Opazo, and Picado, however, are fast becoming dated. Picado's book, which includes the most recent material, covers conditions only up to 1988. Moreover, they are all fairly general studies, dealing with a wide range of time periods, individuals, groups, programs, and issues. While this makes them extremely valuable as introductory and background sources, no one topic is covered in great depth. In this book, by contrast, I analyze the period from 1979 to 1996, and focus in detail on a relatively limited topic: the Costa Rican Catholic Church's *pastoral obrera* (workers' pastorate) and the social justice issues closely related to it.

Costa Rican Church leaders have long seen the importance of addressing the condition of the labouring classes as part of their *pastoral social*. As early as 1893, Monseñor Bernardo Augusto Thiel issued the *carta pastoral* (pastoral letter) entitled *Sobre el justo salario* (*On the Just Salary*), in which he argued that workers should receive a wage that enables them to sustain their lives and their families in a decent manner.[27] I have already noted Sanabria's concern in the 1940s for legislation protecting the rights of the working classes and his role in the development of Costa Rican workers' organizations and the Catholic trade union movement. Since Sanabria's appointment as archbishop, numerous official Church organizations have been created to minister to the spiritual and educational needs of workers, among them: the Liga Espiritual Obrera (LEO, Workers' Spiritual League), the Juventud Católica Obrera (JOC, Young Catholic Workers), the Hermandades de Trabajo (HdT, Brotherhood of Workers), the Escuela Social Juan XXIII (ESJ23, John XXIII Social School), and the Centro Coordinador de Evangelización y Realidad Social (CECODERS, Coordinating Centre for Evangelization and Social Reality). (The latter two entities are discussed in detail, in chapters 6 and 8, respectively.) Clearly, the Church's *pastoral obrera* has long been one of the most important components of the religion and politics nexus in Costa Rica; as such, it warrants a detailed investigation.

Nonetheless, very little published material exists on the Church's relationship with the labour movement in Costa Rica. Eugene Miller's recent book contains information on the relationship between the Church and labour in Costa Rica from 1932 to 1948,[28] and Lawrence Kent's short 1985 article provides some insight into the workings of the ESJ23 in the 1970s and early 1980s.[29] By far the best and most lengthy study of this type, though, is James Backer's *La Iglesia y el sindicalismo en Costa Rica*,[30] which discusses Church leaders' attitudes toward and relationships with the labour movement during the period 1871–1972. Still, as was the case with the studies by Picado, Williams, and Opazo, Kent's and Backer's works are now quite dated; the time spans and topics covered by all these studies mean that such crucial Church actors as CECODERS (founded in 1985) are neglected. The relationship between the Church and the labour movement in late twentieth-century Costa Rica simply cannot be understood on the basis of these works alone.

This book, then, seeks to update these earlier studies. In particular, I focus on four distinct Church bodies. In terms of organizations within the Church's social pastorate, I analyze the ESJ23 and CECODERS. These two are the only well-established and viable organizations within this pastorate that deal specifically with workers' issues. Most importantly for this study, they both have the official mandate from the Church hierarchy to spread and apply the message of Catholic social teaching in Costa Rica. In terms of the hierarchy itself, it is also essential to investigate the words and actions of Monseñor Arrieta and the Conferencia Episcopal de Costa Rica (CECOR, Costa Rican Conference of Bishops). Together these bishops constitute the official face of the Costa Rican Church and they indeed have developed a definable position on social justice and the rights of workers within the Costa Rican context. Finally, I examine the local Church in the Limón region of the country. This examination is crucial because Limón province has been the arena for many of Costa Rica's labour struggles, and because the Limón Church is the only local Church in Costa Rica that has made a sustained effort over the years to develop a *pastoral obrera*. The specific manner in which these cases are approached, however, is best discussed in light of certain guiding theoretical considerations.

Theoretical Considerations

Generally speaking, this study is informed by the work of Italian political theorist Antonio Gramsci,[31] and by that of second-generation Gramscian sociologist Otto Maduro.[32] Gramsci and Maduro together provide us with a neo-Marxist sociology of religion that can give insight into many of the complexities of the relationship between religion and politics in Latin America. Over the years, several scholars have explicitly applied the Gramscian approach to studies of the Church in the region.[33]

More recently, however, such a perspective appears to have fallen out of favour. In some senses, this is not surprising when one considers Latin Americanists' growing fascination with the popular church and CEBs. While the Gramscian framework is particularly useful in examining how and why the Church institution's religious specialists come to promote certain political options and interpretations of religious doctrine, a focus on specialists can imply a more elite-centred or top-down perspective than some scholars feel that a focus on "the popular" demands.[34]

Still, it is worthwhile to point out that, for example, in the case of the country in which many studies of the popular church have been conducted—Brazil—there is no shortage of earlier studies focusing primarily on powerful Church members and national hierarchies. Many scholars today rely on these elite-centred works as they contextualize their portraits of the popular church with a consideration of the institution within which the CEBs operate.[35] In the case of an infrequently studied country such as Costa Rica, a Gramscian perspective can continue to prove useful in establishing and examining the institutional parameters affecting all Church members and structures. Thus, a focus on elites and institutions does not necessarily preclude studies of the popular; it can also function as a preliminary step toward them.

The recent neglect of the Gramscian approach is perhaps also an expression of a broader trend toward Weberian approaches to the sociology of religion—accompanied by, in some cases, a critique of neo-Marxist ones.[36] Several scholars have embraced certain of Weber's insights and concepts and applied them to Latin American religious phenomena; hence, for example, Levine's phenomenological perspective is solidly grounded in the Weberian tradition,[37] as are his uses of the elective affinity, prophetic leadership, and ethical religion concepts.[38] Along with Levine, such scholars as Hewitt and Michael Budde have also employed Weber's observations on congregational religion and Protestant sects in their studies of the CEB phenomenon.[39] In general, the utility of the Weberian perspective in helping to decipher the complex manner in which religious ideas can have practical socio-economic consequences cannot be denied.

Acknowledging this, however, need not involve a rejection of the neo-Marxist framework espoused by Gramsci and developed by Maduro. The argument that the work of Marx and Weber, despite their obviously different political agenda, is "compatible and complementary" has long been established among sociologists.[40] Maduro himself proves this point by drawing on Weber (often via Bourdieu) as he develops his notions of religious labour and prophetic religious innovation.[41] Further, the Gramscian recognition of the relative autonomy of religion (discussed in detail below) easily resonates with one interpretation of the Weberian tradition, provoking in some circles commentary regarding a Marxist-Weberian theory of religion.[42] Weber's influence among observers of the Latin American Church should not therefore imply the dismissal of insights generated by the neo-Marxists.

Ultimately, though, the primary value of the Gramscian perspective rests neither with its potential to frame future studies of the popular church nor with its failure to contradict some of the more frequently used Weberian interpretations in the field. Instead, the richness of Gramsci and Maduro's thought is found in their non-reductionist sociology of religion that acknowledges the importance of three types of variables for the study of religion and social change: the socio-economic context, the nature of the Church as an institution, and the content and qualities of religious discourse itself (in this case, Catholic social teaching). While many scholars do appreciate the importance of one or more of these factors for the analysis of the Catholic Church in Latin America, the Gramscian framework, with its emphasis on the inextricable relation among all three variables, provides the most appropriate categories with which to apprehend the complexity of the relationship between religion and politics in Costa Rica.

Crucially, while the following discussion does explore the Gramscian conceptualization of each of these variables in some detail, it is not my intent to then use such concepts in a mechanistic manner or as rigid pigeonholes into which all the data must be fit. Instead, such theoretical constructs can be used merely as heuristic tools that serve to guide the contours of the study as a whole. This approach, in my opinion, resonates best with the non-deterministic flavour of much of Gramsci and Maduro's work itself.

♦ Religion and Socio-Economic Context

Basic to the work of Gramsci, Maduro, and this study is the assumption that religion is socially embedded, that there are inextricable links between religion and the socio-economic context within which it is located. To put it simply, the socio-economic system of a given society will influence and condition the religious forms expressed in that society.

The classic Marxist perspective declares that religion, as an element of the superstructure, is to a certain extent a reflection of the structure, the social relations of production. Marx views religion as a reflection in consciousness of the social and economic contradictions of the real world. For him, religion can be seen as an indication of human alienation and false consciousness, and it can be used by the ruling classes to serve their own interests and maintain the status quo. Yet this is not to say that, for Marx, religion functions only as weapon in the hands of the dominant classes; the often misinterpreted "opium of the people" quotation in fact reveals that he does at least entertain the idea that religion could express the protests of the oppressed.[43] By extension, the Gramscian analysis suggests that patterns not only of domination and subordination but also of conflict and protest are reproduced in the religious field and will affect religious actors' political options and symbolic production.[44]

This materialist perspective implies that religion cannot be studied in isolation from its social context. It means that, in order to understand the Costa Rican Church's *pastoral obrera*, one must look at the social and economic realities faced by the Church and by the workers to whom it is attempting to minister. Therefore, for example, I discuss the nature and widespread effects of the economic crisis that began to engulf the country in the late 1970s (in chapters 2 and 3). To do so is not merely to provide background to my analysis—it also allows for an exploration of possible motivations for and constraints on Church statements and activism during the same time period. A careful treatment of the socio-historical context of the Costa Rican Church is the logical extension of the presupposition that economic patterns condition religious forms.

By itself, however, the contention that structure determines superstructure is a reductionistic formulation, now dismissed by most sociologists of religion. Crucially, even Engels clarified that he and Marx never said that the economic element was the only determining factor in history; rather, they admitted that various superstructural variables could also affect historical struggles.[45] Gramsci also saw the errors of treating ideology as merely epiphenomenal, labelling as "primitive infantilism" the claim "that every fluctuation of politics and ideology can be presented and expounded as an immediate expression of the structure."[46] As Maduro affirms, structures, conflicts, and changes that are occurring on the level of an entire society do not directly or mechanically influence religious actions. Instead, he argues, the internal characteristics of the religious realm also play a role in determining religious expressions. This recognition—that religion is not unilaterally dependent on the structure, that is, of the *relative autonomy* of the religious realm—represents a crucial advance over reductionistic Marxist theories of religion.[47]

Accepting the relative autonomy of religion means that, to a certain extent, religion must be appreciated on its own terms, within its own specifically religious system of meaning. Without dismissing or discounting a critical sociological analysis of religious expressions, these expressions also need to be understood in light of categories and structures that religious agents themselves define as relevant. Hence, one must always keep in sight the fact that Román Arrieta is not merely an influential public figure who chooses concrete political options at specific historical conjunctures; he is at one and the same time *Archbishop* Arrieta, who is seen by many as a successor of the apostles, a vicar of Christ entrusted with the care and instruction of the Catholic faithful. The Church's teaching on the right to strike, to take another example, is not only a response to the condition of labour in a capitalist society; for many it is also a teaching made in conformity with divine wisdom and made in pursuit of the goal of eternal salvation. To put it another way, one can say that, while religion is always political, it is never purely so.[48] In this sense, religion can never be explained away as simply a tool in the hands of one or another social class. Religion must also be respected as a system of beliefs, practices, and structures that have transcendental significance for those committed to it.

These theoretical considerations influence the way in which I analyze the Costa Rican Church and its *pastoral obrera*. Specifically, this "nonreductive materialism"[49]—a recognition both of socio-economic influences on the expression of faith and of the relative autonomy of religion—has implications for studying the Church as an institution and for studying the ideas this institution transmits.

♦ The Church as an Institution

Andrés Opazo once wrote that "historically speaking, religion is never an incorporeal reality which floats in the consciousness of humans, it is always incarnated in institutions."[50] This contention is confirmed par excellence in the case of Roman Catholicism, which has evolved in the bosom of one of the most highly developed institutions known to humankind. Clearly, the recognition of the importance of the Catholic Church's institutional character has been a guiding force in many of the existing studies on religion and politics in Latin America. This insight also plays a role in my analysis of the Costa Rican Church.

In such an analysis, it is essential to avoid treating the Church in Costa Rica as a monolithic whole and, instead, to respect the complexity of the Church as an institution. Such complexity is in part captured by conceptualizing the Church as an "interclass social space," in which members from a variety of social classes converge and interact.[51] This interclass quality is derived from the nature of the Church as a socially embedded institution, one that reflects the social and economic patterns and conflicts of the larger society. At the same time, this mixed class composition is secured by the universal nature of the Church's mission—the *Catholic* Church preaches that salvation in Christ is offered to all, regardless of social status or class, among other things.[52] Moreover, when competing social groups meet within the Church, they do not acquiesce to the pleas for unity among the faithful (a topic to which I return) but, rather, they seek religious legitimation for their respective political projects.[53]

On the one hand, this process of seeking religious meaning that in some way corresponds to one's social situation occurs spontaneously within all social groups as individuals continually work to struggle through and make sense of the categories, conflicts, and aspirations that colour their everyday lives. In large part, this is the phenomenon that scholars who study "the popular" seek to understand. On the other hand, at a more formal and explicit (and methodologically speaking, more accessible) level, such activity is directed and developed most fully by certain specialists within the religious field. With reference to the Catholic Church in particular, this work generally falls to bishops, priests, and theologians. In line with the Gramscian tradition, these figures can be seen as "organic intellectuals"—that is, as superstructural functionaries whose role it is to give the class to which they are aligned homogeneity and an awareness of its social, economic, and political function.[54]

In this book, I explore the words and actions of some of these specialists within the Costa Rican Church. Hence, I focus largely on official documents and statements issued by ecclesial representatives and related in some way to workers' issues. Of prime importance are the pastoral letters released by Monseñor Arrieta and CECOR from 1979 to 1996 (chapter 5), and by Monseñor Coto and his successor, Monseñor Ulloa, during their time in Limón (chapter 9). Also deserving of special analysis are the publications produced by CECODERS (chapter 6) and the ESJ23 (chapter 8) under the supervision of Padre Orlando Navarro and Padre Claudio Solano, the pivotal figures in these respective organizations. I obtained these materials primarily via library and archival research in San José and Heredia, Costa Rica. Semi-structured open-ended interviews with these five main figures and with other individuals close to them and their organizations provided supplementary material for analysis, as did newspaper and academic articles treating relevant topics. Throughout my discussion, I emphasize how the manifestations of the Church's *pastoral obrera* can be seen as expressions of particular class or political options integrated by organic intellectuals.

Still, if the religious field is seen as relatively autonomous, competing class alliances cannot be simplistically equated with competing forms of religious expression. The characteristics of the religious field—in this case, those of the religious institution—should also be taken into consideration. Gramsci himself wrote: "If, for every ideological struggle within the

Church one wanted to find an immediate primary explanation in the structure one would really be caught napping: all sorts of politico-economic romances have been written for this reason. It is evident on the contrary that the majority of these discussions are connected with sectarian and organisational necessities."[55] More precisely, many actions of the clergy can be linked to the institutional need for self-preservation.

In the specific case of Costa Rica, this institutional imperative can be investigated with reference to three interrelated factors. First, one must consider the possible implications of the Church's constitutional privilege in Costa Rica. In terms of the Costa Rican constitution, the Catholic Church has always been the official state church; even at the height of tensions between the Church and the state in the late 1800s, this constitutional privilege was never abrogated.[56] The current constitution affirms the Church's status in Article 75: "The Apostolic, Roman, Catholic Religion is that of the State, which contributes to its maintenance, without impeding the free exercise in the Republic of other religions [cultos] that are not opposed to universal morality nor good customs."[57] Consistent with this clause, religious education is mandatory in all public schools and Catholic parishes, projects, and buildings are eligible for tax breaks and other financial assistance from the government.[58] The Costa Rican Church, as an institution, will seek to maintain this favourable status vis-à-vis the state.

Second, one must look at the Catholic Church's membership status among the general population. As in other Latin American countries, Catholicism (professed if not actually practised) has long been the religion of the vast majority of Costa Ricans.[59] From the point of view of the Church as an institution, however, this position is never secure. In Limón province, for example, there has always been an uneasy coexistence between the Catholic Church and the numerous "historical" or long-established Protestant churches (i.e., the Baptist, Methodist, Episcopal, and Lutheran churches). In recent years, Catholic Church membership has also been threatened by the dramatic increase in the number of Pentecostal churches—commonly and disdainfully referred to as *sectas*—throughout Costa Rica.[60] Of course, the traditional enemy of the Church throughout Latin America—communism—can also be perceived as threatening the structures and souls belonging to the Church. The days of the unlikely alliance between the Church and the Communist Party in Costa Rica are long past and, although there are no cells of leftist guerrillas practising manoeuvres in the country's rainforests, there is a communist movement in Costa Rica. Further, the unpleasant experiences of the Catholic Church in Cuba and Nicaragua under leftist governments are certainly known among the Costa Rican clergy. It is an institutional imperative, then, for the Church to try to maintain (if not increase) its membership in the face of such threats to its dominance.

A third aspect of institutional preservation relates to the Church's internal organization. The Catholic Church is a hierarchically structured institution in which power is not equitably distributed. Those holding positions of authority generally seek to ensure that the Church's internal structure of religious power is reproduced and that they maintain control over the processes of symbolic production and the distribution of religious goods.[61] This type of centralized and hierarchical authority structure is especially entrenched in the Costa Rican Church, which for the most part has remained immune to the democratizing impulses of the Central American CEB movement. The bishops and priests in Costa Rica are, therefore, motivated to maintain their positions of privilege and status within a Church that has been accorded enormous privilege and status within the general Costa Rican society.

Lastly, the specific nature of the Catholic Church as an institution means that an analysis only of its Costa Rican expression can never be adequate. The *Roman* Catholic Church is a worldwide institution, centred in the Vatican; the national Churches, far from being autonomous or self-contained units, function in inextricable relation and subordination to this governing structure and its leader, the pope. This international or universal Church as a whole, moreover, has institutional needs for self-preservation and reproduction similar to those I have discussed above. The Costa Rican Church, therefore, must always be viewed in light of the larger organizational structure and agenda emanating from Rome.

Given this context, an important task in this study is to investigate to what extent these various institutional characteristics and necessities have an impact on the Costa Rican Church's *pastoral obrera*. Here again, however, it is not possible to plot linear relationships between institutional necessities and pastoral actions. Just as the economic structure is not narrowly determinative of religious expression, neither are institutional exigencies. One remaining variable must also be factored into any analysis of the Church's *pastoral obrera*: that of relevant Catholic social teaching.

♦ Catholic Social Teaching

The Catholic social teaching tradition is generally said to have been inaugurated with Pope Leo XIII's 1891 encyclical *Rerum Novarum*.[62] Known in English as *On the Condition of Labour*, this document warned of the dangers of socialism and was critical of the exploitation of workers under the extremes of industrial capitalism. In it, Leo also advocated for workers' right to a just wage and their right to form "associations." The next major document in this tradition, Pius XI's *Quadragesimo Anno* (1931), also focused on issues concerning workers in industrialized nations and generally expanded on Pope Leo's teachings of forty years earlier. With the papacies of John XXIII and Paul VI, with Vatican II, and with various revolutionary and internationalist currents emerging within and outside of the

Church in the 1960s, Catholic social teaching moved beyond a narrow European perspective and began to deal with social justice in more general and global terms. Development and underdevelopment, conflict and peace, and human rights were issues addressed at length for the first time during this period. These concerns were also treated—with specific reference to Latin America—at the general meetings of the Consejo Episcopal Latinoamericano (CELAM, Latin American Episcopal Council) in Medellín (1968), Puebla (1979), and Santo Domingo (1992). With the papacy of John Paul II, workers' issues were addressed more directly once again in *Laborem Exercens (On Human Work)*, issued in 1981. Since that time, John Paul II's documents have reverted to a consideration of broader social justice issues that nonetheless have implications for the condition of labour in modern societies.

This tradition and its themes help to shape the social justice agenda of local and national Churches the world over, and the case is no different in Costa Rica. There, frequent and explicit references are made to Catholic social teaching documents by the hierarchy and by those involved in the *pastoral obrera*; in fact, both CECODERS and the ESJ23 are considered to be charged with the mission of putting Catholic social teaching into practice. Given these considerations, an examination of Catholic social teaching (chapter 4) is a necessary part of this project.

At this point the reader may question why, given my concern with Catholic thought on social justice, I have chosen to focus on Catholic social teaching and not on liberation theology, which, after all, is centrally concerned with the effort to bring about a more just world. Certainly, liberation theology is known in academic and theological circles in Costa Rica.[63] Still, it is not the direct means through which the Church representatives whom I studied develop their pastoral positions. The famous texts and names of liberation theologians are absent from Church documents in Costa Rica. There is no direct use of works by Gustavo Gutiérrez or Leonardo Boff, for example, in the publications of CECODERS or the Limón Church. And, while Costa Rican progressives may have been influenced by the Latin American liberation theology movement, they see themselves in dialogue with, and as following in the tradition of, Vatican Catholic social teaching and the CELAM conferences at Medellín and Puebla. Often it appears that Costa Rican Church representatives do not venture beyond Catholic social teaching to cite and use liberation theology directly because they interpret Catholic social teaching to be liberationist in itself. In this work, I am more concerned to examine the adequacy of this perception than to discuss liberation theology in its own right.[64] Moreover, I wish to follow the lead of the Church representatives whom I studied and echo their exclusive focus on Catholic social teaching.

A thorough investigation of official Church teachings takes on even greater importance in this context because, surprisingly, most of the existing works treating the Costa Rican Church's *pastoral obrera* do not provide a detailed discussion of Catholic social teaching. Those who do touch on the subject, moreover, often take an uncritical perspective on the tradition. James Backer, for example, takes Catholic doctrine to be "axiomatic."[65] The assumption here is that Catholic social teaching in itself does not need to be critically examined, that on the whole it is pro-union and pro-worker. In this view, any anti-union or anti-worker statements or practices of Church leaders are construed as betrayals of the spirit and letter of the Catholic social teaching tradition. Other scholars present a variation on this theme by portraying conservative or questionable positions vis-à-vis the labour movement as a contradiction specifically of post-Vatican II Catholic social teaching.[66] The premise is that, although the concerns and positions of early Catholic social teaching are now outmoded and unacceptable, since the papacy of John XXIII, Catholic social teaching documents have presented a far more progressive agenda in relation to workers' issues. Hence the conclusion of such scholars is that, if only Church leaders and representatives would put Catholic social teaching faithfully into practice, workers' rights would be respected and justice served.

In contrast, I think it is necessary to take a more critical look at Catholic social teaching itself, to ask whether certain characteristics of or contradictions within the social teaching tradition are related to positions that have a decidedly anti-worker bias. The impetus for this critical analysis is the Costa Rican reality and some of the questions it raises. For example, there is a distinct movement within the Costa Rican *pastoral obrera*—a movement best exemplified in the actions and publications of Padre Claudio Solano and the ESJ23—that seeks to deter workers from unionizing and from exercising their right to strike. On the surface, this appears to be a contradiction of the Catholic social teaching position on the rights of labour. Yet ESJ23 documents are filled with references to and quotations from Catholic social teaching. Does this suggest that Catholic social teaching as a whole is not as supportive of workers and their rights as is commonly believed? One of my aims in this study is to explore this possibility. In other words, instead of assuming the principles of Catholic social teaching to be doctrine invulnerable to challenge, I examine them critically and point out their potential political implications, be they facilitative of justice for workers or not.

This process is especially important because there are pastoral agents and organizations within the Costa Rican Church that do support the rights of workers to unionize and strike, and that more generally support a progressive social justice agenda. Interestingly, these actors—such as Monseñor Coto in Limón and CECODERS based in San José—also look to Catholic social teaching as an inspiration and cite it for legitimation. The question then becomes why and how Catholic social teaching can be used to justify such seemingly contradictory positions on workers' issues. While this question provides a basis for discussion throughout this study, at present certain relevant points can be noted.

First, Catholic social teaching must not be treated as if it is an internally uniform or consistent body of thought. The notion that there would be significant variation within Catholic social teaching is rendered plausible by the mere fact that in the Vatican II and post-conciliar eras alone Catholic social teaching has been generated by the Vatican under three different popes over four decades, and by various constellations of bishops at the CELAM general conferences over the same period. In addition, no one can dispute that, from the 1960s to the 1990s, the world's geopolitical contours and economic patterns shifted significantly, the crumbling of the communist bloc in the late 1980s and early 1990s being the most dramatic of these changes. Therefore, it is hardly surprising that Catholic social teaching, which purports to respond to the "signs of the times," contains a variety of positions. Once one factors in any number of the institutional constraints and influences on religious production discussed above, and the effects of their variable interactions with changing political and economic contexts, a certain measure of plurality within Catholic social teaching appears to be inescapable.

In fact, "conservative" and "liberationist" tendencies can be distinguished within the post-conciliar Catholic social teaching tradition as a whole, with the Medellín documents representing the extreme at the liberationist pole and the teachings issued by the Vatican under Pope John Paul II reflecting the most conservative stance. As will become obvious during the course of this text, I am personally biased in favour of the liberationist perspective. In the context of Costa Rica, I believe that the political options this perspective implies are ones that most fully represent the interests of the majority of Costa Rican workers and citizens in general. Moreover, and in contrast to most analysts of the Costa Rican Church (who do not recognize any distinctions whatsoever within the post-Vatican II tradition),[67] in this work I take care to examine what expressions of the *pastoral obrera* are related to which strands of Catholic social teaching. In other words, I posit that the differing attitudes and actions toward workers on the part of Costa Rican Church leaders and pastoral agents are linked to the differing strands of Catholic social teaching to which they adhere.

By itself, however, this explanation can only be partially correct. As the discussion above has established, no one factor—be it economic context, institutional interest, or in this case Church doctrine—is unilaterally or automatically determinative of pastoral action. Just as those who generate Catholic social teaching in the Vatican and Latin American magisterium are influenced in this production by material and organizational variables, so are the Costa Rican Church representatives in their reception, interpretation, and application of this teaching. The words and actions of the Costa Rican *pastoral obrera* are related to the principles and directives of Catholic social teaching, but they are not reducible to them.

Overall, then, the task of this book is not only to tell the story of the Costa Rican *pastoral obrera* from 1979 to 1996 but also to do so in such a way that does justice to the complexity of all these variables and the relationships among them. The theoretical framework I employ provides space for an analysis of the political-economic and religious-institutional conditions motivating the words and actions of Church representatives, but also allows for the examination of the implications of such documents and programs for those at lower levels of the Church and for those within the society at large. Hence, I recognize—with Gramsci—the "necessary reciprocity," or the dialectical relationship, between structure and superstructure.[68] In more general terms I illustrate—as Maduro would suggest[69]—how, in Costa Rica, society acts on religion, religion (as relatively autonomous) acts on itself, and religion acts on society and social conflicts.

Chapter Outline

In the next chapter, I begin with a discussion of the political-economic conditions that prevailed in Costa Rica during the period under investigation. A focal point of this analysis is the economic crisis that started to affect Costa Ricans in the late 1970s, along with the more recent embracing of neo-liberal economic policies by the country's leaders. Exploring the characteristics and implications of these and related phenomena will help to illustrate the deteriorating living conditions of Costa Ricans in recent decades; it will also suggest some of the constraints and influences on the pastoral agents seeking to minister to these workers.

Chapter 3 contains an examination of how Costa Rica's union movement and workers have fared in the face of the economic crisis. While in many respects the strength of *sindicalismo* in Costa Rica has waned over the past few decades, new forms of union co-operation and protest have arisen in response to the demands posed by the country's worsening economic straits. This chapter explores the complexities of this situation and discusses how the fate of the Costa Rican union movement is tied to a competing form of labour organization known as *solidarismo*.

This is followed in chapter 4 by an examination of the Catholic social teaching tradition and its treatments of the rights of workers. Issues narrowly related to workers' concerns, such as the right to a fair wage, the right to strike, and the right to form unions, are discussed. I also analyze more general teachings on social justice (e.g., those related to the nature of social problems and to the means to enact social change) that can be shown to have implications for the condition of workers in Costa Rican society. Finally, in this chapter, I delineate conservative and liberationist categories within post-Vatican II Catholic social teaching, and suggest how these can be used to illuminate corresponding tendencies within the Costa Rican *pastoral obrera*.

In the next two chapters, I show in detail how specific Church representatives are situated within Costa Rican political-economic and religious-institutional contexts, and I analyze the nature and effects of these actors' participation in the *pastoral obrera*. In chapter 5, I discuss the words and actions of the most powerful religious figure in the Costa Rican Church, Monseñor Román Arrieta, and examine the position of the Costa Rican hierarchy as a collective. In chapter 6, I look at CECODERS, an organization that operates in San José and under the jurisdiction of Monseñor Arrieta.

The following three chapters discuss the particular situation of workers and the Church in the province of Limón. Chapter 7 outlines the social, political, religious, and economic peculiarities of Costa Rica's "province on the periphery." In chapter 8, I examine the case of the ESJ23, an archdiocesan organization that carries out the bulk of its activities on the banana plantations in Limón. The final case study, presented in chapter 9, looks at the official Church in Limón and its counterparts to Monseñor Arrieta in the hierarchy, Monseñor Coto and his successor, Monseñor Ulloa.

The concluding chapter contains a brief summary of the most important points of the study, and suggests the implications of my research for the future analysis of the Catholic Church in Costa Rica and in Latin America.

Crisis in Costa Rica 2

At first sight, Costa Rica appears almost too good to be true.
—Christopher P. Baker, *Costa Rica Handbook*

During the 1970s, Costa Rica was often considered to be exceptional among Central and South American nations. Costa Rica was the *suiza centroamericana* (Central American Switzerland) without an army. It was a "showcase for democracy" without dictators. It was an economic development success story, with a standard of living and social development indicators that were the envy of much of the rest of Latin America. And while many would argue that these accolades remain well deserved, the experience of many Costa Ricans since the 1970s suggests that their country is not as pacific, democratic, or prosperous as is often believed.

The downturn in Costa Rica's fortunes began in 1978, when the country started to slide into a severe socio-economic crisis. While in certain respects the nation experienced a slight reprieve from its troubles after 1983, Costa Rica has still not fully recovered. This chapter examines the crisis and various reactions to the crisis in depth, thereby establishing the historical context, influences, and constraints experienced by Church agents as they sought to develop their *pastoral obrera*.

Post-Civil War Economic Development

The social legislation promoted by Monseñor Sanabria and political leaders during the early 1940s formed the foundation of Costa Rica's welfare state and contributed to the comparatively high standard of living enjoyed by Costa Ricans prior to the economic crisis of the late 1970s. However, Costa Rica's relative socio-economic successes, as well as its eventual and devastating socio-economic crisis, cannot be fully understood without also considering the programs of economic development implemented by Costa Rican leaders in the decades following the 1948 civil war.[1]

José Figueres, a key figure in this war, won the presidency in the elections of 1953 and embarked on an explicitly Keynesian development policy. Figueres's drive toward modernization was impelled by state intervention in the economy and financed by a combination of the national-ization of the banking system, the imposition of indirect taxes, and the incurring of internal and external debt.[2] The resources generated by this program allowed for both a substantial expansion of the central civil service and the creation of numerous "autonomous institutions" (decentralized public agencies). By the end of the decade, the large state bureaucracy was a major employer of Costa Ricans; through these state and autonomous institutions, significant advances were recorded in such areas as housing, communications, education, and road construction.

The 1960s were marked by Costa Rica's entry into the Central American Common Market and its adoption of an import substitution industrialization strategy aimed at reducing dependence on imported goods. Initially, Costa Rican industry flourished under the protectionist policies and tax exemptions offered by the government. Eventually, however, competition among common market members forced Costa Rica to attract increased foreign investment by extending tax breaks to other parties. As a result, capital from the United States came to dominate manufacturing.[3] Further, and despite its efforts toward urban industrial development, Costa Rica continued to promote its agricultural export sector. Traditional exports, such as coffee and bananas, remained a chief source of foreign exchange, while an agricultural diversification program led to ventures into sugar, cotton, pineapple, and livestock production for export.[4] By the end of the decade, Costa Rica's dependence on foreign capital and markets was substantial.

Social services were expanded considerably in the 1970s, initially during the term of Figueres's second presidency (1970–74) and then under the administration of Daniel Oduber (1974–78). Relying heavily on internal and external credit, between them, Figueres and Oduber universalized social security, implemented family allowances, extended health, transportation, communication, and electrical services, and further developed the country's post-secondary education system. The 1970s also witnessed the birth of the entrepreneurial state in Costa Rica; a key role here was played by the Costa Rican Development Corporation, an autonomous institution devoted to creating state enterprises with the same legal status as private corporations.[5] The administrative needs of the enlarged social safety net and the new form of government economic intervention made for an even bigger state bureaucracy; by 1978 there were almost 130,000 state employees — nearly 19 percent of the economically active population.[6]

At a certain level, the results of these economic and social development programs were truly impressive. For example, between 1960 and 1978 the gross domestic product (GDP) grew approximately 3 percent per year and inflation was controlled. In the 1970s, the rate of unemployment averaged only 3 percent a year, in large part owing to the high state demand for labour.[7] The education system had reduced the rate of illiteracy to one of the lowest in the Americas. Moreover, by 1978, basic health services had grown to cover 86 percent of the population, average life expectancy had risen past seventy years, and infant mortality had fallen to 21 per 1000.[8] Add to all this the relative tranquillity of Costa Rica in a region otherwise marred by civil strife, repression, and insurrection, and the country certainly appeared as the Central American success story of its time.

The Crisis and Government Policies

◆ The Crisis Hits

Exceptional though they were, however, such indicators could only compensate for the structural vulnerability of Costa Rica's development model for so long. In reality, the Costa Rican economy was excessively foreign-oriented. On the one hand, Costa Rica continued to rely heavily on the exporting of primary agricultural products, such as bananas and coffee; on the other, the industrialization strategy—while successful in reducing the need to import finished goods—nonetheless called for the importing of large amounts of raw materials, intermediate technological products, and capital goods. Significantly, the value of these imports greatly exceeded that of the country's exports, and this trade deficit grew throughout the 1970s. At the same time, the dependence on external borrowing to compensate for the trade imbalance and to maintain and expand social programs led to a rapidly increasing debt.[9] Thus, by the late 1970s, Costa Rica found itself in an extremely precarious position, and a series of events on the international front were enough to trigger the economic crisis.

The blows to the Costa Rican economy came fast and furious.[10] First, coffee prices plummeted in 1978. Then the price of imported oil, on which Costa Rica had long been dependent, jumped in 1979. Also in 1979 the Nicaraguan Revolution and increasing conflict in El Salvador seriously disrupted commerce in the Central American Common Market and reduced regional demand for Costa Rican exports. Further, the world economic recession at the end of the 1970s led to a decreased demand for Costa Rican products in other markets. With these events, the Costa Rican economy was severely strained and the flaws of an externally dependent development program were exposed.

Unfortunately, the Costa Rican government's reaction to the onset of the crisis made matters worse.[11] In an effort to keep the economy afloat, President Rodrigo Carazo (1978–82) continued to borrow money on international markets. By this time, however, loan conditions were becoming more stringent, with shorter payment terms, higher interest rates, and increased debt service demands, all of which added to the stress on the Costa Rican economy. The government also attempted to print money to pay its debts but, since the Central Bank had no backing to support such a move, inflationary pressure increased. Moreover, the weak and inefficient government proved unable to collect taxes in some cases; in other cases, officials capitulated to elite demands and neglected to do so, causing a further shortage of revenue. Finally, in the fall of 1981, Carazo resorted to halting payments on the debt. In response, international lending institutions suspended further aid to Costa Rica. By the end of Carazo's term, the country's economy was in dire straits and Costa Ricans were suffering accordingly.

The severity of the situation in Costa Rica was evident in a variety of measures. In the early and mid-1980s, the foreign debt exceeded 100 percent of the country's GDP for seven consecutive years.[12] In 1982, for example, Costa Rica owed over US$4 billion to external creditors, a factor that gave the nation one of the highest per capita debts in the world. Inflation, long kept relatively low in Costa Rica, climbed to 65 percent in 1981 and reached nearly 100 percent in 1982. The Costa Rican *colón*, meanwhile, took a battering in devaluation, falling from 8.6 to a low of 65 to the dollar between 1980 and 1982.[13] In terms of production, the rate of growth in the GDP had begun to slow after 1977, but it fell 4.6 percent in absolute terms in 1981 and 7.3 percent the following year.[14] Costa Rica's once impressive health care system and statistics also revealed the magnitude of the crisis: in the late 1970s and early 1980s, the rates of malnutrition, infectious diseases, and infant mortality all increased and medical services and supplies were cut or in short supply.[15] In addition, throughout this period, income distribution became increasingly skewed in Costa Rica as the gap between the rich and poor widened.[16] Most telling, however, were Costa Rican poverty rates. According to one measure, in 1977, 24.8 percent of families were living in poverty; this figure rose to 41.7 percent in 1980 and up to 70.7 percent in 1982.[17] By this time, then, economic indicators and the dramatic drop in Costa Rican living standards were enough to challenge any notions of Costa Rican prosperity or development success. By all accounts, Costa Rica was experiencing a serious crisis.

♦ Government Attempts to Combat the Crisis

President Carazo had proven unable to quell the crisis and stabilize the economy. His successor, Partido Liberación Nacional (PLN) leader Luis Alberto Monge, chose to approach the nation's problems in a different and more systematic manner after he took office in May 1982. As early as his inauguration, Monge was calling on all Costa Ricans to work together and to tighten their belts in a hundred-day emergency period, assuring the population that the sacrifices they made were for the good of the nation. Monge also strove to encourage unity among the various social and political actors in the country; this included his negotiation with the opposition and his support for the merger of four opposition parties into one larger party (the Partido Unidad Social Cristiana, PUSC).[18] In the end, Monge's manoeuvres helped pave the way for the acceptance of his anti-crisis strategy—the so-called bitter pill of structural adjustment. With this strategy, Monge was to inaugurate a shift from the welfare state to the neo-liberal era in Costa Rican economic policy, an era which lasted throughout the 1980s and persists into this millennium.

Carazo had alienated financial institutions such as the World Bank and the International Monetary Fund (IMF) by suspending debt payments. Monge and his successors, however, saw better relations with, and further assistance from, such organizations as the key to combatting Costa Rica's economic problems. To this end, Monge signed two letters of intent with the IMF, in 1982 and 1985, and the first structural adjustment agreement with the World Bank, also in 1985. The government of Oscar Arias (1986–90) continued in this vein by signing two further IMF letters of intent, in 1987 and 1989, and by supporting a second World Bank structural adjustment program in 1988. The Calderón administration (1990–94) also signed IMF letters of intent, in 1991 and 1992, and a third structural adjustment agreement in 1993. The terms of this latter agreement were eventually accepted by the administration of José Figueres, Jr. (1994–98); Figueres, Jr. himself signed another agreement with the IMF in 1995. In addition, it was not only the IMF and the World Bank to whom Costa Rica turned for help. Beginning in 1982, the U.S. Agency for International Development (USAID) also became a key player in countering the crisis, tying its assistance to Costa Rica's compliance with some of the international agreements.

All these agreements made economic aid for stabilizing the economy and for debt payments contingent on the fulfilment of certain demands. Although each letter or program was slightly different,[19] in general they included calls for decreasing the size of the state (for instance, through layoffs and through the privatization of certain state agencies) and for cutting public spending on education, social programs, and price subsidies for basic necessities. These agreements also included demands to place salary caps on public sector jobs and to increase consumption taxes and tariffs on such public services as water and electricity. While requiring downsizing in the public sector, however, the structural adjustment programs focused on strengthening the private sector. Further, the economic structure was to be reoriented so as to decrease production for domestic consumption and to increase production (particularly of such non-traditional goods as ornamental plants and textiles) for export. Reducing or eliminating trade barriers also went along with such restructuring, as a chief aim of these programs was to push the country to become more open to and integrated in world markets. These policies, which essentially allow the market to become the dominant force in the structuring of society with as little state interference as possible, are generally referred to as "neo-liberal."

By some accounts — most notably those of the international financial institutions themselves — this neo-liberal medicine did cure Costa Rica's economic ills. Certainly, the infusion of such large amounts of money did help to stabilize the economy and lift it out of the crisis lows of 1981 and 1982. Shortly after this point, for example, inflation and unemployment dropped, and economic growth was restored.[20] Nonetheless, as is especially evident when viewed from the longer-term perspective of the late 1990s, in many respects the neo-liberal economic adjustment strategies have done far more harm than good in Costa Rica.

♦ Side Effects of Neo-Liberalism's "Bitter Pill"

The disconcerting implications of loans and structural adjustment programs come to light once one probes a little deeper into the various politics and policies involved. Take for example the substantial assistance provided by USAID: by 1985, the United States, through this agency, was contributing loans and outright grants to Costa Rica at the rate of US$1.2 million per day.[21] Important though this financial help may have been, it also reflected the clear geopolitical motivation of the United States government, which saw the strategic value of a stable Costa Rica in the land of the Panama Canal, the *contra* war in Nicaragua, and the civil war in El Salvador. It is also revealing that, during the 1982-89 period, Costa Rica — the "country without an army" — received more than US$27 million in military assistance and training from the United States.[22] Moreover, it is no coincidence that various right-wing paramilitary groups (several with links to the United States) flourished in Costa Rica during this period, aiding the *contras* to the north and persecuting leftists at home.[23] Throughout the 1980s, Costa Rican dependence on the United States grew dramatically and the seamy side of U.S. charity was becoming increasingly exposed.

United States intervention and the militarization of Costa Rican society are not the only signs that Costa Rica is not the debt relief success story that the international financial institutions make it out to be. Consider, for instance, the shifts in the Costa Rican economy from the mid-1980s onward. The government has increased its support for agro-export production, largely through the reduction of export taxes and the provision of subsidies to export industries. These benefits to the export sector have come partially at the expense of small-scale basic grain producers, many of whom have been forced off their lands as a result of the government's reduction of price subsidies for their products. This process, because it has led to a drop in production of food staples (such as corn, beans, and rice), jeopardizes the ability of Costa Ricans to feed themselves. Nonetheless, the displacement of independent farmers frees up land and labour needed for large-scale agro-export enterprises.[24]

The country's increased bias toward export production, however, has not meant that the other risks associated with this type of economic activity have been eliminated. Costa Rican exports are just as vulnerable to international fluctuations in prices and demand as they have always been (the 1993 cuts in European banana quotas and their devastating effects on the Costa Rican banana industry are a case in point). Further, Costa Rican reliance on non-traditional exports is particularly unstable, largely because such production is often subsidized by foreign aid and dependent on preferential access to U.S. markets.[25] Yet, even with the drawbacks inherent in this type of export-oriented economy, Costa Rica's pattern of dependent development continues.

Despite — and in part because of — this export-based pattern of agricultural production, Costa Rica still has not been able to eliminate its large trade deficit nor substantially pay down its foreign debt. For one thing, the drop in the domestic production of basic grains has meant that Costa Rica has had to import staple food products, such as wheat from the United States. As well, the country must still import the technology and pesticides essential to its agro-export enterprises. Moreover, in recent years the Costa Rican market has been flooded with foreign-produced luxury items, such as cosmetics and cars, further contributing to a skewed import-export ratio. Therefore, even though the adjustment strategy of expanding exports was designed to reduce the trade deficit and to generate the foreign exchange needed to service the external debt, the commercial deficit has not been reduced. Costa Rica has actually been forced to borrow more from international institutions in order to maintain imports and pay its foreign creditors.[26] This vicious circle meant that, in the mid-1990s, Costa Rica still carried well over US$3 billion in external debt and, by 1996, was devoting 27.6 percent of the public budget to debt service.[27]

Further, analysts argue that an even larger problem for Costa Rica in recent years has been its internal debt — the amount by which the government's internal expenses exceed revenues. In Costa Rica, this debt is expressed as the amount of money the central government and government banks owe (mainly in the form of bonds) to internal creditors, which are generally public institutions. The internal debt grew steadily throughout the early 1990s, in part owing to the tax breaks, subsidies, and other costs associated with the government's promotion of the export sector. It reached an alarming 38.5 percent of the country's gross national product (GNP) by 1995.[28]

An internal debt of this size is problematic because it leads to increasing interest rates. Not only do high interest rates drive up the cost of housing for the general population, they also discourage private investment and reduce the level of production, which in turn cause unemployment to rise. Moreover, the government has attempted to cope with this deficit by once again cutting spending in such areas as social programs, health care, and education. Social spending as a percentage of the GDP dropped by a quarter from 1980 to 1989, with education spending falling 43 percent and health care expenditures plummeting 54 percent.[29] The population once more suffers the consequences as school days are shortened, and as the quality and availability of health care supplies and services has declined. Finally, not only have Costa Ricans witnessed this dismantling of their welfare state, but inflation has spiked upward, exceeding 20 or 25 percent, in several of the years since the late 1980s.[30] In effect, the excessive internal debt has a near stranglehold over Costa Rica's economy and its people.

Overall, the various debt relief, structural adjustment, and deficit-fighting schemes of the 1980s and 1990s have not solved Costa Rica's economic and social problems. More than ten years after the alleged end to the Costa Rican crisis, two key measures of living standards, per capita GDP and per capita real private consumption, still have not recovered to their pre-crisis levels.[31] Moreover, the country is still deeply indebted and dependent, and landlessness has increased markedly in the rural areas. In light of these circumstances, and given that, by some estimates, up to 38 percent of the total population now lives in a condition of poverty,[32] Costa Rica can hardly be considered the democratic and prosperous paradise that some proclaim it to be.

Popular Reactions to the Crisis

While the foregoing may imply that ordinary citizens were passive victims of the crisis and the government's neo-liberal policies, the level and nature of popular protests during the 1980s and 1990s suggest otherwise. Costa Rica's economic problems and the various attempts to remedy them provoked strong reactions during this period as some of the people most affected by the changing socio-economic structure began to organize and mobilize. Beginning in the 1980s, there was a dramatic surge in political activism among the urban poor, as well as among poor *campesinos*. Instead of simply acquiescing to the demands of the government and international financial institutions, these groups played important roles in contesting the biases of the changing Costa Rican economic order.

♦ The Electricity Rate Protests

The earliest and most noteworthy instances of popular mobilization originated in the cities with the 1983 protests against rising electricity rates.[33] In November 1982, as a condition of a government agreement with the IMF, the public utility companies began to implement a plan to increase the cost of electricity by 92 percent. This was a vicious hike, especially harsh since rates had already been raised by more than 70 percent a few months earlier. A basic public service had become unaffordable for many people. As the increase was phased in over the following months in increments of 10 and 13 percent, and as more and more Costa Rican individuals and organizations were affected, people began to voice their discontent. When complaints among neighbours and individual petitions to the electric companies proved fruitless, organization at the community level began to take place. Among the first to hold meetings were residents in Hatillo 5 and Hatillo 6, two poor neighbourhoods on the outskirts of San José. From these meetings arose the first *comités de lucha* (struggle committees), local groups that would play an important role as the protest movement spread. These Hatillo committees were already in place when the straw that broke the camel's back came with the April 1983 power rate jump of 24.25 percent. When the electricity bills reflecting this increase were distributed, popular discontent erupted.

The organized protests began with a May 2 march from Hatillo to the offices of one of the electrical companies in San José. Demonstrators burned their light bills and demanded a meeting between community representatives and company officials. When the meeting resulted in no concessions from the company, the Hatillo committees set about organizing a National Coordinating Committee to facilitate the establishment of committees in other regions of the country and to co-ordinate the efforts of various community organizations that were expressing interest in the cause. In the days that followed, members of the existing and newly formed committees began to go door to door, urging people to default on their electricity payments and collecting light bills to return to the electric companies. Everywhere, signs in windows and on placards declared: *"YO NO PAGO EL RECIBO DE LA LUZ"* (I don't pay my electricity bill). Many people remained resolute in their protest even after the electric companies began to cut the power to the strikers' homes and workplaces.

At the same time, witnessing the escalating tensions and hoping to forestall further protests and conflict, the government announced that it was forming a commission to study the problem. The commission, however, refused to negotiate with the National Coordinating Committee, discrediting it by labelling it communist. (In fact, although members of the Popular Vanguard Party—the Costa Rican communist party—were involved in the committee, it was a truly cosmopolitan group composed of representatives from many different grassroots organizations.) Instead, the government began to deal with a separate committee (made up of certain union leaders and PLN allies) that had little popular support. When the government and negotiating committee announced an agreement to lower rates to the February 1983 level and to stop cutting electrical service to the homes and businesses of strikers, the popular protests were temporarily dampened.

The protests were not completely extinguished, however. By early June, the companies were once again cutting the electrical service of the strikers, a move that served only to reinvigorate the protests. Struggle committees began to organize teams to reconnect the power lines and "defence committees" (largely made up of female homemakers) to stand guard against the disconnection of power in other areas. More visibly, traffic barricades were erected in more than forty communities, and blockades almost completely cut San José itself off from the rest of the country. By this point, the protest movement had become so intense and so widespread that the government had no choice but to negotiate with the National Coordinating Committee. In the end, the national committee attained an impressive series of concessions from the government and utility companies, including the lowering of rates to their December 1982 levels, further rate concessions to schools and nutrition centres, preferential rates to small businesses, and the restoration of power to those behind in paying their bills. The struggle and sacrifices made by the members of the movement had not been in vain.

♦ The Rural Squatter Movement

In the countryside, popular protest has been most clearly expressed in the illegal land invasions of the *movimiento precarista* (squatter movement).[34] This type of activism began to expand most noticeably after mid-1983, and is still a visible facet of rural life in Costa Rica. Generally, the *precarista* movement has consisted of families, sometimes in groups of up to six hundred people, who invade and erect makeshift shelters on uninhabited tracts of land (often the unused portions of the large farms owned by multinational agro-export companies). Sometimes, these people have been displaced from their own small plots of land because of agribusiness expansion; often they are the families of migrant workers who move from region to region in search of temporary employment on banana plantations. In general, the *precaristas* are not allowed to stay on the land for any length of time; usually, within days or weeks, the Rural Guard expels them and destroys their tents and any rudimentary infrastructure they may have set up. When thrown off such land, many return to squat again, only for the guard to come and begin the expulsion anew.

While such land invasions are typically spontaneous actions taken out of desperation by poor families, other protests related to the *precarista* movement are co-ordinated by larger *campesino* organizations.[35] The Federaciones Campesinas (Campesino Federations), many of which are tied to the Costa Rican union movement, have launched various publicity campaigns, legal appeals, and negotiations with the state and with farm owners in attempts to secure land ownership for the *precaristas*. When such measures fail, however, members of these organizations have resorted to occupations of government and Church buildings, hunger strikes, protest marches, and road blockades in order to have their demands heard.

Unlike the case of the electricity rate protests, which were for the most part peaceful and did not incur repressive measures from the government, violence and persecution have often plagued the *precarista* movement. While many *precarista* families try to live and tend their gardens peacefully on the patches of land they inhabit, other squatters have been combative, destroying property and bridges during land invasions. More often, however, it has been the Rural Guard's members who have exercised excessive force, using bullets and bulldozers to drive the *precaristas* away. Various participants in other protests of the movement have also been fired on, forcibly evacuated, or jailed by Costa Rican security forces. Overall, in contrast to the eventual success achieved by the electricity rate protesters, the *precaristas* remain on the losing end of the battle for land in Costa Rica and continue to be persecuted by state authorities.

Conclusion

Prior to the 1980s, Costa Ricans, living in a peaceful and prosperous oasis relative to the rest of Central America, had come to accept the ideology of Costa Rican exceptionalism. The prevailing interpretation attributed the country's idiosyncratic circumstances to its "curious colonial history" as a poor and relatively isolated colony with few precious metals or indigenous peoples to exploit and, as a result, no warring social classes or despotic rulers.[36] It is argued that, from this situation, the noble yeoman farmer emerged in the eighteenth century as a hardworking man of the land, struggling to subsist, yet free from domination and obligation to large landowners. From him, the traditional historians claim, arose Costa Rica's long-standing rural democracy, persistent pacifism, and characteristic respect for law and liberty. While this reading of history has been shown by more critical analysts to be wanting,[37] and, while changes in modern agriculture have made the yeoman a nearly extinct species, the portrayal of their nation as democratic, pacifist, and egalitarian has nonetheless been proudly and widely adopted by Costa Ricans.[38]

An important buttress to the legend of the idyllic *campesino* lifestyle arose in connection with the development of the benefactor state in Costa Rica from the 1940s onward. As the state grew and grew, providing more jobs, benefits, and social plans to its citizens, further proof of Costa Rica's exceptional egalitarianism and democracy was amassed. Crucially, though, this political model also played an important role in maintaining social stability. The paternalistic state — the *"gran padre providente"* (great provident father), as Opazo has called it — successfully minimized social conflict for a long time by preventing the development of an extreme polarization of wealth.[39] The state responded to the material needs of the popular classes not by repression but by creating numerous government and autonomous institutions, which succeeded in institutionalizing conflict and relieving tensions before they could build to a point where the status quo was threatened.[40] A prime example of this stability-creating mechanism was Costa Rica's agrarian reform program of the 1960s, co-ordinated by the Instituto de Tierras y Colonización (ITCO, Lands and Colonization Institute) and influenced by the strategy of the U.S. Alliance for Progress (implementing reform from above in order to forestall revolution from below).[41] As many of Costa Rica's socio-economic problems were handled in this fashion, popular passivity predominated. Those who did attempt to protest conditions were usually drawn into bureaucratic channels for redress, rather than forced to demand changes in the streets.[42] Orchestrated by the country's leaders, gratefully accepted by the majority of citizens, and handily reinforced by the ideology of exceptionalism, this social pact persisted for many years and paid handsome dividends in the form of social order for Costa Rica.

The turning point came as this pact was broken by the economic crisis and the substitution of neo-liberalism for social reformism. While the economic crisis generally made life more difficult for Costa Ricans, moves such as the hike in electricity rates threatened to make conditions intolerable for the country's most vulnerable citizens. Worse, the source of the hikes and other structural adjustment measures was the state — the very state that Costa Ricans had been conditioned to believe would take care of them. Not only was *el gran padre* no longer doing a good job taking care of his children, but he now appeared to be turning against them. And in contrast to what Costa Ricans had long been taught about the superiority of dialogue and negotiation as means to resolve difficulties, these tools proved ineffective when tested at the beginning of the electricity rate protests and throughout the *precarista* activism. The worsening conditions in the countryside had the additional effect of dispelling any residual myths about rural families contentedly working their own land, while the violent treatment of the squatters helped to disprove the claim that no army exists in Costa Rica.[43] Prosperity, pacifism, and democracy had long been touted as the hallmarks of the Costa Rican national character and were supposedly writ large in the benefactor state. But the economic hardships, neo-liberal policies, and popular protests during the 1980s proved the predominant assessment to be false. Costa Rica's image was, unfortunately, too good to be true.

The Unions in the Face of the Crisis 3

A strike is a strike from a political perspective,
but not from a juridical-legal perspective.
—Costa Rican Labour Minister Farid Ayales,
in a 1995 interview with *La República*

But the spirit of the laws is one thing and reality is another.
—Elisa Donato M. and Manuel Rojas B., *Sindicatos, política y economía, 1972–1986*

The economic crisis in the late 1970s did not come at the best of times for the Costa Rican union movement. Having peaked in influence among workers, in organization, and in strike activity during the first half of the century, the movement entered into a period of decline in the 1950s and 1960s, experienced a slight resurgence (mainly in the banana sectors) in the 1970s, and had begun to lose ground again by the onset of the crisis.[1] As well, according to almost all accounts, the union movement could be best characterized as "weak" or "passive" as it faced the crisis and its aftermath throughout the 1980s and into the 1990s. Analysts point out that, during these years, not only did the overall level of unionization among workers remain relatively low and stagnant,[2] but the union movement as a whole was unable to respond effectively enough to derail the privatization process and the other programs of the government's neo-liberal agenda.[3]

Despite the very real and serious problems experienced by the Costa Rican labour movement in recent decades, however, union activism has not completely disappeared from the political landscape. In the 1980s, and particularly the 1990s, new forms of union protest and collaboration have also arisen in Costa Rica. In fact, there is ample evidence to suggest that workers' organizations have not taken the economic crisis and the government's neo-liberal remedies for it lying down. In this chapter, I discuss both the problems and the promise of the Costa Rican union movement after 1979 and thus provide more of the historical context needed to understand Costa Rican Church leaders' varied approaches to workers and the issues affecting them.

Notes for chapter 3 start on page 206 33

Problems for the Costa Rican Union Movement

♦ Internal Weaknesses

One of the most commonly cited causes of the relative impotence of the unions during the 1980s and 1990s has been the "atomization," or excessive fragmentation, within the union movement itself. This phenomenon is most noticeable in the public sector, where the workers of even a single institution may find themselves split among a dozen or more unions; the Caja Costarricense de Seguro Social (CCSS, Costa Rican Social Security Bureau), for example, contained thirty-six different unions in 1997.[4] New unions continually appear, often as groups within existing unions attempt to break away and form their own organizations. Sometimes these new unions fail and vanish, but more often they remain as small units unto themselves. In 1993, 45 percent of unions recorded fewer than fifty registered members, while 24 percent had between fifty and ninety-nine members.[5] As well, because a substantial proportion of unions in Costa Rica have elected not to affiliate themselves with one of the existing union federations or confederations (the latter are also known as "union centrals"), the isolation and lack of co-ordination among many of these small independent unions is even more pronounced.[6]

The fragmentation of the union movement can be attributed to a number of factors, including: ideological dogmatism or sectarianism; elitism, in evidence when groups of engineers, for example, refuse to affiliate with groups of bus drivers or other manual labourers; and *gremialismo*, a "guild mentality," in which workers associate only with other workers in the same, very narrowly defined, trade.[7] Regardless of the exact causes responsible for atomization, this division in the movement has had harmful effects on Costa Rican workers. On the one hand, many of the unions are too small and have too few resources to be able to muster significant bargaining power vis-à-vis employers. This is particularly serious during a period when social and economic conditions indicate that workers can least afford to be losing ground as far as wages, job stability, and similar matters are concerned. More generally, atomization has reduced the level of influence of the union movement as a whole, with dispersion and infighting among unions hindering them from forming a united front able to contest the government's neo-liberal policies and the changes in working conditions such policies imply.

♦ External Factors

While atomization is a problem internal to the union movement, there have also been influences from outside the movement that have eroded the power of Costa Rican unions in the 1980s and 1990s. Some have observed, for example, that the 1982 division within the Partido Vanguardia Popular, the crisis and/or disappearance of other leftist forces in

Costa Rica, and the disintegration of the world socialist system have all taken their toll on the militancy of the Costa Rican union movement.[8] Others note that the dramatic downsizing of the public sector in Costa Rica has also affected labour's power. Since the public sector in Costa Rica has been heavily unionized, the government's various structural adjustment and privatization schemes—which have resulted in the loss of thousands of public sector jobs in the 1990s alone—have struck at the heart of union influence.[9] Simply put, as more workers are drained from the state and its institutions, more power is drained from the unions.

Aside from the general political climate and the decreasing size of the state in Costa Rica, other factors related to the weakness of the union movement can be pinpointed. In the last twenty-five years, for example, a form of labour organization known as *solidarismo* has grown dramatically in the country—largely at the expense of *sindicalismo* (unionism). Founded in Costa Rica in 1947 by Alberto Martén,[10] the solidarity movement emphasizes the common interests and co-operation of labour and capital. Under *solidarismo*, owners and workers of a given company contribute equal amounts, usually 5 percent of a worker's salary, to a savings fund. This fund, which is administered by the company's "solidarity association" (composed of both management and workers), is used to finance health care, housing, and education for workers, as well as to provide recreational opportunities and commercial services (such as a store or cafeteria) for them. Consistent with the ideology of collaboration, workers of solidarity associations also renounce their right to strike. Further, under *solidarismo*, collective agreements negotiated by unions are replaced with *arreglos directos* (direct agreements) arrived at by workers' committees (composed of no more than three people) in consultation with company owners or their representatives. Since *solidarismo* has proven to be a cost-effective way to cope with workers' demands and to reduce labour strife, it is hardly surprising that owners have been among the strongest supporters of the solidarity movement and have basically underwritten its spread.

A more detailed analysis of the solidarity movement, its ideology, and its close links to Costa Rica's business class and the Church's ESJ23 is provided in chapter 8. Here, I briefly examine the relationship between *solidarismo* and the weakness of the union movement in Costa Rica. In the first place, it is notable that, while the level of unionization has remained relatively stagnant in Costa Rica throughout the 1980s and 1990s, the number of solidarity associations has been rising steadily: before 1972, there were only 30 solidarity associations in Costa Rica; in 1996, more than 1,800 existed.[11] Much of the growth of *solidarismo* has occurred on the transnational banana company plantations, particularly those in the Limón region on the Atlantic Coast. There, solidarity associations have largely supplanted the once powerful unions. Today, *solidarismo* is reported to be the most common form of labour organization in the country, with more than 15 percent of private-sector workers and 7 percent of public-sector employees affiliated with the solidarity movement.[12] In so far as there is competition between the solidarity movement and the union movement for the allegiance of Costa Rican workers, the *solidaristas* appear to be winning the battle.

The relevant issue, however, is whether there is some sort of causal relationship between the growth of *solidarismo* and the decline of *sindicalismo* in Costa Rica. On the one hand, as discussed, several variables aside from *solidarismo* have contributed to the weakness of the union movement in Costa Rica; on the other, certain *solidaristas* are doing far more than merely taking advantage of the fallout from a weak and divided union movement. In fact, ample evidence indicates that *solidaristas* have used propaganda, pressure, and outright persecution against unionists in order to increase membership in the solidarity movement. As a result, a coalition of Costa Rican union confederations has argued that "*solidarismo* and the violation of union freedom in Costa Rica turn out to be two intimately linked phenomena. Like Siamese twins, the violation of the right to free unionization is the *sine qua non* of the rise and development of *solidarismo* in Costa Rica."[13]

Dubious and coercive *solidarista* recruiting tactics and the blatant infringement of union liberties are particularly well documented in relation to the banana plantations of Limón.[14] Unions are vehemently condemned as corrupt, violent, and communist—qualities said to be at odds with the peace-loving and democratic Costa Rican character—in *solidarista* speeches, pamphlets, and posters. In addition, workers are pressured to join solidarity associations either as a condition of employment on plantations or to ensure continued employment or benefits. Those workers refusing to renounce their union affiliation or who otherwise criticize or doubt the solidarity movement risk ending up on the infamous *listas negras* (blacklists) maintained by the banana companies and *solidarista* promoters.[15] People whose names are included on such lists are harassed and frequently fired, only to find themselves discriminated against when they apply for other jobs in the region. Such sordid tactics have obvious and negative repercussions for the strength of the union movement in the country.

It is important to note, moreover, that the Costa Rican government has been unable and, it appears, unwilling to protect unionists from this type of persecution. Granted, Article 60 of the Costa Rican constitution and Articles 363–70 of the Labour Code clearly imply that, in Costa Rica, union liberties are protected by law: workers in Costa Rica have the right to organize and join unions.[16] In fact, even the Ley de Asociaciones Solidaristas (the 1984 legislation that gave juridical sanction to *solidarismo*) states that any form of activity by solidarity associations or their representatives that hinders the formation or function of union organizations is "absolutely prohibited."[17] Nonetheless, the state has done little, if anything, to censure representatives of the solidarity movement for their obvious disregard of such legislation, even when the government has been pressured to act on this matter by the International Confederation of Free Trade Unions (ICFTU) and the International Labour Organization (ILO).[18] Without the appropriate enforcement, the laws intended to safeguard union liberties in Costa Rica exist on paper only.

There are also other instances, quite apart from those related to the solidarity movement and its actions, in which Costa Rican legislation and its application appear to have an anti-union bias. Most relevant here are the provisions regarding workers' right to strike. The right to strike — for all except those employed in public services — is guaranteed by Article 61 of the Costa Rican constitution.[19] However, between 1969 and 1996 all but three strikes were declared illegal.[20] The fact that almost all strikes are illegal suggests that the right to strike is more an illusion than a reality in Costa Rica; examining some of the specific requirements for a legal strike reveals the extent to which Costa Rican law hinders the ability of unions to mobilize their workers.

First, one must examine the definition of "public services" in the constitutional clause cited above. As might be expected, strikes in certain essential public service settings, such as health care clinics or hospitals, are disallowed. As Article 376 of the Labour Code reveals, however, public service workers also include employees of the state and its institutions, and workers in agriculture (including workers on banana plantations), transportation, and the stevedore industry.[21] When this broad definition of public services is taken into account, relatively few Costa Rican workers actually have the right to strike.

In effect, only Costa Rican workers in certain private enterprises can strike legally. Even in these cases, however, the chances of a strike being declared legal are extremely slim. For one thing, at least 60 percent of the workers must support a strike for it to be deemed legal. This does not seem an overly stringent requirement in itself — until one considers that, in Costa Rica, the workers in favour of such labour action must sign their names on a list to be registered with the labour tribunals. Because this type of public declaration of support for union actions will often lead to a worker being fired by his or her employer, it is not surprising that the necessary number of workers' signatures is almost impossible to collect.[22] Additionally, a strike will only be classified as legal once all other avenues (e.g., conciliation) for settling the differences between employer and employees have been exhausted. Again, this does not appear to be unreasonable, except for the fact that, under Costa Rican law, the conciliation process can last up to forty-five days. During this phase, the employer often stalls, intimidates workers, and otherwise interferes with the momentum of the pro-strike agitators — so much so that unions can rarely afford to wait the legally prescribed amount of time to declare a work stoppage.[23] Conciliation in Costa Rica very rarely ends in a resolution of labour disputes. Overall, with such requisites built into Costa Rican labour law, it is easy to see why so few strikes in Costa Rica are legal. In the end, moreover, this anti-union characteristic of the Costa Rican legal system constitutes yet another blow to the strength of individual unions and to the overall union movement in Costa Rica.

♦ The Crisis and Workers' (Mis)Fortunes

A final area of concern for labour activists and labourers alike involves the effects of the Costa Rican crisis, and the neo-liberal reaction to the crisis, on economic indicators that are specifically relevant to workers and their living standards. Importantly, workers' earnings were undeniably and negatively affected at the height of the economic crisis, leading one ILO analyst to declare that a "veritable collapse of the wage structure" had occurred in Costa Rica.[24] From 1979 to 1983, for example, the real wages of workers in all sectors of the economy dropped dramatically. Workers in the private sector fared the "best," experiencing "only" a 21 percent drop in their real wages during this period. Workers in the public sectors and autonomous agencies saw their real wages decrease by 34 percent and 31 percent, respectively, while central government workers suffered an astonishing 39 percent decline.[25] Another indicator of the severity of the situation was the sharp decrease in the difference between the minimum and average Costa Rican wages. In 1980 the difference was 70 percent but, by mid-1982, this figure had sunk to under 10 percent.[26] Given the drop in wages and concurrently rising prices of consumer goods and basic necessities, workers' purchasing power and their very ability to subsist were severely compromised.[27]

Other measures speak further to the dire straits of workers during the crisis. Of these, the levels of open unemployment, underemployment, and hidden unemployment deserve consideration. Open unemployment peaked at 9.4 percent in 1982 and disproportionately affected women, youth, and migrant workers, particularly the less educated and less skilled among these groups.[28] Underemployment in terms of insufficient hours worked (i.e., less than a full work week) plagued one-quarter of those employed, while underemployment in terms of insufficient income earned (i.e., less than minimum wage) affected more than a quarter of all workers. In addition, the number of hidden unemployed (i.e., potential workers, usually spouses and school-aged youth, who are classified by the government as inactive but would work if given the chance) more than doubled between 1979 and 1982.[29] All told, according to one estimate, in 1982 open unemployment, underemployment, and hidden unemployment hit 55 percent of the labour force, or 482,000 Costa Ricans.[30]

Despite the improvement in certain economic indicators after 1983 and the supposed success of neo-liberal programming, many Costa Rican workers continued to face tough times. Thus, while unemployment levels fell after the mid-1980s, many of the new jobs created were low-paying and low-skilled, concentrated as they were in assembly industries and agro-export enterprises.[31] In the years after the crisis, the percentage of underemployed workers actually rose, with an estimated 37 percent receiving below minimum wages in 1991.[32] Real wages have also fluctuated since the crisis. Instead of a slow and steady increase, some analysts have noted that gains made in this area under vote-seeking governments tend to evaporate in non-election years.[33] One telling indicator of the condition of workers in Costa Rica since the crisis was the fact that, in 1991, almost 40 percent of wage workers were living below the poverty line.[34]

A final phenomenon with troubling implications has been the increasing "informalization" of Costa Rican workers. The informal sector of the economy began to grow during the crisis[35] and continued to expand throughout the 1980s and into the 1990s.[36] By far the most visible workers in this sector are the *vendedores ambulantes* (street vendors) in San José. These men, women, and children may shine shoes or sell their wares (anything from fruit, vegetables, and prepared foods to crafts, clothing, and cosmetics) out of bags or makeshift stalls. Mass layoffs in the banana industry and the drastic downsizing of the state have forced thousands of extra workers into such informal sector activities, which also include other self-employed workers and the employees of very small businesses known as *microempresas*. Workers in this sector, who made up almost one-quarter of the labour force by 1991, are particularly vulnerable; since most are not protected by labour regulations and are less likely to be covered by social security, their ability to guarantee a minimum subsistence level for their households is jeopardized. In fact, 53.5 percent of such workers fell below the poverty line in mid-1991.[37] Given all this, it appears that the end of the economic crisis did not spell the end of the troubles for many Costa Rican workers.

Promise in the Costa Rican Union Movement

In light of these weaknesses in the union movement and the problems plaguing its members, one may wonder whether there were any signs of hope for Costa Rican unions and workers after the crisis began, or whether the labour movement was doomed to still further difficulties as neo-liberal policies became even more entrenched in Costa Rica late in the century. In fact, and despite the serious problems and persecutions discussed above, there were some indications of a reinvigorated union movement during the 1980s and 1990s.

In spite of the considerable legal bias against unions and strikes, workers in Costa Rica continued to use strikes as a means to place pressure on their employers and the state. Interestingly, some of the most pronounced strike activity occurred in the thick of the economic crisis in 1980. In that year alone, workers waged 63 strikes in Costa Rica (by contrast, from 1972 to 1979 there were 110 strikes in total).[38] Most of the 1980 strikes were in the agricultural sector, and the most significant of these was the banana strike in Golfito of the Zona Sur; in fact, many of the other strikes of this year were waged in solidarity with the workers of that region. Other important banana strikes occurred in 1982, in Limón, and 1984, again in the Zona Sur. But, by the mid-1980s, the agricultural sector had ceased to be the focal point of union activity.

In the late 1980s, strikes among government employees, teachers, and non-agricultural labourers in the Limón region became more frequent. Of note were the August 1989 general strike in Limón; the July and August 1993 strikes of government workers, educators, and Limonense labourers (with a total participation of approximately 97,000 workers);[39] and the strikes that sprung up in relation to the massive teachers' strike in July 1995. These and some other strikes during this period often included specific demands for better wages and benefits; teachers, for example, have struck for salary increases and against proposed changes to their pension plan. The strikes were more generally aimed, however, at protesting the government's programs of privatization and structural adjustment, and at contesting the layoffs, decimated social programs, and increases in the cost of living that resulted from these programs. In spite of the various woes of the union movement during this time, workers still attempted to register their dissatisfaction by stopping work and taking to the streets.

Aside from the fact that union activism has persisted throughout the 1980s and 1990s in the face of the obstacles provided by the law and *solidarismo*, the changed nature of this activism during this period also deserves comment. The shift in the locus of union activity from the private to the public sector and, to a certain extent, from manual labourers (such as *bananeros*) to professionals (such as teachers and government bureaucrats), indicates the beginnings of a deeper ideological and political realignment in Costa Rican society.

In earlier times and in the context of a burgeoning benefactor state, professionals in the public sector could count on a relatively stable and comfortable existence in Costa Rica. The government, for its part, could count on these professionals to reinforce its rule through their compliance, silence, and, especially in the case of teachers, through their transmittal of the predominant ideological biases in Costa Rican society. Although strikes in the public sector (among doctors, for example) were not unknown during this period, they were generally infrequent and of short duration. Even when the economic crisis hit Costa Rica in the early 1980s, these professionals remained relatively complacent. It was only when the socio-economic repercussions of the neo-liberal *solutions* to the crisis were revealed in the late 1980s that discontent among professionals began to show. At that point, even though the government declared the crisis to be over and certain economic indicators had rebounded, these professionals did not witness any attendant increase in their standard of living. Instead—opposite to what they may have expected, but similar to many other Costa Ricans at that time—they began to feel the pinch of structural adjustment. With government downsizing and privatization schemes further threatening their very jobs, these professionals had little motivation to continue legitimating the government's rule with their passivity. Disaffected with neo-liberal policies and detached from their traditional functions in the state, these public-sector professionals started to protest against the government in unprecedented numbers. While with these protests the government was losing an essential source of ideological support at a time when its controversial policies most needed confirmation, the union movement gained some much-needed and high-profile momentum in the public sector.

Importantly, while such public-service strikes were still classified as illegal, after 1993 the individual instigators of and participants in such actions could no longer be punished with jail terms. Once the legislative assembly voted to repeal Articles 333 and 334 of the Penal Code in June 1993 (albeit after a seven-year delay), participation in strikes was effectively "de-penalized."[40] This may appear to be a small consolation in light of the otherwise anti-union bias of the Costa Rican legal system, but the de-penalization does provide some measure of protection for union leaders and members and constitutes an encouraging advance for the union movement.

Unionists can also be heartened by the collaboration and coalition building within the union movement, phenomena that have helped to offset the process of atomization discussed above. In 1986, for example, six major union centrals in the country joined together under the name Consejo Permanente de los Trabajadores (CPT, Permanent Workers' Council). Although the individual confederations within the council still remain, the CPT as an umbrella organization has proven to be an important protagonist in the strikes and protests against privatization and structural adjustment.[41] While this council is an instance of co-ordination across various labour sectors, other smaller coalitions of note have been formed within individual sectors, such as the Consejo Intermagisterial Asociado (CIMA, Associated Inter-Magisterial Council, an organization for the country's teachers) and the Frente de Organizaciones Laborales del Sector Agropecuario (FOLSA, Front of Labour Organizations of the Agricultural Sector). Interestingly, one of these sectoral organizations, the Frente de Organizaciones Sindicales del Sector Salud (FOSSS, Front of Health

Sector Union Organizations) has worked extensively with the Church organization CECODERS in protesting the proposed reform and privatization of the health care system in Costa Rica. Such collaboration among unions compensates for some of the effects of fragmentation in the union movement and helps to provide workers with a stronger voice in the face of the government's neo-liberal agenda.

On a different level, some union leaders have recently begun to participate in the development of a new political party in Costa Rica, the Partido Rescate Nacional (PRN, National Recovery Party).[42] These *sindicalistas* recognize that strikes and other labour actions can only go so far in challenging the government's anti-union bias; they argue that the best way to protect and promote the interests of workers is to seek direct representation in the country's legislative assembly. Strictly speaking, the proposed PRN will not be a party of unionists but, rather, an alternative coalition drawn from various sectors of civil society. However, by developing a formal political presence in Costa Rica, union leaders hope to shape government policy from the outset, as opposed to merely protesting its implications after the fact. To date the party has not yet received official recognition from the Tribunal Supremo de Elecciones; however, the very efforts of *sindicalistas* to employ broad political means to confront the problems facing workers is another indication that the Costa Rican union movement is by no means in complete decline.

Limón en Lucha

The 1996 protest movement referred to as "Limón en Lucha" (Limón in Struggle) deserves special mention at this juncture for a number of reasons. This movement is noteworthy because it illustrates some of the recent developments in the Costa Rican union movement discussed above. Further, it reinforces the point that Costa Rica is a more conflict-ridden nation than is commonly assumed. The Limón en Lucha movement is also significant because, as will eventually be shown, it involved the considerable participation of several pastoral agents of the Catholic Church in Limón. Finally, Limón en Lucha is important quite simply because it was the most impressive, widely based, and, in certain respects, effective union-led protest movement to occur in Costa Rica in recent decades.

Limón en Lucha was a coalition built in May 1996 and based largely in Puerto Limón (the capital city of Limón province, the poorest region in Costa Rica). Unions and their leaders formed the heart of the coalition and its co-ordinating committee. Key roles in the alliance were played by union representatives from the stevedore industry; the main hospital in Limón (Hospital Tony Facio) and, more generally, the medical sciences profession; the municipality of Limón; and the University of Costa Rica. The coalition of fifty-seven members also incorporated various community associations, women's organizations, and *campesino* organizations, as well as certain representatives from the Catholic Church and several Protestant churches in Limón (most notably the Baptist and Adventist churches, and the Salvation Army).[43] Significantly, then, not only was Limón en Lucha an example of coalition building within the union movement, it was also an instance of labour's collaboration with various popular sectors under a common banner.

Once formed, the leaders of Limón en Lucha began to pressure the Costa Rican government on a number of fronts.[44] They demanded, for instance, that dockworkers be guaranteed a fixed minimum wage and workday length, and that measures be taken to ease the hardships faced by workers laid off from the stevedore industry. Further, the Limón en Lucha committee called for a halt to government plans to amend the constitution to allow for the privatization of the country's ports, airports, and railway system. The movement's members also sought a variety of improvements in housing, education, public health care, sanitation, and infrastructure, all aimed at redressing the long-standing conditions of poverty in the country's most disadvantaged region. Overall, therefore, and despite the heavy labour representation in the movement, Limón en Lucha was not just a struggle for better wages or working conditions. It was, instead, *de todo y para todos* (from all and for all): a broadly based movement protesting injustice and government policy in the region and seeking a better quality of life for all Limonenses.

The leaders of Limón en Lucha began by petitioning the central government to fulfil the movement's demands and, when they received unsatisfactory responses, turned in mid-August to other pressure tactics. The co-ordinating committee first called for the paralyzing of the Moín and Alemán docks, two of Costa Rica's key commercial ports on the Atlantic.[45] Soon, strike activity spread to other sectors, as commercial establishments closed their doors and workers at Hospital Tony Facio scaled back services. Roadblocks and protest marches were also employed and these further disrupted traffic and commerce in the region. From the outset, there were considerable numbers of police in the area and they used gunfire and tear gas to quash the rioting that broke out on several occasions. At least one death and hundreds of injuries were reported.[46] For a two-week period, the Limón en Lucha protests captured the attention of the nation and the headlines of the media—Costa Ricans were reminded yet again that theirs was not a country immune to violence.

Finally, in early September, after discussions had been repeatedly launched and broken off, government representatives and the Limón en Lucha negotiating committee settled on over two hundred points of agreement. The members of Limón en Lucha had succeeded in voicing their demands and in bringing the government to the table. And, while the longer-term efficacy of the protests and negotiations remains unclear,[47] the union movement in Limón, in an alliance with the popular sectors of the region, showed a vitality and unity of purpose not expected by observers preoccupied with tales of unionism's fragmentation and decline.

Conclusion

It is difficult to describe the status of the Costa Rican union movement from 1979 onward in a straightforward manner. Certainly, serious problems have plagued the unions and have hampered their ability and freedom to act in the interests of workers. Yet, for every charge of atomization, there is a countervailing example of collaboration, and for every lament about union passivity, a protest that proves the contrary. The 1980s and 1990s brought mixed fortunes for the union movement in Costa Rica; that the overall condition of the union movement defies clear categorization is not surprising. Still, some general observations can be made about recent changes in the tenor of union activity and their significance. If the popular protests described in the last chapter represented a challenge to the government and its long-standing reliance on the myth of Costa Rican exceptionionalism, the phenomena treated in this chapter reveal that this challenge is deepening.

Specifically, the ignition of union activism among public-sector professionals indicates that a larger segment of Costa Rican society is opting to contest the bases of governmental rule. These recently mobilized professionals are not only articulating workplace- or industry-specific concerns but they are also protesting the broader economic and political policies on which the neo-liberal government rests. In the 1980s and 1990s, they demanded change from the very order that, formerly, they apparently felt no need to question. Importantly, since these intellectuals have become unmoored from their traditional ideological function in favour of the state, there is the potential for them to be converted into allies of the popular classes in Costa Rica. Some alliances are already being forged as witnessed, for example, in the participation of public-sector unionists alongside popular organization members in the Limón en Lucha struggles. Many of the Costa Rican teachers on strike—in so far as they move beyond demands for better wages and pensions to defend all those affected by the biases of neo-liberalism—can also be seen as participants in a much wider effort to transform the existing social order.

Perhaps just as significantly, these more heterogeneous protests hold promise for the Costa Rican union movement as a whole. Whereas earlier, more narrowly based and sector-specific strikes (such as those on banana plantations) were justified, their long-term efficacy was severely limited in the context of anti-union legislation and the rise of *solidarismo*.

A more broadly based movement, such as Limón en Lucha, is less vulnerable to persecution and, if successful, will manage to address both detestable working conditions *and* the political/economic models that ultimately give rise to and sustain them. Moreover, although to date unionists in Costa Rica have been unable to derail the *solidarismo* phenomenon directly, their continued support for and participation in anti-government protests will indirectly challenge the ideological underpinnings of the solidarity movement. Since *solidarismo* (like the government) depends on people's willingness to value consensus and collaboration in society regardless of existing injustice and inequity, any visible and repeated contradiction of these values—such as occurs with the widespread and high-profile protests I have discussed here—will eventually help to erode the solidarity movement's credibility. As many unionists have come to acknowledge themselves with their attempt to create an alternate political party in Costa Rica, the struggle for workers' rights must take place on various ideological, political, and economic levels.

In the end, it is obvious that opinions differ in Costa Rican society about whether and how and when workers should be allowed to unionize and to express their grievances in protests and strikes. Crucially, some of these same differences of opinion are reflected within the Costa Rican Catholic Church. Church leaders and pastoral agents struggle, for example, over whether *sindicalismo* or *solidarismo* best represents the interests of workers. Or they work to define through their words—and confirm by their actions—whether the use of strikes is legitimate. In such efforts, however, Church agents not only observe and are influenced by the sociohistorical context around them, they also look to the Church magisterium for inspiration and guidance. Hence, this study turns to the Catholic social teaching tradition, which contains ample material related to the condition and the rights of workers, as yet another phenomenon that needs to be examined in order to understand the types of *pastoral obrera* that exist in Costa Rica.

Official Catholic Social Teaching on Workers' Issues 4

> Human work is a key, probably the essential key,
> to the whole social question.
> —Pope John Paul II, *Laborem Exercens*

Since Leo XIII issued his famous encyclical *Rerum Novarum* (*On the Condition of Labour*)[1] over one hundred years ago, the theme of work has figured prominently in the Catholic social teaching tradition.[2] While Catholic social teaching documents have routinely condemned the overly harsh or unjust conditions to which workers are often subjected, work in itself has always been ascribed a positive value by the magisterium. At a most basic level, work is said to be a duty and a right,[3] the means by which an individual sustains life and contributes to his or her family, community, and nation.[4] According to Catholic social teaching, there is dignity and honour in work,[5] labour being the means through which one realizes, maintains, and develops one's humanity.[6] Yet work is also said to have theological significance: it is through work that humans can participate in the activity of the Creator,[7] it is through toil that the worker can share, in some small way, in the cross of Christ.[8] In fact, as Pope John Paul II reminds his readers in *Laborem Exercens*, Jesus Christ himself was a working man, and Christ looks on human work with love, appreciation, and respect.[9]

In light of my discussion, however, more relevant in Catholic social teaching is the treatment of workers' rights, not the issue or definition of work per se. Significantly, the rights of workers to strike and to form unions have been contested in Costa Rica over the years, regardless of the juridical protection such liberties appear to be given. For their part, Church leaders in Costa Rica have turned to the Catholic social teaching tradition for inspiration and legitimation as they minister to workers and attempt to clarify their rights. Interestingly, though, often the very same Church documents are used to justify opposing pastoral positions on labour in Costa Rica. A first step in discovering why this is the case is to uncover precisely what the magisterium has taught in regard to workers' rights over the years.

Notes for chapter 4 start on page 208

A simple chronology of Church teaching on strikes and unions is not enough, however. The "condition of labour" in society is dependent on far more than simply the right to association or to strike. The characteristics of the overall social structure, the available mechanisms for remedying social injustice, the role of the lower classes in social change: these are just some of the factors that also have implications for workers and their well being in any given society. Since the Catholic social teaching tradition has concerned itself with such issues in the past century, I also consider the Church's broader social justice perspectives as part of my analysis. As the following survey indicates, two patterns in Church history can be delineated: the conservative and the liberationist.

Strikes and Unions in Catholic Social Teaching

In general, Catholic social teaching on workers' issues appears in two sets of documents: statements from the Vatican (i.e., documents issued by individual popes and by the conciliar fathers at Vatican II), and documents issued by CELAM (i.e., the Latin American bishops' council) at its general conferences.

♦ Vatican Statements

In 1891, Leo XIII issued the first encyclical that dealt extensively with workers' issues in modern society. A startling Church pronouncement for its time, *Rerum Novarum* was a strong and unprecedented papal critique of the miserable condition of workers under industrial capitalism. While also warning against the dangers of socialism (to which he feared the Church was losing the lower classes), the pope in this encyclical eloquently promotes such workers' rights as the right to a just wage and to regulated hours of labour. In addition, Pope Leo touches on the issue of strikes and on the workers' right to form "associations." Significantly, however, his message on these latter two themes is rather ambiguous and would probably prove disappointing to the present-day unionist.

On the matter of strikes, as Donal Dorr notes,[10] Leo emphasizes what makes a strike wrong, as opposed to what would justify one. The pope states, for example, that a strike is a "grave inconvenience" that hurts trade and the public interest, and that frequently leads to violence. Although the pope acknowledges that the grievances leading to a strike (such as overwork or insufficient wages) may be legitimate, he places the onus on the state to enact the appropriate laws so that such labour conflicts need not arise.[11] For their part, workers are, in the pope's words, "never to injure capital, nor to outrage the person of an employer; never to employ violence in representing [their] own cause, nor to engage in riot or disorder."[12] While strikes are not mentioned by name at this point, this passage certainly implies that strikes with such characteristics should not be allowed. In fact, since Leo's overriding concern in *Rerum Novarum* is with the maintenance of harmony and order in society (a theme treated at length below), strikes—in so far as they disrupt social stability—appear to be frowned on. In the end, nonetheless, since strikes in themselves are never explicitly condemned in the document, Leo's exact position on the issue (or, for that matter, on more tranquil work stoppages) remains unclear.

The pope's stance on the right of workers to unionize is also ambiguous. Granted, he lauds "workmen's associations" as the most important of all social assistance organizations and states that it is a natural right of citizens to form associations.[13] Leo further points to the potential importance of such organizations in helping members resolve disputes with their "masters," in arranging for a continuous supply of work, and in creating a contingency fund to help sick, injured, or elderly members.[14] Still, nowhere in the encyclical is it entirely clear that it is in fact *trade unions* (understood as organizations restricted to wage workers only) to which Leo is referring. As several scholars have pointed out, the terminology used in this section of the encyclical is vague and inconsistent, with the use of various terms (in the original Latin, *associationes, collegia, sodalitia, sodalitates, societates*, and *communitates*) that leave the reader uncertain as to whether the pope is discussing mixed groups of workers and employers, or groups of labourers alone.[15] Moreover, Leo warns against associations based on un-Christian principles;[16] and, true to his emphasis on harmony and order in society, he does not in the slightest encourage such "workmen's associations" to undertake resolute or militant action to further the workers' cause. Thus, those who look to *Rerum Novarum* for the unconditional support of unions and their activities will likely be disappointed.

After *Rerum Novarum*, the next major document in the Catholic social teaching tradition was Pius XI's *Quadragesimo Anno* (*After Forty Years*, sometimes also referred to as *On the Social Order*). Issued in 1931 to commemorate the fortieth anniversary of Leo's influential encyclical, *Quadragesimo Anno* sought to reaffirm and update the principles laid out in *Rerum Novarum* and to encourage a Christian reconstruction of society, beginning with the renovation of morals. Clarifying Leo's teaching on workers' associations, Pope Pius comes out strongly in favour of trade unions.[17] He leaves no question that the Church supports the formation of associations restricted to workers only, and he stresses the importance of such unions in protecting the rights and interests of the working classes. Nonetheless, Pope Pius also promotes a corporatist model of social organization based on occupational/vocational "groups." He saw such groups, composed of both employers and employees, as essential in promoting harmony among the various "ranks" in society.[18] Finally, although Pius is brief and indirect on the matter of strikes,[19] he does appear to uphold the prohibition of strikes made by his immediate predecessors, Pius X and Benedict XV. This position would certainly be in line with the emphasis in *Quadragesimo Anno* on social harmony and the mutual collaboration between capital and labour.

Pope John XXIII was next to broach the subject of workers' rights in his 1961 encyclical, *Mater et Magistra (Christianity and Social Progress)*.[20] While the novelty of *Mater et Magistra* lay in its relatively detailed treatment of international social and economic development issues, Pope John's discussion of unions in this document is also noteworthy. Cognisant of the reasons earlier Church leaders were wary of union organizing, the pope notes that "these bodies no longer recruit workers for the purposes of strife, but rather for pursuing a common aim."[21] He praises those who strive "to vindicate the rights of workingmen and to improve their lot and conduct"[22] and even applauds the "effective and valuable" work of the ILO.[23] Although in this encyclical the pope did not directly address the issue of the right to strike, a discussion of this matter was soon to follow in one of the core documents of the Second Vatican Council (1962–65).

The monumental *Gaudium et Spes (Pastoral Constitution on the Church in the Modern World)* was released near the close of Vatican II and can be considered a cornerstone of the council's process of *aggiornamento* (updating or renewal) of the Roman Catholic Church. A wide-ranging document that covers all manner of themes from international peace and poverty to politics, marriage, culture, and the economy, *Gaudium et Spes* also manages to address the issues of unions and strikes. On the matter of unions, the conciliar fathers are succinct: "Among the basic rights of the human person must be counted the right of freely founding labour unions. These unions should be truly able to represent the workers and to contribute to the proper arrangement of economic life. Another such right is that of taking part freely in the activity of these unions without risk of reprisal."[24] This final sentence can be taken to imply that strikes too are permissible and, indeed, the document affirms that the strike can be a legitimate means to defend workers' rights and to fulfil their just demands. Overall, however, the document cautions that a strike is to be a mechanism of last resort only, with sincere discussion and negotiation the preferred means of resolving disputes.[25] Hence, with *Gaudium et Spes*, the Second Vatican Council reaffirmed the Church's approval of trade unions and attempted to set certain guidelines for their activities.

Pope Paul VI, who presided over the sessions of Vatican II after John XXIII died in 1963, further developed the Church's position on workers' organizations in his own writings. While there are some positive allusions to unions in *Populorum Progressio (On the Development of Peoples)*,[26] a more explicit teaching can be found in the pope's apostolic letter of 1971, *Octogesima Adveniens (A Call to Action)*.[27] In this latter document, the pope notes the important contribution that unions can make to society and affirms the conciliar position on strikes (i.e., that a strike is recognized as legitimate when used "as a final means of defence").[28] Yet, in a manner reminiscent of Leo XIII's *Rerum Novarum*, Paul appears to be more concerned with pointing out the potential dangers of union activism and strikes, as opposed to promoting their legitimacy. He states that the activity of unions "is not without its difficulties," including the temptation to impose conditions that would burden the economy or the "social body" and the desire to obtain demands of a "directly political" nature.[29] The implication here is that unions are to restrict their activities to those involving specifically economic issues and that, even then, they are not to ask for too much.

One problem with this position, however, is that it is often difficult to delineate a specifically "economic" as opposed to a "political" realm in modern society. The privatization of the Costa Rican public sector, for example, has both political and economic aspects. Privatization is a government-initiated process involving a reorganization of the state and its services; in this sense, it is certainly a political issue. Yet privatization also involves economics, for not only is the matter of ownership involved, the privatization process often has an impact on the condition of workers by affecting the availability of employment and the level of wages offered. Although this example simplifies the mechanics of Costa Rican privatization, it is sufficient to indicate how problematic it can be to speak solely of its economic or political underpinnings. Restricting the activity of unions to the economic sphere, therefore, implies that unionists are only to involve themselves with the narrowest of bread and butter concerns, regardless of the broader political policies or laws that contributed to such concerns in the first place. In a society in which economics and politics are combined, disallowing the participation of unions in politics robs them of much potential efficacy and force.[30] Still, serious as the implications of this teaching may be, the fact remains that workers' issues were not a central theme of either Paul VI's papacy or his writings.

The same could certainly not be said of Pope John Paul II, who in 1981 issued the first papal encyclical to deal primarily with the question of work since *Rerum Novarum*. His *Laborem Exercens (On Human Work)* is an aptly named and complex treatise that explores the process of work and the dignity of the worker from a historical, philosophical, and theological viewpoint. The pope does treat workers' issues in his other two major social encyclicals, *Sollicitudo Rei Socialis (On Social Concern)*[31] and especially *Centesimus Annus (On the Hundredth Anniversary of Rerum Novarum)*,[32] but *Laborem Exercens* remains the most explicit and detailed statement of his views on the topic.

John Paul's specific teachings on unions and strikes are gathered under one lengthy subsection of his encyclical.[33] Consistent with most of his predecessors, John Paul comes out clearly in favour of the right of workers to form unions. Labelling them "an indispensable element of social life," the pope argues that unions function "to defend the existential interests of workers in all sectors in which their rights are concerned." He clarifies that all types of workers—not just industrial labourers—can form unions and that employers may also set up their own associations. On the issue of politics, the pope claims that, while union activity does enter the field of politics (as long as politics is "understood as prudent concern for the common good"), unions themselves should not "play politics," should not act like political parties struggling for power, and should not have too close ties to existing parties. In addition, Pope John Paul II sees strikes as legitimate "in the proper conditions and within just limits." Once again they are viewed as an "extreme" means that must not be abused—especially, John Paul emphasizes, for "political" purposes. The pope also argues that strikes should not endanger essential community services. Finally, he warns that misuse of the strike as a weapon can paralyze the whole of socio-economic life, a situation at odds with the common good of society. Like Leo XIII and Paul VI before him, Pope John Paul II seems more concerned to spell out what would make a strike wrong than to promote the idea of the strike as a right.

The treatment of unions and politics in this section of *Laborem Exercens* presents certain difficulties. To begin with, the pope's use of the term "politics" is imprecise. He jumps from a general definition of politics as concern for the common good to a reference to party politics to the vague notion of "political purposes"—and he evaluates the participation of unions in each type of activity differently. Similarly, what exactly does "playing politics" mean? On the one hand, the admonition against playing politics can be taken to mean that the pope is warning union leaders to focus on protecting the rights of workers instead of being preoccupied with their own personal quests for power and social influence. On the other hand, the whole notion of prohibiting union activism in the political sphere once again brings up the issue of the impossibility of strictly separating the economic and the political in modern society. By prohibiting unions from playing politics, is the pope thereby saying that government policies and legislation are not legitimate targets for union concern? In many countries, union political activity is precisely the means by which workers' rights are secured;[34] in some cases (e.g., the British Labour Party), unions are constitutionally linked with political parties.[35] When considered in this light, the pope's prescription regarding politics seems unrealistic at best and detrimental to workers' rights at worst.

Nonetheless, the full implications of Pope John Paul's teachings on workers' rights can only be understood in light of his more general positions on such matters as the relationship of labour and capital, or the mechanisms for social change. Before turning to discuss these issues, however, it is first necessary to examine one other major body of Catholic social teaching relevant to the Costa Rican situation—that produced by CELAM.

♦ CELAM Documents

The creation of CELAM in 1955 was one of the most important events in the history of the Latin American Roman Catholic Church. Until that time, no formal collective expression of the continent's Catholic Church existed. A meeting of Latin American bishops had been held once before, in Rome, in 1899. But not until the First General Latin American Episcopal Conference met in Rio de Janeiro and formed CELAM was there an actual episcopal organization devoted to studying the affairs and co-ordinating the activities of the Church throughout the region as a whole. As such, over the years, CELAM came to be an extremely powerful force in the operation of the Latin American Church.[36]

CELAM's second general conference in Medellín, Colombia, in 1968, was a watershed event for the Latin American Church that provided legitimation and inspiration for the emerging liberation theology movement on the continent. At Medellín, the bishops documented and denounced the injustice they saw around them, they promoted the Church's option for the poor, and they committed themselves to working for both spiritual change and the radical transformation of societal structures.[37] Significantly, the bishops saw workers and workers' unions as principle agents in this process of social change.[38] Not only do workers have the right to unionize, according to the Medellín documents, but their unions should also acquire "sufficient strength and presence" and should participate in all levels of production and in the areas of national, continental, and international trade. In addition, the bishops counsel that union members should exercise their right to be represented "on the political, social and economic levels, where decisions are made that are related to the common good."[39] In contrast to the papal teachings on unions and their activities, then, the bishops at Medellín appear to give unionists the right—and the responsibility—to become involved in social movements and political debates that extend beyond narrow "economic" issues.

The final document from CELAM's third general conference,[40] held in Puebla, Mexico, in 1979, is markedly different in tone from the Medellín texts. The Puebla conference came at a time when many Church officials had grown wary of the revolutionary political implications of liberation theology; in large part, the Puebla document exhibits the reserve of these more conservative factions. Such restraint can also be detected in the bishops' treatment of workers' issues. While in the final document the bishops affirm the right to unionize and comment on the frequent disregard for labour legislation in Latin America,[41] bold calls for workers' participation in the transformation of society are absent. In contrast to the Medellín bishops' view of workers as agents of social change, the bishops at Puebla see working people as victims of poverty and repression or as objects of the Church's evangelization.[42] Granted, the Puebla bishops call for workers to "contribute responsibly to the common good" and to the construction of "the Latin America of tomorrow,"[43] but even these phrases seem rather weak and vague. In combination with other comments and the bishops' warning against the "exasperated politicization" of the top union levels,[44] however, the implication becomes clearer. It appears that, much as Pope John Paul II was to do in *Laborem Exercens* two years later, the bishops in the Puebla document are attempting to de-politicize the role of workers and unions in Latin America.

The last text to be examined in this history of Catholic social teaching was issued by CELAM in Santo Domingo during its fourth general conference.[45] The conference began in 1992 (exactly five hundred years after the day Columbus first sighted land in the Americas) and was intended as a celebration of Jesus Christ and the Church's evangelization on the continent. Although in the conclusions from the conference the realm of work is delineated as an area of great pastoral concern,[46] the treatment of workers' issues is one of the weakest in the entire Catholic social teaching tradition. In the Santo Domingo document, for example, the bishops do not repeat the by-then standard Catholic social teaching confirmation of the right to unionization or even refer to unions by name; the document alludes instead to "organizations of workers."[47] The bishops' conclusions do, however, note the lack of respect for workers' rights and the setbacks in labour legislation in Latin America.[48] Yet the emphasis there is on the rights of individual workers very narrowly defined (e.g., the right to sufficient pay and to protection for old age, illness, and unemployment),[49] and there is the assumption that adequate — and adequately enforced — legislation is the key to securing justice for workers. While these matters are undoubtedly important, the bishops at Santo Domingo give no recognition of the role of workers or unions themselves in the broader political environment. Lawmakers and law enforcers appear to be the key agents in change, while the potential activism of workers at the grassroots level is ignored.

Finally, it should be acknowledged that part of the reason that workers and their families are poor is because of the overall socio-economic conditions in which they attempt to subsist. The Santo Domingo bishops appear to recognize this, but their suggestion that increased economic growth will increase the welfare of the poor (through just distribution)[50] is problematic. By concentrating on improving productivity within the present economic framework instead of questioning whether the framework itself is a hindrance to fairer distribution,[51] the bishops appear to misplace the emphasis again. An essential part of securing workers' rights is transforming exclusionary and inequitable social structures as a whole, not merely remedying employers' lack of compliance with labour laws or stimulating economic growth. The bishops at Santo Domingo do not make these connections strongly enough in their treatment of work and, as a result, their teachings on workers' issues suffer.

As a matter of fact, any treatment of workers' issues will be incomplete if it remains narrowly concerned with the rights of workers to form unions or to strike. A thorough understanding of the various positions on workers within Catholic social teaching can only be sought in the context of the Church's overall discussion of social justice.

Contrasting Approaches to Social Justice

Put simply, Catholic social teaching cannot be considered an internally uniform or consistent body of thought. The perspectives on social justice represented in Catholic social teaching documents run the range from conservative to liberationist in nature. In this section, I define the terms "conservative" and "liberationist," and provide the clearest examples of such positions from the Catholic social teaching corpus. Overall, conservatives and liberationists can be distinguished by their opposing positions on three key measures: their general view of society, their diagnosis of social problems, and their proposed strategy for overcoming such problems.

♦ Conservative Catholic Social Teaching

The classic conservative position in Catholic social teaching can be characterized by a functionalist or organic view of society, by a diagnosis of social problems that emphasizes individual attitudes and behaviours and that is reluctant to criticize the structures of capitalism itself, and by a model of social change that is top-down, non-violent, and based on consensus and collaboration as opposed to conflict. These characteristics are best illustrated with reference to the main Catholic social teaching encyclicals of popes Leo XIII and Pius XI.

▶ *Leo XIII and Pius XI*   To begin, it is clear that *Rerum Novarum* and *Quadragesimo Anno* are both based on a functionalist view of the social order. Here, society is seen as an organic whole, much like the human body, in which all the parts function in unison to contribute to the operation of one another and to the overall life of the organism. From this perspective, inequities and social stratification are a given; each social group has its own particular role to play in order to keep society functioning smoothly. In *Rerum Novarum*, for instance, Pope Leo explains that: "Such inequality is far from being disadvantageous either to individuals or to the community; social and public life can only go on by the help of various kinds of capacity and the playing of many parts, and each man, as a rule, chooses the part which peculiarly suits his case."[52] From this perspective, abolishing differences among humans or classes would be impossible; to try to do so would be a vain effort against natural law. By extension, for both Leo and Pius, harmony and collaboration among the various social groups are the proper foundations of social life, with stability and order in society prized above all.

Nonetheless, despite this ideal of "blessed social peace"[53] for which both popes longed, Leo and Pius recognized the tensions and strife in the societies of their day. Leo commented on the "conflict" and "evil" around him, in which "a small number of very rich men have been able to lay upon the masses of the poor a yoke little better than slavery itself."[54] Pius, for his part, lamented the "grave disorder" of class "combat" in his own time, so greatly at odds with the well-ordered social body he and his predecessor sought.[55] Importantly, however, although Leo and Pius decried the condition of workers under industrial capitalism, they did not lay the blame for social problems on capitalism per se. Pius, for example, noted: "[I]t is clear then that the system as such is not to be condemned. Surely it is not vicious of its very nature."[56] Instead, Leo and Pius criticized only the extremes of modern capitalism as seen, for instance, in the enormous gulf between rich and poor,[57] in the "despotic economic domination ... concentrated in the hands of a few,"[58] or in the "economic dictatorship [that] has replaced a free market."[59]

Ultimately, both Leo and Pius argued that un-Christian principles and mistaken ideas were at the root of society's ills. To Leo, employers were greedy, grasping, and callous, oblivious in their pride to the plight of the worker. The workers themselves were often envious and impatient, unwilling to accept their lot in life and all too susceptible to misguided calls for social equality and to the revolutionary rhetoric of "crafty agitators."[60] Similarly, Pius condemns those who are "swept away by selfishness, by unbridled and sordid greed,"[61] and pinpoints original sin as the source of this lack of morals in economic life.[62] Hence, for Leo and Pius it was not the structure of capitalist society itself, but the sinful attitudes of and the abuses by its members that led to the shameful poverty among workers and the social conflict that they denounce.

These popes' prescriptions for social change follow logically from their perception of the nature of society and the causes of its problems. The solution, as implied above, is not to abolish the fundamental structures of capitalism. Neither are socialism and communism viable paths to follow, because, among other reasons, they foment the very type of class conflict and social disorder that the popes seek to remedy.[63] The changes the popes call for do not take place so much in the structures of society as they do in human hearts and consciences. Leo and Pius seek an end to social strife and the re-establishment of order and harmony in society through a "renewal of the Christian spirit."[64] The Church obviously plays a key role in this moral renovation, serving to teach the precepts of the Gospel and trying "to bind class to class in friendliness and good understanding."[65] This Christian-inspired unity extends to all social relations, including those in the workplace where the classes should collaborate in their recognition that "capital cannot do without labor nor labor without capital."[66] Granted, there are workers' groups or corporative structures that the popes also believe will contribute to the betterment of society; but these too must first and foremost be imbued with Christian virtue. As both Pius and Leo repeatedly emphasize, above all it is charity that should undergird social relationships.[67] In the end, nonetheless, if charity and co-operation should fall short in some way, if the poor continue to be mistreated, or if the workers' agitation for rights threatens to disrupt peace and order, the encyclicals counsel that the state should step in to protect the weak and to safeguard social stability.[68] In general, then, Leo and Pius call for a spiritual transformation in society, reinforced by the institutional authorities of the Church and, when necessary, the state.

▶ *Assessing Conservative Teaching*   The implications of this conservative perspective are problematic in several respects. First, the structural components of injustice in capitalist society are largely overlooked, as the popes concentrate instead on the interior qualities and attitudes of individuals. There is no questioning of the fundamental dynamics of the capital-labour relationship, no deep analysis of the economic or political mechanisms by which the "sinful" extremes of wealth and poverty arise and are maintained. In this extremely spiritualistic rendering of the roots of social conflict and of the impetus for social change, the conversion of hearts and minds is rather naively assumed to be sufficient to overcome complex and ingrained patterns of inequality in industrial society. The shallow inspection of capitalism and unwarranted optimism in the encyclicals of Leo and Pius detract from the strength of their critique on the condition of workers. The popes' teachings also help to sabotage calls for more thoroughgoing structural transformations in society.

Also questionable in this conservative perspective is the exaltation of social stability as a value or condition to be preserved at all costs. Dorr correctly notes that: "Stability is a very good thing in a society which is reasonably just. On the other hand stability may not be a good thing in a country that is highly stratified socially and economically, a society built on flagrant social injustice. In this situation radical change may be a higher priority than stability."[69] In *Rerum Novarum* and *Quadragesimo Anno*, the popes appear to place the need for order in society above the need for justice. Despite the condemnations of the suffering of the poor under the extremes of industrial capitalism, their emphasis on order and harmony implies that, if a change in society cannot come about peacefully and without disturbing social stability, then it should not occur at all. Put another way, according to the logic of the encyclicals, stability may mean that the poor will just have to tolerate injustice.[70]

These two encyclicals encourage a passive or fatalistic attitude for the poor in other manners as well. As discussed, inequality in the social order is characterized by the popes as natural, as beneficial to the operation of society, and as impossible to abolish. Also in line with this perspective, the poor are counselled that "in God's sight poverty is no disgrace"[71] and reminded that "to suffer and endure ... is the lot of humanity."[72] Granted, both Leo and Pius support the formation of workers' organizations. Yet their restrictions on these groups' activities, their insistence on social stability, and their notion that "tranquil resignation"[73] is the appropriate attitude for the poor to assume are all ways in which the popes discourage social activism by those at the base of society. Suffer though they may, the poor are not given the right—nor acknowledged to have the ability—to mobilize for significant change.

Instead, the popes promote a distinctly top-down vision of social change in which the wealthy and powerful members of society hold the responsibility to care for the poor and to effect reform; this can be seen in the repeated references to charity in the encyclicals. In addition, the top-down model is evident in the frequent and direct appeals to rich men, "masters," and public leaders to remind them of their duties to watch over the poor. These pleas lend the encyclicals a distinctly paternalistic tone.

Certainly, I do not mean to suggest that the state and the more influential members of society should bear no responsibilities toward the poor; in fact, social justice demands that they should have great obligations in this regard. I would argue, however, that without genuine moves to empower the poor themselves and to respect them as agents of social change, another form of inequality is perpetuated. Further, and from a more pragmatic point of view, reforms sponsored only by people in the upper social strata — changes that disregard the opinions and participation of the poor—will likely do little to modify the system that led to widespread impoverishment in the first place. Those in positions of privilege have a vested interest in maintaining the structures that have made them successful; as such—and whether consciously or not—many will not propose remedies for poverty that will threaten their own status and wealth. Since it lacks the authentic inclusion of the poor, the top-down bias of the conservative model functions to undermine attempts to achieve social justice.

♦ Liberationist Catholic Social Teaching

In clear contrast to the conservative approach to Catholic social teaching stands what I label as the "liberationist" approach. Whereas conservatives see the basis of society in harmonious and organic terms, liberationists view the social order as torn by conflict and violence. When conservatives focus more on attitudes and individuals in their examination of the root of society's problems, liberationists expose the structural components and international dynamics of injustice in modern capitalism. Finally, while conservatives promote a top-down program of reform based on consensus, liberationists adhere to a bottom-up model of societal transformation (sometimes explicitly labelled "liberation") that encourages the activism of the poor and that admits the possibility that confrontation may be a necessary part of the process. While the early work of the liberation theologians certainly embodies many of these themes,[74] the Medellín conference documents represent the best example of the liberationist perspective as it exists in official Catholic social teaching.

▶ *CELAM and the Medellín Documents*   Significantly, the bishops at Medellín perform a structural analysis of Latin America's problems and thereby acknowledge fundamental conflicts in the social order. They discuss the extreme inequality between the classes within Latin American countries and attribute the widespread poverty to the unjust nature of certain political, economic, and cultural structures, as well as to the insensitivity and wilful oppression displayed toward those who have been marginalized within those structures.[75] What the bishops label "international tensions and external neo-colonialism" compounds the problems generated by this internal injustice.[76] Here the bishops concentrate on the relative poverty of Latin American countries in the global market, arguing that this impoverishment is largely owing to Latin America's dependence on a centre of economic power outside itself. They identify distorted terms of exchange, the tax evasion of multinational companies, and growing external debts as aspects of the inequitable international relations that have had grave consequences for poor Latin Americans.

It is through this analysis that the bishops reveal the conflictual nature of Latin American society. In fact, the Medellín bishops go so far as to view these injustices as a negation of peace, as *violence*.[77] According to the documents, when structural deficiencies of agriculture, industry, national and international economies, and cultural and political life deprive people of their independence, initiative, and basic life necessities, then "institutionalized violence" exists.[78] In this understanding, the inhuman and destructive structures themselves are diagnosed as violent. "Repressive violence" is closely related to institutionalized violence, as the groups who benefit from the violent structures of the established order use force in order to prevent the alteration of these structures. These elites repress attempts at opposition and, although such measures are often masked as "anti-communist" or as necessary to maintain "peace and order," repressive force is nonetheless violent.[79] Like institutionalized violence, repressive violence has as its victims the impoverished masses. This being the case, the bishops are not surprised that there is the "temptation to violence" among the people. "Revolutionary violence," therefore, is directly provoked by the institutionalized and repressive violence to which people are subject and is fuelled by their increasing awareness of their situation. Referring to the "explosive consequences" of socio-economic problems and the "climate of collective anguish" among the poor, the bishops powerfully indicate the potential for revolutionary violence in Latin America.[80] When these descriptions of violence are taken together with the discussions of injustice, tensions, inequality, and colonialism in the Medellín documents, one conclusion is inescapable. The participants at Medellín, in attempting to outline the nature of reality in Latin America, assess it to be pervaded with conflict.

The bishops at Medellín, however, do more than simply discuss the injustice and violence in Latin America. They are also prepared to promote changes to this situation. Echoing some of the language and concepts of the incipient liberation theology movement of the time, they announce a message of liberation for Latin America that involves both an attitudinal conversion among individuals and the transformation of societal structures.[81] Importantly, liberation in this context is at once spiritual and social; at Medellín the bishops refuse to separate the spiritual and temporal realms. According to the teaching in these documents, it is artificial to make a separation between temporal tasks and religious commitments, because, after all, God's salvific work in Christ is performed in the course of human history. For the Latin American episcopate, therefore, there is no excuse for the Church to remain aloof and separate from the world: it is a Christian responsibility to work for justice in society.[82]

Consistent with this conviction, the bishops in their pastoral recommendations outline the various types of social transformations they support. These changes — to take place in the economic, industrial, agricultural, judicial, and political realms — include such things as agrarian reform, ensuring just prices for exported raw materials, and incorporating peasant and other marginalized populations into political and economic decision making.[83] Such recommendations do appear to be far-reaching and, in fact, the bishops fit into the "revolutionary" (as opposed to the "traditionalist/conservative" or "developmentalist") category of their own classification system because they "question the socio-economic structure ... [and] desire its radical change, in both its goals and means."[84]

There remains, of course, the question of who is to orchestrate such transformations. In contrast to the top-down model of reform in conservative Catholic social teaching, the Latin American bishops at Medellín view social change in more broad-based and participatory terms, with the poor emerging as the central agents of the process: "all of the population, [but] *most especially the popular classes*, have, by means of territorial and functional structures, a receptive and active, creative and decisive participation in the construction of a [new] society"[85] (emphasis added). In this view, the elites with formal political power, and those with more education or economic resources, are not excused from their responsibility to assume the struggles of the poor and to foment structural change in society. Nonetheless, it is the poor themselves who are the central architects of their own liberation. By supporting the formation of CEBs[86] and other grassroots organizations, and by promoting a form of "liberating education" (or, in effect, "conscientization")[87] for the lower classes, the bishops further reinforce the notion of the poor as social activists.[88] These components of the bottom-up model of social change are an essential part of Medellín's option for the poor and comprise some of the most vaunted and controversial contributions to the Catholic social teaching tradition.

▶ *Assessing Liberationist Teaching*   One of the most polemical implications of the message from Medellín is related to the power structure of the Church. If Medellín's option for the poor is taken seriously, the poor become active not only in the transformation of the larger society but also within the Church itself. This option, particularly as it is presented in the bishops' support for the CEBs, reveals the potential for what Leonardo Boff has called a "reinvention of the Church." Such a reinvention implies a shift away from the authoritarian and monarchical model of the Church and a move toward a model of the Church as the "People of God," a Church that is *from*, *of*, and *with* the poor. Historically in the Church, as Boff points out, the bishops and the priests received all the religious "capital" and produced all the religious "goods," with the faithful relegated to "consumer" status only. In a reinvented Church, this religious production is no longer the monopoly of the hierarchy but can and also should originate "from below." With this reinvention, sacred power is redistributed in the Church, and new energy would be directed toward the essential task of spiritual and political liberation.[89] By affirming the need for CEBs, the bishops at Medellín are suggesting a reform and renewal of the long-standing Church structure—changes that could certainly be viewed as threatening by many of those whose power and status are linked to the traditional institutional form.

In addition, if one is to take the Medellín bishops' bottom-up program for societal transformation seriously, it must be admitted that confrontation may be an inescapable part of the process of social change. If, as the option for the poor implies, the popular classes are to play such a key role in determining a course of action—if their needs and expectations are truly to be addressed—conflicts with other segments of society will arise. Fulfilling the demands of the poor will often entail a redistribution of resources to such an extent that it will be unlikely that those at the top of society will be able to maintain the positions of privilege to which they have become accustomed. Given this scenario, the conservative model of change through consensus appears quite unrealistic. The resistance to change that many in power will provide means that for the poor, a degree of militancy, protest, organization, and action—in other words, a degree of conflict and confrontation—will be necessary in order to carry out a genuine transformation of the social order.

The bishops themselves understand this and, although they generally assume that the process of change should not be violent, they also admit that, in certain circumstances, even violent confrontation may be justified. The oft-cited Medellín loophole for revolutionary violence is found in the document on peace:

> If *it is true that revolutionary insurrection can be legitimate* in the case of "evident and prolonged tyranny that seriously works against the fundamental rights of the person and dangerously damages the common good of the country", whether it proceeds from one person or from evidently unjust structures, it is also certain that violence or "armed revolution" generally "generates new injustices, introduces new imbalances and causes new disasters; one cannot combat a real evil at the price of a greater evil."[90] (emphasis added)

Although here the Medellín bishops are borrowing words from Pope Paul VI's *Populorum Progressio*, the sense imparted is much different.[91] Unlike Paul, the bishops actually make the explicit and audacious statement that revolutionary violence can be legitimate. In the context of Latin America (which by the late 1960s had witnessed more than its share of revolutionary movements and uprisings), and when contrasted with the dominant pacifist stream of the broader Catholic social teaching tradition (discussed below), it is not difficult to see why the Medellín position on violence remains controversial.

Persistent Conservatism in Catholic Social Teaching

That the social teachings of Leo XIII and Pius XI occupy the conservative end of the Catholic social teaching spectrum is hardly disputable, as is the fact that the Medellín conference documents represent the most liberationist views in the same tradition. Beyond this, however, many scholars assume that the Medellín conference (or, as some would argue, Vatican II a few years earlier) ushered in a new era of progressivism in Catholic social teaching. They frequently refer, for example, to the tradition of "Medellín and Puebla," based on their perception that the latter conference represented a reaffirmation—even a deepening—of the liberationist tenets of the former.[92] Analysts of the Costa Rican Church have also portrayed post-Vatican II Catholic social teaching in homogeneous terms as pro-union and pro-worker. This type of analysis sets up a simplistic dichotomy in Catholic social teaching, one that is based on the assumption of a rather arbitrary 1960s divide between the old-fashioned conservative and the progressive contemporary eras.

Such assumptions, however, are largely unwarranted. Catholic social teaching since Vatican II cannot be so easily categorized, containing as it does elements that resonate with both the liberationist and the conservative perspectives on social justice. If anything, I would argue that in this mix the conservative perspective is by far the dominant one, with several parallels existing between the pre-conciliar social teachings and those issued during and since the 1960s. The basis for such assertions will become evident through a critical examination of conciliar and post-conciliar positions on four issues suggested by my discussion of the conservative and liberationist Catholic social teaching models: unity and conflict, social change and solidarity, liberation, and the option for the poor. In this analysis, I pay special attention to the documents issued during the tenure of Pope John Paul II, as this period most closely corresponds to the period of Costa Rican Church history covered by this study.

◆ Unity and Conflict

In many documents issued during and since the conciliar era, one can detect a stress on social harmony and collaboration. The focus, reminiscent of the conservative encyclicals of Leo XIII and Pius XI, is on the fundamental unity of the human race with a frequent failure to admit, or to acknowledge the importance of, the existence of serious conflicts in society. Emphasis is placed on the mutual rights, respect, obligations, and love that members of society should have for one another, and great value is ascribed to the ideal of co-operation within and among nations.[93] Consistent with this perspective, the image of the human family is commonly employed in these documents, with repeated references to "brotherly love," "universal brotherhood," and the "fraternal unity of one human family" that reinforce an organic view of society.[94] The bishops at Santo Domingo illustrate this view succinctly when they write that "in Latin America many people live in poverty, which frequently reaches shocking levels. However, even in limit-situations, we are able to love one another, to live in unity despite our differences, and to show the whole world our radiant experience of brotherhood."[95] Hence, in spite of the grave problems and inequities in the modern world, such documents showcase a concentration on unity rather than an understanding of confrontation or conflict. In the end, the sanction for this concept of unity often comes through direct appeals to theology, evident in such papal statements as "the Son of God has saved mankind and at the same time has united all people,"[96] and "the Lord *unites us with himself* through the Eucharist ... and he *unites us with himself and with one another* by a bond stronger than any natural union"[97] (emphasis in original). Once it is cast in this way as "God's will," the value of the unity in the Catholic social teaching tradition cannot be underestimated.

This conservative emphasis on unity, however, proves troublesome from the perspective of social justice. This is certainly true in the case of Latin America, where the poverty and oppression suffered by so many people belie any idealistic notion of humankind's unity. Far from existing as a radiant and unified family, Latin American society is at present deeply divided, where "the basic difference is between being close to life or close to death."[98] In such a context, the above-cited Catholic social teaching texts simply falsify reality. Further, and as the work of Otto Maduro suggests, downplaying or denying social conflict and trying to unify the dominant and dominated religiously within the Church contribute to the symbolic concealment and transcendence of the socio-political struggles that persist in Latin America. The failure to acknowledge such conflicts adequately hinders and contradicts the recognition by the poor of the injustice of their condition.[99] An overemphasis on unity thereby provides support for those who benefit from the maintenance of the existing order, as opposed to those whose hopes lie in its transformation.

Before moving on to the next theme, it is necessary to discuss the notions of unity and conflict presented in Pope John Paul II's *Laborem Exercens*. Although this encyclical is frequently applauded for its progressive social analysis and political positions,[100] it nonetheless contains material that resonates more with a conservative than a liberationist point of view. For instance, John Paul does present a concept of class unity consistent with the conservative position already described, as is evident in his discussion of the world of work. Work, the pope argues, "first and foremost unites people"—workers, managers, *and* owners.[101] In his view of society, since work is considered a universal calling, virtually all people can be considered workers and, as such, they are bound together.[102] On a related note, John Paul also argues that the link between workers and owners is an inseparable one, that there is no inherent opposition between labour and capital: there is no fundamental distinction because, simply stated, capital is merely the accumulated result of labour. Since it is the human being and his or her labour that are the source of the entire economic process, for John Paul, it is erroneous to posit a necessary division or opposition within the economic arena.[103]

This "personalist" perspective, although it is important in supporting John Paul II's contentions about the dignity of the worker, also serves to reveal the conservatism in *Laborem Exercens*. With his portrayal of labour and definition of capital, and his argument about the unity between the two, the pope neglects fundamental truths about the structure and nature of capitalist society. True, capital is labour on labour (i.e., accumulated labour), but it is not merely so, as the encyclical suggests. Specifically, capital is amassed through a process whereby the owners of the means of production appropriate the value produced by the workers in their employ. The relation between capital and labour is therefore not merely quantitative, it is also exploitative, since the owners are reaping profits from the labour power of others.[104] Given this exploitation, to posit an underlying unity of labour and capital does not make sense. By insisting on the unity of labour and capital, the pope glosses over the structural contradiction that is at the core of the capitalist mode of production.

Despite his emphasis on an ideal or theoretical unity in the world of work, however, the pope does not deny that social conflict has existed since the early stages of industrial development. In fact, John Paul devotes a considerable amount of space in his encyclical to the "Conflict between Labor and Capital in the Present Phase of History."[105] Yet if, as the pope argues, "opposition between labor and capital does not spring from the structure of the production process or from the structure of the economic process,"[106] how does this conflict arise? The pope's answer reveals a further conservative bias in *Laborem Exercens*.

John Paul II argues that the conflict first arose during the birth and rapid development of industrialization, when small groups of greedy entrepreneurs exploited their employees in an attempt to maximize profits and so provoked a "justified" reaction from these workers.[107] He goes on to state that this strife soon became cast as a socio-economic class conflict that was expressed in the ideological and political struggle between liberalism and Marxism. This interpretation, however, was based on false theoretical systems (i.e., economism and, eventually, materialism) that reduced labour and capital to two impersonal forces that could be separated and set in opposition to one another. Thus, for the pope, the "practical error" of conflict—a reality since early industrial society—is misrepresented and exacerbated by the "philosophical error" of Marxism which, because it ignores the primacy of the personal element in the economic process, interprets class struggle as inevitable. For the pope, then, class conflict is not a necessary or unavoidable aspect of the capitalist system: it is instead the unfortunate byproduct of human greed, immorality, and distorted thinking.

Several points must be made about the treatment of class conflict in *Laborem Exercens*. The first is that John Paul II rests his argument on an inaccurate characterization of Marxism. He implies that in their theories of class conflict, all Marxists would subscribe to materialism as *he* defines it, a "non-humanistic way of stating the issue [of work in which] man is not first and foremost the subject of work and the efficient cause of the production process, but continues to be understood and treated, in dependence on what is material, as a kind of 'resultant' of the economic or production relations."[108] The pope here associates Marxism with a narrow economic determinism, a doctrine that denies human agency and instead posits that human consciousness and behaviour are dictated solely by the socio-economic structure of a society. While this view may bear some relation to the interpretation of Marxism as it has been imposed under certain communist regimes (e.g., the Soviet Union), it certainly does not correspond to the work of many Marxist thinkers—whether they are labelled "critical," "revisionist," or "neo-" Marxists—who do place emphasis on the role of humans as subjects and shapers of the world around them.[109]

Perhaps more importantly, even Marx himself, when his work is taken as a whole, cannot be accused of expounding a determinist view. As analysts such as José Porfirio Miranda have so persuasively drawn out, Marx (particularly in works such as *Theories of Surplus Value, Contribution to the Critique of Political Economy,* and the *Grundisse*) rejects any mechanistic determinism, insisting instead that humans are free subjects who are both products of history and producers of history.[110] Further, and in contrast to what the pope implies in *Laborem Exercens,* Marx also applies this principle of human agency to the production process itself. Consider what he wrote in *Theories of Surplus Value*:

> Man himself is the basis of his material production, as of any other production that he carries on. All circumstances, therefore, which affect man, the *subject* of production, more or less modify all his functions and activities, and therefore too his functions and activities as the creator of material wealth, of commodities. In this respect it can in fact be shown that *all* human relations and functions, however and in whatever form they may appear, influence material production and have a more or less decisive influence on it.[111] (emphasis in original)

Thus, for Marx too, it is the human being who produces, who is the true subject of production.

John Paul II, however, does not recognize this subtlety in Marx's thought, much as he does not acknowledge the variety among those who belong to the broader Marxist tradition. The pope, who indiscriminately refers to "Marxism," the "Marxist program," and "Marxist ideology" without qualification, is therefore attacking only a caricature, an exaggerated and grotesque representation of what Marxism actually professes. And while painting this picture of an unsophisticated and monolithic Marxism may correspond with certain historic institutional necessities for the Church,[112] such inaccuracies also serve to undermine the pope's claims about Marxism in this encyclical.

Finally, and aside from the issue of accuracy, it can be noted that once the pope does set up this version of Marxism as deterministic and antihumanistic, it becomes that much easier for him to contrast it with his own personalistic interpretation of economics and labour. Yet, with all the attention paid to personal characteristics of owners (i.e., as greedy and exploitative) or workers (i.e., as conscious of their position in society and free to choose their [re]actions), *Laborem Exercens* fails to analyze the structural basis of poverty and social injustice. As discussed earlier, John Paul emphasizes the unity between labour and capital to the neglect of the deeper conflict of interest between the two groups. Here, it can be seen how, as Hobgood perceptively notes, *Laborem Exercens* "make[s] individual ethical choice the primary factor in determining the justice of an economic system."[113] Thus, not only in its unyielding attack on Marxism but also in its emphasis on the moral and personal at the expense of the structural and objective, John Paul II's supposedly progressive encyclical in fact echoes the conservatism of Leo XIII's *Rerum Novarum* and Pius XI's *Quadragesimo Anno*.

♦ Social Change and Solidarity

Regardless of their sometimes idyllic view of human society and their inadequate analyses of conflict, official Catholic social teaching statements since the 1960s have emphasized the need for social change. Nonetheless, much as in the pre-conciliar period, the authors of these documents indicate that consensus and co-operation are sufficient to bring about greater justice in society. In John XXIII's encyclicals, for example, the position taken is most optimistic, exhibiting the pope's hopeful belief that love and charity can conquer all.[114] Even Paul VI's *Populorum Progressio*, despite its urgent calls for bold social transformations and subtle reference to rebellion, ultimately reverts to the position that change can be effected by a process of dialogue and negotiation in which the generous efforts of the rich and ruling play the central role.[115] In these documents, John XXIII and Paul VI appear to share Leo XIII and Pius XI's impression that goodwill can be an effective antidote for society's ills.

With this renewed emphasis on consensus and collaboration in Catholic social teaching, it is not surprising that the authors of such documents envision a strictly non-violent process of social change. In fact, the Medellín document on peace is one of the few texts in the Catholic social teaching tradition that suggests that revolutionary violence may be seen as legitimate in the eyes of the Church. Pope Paul VI, whose passage in *Populorum Progressio* provided some argument for the Medellín loophole justifying revolutionary violence, soon afterward recanted his original position. In his addresses in Colombia preceding and inaugurating the Medellín conference, the pope repeatedly stressed that revolution and violence were un-Christian,[116] a position he continued to support in his later teachings.[117] In 1979, the Latin American bishops at Puebla reversed the Medellín position on revolution by unequivocally condemning all forms of violence, including "subversive" violence.[118] Pope John Paul II has also continued in this vein by consistently refusing to endorse any violent means for social change.[119] Overall, these judgments on revolution provide a further link between pre- and post-conciliar thought. The Church's recent prohibitions on revolutionary violence are consistent with Leo and Pius's non-violent approach to social change, and with their fear of revolution and the social disorder that accompanies it.

The essentially conservative view of the post-1960s Church on social change is further bolstered by John Paul II's teachings on solidarity. In *Laborem Exercens*, John Paul presents solidarity in a historical context as the justified reaction of workers against exploitation during the early period of industrialization. But he also argues that "movements of solidarity of the workers and with the workers" are the means to achieve justice in the world today, both in working conditions and in society in general.[120] Interestingly, scholars such as Donal Dorr contend that, in using this notion of solidarity, the pope admits that a certain degree of struggle or confrontation may be necessary for justice to be served.[121] This interpretation has contributed to the perception that, with *Laborem Exercens*, the pope moves to "the left," in effect adopting a position that resembles that of the liberationists. I would argue, however, that this perception is an inaccurate one. Once John Paul II's notion of solidarity is examined more closely, both within the context of *Laborem Exercens* and as the pope elaborates on it in two later social encyclicals, the continuity between John Paul's teachings and the conservative pre-conciliar encyclicals becomes evident.

In *Laborem Exercens*, for example, the actual link between solidarity and struggle or confrontation is tenuous at best. As Dorr himself points out, in the passage where John Paul discusses solidarity most thoroughly, the pope does not once refer to "struggle."[122] Nor does the pope mention solidarity when he does bring up struggle in his comments on trade unions, and he is quick to point out that this struggle is "for" the just good and not a struggle "against" others.[123]

In fact, it appears that the linking of solidarity and confrontation in the pope's thought comes not from *Laborem Exercens* itself, but only from a study Karol Wojtyla published in 1969 while he was archbishop of Krakow.[124] Granted, in this work Wojtyla does argue that opposition may be compatible with solidarity and, of course, Karol Wojtyla became Pope John Paul II. Nonetheless, the fact remains that over a decade elapsed between the two documents in question and, during that time, the Church and Karol Wojtyla's role and responsibilities within the Church changed dramatically. That a philosophically minded archbishop in Poland once wrote an essay that incorporated the notion of conflict into a discussion of solidarity is perhaps a point of interest for the pope's biographers; it is not a hermeneutic key to an encyclical written twelve years later by the leader of the world's Catholics. The assumption that the term solidarity retained its confrontational connotation when it was used in *Laborem Exercens* is therefore quite unwarranted, especially in light of the absence of a direct tie between solidarity and struggle in the latter document.

The manner in which John Paul II uses solidarity in his other social encyclicals, and particularly in *Sollicitudo Rei Socialis*, further reveals his conservatism. In *Sollicitudo Rei Socialis*, the pope presents solidarity as the appropriate response to the recognition of interdependence among individuals and nations in the world today.[125] More precisely, for John Paul II, solidarity is the means through which justice in the world can be achieved: it is, according to him, *"the path to peace and at the same time to devel-*

opment"[126] (emphasis in original). Since, for the pope, obstacles to social and economic development are rooted in sinful attitudes such as the "all-consuming desire for profit" and "the thirst for power,"[127] solidarity responds on the same moral level as it aims for a spiritual conversion among society's members. In place of selfishness, solidarity calls for the rich to be responsible for and to share with the poor, and for the poor to be neither passive nor destructive in their work for the common good. According to both *Sollicitudo Rei Socialis* and *Centesimus Annus*, the acts proper to solidarity are therefore peaceful collaboration and dialogue.[128] In the end, solidarity, as a "Christian virtue," is inspired by a model of human unity, which is a reflection of one God in three persons, and takes on the elements of charity and of "total gratuity, forgiveness, and reconciliation."[129]

Even beyond the discussion of solidarity, the conservatism of John Paul II's thought is evident in several respects. First, the problems and poverty in society are portrayed in individualistic and spiritualistic terms. The pope makes it clear that underdevelopment is above all a moral problem,[130] one that can be traced to the attitudes and shortcomings of individual actors. In this view, a structural analysis of social injustice and the corresponding need for socio-economic transformation are bypassed — even the "structures of sin" that the pope critiques are "rooted in personal sin."[131] While selfishness is mentioned most often in this regard,[132] the pope argues that development may also be blocked "through fear, indecision and basically, through cowardice"[133] or even by the "laziness"[134] of responsible persons. For John Paul II, then, there is "the urgent need to *change the spiritual attitudes*"[135] of individuals (emphasis in original).

With personal as opposed to structural transformation being John Paul II's focus, it is not surprising that the social changes he does propose are reformist as opposed to revolutionary. For him, capitalism itself is not the problem, even though the excesses and consumerist attitudes that accompany the free market system may need to be corrected.[136] Other changes that are suggested are of a top-down variety, since "a greater responsibility rests on those who have more and can do more."[137] In the place of receiving unequivocal empowerment in the pope's scheme, the poor are counselled to avoid violence and destruction.[138] Instead of emphasizing the potentially liberating value of basic education programs or grassroots political mobilization,[139] the pope falls back on the principle that "the more individuals are defenceless within a given society, the more they require the care and concern of others, and in particular the intervention of governmental authority."[140] In this model, collaboration and consensus are expected to suffice to foment social and economic development, and the charity of the rich once again is assigned a key role in place of encouragement to the poor to struggle for their own advancement. Given all of this evidence, the similarities between John Paul's social teachings and the earlier documents of Leo XIII and Pius XI are obvious.

♦ Liberation

In the discussion of key themes to this point, one can note a certain consistency between the terminology used in many of the Catholic social teaching documents and their conservative bias. To some extent, one could perhaps predict a pre-conciliar style emphasis on harmony and repudiation of conflict by observing the repeated use of the terms "unity" and "solidarity" in the documents of the conciliar era and beyond. The use of the term "liberation" in a document, in contrast, prompts an opposite prediction. Surveying the frequent use of "liberation" in major Church documents since the conference at Medellín, one could conclude, contrary to what I have been arguing so far, that the liberationist model has been adopted in important ways in recent Catholic social teaching. The matter is not so simple, however. For once one sees exactly how "liberation" is employed in these various documents, other aspects of conservatism emerge.

As I explained above, the bishops at Medellín were among the first to use the term "liberation" in their prescriptions for social change. For them, liberation involved both a spiritual and a social aspect — individual conversions and profound structural transformations in society were to take place at the same time, with the Church and its members fully involved in these tasks. Put another way, the Medellín bishops were proclaiming the unity of the religious and temporal realms (or of the Church and the world), a concept they developed in conscious relation to Vatican II ecclesiology.[141] Citing *Gaudium et Spes*, they arrive at the same essential conclusion as Pope Paul VI did at the end of that council when he spoke of "the *intimate union, constantly affirmed and upheld* by the Council, that exists between *human and temporal values* and properly spiritual, religious, and eternal values. The Church is inclined toward man and *the earth*, but in so doing, raises it toward *the Kingdom of God*"[142] (emphases in original). Following this principle means that liberation cannot possibly be reduced solely to its political dimension, nor solely to its spiritual one.

Nonetheless, when the Vatican began to use the language of liberation as its own in the early 1970s, a definite emphasis on the spiritual aspects of liberation could be detected. In so far as the term "liberation" is used in Paul VI's *Octogesima Adveniens*, it is primarily connected with the internal conversion of humans.[143] In *Evangelii Nuntiandi*, moreover, Pope Paul defines liberation according to its links with the Gospel obligation of evangelization — the bringing of the Good News (the centre of which is the proclamation of God's great gift of salvation). While evangelization *is* a message of liberation, Paul stresses that it is not limited to the economic, social, or cultural spheres, but that it concerns the whole person in every dimension, including his or her relation to God. Therefore, the pope states, while the Church has the duty of proclaiming liberation and of working for its completion, this liberation is not purely human: the Church reaffirms the primacy of her spiritual role.[144] As Donal Dorr once suggested, through its location within a network of established theological concepts (i.e., evangelization and salvation), the term "liberation" is accorded a certain amount of "theological respectability" in *Evangelii Nuntiandi*. In this way, liberation cannot be narrowly defined as revolution in a purely politico-economic sense, but is primarily seen as a spiritual concept.[145]

This emphasis is reinforced by the pope's treatment of those who adhere to a liberationist perspective, who of course also maintain that political and spiritual liberation are inseparable. In *Octogesima Adveniens*, for example, Paul distinctly warns against the political liberation promised by revolutionary ideologies, which he argues enslaves humans, curtails freedoms, and establishes new injustices.[146] In *Evangelii Nuntiandi*, moreover, he clearly distinguishes his liberation from that of "all temporal liberation, all political liberation," stressing the latter's inadequacy "even if it endeavours to find its justification in such or such a page of the Old or New Testament, even if it claims for its ideological postulates and its norms of action theological data and conclusions, even if it pretends to be today's theology."[147] The Vatican's post-conciliar move toward distinguishing between the two aspects of liberation was therefore first seen not only in its emphasis on the spiritual, but also in its critique of those who themselves explicitly combined the spiritual and the political.

This dualism resurfaced in CELAM's 1979 Puebla conference document. However, it did so in a subtle manner missed (or perhaps ignored) by those positing Puebla's "confirmation" of the teachings from Medellín. Granted, in the Puebla document liberation is said to include spiritual, interpersonal, and social dimensions.[148] Further, the Puebla document also picks up Medellín's assumption that temporal tasks are related to the spiritual realm: the bishops argue that, since justice in the world is related to the Kingdom of God, the Church must necessarily be involved in worldly affairs.[149] However, the bishops at Puebla emphatically and repeatedly mention one additional component of the Church's mission that was barely articulated at Medellín: evangelization. In fact, the descriptions of liberation and its links to evangelization in the Puebla document are taken almost completely from Paul VI's *Evangelii Nuntiandi*. Hence, while at Puebla the need for the Church's involvement in worldly affairs is noted, the emphasis is once again on the spiritual component of liberation.[150]

In this definition the political facet of liberation, although minimized, still appears to be preserved in line with the conciliar conception of the Church and the spiritual realm as wholly bound up with the temporal. However, for the bishops at Puebla, evangelization means that the Church's involvement in the socio-political arena should be exclusively religious and "not driven by any intention of a political, economic or social nature."[151]

Here, bishops, priests, and religious are forbidden to exercise or to support partisan political options within the Church. While the CEBs are labelled "motors of liberation and development," attention is focused more on the experience of the Word of God and of the Eucharist in these groups than on world-transforming action. In fact, the bishops express their regret that sometimes political interests manipulate the CEBs.[152] At Puebla, the distinction between the spiritual and the political in the struggle for liberation is widened through the critique of the political nature of the CEBs and by the attempted removal of all actual political activity from the sphere of the Church.

Interestingly, Pope John Paul II tends to shy away from treating the theme of liberation at length in his encyclicals. In *Sollicitudo Rei Socialis*, for example, the pope is more concerned with expanding on his predecessor Paul's teaching on "development" through his own concept of solidarity. This is not to imply, however, that Pope John Paul did not feel the issue of liberation to be worthy of comment: nothing could be further from the truth. In fact, one could say that one of the pope's chief concerns throughout his papacy has been to set the record straight on the concept of liberation and its proper use within the Church. But in place of detailed expositions on the topic in his own encyclicals, the pope, when he does refer to what he calls "authentic" liberation, instead directs his readers to the position spelled out in the *Instruction on Christian Freedom and Liberation*.[153] The Vatican Congregation for the Doctrine of the Faith issued this document in 1986 as a companion piece to the 1984 text, *Instruction on Certain Aspects of the "Theology of Liberation."*[154] Although Cardinal Ratzinger (the prefect of the congregation) wrote these two Instructions, the pope approved them, ordered their publication, and repeatedly cited them as the Church's official statements on the matter.

Both Instructions exhibit the Vatican distinction between the spiritual and political planes of reality. In both documents, for instance, sin is treated primarily as an interior moral condition of individuals and thus a purely religious phenomenon, in contrast to the view of the liberationists, in which sin is viewed as both collective (i.e., social and structural) as well as personal.[155] The dualism implicit in the Vatican's conception of sin further manifests itself in the fundamental distinction made between "liberation [as] first and foremost liberation from the radical slavery of sin" and "liberation from servitude of an earthly and temporal kind."[156] While Vatican II's conception of the intimate union between the two realms suggests that such a distinction is impossible to make, this separation is nonetheless reinforced at various points throughout the Instructions. Pope John Paul, through his citation of some of these same passages and through his own direct use of a very individualistic and spiritualistic notion of sin, also helps reinforce a conception of liberation considerably at odds with that originally proposed by the Latin American bishops at Medellín.

Ironically, the biggest change in the use of the term "liberation" came from the Latin American bishops themselves when they broached the subject again at their fourth general conference in Santo Domingo in 1992. The references to liberation in the Santo Domingo conclusions are few and far between, but when an attempt is made to elaborate on the meaning of the term, the connotation given to it is overwhelmingly spiritual. At one point, for example, the bishops "testify with joy that in Jesus Christ we have integral liberation for each one of us and for our peoples; liberation from sin, from death and from slavery, which consists of forgiveness and reconciliation."[157] In their most thorough treatment of the topic, the bishops quote extensively from Pope John Paul II's *Redemptoris Missio* (*On the Permanent Validity of the Church's Missionary Mandate*), a 1990 encyclical not considered to be part of the Catholic social teaching corpus. They note that: "the Church offers a force for liberation and promotes development precisely because it leads to conversion of heart and of mentality; aids the recognition of each person's dignity; [and] encourages solidarity, commitment, [and] service of one's neighbour."[158] Immediately after, they again quote John Paul II that the Church "always safeguards the priority of transcendent and spiritual realities, which are premises of eschatological salvation."[159] At these points, no direct mention is made of socio-economic change or structural transformation; liberation essentially appears as a spiritual process of conversion.

Strictly speaking, there is nothing inherently conservative or anti-liberationist about emphasizing the spiritual component of liberation. The Medellín definition of liberation itself assumed that the spiritual and political were different aspects of the same struggle. However, increased spiritualization does become problematic if it is related to a corresponding shift away from the concern with political activities, something witnessed in recent Catholic social teaching documents with their tendency to separate the spiritual and temporal realms and to critique the political activism of members of the popular church. Hence, even though the term "liberation" becomes relatively commonplace in the official Church literature after the 1960s, the sense imparted to it is much different than what the authors of the Medellín texts originally suggested. Contrary to first appearances, then, the use of the concept of liberation reveals yet another manner in which a pre-conciliar conservatism surfaces in much more recent Catholic social teaching.

♦ The Option for the Poor

The phrase "option for the poor" arose in connection with the Medellín documents and the early writings of the liberation theologians.[160] Originally, the option meant that the movement for liberation was to begin and end with the poor and the oppressed. The Church was also to side with the poor in the struggle for social change and to respect the fact that the poor themselves were to be the central architects of this change. As I noted above, this option for the poor further involved support for the CEBs and their reinvention of ecclesial structures.

Since its earliest formulation in the late 1960s, however, the concept has lost much of its force and specificity, as is especially evident in its significant linguistic dilution over the years. Nowhere now is there a straightforward mention of the option for the poor in Catholic social teaching. Instead, the notion emerges in the conference documents from Puebla and Santo Domingo as the "preferential option for the poor," the "preferential love and concern for the poor and needy," and the "preferential option for the poor and young."[161] Pope John Paul II, for his part, refers to "the *option* or *love of preference* for the poor" which is "an option, or a *special form* of primacy in the exercise of Christian charity"[162] (emphases in original). Clearly, a softening in phraseology has occurred.

Liberation theologian Juan Luis Segundo points to some of the implications of such changes:

> To opt (or to choose sides) in a conflict means to enter into it and to accept the inherent partisanship of one of the two sides—in this case, that of the poor. Every option limits. And that limitation is even greater, the deeper and more crucial the conflict. But at the same time the strength and efficacy of the option comes precisely from its partiality.[163]

Thus, even appending the word "preferential" to the option phrase already implies a compromise, because it excludes the possibility of unequivocal solidarity with the poor by implying that one opts for *both* the poor and the rich and just gives preference to the former. The further the option devolves into "a special concern" or a "love of preference," the further the conflictual meaning of the phrase recedes.[164] Granted, Segundo's reading here is based on a limited examination of word choices and phrasing. Nonetheless, his suggestion—that these reformulations indicate a withdrawal from the crucial elements (i.e., conflict and partiality) of an efficacious option for the poor—can be corroborated by other means. Once one sees that the changed option corresponds to and is reinforced by an emphasis on a particular ecclesiological model—that of the Church as unified and universal—one comprehends that the shifts in the option for the poor do go deeper than diction.

Of the traditional defining marks of the Catholic Church, Vatican and Latin American Church leaders in recent decades have emphasized unity and universality the most. Church unity, for example, was a key theme at Vatican II and since has played an important role in the teachings of Pope John Paul II.[165] It is based on the belief that there is "one Lord, one faith, one baptism, one God and Father of all, who is over all, and works through all, and is in all" (Eph. 4:5-6). Universality is, of course, a hallmark of the

Catholic Church, which believes its mission is to direct its message of salvation to all people in all nations. Also treated in the texts of the Second Vatican Council, the value of universality is more noticeably emphasized in later documents, such as Paul VI's *Evangelii Nuntiandi*.[166]

The concentration on a unified and universal Church contradicts the original liberationist option for the poor in several ways. A focus on unity, for example, can obscure the extent to which the Church, as fully present in society, is traversed by the same conflicts and struggles as is the larger social order. The idea of a unified Church is not only inaccurate, but unduly emphasizing this value also detracts from the call to struggle against injustice and those responsible for it. As Segundo implies above and as Gutiérrez once affirmed, the decision to be with the poor and to opt for them inevitably involves an element of conflict: "to be with the oppressed is to be against the oppressor."[167] An artificially unified institution in which conflict is suppressed is an institution in which the injustice of inequality is denied and is thereby perpetuated. Church leaders' appeals to unity are based on a denial of the nature of the Church as it exists in a class society, and on a denial that, within such a society, when the Church professes to be free of conflict, it is actually taking the side of the elite against the majority.

Emphasizing the Church's universal nature has related implications for the option for the poor. A conservative focus on the Church as universal implies that all groups must be included in any social or political program undertaken. In so far as an option for the poor involves an option against the oppressors, then, it can become equated with exclusivity or even sectarianism—an affront to the universal character and mission of the Church.[168] As a result, Church documents may only go so far as to promote a "preferential" option for the poor that "does not suppose the exclusion of anyone."[169] Ironically, however, through the very careful promotion of this preferential-but-not-exclusive option for the poor, Church leaders ultimately contribute to a system that conspires against—and even excludes—the poor. As Segundo notes, the force of an option is derived precisely from its partiality. When an unequivocal stand for the poor is not taken, the threat to existing structures of sin and injustice diminishes correspondingly. In highly stratified societies, such as those in Latin America, the attempt of the Church to be non-partisan cannot succeed. Not opting for the poor is the same as opting against them.

▶ *The Poor within the Church Structure*   An ecclesiological model that posits the Church as united and universal can contradict a genuine and effective option for the poor in additional ways. Consider that, although the unity of the Church may be based on the belief in one faith and one God, it is above all maintained, as Pope John Paul II stresses, by "obedience to the bishops and to the pope."[170] This hierarchical structure is reinforced by the emphasis on the universal Church as a church with only one accept-able organization, magisterium, and doctrine—the one centred in Rome.[171] Pope John Paul II confirms that: "Dissent ... is opposed to ecclesial com-munion and to a correct understanding of the hierarchical constitution of the people of God. Opposition to the teaching of the Church's pastors can-not be seen as a legitimate expression either of Christian freedom or of the diversity of the Spirit's gifts."[172] Given this, certain questions logically arise. For example, does this emphasis on obedience to the magisterium conflict with the need of the poor to be central to the reflection on, and to the struggle for, liberation? Further, does this emphasis also conflict with the need for a redistribution of power within a Church that opts for the poor?

One way to broach the first question is to investigate the extent to which the historical experiences, perspectives, and needs of the poor are considered in the generation of theological reflection on liberation. Rele-vant here is Pope John XXIII's introduction of the "signs of the times" approach in Catholic social teaching during the 1960s. According to him, the signs of the times are distinctive characteristics of the current histor-ical situation: political, economic, or social in nature, these signs can be positive or negative, representing justice or injustice.[173] With the Vatican II document *Gaudium et Spes*, the signs of the times became the starting point in the process of moral discernment on social matters. Thus, the concrete historical situation and its crises were chronicled and analyzed first, were then followed by an interpretation in the light of the Gospel, and were finally followed by suggestions for pastoral action. The same induc-tive methodology of "see, judge, act" was also adopted in Paul VI's *Popu-lorum Progressio* and in the documents of the Medellín conference. The Latin American bishops in particular exemplified this manner of approach-ing social issues. By beginning each of their documents with detailed descriptions and denunciations of the injustices and inadequacies in Latin American societies, the Medellín bishops grounded their social teachings on the demands of the historical context. This inductive formulation is one way to give priority to the poor and their struggles in the creation of the-ology and the quest for liberation.

In more recent times, however, the emphasis has shifted. In several Catholic social teaching documents since Medellín, conformity to ortho-doxy appears to take precedence over the life experiences of the poor. For example, Pope Paul's *Evangelii Nuntiandi*, John Paul II's *Laborem Exercens*, and the document of the Latin American bishops at Santo Domingo all adopt a "theology, world, action" formula. Such texts begin with lengthy theological expositions that are only then followed by discussions of cur-rent social problems and, finally, by suggestions for appropriate remedy-ing actions. More than just organizational formalities, however, the teaching itself is also significant. Thus, for example, in John Paul II's *Centesimus*

Annus the aim is to apply the century-old teaching of *Rerum Novarum* to the conditions of the world in 1991. While the pope indicates he is performing a "re-reading" of the text and is giving "careful consideration to current events," his point is not to bring Leo's encyclical up to date but, rather, to "discover anew the richness of the fundamental principles which it formulated ... [and] confirm the permanent value of such teaching."[174] Modern historical circumstances apparently have no determinative influence on social teaching; instead, it is "the church's tradition, which contains what is old...which enables us to interpret the 'new things.'"[175] Here the procedure is not a historically relevant reinterpretation of traditional social teaching but, rather, a reapplication of dogma to modern historical circumstances.

These documents represent a reversion to a distinctly pre-conciliar methodology. Prior to the 1960s, the institutional Church, viewed as the privileged and exclusive guardian of the truth of revelation, was accorded prime responsibility for moral teaching. In the pre-Vatican II vertical authority structure of the Church, the hierarchical magisterium, headed by the pope, was seen as the infallible interpreter of the revelation of Jesus Christ and therefore as the unquestionable authority on all social and economic matters.[176] Regardless of new demands and changed historical conditions, the teaching of the magisterium was not to be altered, but only adapted carefully or applied precisely to the needs of time and circumstance.[177] With this dogmatic methodology, the magisterium's authoritative expression of the immutable and eternal truth was the starting point for all social teaching pronouncements that could then be surely applied to any number of historical situations.

While the documents cited above certainly employ this type of deductive reasoning, the two Vatican Instructions on liberation theology issued in the mid-1980s emulate the pre-conciliar approach most closely. In these texts, social teaching is not said to be based on the historical context. Instead, the truth of divine revelation, as interpreted by the Church's hierarchical magisterium, is pronounced as the starting point for all theological reflection on human liberation:

> Through the mystery of the Incarnate Word and Redeemer of the world, she [the Church] possesses the truth regarding the Father and his love for us, and also the truth concerning man and his freedom .... It is from Christ the Redeemer that her thought and action originate when, as she contemplates the tragedies affecting the world, she reflects on the meaning of liberation and true freedom and on the paths leading to them.[178]

As in the pre-conciliar era, historical conditions and actions are evaluated against an unquestionable orthodoxy, instead of forming the dynamic theological locus themselves. With these deductive processes, the poor and their experiences in history are devalued in relation to the need for obedience to the hierarchical magisterium and to its infallible interpretation of revelation.[179] Such a methodology thus conflicts with the option for the poor's demand that the poor and their needs be placed front and centre in the process of liberation.

▶ *Activism by the Poor*   Turning to some final questions, what of the poor as the "architects of change" themselves? Has there been a reinvention of the Church along the lines indicated by the original option for the poor? The answers to these queries may be predictable in light of the above comments on methodology, but the evidence merits reviewing nonetheless.

Consider, once more, the Church's prohibition on revolutionary violence after the Medellín conference. Extreme though it may sound, forbidding the use of force by the oppressed is a matter of restricting the role of the poor as agents of change. By not granting any legitimacy to the violent means the poor have sometimes felt impelled to use in the struggle for liberation, Church leaders are withdrawing from an option from the poor. It is a question of the distribution of authority within the Church. In a truly reinvented Church, one in which authority can originate from the base, the decision of those at the base (who also form the majority in the Church)—even if it is a decision to use violence—cannot be unequivocally denied. A predetermined and absolute prohibition of revolutionary violence in effect rescinds the right of the poor to determine for themselves the path to their own liberation.

Consider also the reaction of the Church hierarchy to the CEBs over the years. As early as Pope Paul VI, the CEBs were admonished to remain "firmly attached to the local Church" and "never sectarian." According to Pope Paul in *Evangelii Nuntiandi*, those "communities which by their spirit of opposition cut themselves off from the Church, and whose unity they wound, can well be called *communautés de base*, but in this case it is strictly a sociological name. They could not, without a misuse of terms, be called ecclesial *communautés de base*."[180] It is worth noting that in this same passage Paul also appeals to the value of Church universality in support of his position on CEBs. In the Puebla conference document too, as I noted above, the Church's position on CEBs is restrictive, as the bishops attempt to indicate what types of activity are not acceptable in these groups. Significantly, the delegates at Puebla also appeal to unity and universality in their treatment of the "popular church" (i.e., the CEBs). They argue that the popular church is problematic because it "implicates a division within the bosom of the Church and an unacceptable denial of the hierarchy's function."[181] Moreover, they cast the popular church in terms of the issue of "parallel magisteria,"[182] another way of implying that CEBs are a divisive phenomenon. In these cases, the hierarchy demonstrates their lack of willingness to relinquish authority to the laity in the CEBs.

This conservative theoretical position on CEBs has been reinforced by Rome's actions vis-à-vis the popular church's supporters in Latin America. During John Paul II's tenure, the Vatican has censured the pro-CEB Latin American Conference of Religious and has further "questioned, controlled, or quashed" many other progressive Church experiments.[183] Pope John Paul II himself has replaced several progressive Latin American bishops with conservative ones (including members of the ultra-rightist Opus Dei movement), often over the protests of the local Churches.[184] Rome has also blocked the appointments of progressive professors to Latin American theology schools. And finally, of course, Rome has persecuted, censored, and silenced certain liberationist theologians, including Leonardo Boff who, significantly, has written extensively on the reinvention of the Church.[185]

Authoritarian actions of this nature do not signify a transformation of traditional Church structures. If anything, they represent a return to a pre-conciliar authority structure that is far from a democratized Church of the poor. Add to these facts the other implications of an overemphasis on the unity and universality of the Church, and a pre-conciliar style conservatism is evident again. Hence, over the years and through to its expression as a "preferential love and concern for the poor and needy," the bold and precise commitment of the original option for the poor has devolved into a vague and subdued platitude.

Conclusion

Pope John Paul II, in his introductory comments to *Laborem Exercens*, noted that his reflections on work were intended to be "in organic connection" with the Church's whole social teaching tradition.[186] The above analysis shows that the pope did follow through with his intention, not only in *Laborem Exercens* but also in his later social encyclicals. In fact, on the crucial issues related to social justice discussed above, the other documents surveyed would also fit in with the fundamentally conservative heritage passed on from Pope Leo XIII in the last century.

Perhaps this is not surprising, given that Tradition is considered to be one of the anchors of the Catholic faith. The conservative tradition that influences much of the official Church's position on social justice does, however, provide cause for a re-evaluation of the Medellín conference and of its significance to the larger body of Catholic social teaching. Seen from this perspective, the Medellín conference does not quite fit in. The bishops there did not inaugurate a new era in Church progressivism; rather, their conference document remains an exception in the otherwise conservative trajectory of Church teachings. Still, Medellín did make a mark. Medellín introduced Latin American liberation theology to the worldwide Church and to official Catholic social teaching. Medellín also inspired and supported militants in the Latin American Church who struggled for social change. Most importantly, the words and actions associated with Medellín caused a backlash.

Once the CELAM bishops introduced their liberationist model at Medellín, it could not be ignored. The impression that the bishops helped to make can be seen in the various popes' admonishments about the "liberation movement" and their critiques of the popular church. It can be seen in the silencing of Leonardo Boff, in the careful adoptions and adaptations of the terms "liberation" and "option for the poor," and in the very fact that the two Instructions on liberation were deemed necessary. With Medellín, the conflict between liberationists and conservatives in the Church hierarchy was revealed. With these subsequent events and activities, this same struggle was proved present at other levels of the institution as well.

Costa Rican Church agents are both witnesses to these liberationist-conservative struggles and participants in them. They seek to understand and implement Catholic social teaching as they develop their own versions of a Catholic *pastoral obrera*, which in turn can be liberationist or conservative in orientation. Church actors do not simply translate Catholic social teaching into theoretical positions and practical programming, however. Rather, as the following case studies will demonstrate, Catholic social teaching is appropriated and employed in ways that are related to these actors' needs, experiences, and alliances within the Costa Rican Church and society.

Monseñor Arrieta and CECOR 5

Only the union of all Costa Ricans, without social, political or religious
distinctions, can move us forward and free us from a social cataclysm.
—Monseñor Arrieta, "United to Save Costa Rica" (a 1982 editorial)

Where there is work there is bread, and where there is bread there is peace.
—Frequent expression of Monseñor Arrieta

After the 1952 death of Monseñor Sanabria, the outspoken Church
leader and vigorous proponent of social reform, the Costa Rican
bishops (collectively known as CECOR) fell into a so-called long
period of silence regarding social and political issues. This era, which
spanned the tenures of both Monseñors Odio (1952–59) and Rodríguez
(1960–79), can be best characterized as one of extreme Church complacency
with regard to social problems. Although the imagined threat of communism did occasionally rouse the bishops to heated commentary, in general the Costa Rican episcopate displayed little public concern for social
justice during this period. Not even the currents of change in the worldwide Church in the 1960s had much effect on the Costa Rican episcopate: as some have remarked, all Vatican II meant in Costa Rica was that
priests could now turn around and speak Spanish when saying Mass.[1] The
1968 Medellín conference had even less of an impact, as was perhaps predictable with the arch-conservative Monseñor Rodríguez leaving the conference before the closing ceremony and refusing to sign the liberationist
final document.

All this appeared to change, however, with the 1979 appointment of
Monseñor Román Arrieta Villalobos. Since that time, Monseñor Arrieta
and CECOR have issued numerous noteworthy pastoral letters on social
justice. The Costa Rican bishops have also taken some significant public
stances in relation to workers' associations and activism in Costa Rica.
By examining the political, economic, ideological, and institutional variables affecting Monseñor Arrieta and the Costa Rican Church hierarchy,
I demonstrate why the bishops chose to speak out when and how they
did, and what functions their pronouncements performed in the context
of Costa Rican society and of the Church itself.

The Man They Call *Manzanita*

It came as no surprise that the Costa Rican Church found its voice again after Monseñor Arrieta's appointment as archbishop. As bishop of Tilarán (1961–79), Monseñor Arrieta had been known as an exception, as one of the few Church leaders who would publicly involve himself in social justice issues during the long silence.[2] Perhaps most notably, Arrieta achieved national attention in 1975 for his statements in support of the PLN government's controversial irrigation and agrarian reform proposal for the Guanacaste region.[3] Because of the bishop's tenacity in promoting the project's benefits for poor *campesinos*—even in the face of harsh criticism from the cattle-ranching *latifundistas* of the area—it appeared that the Costa Rican Church had finally found a worthy successor to Sanabria.

Still, in spite of—or, more likely, because of—the leadership he had shown on the Guanacaste issue, Arrieta was not appointed archbishop when the time came. Although Monseñor Rodríguez's failing health meant that the Church was effectively leaderless in 1978 and early 1979, and although Arrieta appeared to be well respected in Church circles as president of both CECOR and the Secretariado Episcopal de América Central y Panamá (SEDAC), Arrieta's widely expected ascension to the archbishop's position was delayed. The resistance to Arrieta came primarily from the newly elected Partido Unión Nacional (PUN) government of Rodrigo Carazo.[4] Aware of Arrieta's close ties to the PLN and witness to the effects of such ties in the irrigation and land reform debate, President Carazo succeeded in convincing the Vatican to postpone naming a new archbishop until he could visit Rome to discuss the issue in person. When Carazo could not find another suitable candidate for archbishop and then became otherwise occupied with the worsening economic crisis in Costa Rica, Monseñor Arrieta was finally named archbishop of San José in July of 1979.

In the years after his appointment, Monseñor Arrieta took on even more responsibilities in the international Catholic Church.[5] Once a long-serving president of CELAM's department of vocations and ministries, he was elevated to the role of second vice-president of the council from 1980–83. For the Vatican, Arrieta served as a consultant on the Pontifical Commission for Latin America and, in the early 1980s, was named as a member of both the Commission for the Revision of the Code of Canon Law and the Sacred Congregation for the Evangelization of Peoples. At the same time, Arrieta grew to become a respected public figure at home, receiving high approval ratings in Costa Rican public opinion polls.[6] Before long, the archbishop came to be known colloquially and affectionately as *Manzanita* (little apple), a reference to his rather round and red face (and definitely not to any communist convictions). Biographical details aside, however, my focus here is on Arrieta's socio-political positions and those of the CECOR bishops as a collective.

The Church Hierarchy's Political Pronouncements and Preferences

During the time period under study, the Costa Rican bishops collectively and Monseñor Arrieta as an individual released nine major pastoral letters and numerous shorter pronouncements on topics related to politics and social justice. The similarities and often subtle differences in the content, tone, and targets of the bishops' analyses can be best discussed in terms of three specific periods: 1979–81, 1982–89, and 1990–96.

♦ Liberationist Language but Conservative Concepts (1979–81)

In the period immediately following Monseñor Arrieta's appointment, the bishops issued three major pastoral letters addressing the country's severe economic crisis. The first and, arguably, most important of these was *Evangelization and Social Reality in Costa Rica*,[7] the document that definitively broke the bishops' long silence in December 1979. This missive was followed by *The Church and the Current Moment* in August 1981,[8] and by the aptly named *United in Hope*,[9] a Christmas message for the same year. Throughout this period, moreover, Arrieta also released certain individual statements in which he sought to clarify the meaning of the socio-religious themes of liberation and the preferential option for the poor.

▶ Breaking the Long Silence on Social Justice

Evangelization and Social Reality in Costa Rica represents the conscious effort of Monseñor Arrieta and the CECOR bishops to apply the categories and teachings of that year's CELAM conference in Puebla to the Costa Rican crisis. In the letter, the bishops recognize that one-third of the population lives in state of "misery" and they pronounce this to be "a grave negation of the Kingdom of God."[10] The Costa Rican hierarchy also condemns the "social breach between the rich and poor," in which the privileged minorities live in "the offensive ostentation of superabundance." Directly citing the Puebla document, the Costa Rican bishops classify this situation as one of "social sin" and "a scandal and contradiction of the essence of Christianity."[11]

When it comes to laying blame for the "asphyxiating economic situation and distressing social reality"[12] in the country, the bishops point both to sinful attitudes and structural flaws in the socio-economic system. Singled out on the one hand are the "materialistic selfishness and an unbridled urge for luxury,"[13] along with the "uncontrolled ambition" of a consumerist society.[14] On the other hand, the bishops refer to the "structures and mechanisms" of a socio-economic development process that has benefitted the middle and upper classes more than the popular classes.[15] The bishops are rather vague about how these structures and mechanisms function; however, they do accuse the "privileged groups" and powerful political "plotters" of orienting the structure of commerce and production in their favour and of controlling public opinion through their influence over the mass media.[16]

This denunciation of the Costa Rican social reality is strong, as is the language used to delineate what must change. Once again citing phrases from the final document of the Puebla conference, the bishops call for both a "personal conversion and profound changes of structures."[17] Along with the CELAM bishops, the Costa Rican hierarchy aims to support the "integral liberation of the human person,"[18] as well as Puebla's "unambiguous preferential option for the poor."[19]

Yet, in spite of the impression given by the use of such liberationist language, the remedies actually proposed by the bishops are quite weak. As other analysts have also recognized,[20] the bishops do not point to any specific alternatives to the current structures, nor to any concrete strategies for overcoming societal inequities. In fact, they stress that their role is not to promote specific forms of social organization or economic models,[21] and they qualify their support for liberation by saying that "it is not technical, but moral and from faith."[22] Moreover, the bishops appeal almost exclusively to the wealthy in society in their letter, calling on the privileged to act as "Good Samaritans" and to "exercise love and practice justice towards [their] needy brothers."[23] Quoting the document from Puebla yet again, the bishops call for the rich to be "converted and liberated" from their slavery to riches and from their selfishness. The poor, instead of being empowered to change the world around them, must be "freed" from individualism and from being "attracted and seduced by the false ideals of a consumer society."[24] This emphasis on attitudinal as opposed to structural change, and on the rich as opposed to the poor as the prime agents of change, contrasts with the almost strident tone of the phrasing the bishops use in their document. Despite some of the liberationist overtones implied by the language of the letter, the underlying message of the document falls closer to the conservative end of the Catholic social teaching spectrum—much as I have indicated is the case with the Puebla document itself.

Many of the same biases are evident in the other two pastoral letters released by the bishops. In both *The Church and the Current Moment* and *United in Hope*, the bishops condemn the crisis and its characteristics (e.g., unemployment, inflation, corruption, the growing gap between rich and poor); yet, the solutions they propose do not seriously challenge the current socio-economic structure or the privileges and power of those in charge of it. Avenues for the structural renovation of society are ignored in favour of calls for a "radical change of attitude"[25] and appeals to "Christian sentiments"[26] and "conscience."[27] Once again, the remedies for the crisis involve mainly the powerful in society, as the bishops express hope that Jesus will "with celestial brilliance illumine the mind and heart of our government leaders, politicians, businessmen, and all those who can do as much to improve our current situation."[28] Hence, the Church hierarchy appeals to the privileged of the social, political, and economic hierarchy to contribute generously to Church programs for the poor, to live austerely, to be content with what they have and not press for more, and to pay higher taxes so that the government can redirect resources and fund programs for those most in need.[29] In all of this, the poor themselves are not accorded much agency but are treated more as victims needful of help from above.

▶ *Preserving Social Peace and Unity*   Two other important themes in the pastoral letters issued between 1979 and 1981 merit comment. The first is the bishops' preoccupation with preserving social peace in Costa Rica. They repeatedly warn that the characteristics of the crisis present "a grave threat" to social harmony.[30] Here, the hierarchy views the crisis as potentially initiating some sort of dangerous chain reaction, as they pray to "let us maintain a Costa Rica free of the violence that hunger can provoke."[31] At another point, they plead that God will "not permit that, due to the selfishness, indifference, or short-sightedness of some, the situation will deteriorate even more, violence will arise, chaos will reign and the country will perish."[32] In this plea, the injustice and poverty characteristic of the crisis are not defined as violent in themselves; instead, the bishops argue that only if such inequality and suffering are not ameliorated might violence erupt. This categorization stands in contrast to that of the Medellín conference, where the definition of "institutionalized violence" condemns the very structures of an unjust society as a negation of peace. By refusing to acknowledge the inequality of the crisis as a form of violence in itself, the CECOR bishops are minimizing the severity of the situation in Costa Rica. Moreover, with their insistence that social peace must be preserved at all costs, they are communicating to their constituents that violence is an unacceptable reaction to social problems.

This last point is certainly consistent with a final theme that comes to the fore in these pastoral letters, that of social unity. The unified efforts of Costa Ricans are, for the bishops, the key to overcoming the economic crisis. All Costa Ricans, regardless of social, political, or economic differences, must work together in solidarity and fraternity to resolve the nation's problems.[33] They must overcome any political and ideological barriers to confront their challenges together, "forging [their] common destiny as one big family."[34] As a corollary to this position, the bishops condemn struggle and polarization as anti-Christian and warn against the "exacerbated hatred that is leading peoples dear and near to us to genocide and self-immolation."[35] With this tacit reference to the Nicaraguan Revolution, the Costa Rican bishops' message is clear: it is Christian collaboration—not conflict and confrontation—that will resolve Costa Rica's crisis. Overall, the bishops' emphasis on unity and collaboration, in the face of an economic crisis characterized by the fact of conflict, also places the Costa Rican Church hierarchy within the conservative Catholic social teaching tradition.

This interpretation is borne out by a closer examination of the way in which the bishops use the concept of the preferential option for the poor. The careful observer, for example, will note that the 1979 letter refers to an "unambiguous" preferential option for the poor.[36] Yet, as I outlined in the previous chapter, by merely appending the qualification "preferential" onto the phrase "option for the poor," ambiguity—or at least a degree of equivocation—is introduced; the implication then is that one opts for both the rich and the poor, and just gives preference to the poor. The bishops themselves confirm that they do not intend to promote exclusivity or side-taking, as they state that "this option for the poor does not mean, in return, the undervaluing, or even less the rejection of the rich."[37] Monseñor Arrieta also made an individual statement on the option for the poor, tying it to the preservation of social peace. In it, he takes care to stress that above all the option for the poor should be an authentic "option for Christ." For the archbishop, this means that Marxism and its method of analysis—with its acceptance of class struggle and violence—must be rejected. Otherwise, he warns, the unity of the Church and the communion of all its members are threatened.[38]

Arrieta cites similar principles to clarify what the term "liberation" should mean for Christians. He obviously felt the need to stipulate what liberation was and what it was not, much as Pope John Paul II and Cardinal Ratzinger were soon to do with their infamous Instructions on liberation theology. According to Arrieta, "authentic" or "Christian" liberation (the term is almost never left to stand on its own) has four key characteristics. Liberation should be based in faith and not ideologies. Liberation should begin with the conversion of individual hearts and one should begin with oneself before attempting the liberation of the world. Liberation should employ only "evangelical" means and never violence. And liberation should be "rectilinear" and should involve only an option for Christ, since anything else—such as opting for an idolatrous socio-economic system—would destroy Christian unity.[39] Much as was the case with the collective pastoral letters, then, Arrieta's definitions of liberation and the preferential option for the poor emphasize the political and socio-religious convictions that are the hallmarks of conservative Catholic social teaching.

♦ Continuing Conservatism (1982-89)

In the second period, Monseñor Arrieta and the CECOR bishops collectively issued four further pastoral letters. The most relevant to the present discussion are *Blessed Is He Who Comes in the Name of the Lord*,[40] which was released shortly before the pope's 1983 visit to Costa Rica; *The Church in the Face of the Electoral Process*,[41] which was circulated in late 1985 in anticipation of the elections slated for the following February; and *A Call from the Bishops of Costa Rica to the Conscience of the Country*,[42] which was published in March of 1988. Only the 1988 call from the bishops focused centrally on overcoming the country's economic woes; yet all three pastoral letters contain material of relevance regarding the Church's position on social justice. Overall, the bishops in these documents fall into their earlier patterns when it comes to offering opinions about how best to solve the Costa Rican crisis.

Once again, no real changes of a structural nature are recommended. Instead, for example, the bishops ask public sector workers to work more conscientiously and efficiently, and to treat their office machines more "delicately" and maintain them regularly, so that the money saved can be directed to the needs of the poor.[43] In other cases, the bishops concentrate on such factors as the "reform of customs" or the "reconstitution of man" as the means to societal improvement.[44] Indeed, in this period the myth of the noble Costa Rican *campesino* seems to have been resurrected, as the bishops appeal to individuals to "project the authentic *campesino* soul, so full of values, that has forged the history of our people."[45] Here, the focus is on the moral renovation of citizens and not, as the bishops emphasize, on any ideology or socio-economic "system."

The Costa Rican hierarchy also remains biased toward a top-down model whereby the country's elites direct social change. The letters ask those with economic and political power to help the needy or, as in the case of the *carta pastoral* released during the mid-1980s election campaign, they ask the faithful to elect representatives who will "opt preferentially for the poor and fully dedicate themselves to their integral promotion."[46] Monseñor Arrieta, in his individual statements, reinforces this rather paternalistic *compromiso con los pobres* (obligation to the poor) by "calling for the rich to not forget the poor, and for selfishness to die so that they can open themselves to their brothers with generosity."[47] For all their rhetoric about committing and opting for the poor, none of the bishops' statements during this time incorporates the necessary actions of encouragement or empowerment for the poor—actions that would make such commitments and options truly effective.

▶ *Conforming with the Vatican*   A final set of similarities between the bishops' documents from 1979 to 1981 and from 1982 to 1989 relates to the themes of social peace and unity. As seen in my previous analyses, ensuring peace, love, and order—as opposed to "war, hatred, and chaos"—is portrayed as the prime motivation for caring for the poor and for overcoming the gap between the rich and poor.[48] Especially evident, however, is a stress on Christian unity (specifically Church unity above all) in *Blessed Is He Who Comes in the Name of the Lord*. In this 1983 document, the bishops, who define themselves as "pastors at the service of unity and truth,"[49] affirm that it is the pope who is the guarantor of unity in the Church, the "visible and lasting source and foundation of the unity of faith and of communion."[50] Here the bishops are explicitly promoting a hierarchical ecclesiological model, and they emphasize that it should not be confused with civil society and its democratic characteristics.[51] Likewise, they discredit the notion of the "wrongly named" popular church, arguing that it is "neither Church nor popular."[52] In the CECOR bishops' institutional model, there is only one path to follow—that laid out by the pope: "to separate oneself from him is to separate oneself from Christ."[53]

As I discuss below, these comments can be related to the situation of the Church in neighbouring Nicaragua. Nonetheless, they are also consistent with the statements that Monseñor Arrieta made on the importance of Christian unity earlier in the 1980s. Given such concerns for unity, moreover, and given the archbishop's position on liberation as outlined above, it is not surprising that the archbishop displayed strong support for the 1984 Instruction on liberation theology issued by the Sacred Congregation for the Doctrine of the Faith. In his formal declaration on the topic, Arrieta echoes the Vatican document in all its key points: the definition of liberation as a "liberation from the radical slavery of sin," the rejection of a principally political form of liberation, and the warning of the dangers of using Marxist analysis.[54] This statement of solidarity with the Instruction provides one more link between the Costa Rican Church hierarchy and the conservative project of the Vatican.

▶ *Preference for the PLN*   For all the consistencies in the bishops' statements from 1979 to 1989, however, one important new element can be detected in the public position of the Church. Beginning with the 1982 election of Luis Alberto Monge, the Church—and particularly Monseñor Arrieta— made clear its support for the PLN government. From this point, through to the election and presidential term of Monge's successor Oscar Arias (1986–90), the official Costa Rican Church played a crucial role in supporting the PLN government in both its anti-crisis strategy and its foreign policy commitments.

Clues about the forthcoming collaboration came as early as the morning following Monge's election victory, when Arrieta hosted the ceremony proclaiming the new president in the atrium of the Metropolitan Cathedral (the archbishop was to continue this new tradition when Arias was elected four years later). During his remarks to the nation, the archbishop invoked the nation's "sacred heritage" and "exemplary" traditions of peace and democracy, while also warning that these were threatened by the effects of the crisis and by those associated with "terrorism, social instability, and intimidation." Significantly, he called on Costa Ricans to "close ranks" (*cerrar filas*) around the new government and work together with the newly elected leaders to overcome the economic crisis.[55] At the ceremony, Monge also emphasized that all Costa Ricans needed to pull together in a spirit of solidarity to confront the crisis. The president-elect closed his speech by stating his desire to serve the people of Costa Rica as well as God; he referred to the "heavy cross" that he had been given and that he would carry on his shoulders with discipline and humility.[56] With this event, a significant alliance came to light, featuring the nation's highest-ranking religious leader speaking in clearly political terms and its future political leader openly adopting religious symbolism.[57]

The Church's pastoral letters during the eight years of PLN rule in the 1980s display further evidence of this relationship between Church and state. Whereas during President Carazo's tenure the Church's critique of the economic crisis was pointed and unforgiving, the pastoral letters during the time of Monge and Arias took on a more conciliatory tone. The 1983 and 1985 letters contain a relatively weak critique of social conditions and, as noted, were not primarily concerned with the country's economic conditions anyway. Moreover, even the hierarchy's 1988 letter on the crisis was worded to avoid offending those in political power. In the preamble to the document, the bishops stress that by pointing out problems they did not mean "to humiliate anyone, whether that be the government, its institutions, or private initiative."[58] They further preface their comments on reducing public spending by acknowledging the government's efforts in that area, even though they recognized that more needed to be done.[59] By muting their criticism of the economic crisis and by softening their direct comments toward the government in this way, the bishops helped the government to disassociate itself from the causes of the crisis. Perhaps more importantly, they helped to reinforce the notion that the government was effectively working to overcome the nation's problems.

This latter point is especially important since both Monge and Arias sought to portray themselves as leaders capable of competently combatting the crisis. The structural adjustment agreements these presidents signed with the IMF and the World Bank were part of their strategy to restabilize the Costa Rican economy through neo-liberal policies. And, while the government attempted to impose the structural framework for neo-liberalism, the Church provided important ideological and practical backing for the project.

Nowhere is this relationship seen more clearly seen than in Monseñor Arrieta's *Decálogo de la austeridad* (*Ten Commandments of Austerity*). Widely publicized in the Costa Rican media during 1984, these commandments represented another merging of religious symbolism with a frankly political agenda in the Church's discourse. Explicitly referring to the government's calls for austerity as a means to overcome the crisis, the archbishop reinforces this strategy by asking Costa Ricans to avoid spending money on vices and luxuries, to save as much as possible, to use public services sparingly, and to conserve petrol by walking instead of driving.[60] Such a program, beyond helping to instill among the population a mindset of making sacrifices for one's country, was also a means to soften the side effects of the "bitter pill" of structural adjustment. By promoting these austerity measures, then, the archbishop helped the government to maintain social stability during a period of widespread economic hardship.

A related joint venture of the Church and state during this period functioned in a similar manner. In 1982, the Monge administration proposed that the Church assist in the implementation of a new National Food Distribution Plan intended to alleviate the poverty of approximately 25,000 of Costa Rica's poorest families. The Church agreed, and through Cáritas (its social assistance agency) and local parishes it began to assess the needs of families and distribute staple food items. While undoubtedly this program helped to satisfy the basic needs of many poor families, this type of *asistencialismo* also fit in with the Costa Rican Church's preference for a top-down approach to social problems. Moreover, the Cáritas program was another means through which the Church acted as an accomplice in the government's program of "social containment" during a time of crisis.[61]

A final form of Church support for the state came in relation to the Costa Rican government's various approaches to the increasingly complex Nicaraguan situation.[62] By the time Monge was elected in 1982, the Nicaraguan counter-revolution was already underway. Although at the beginning of his term Monge proclaimed Costa Rica's neutrality on Nicaragua, because of the importance of his alliance with the United States (which provided much-needed economic aid for Costa Rica during the crisis) he also allowed the anti-Sandinista *contra* rebels to operate from Costa Rican territory with little or no interference. After 1984, the Monge administration's support for Ronald Reagan's campaign against the Sandinistas became more overt. Thus, military aid — and a group of U.S. Green Berets — poured into Costa Rica, and the "neutral country without an army" became fully embroiled in what was threatening to become an all-out war in the region. Only with the 1986 election of Oscar Arias and the 1987 acceptance of his Esquipulas II peace plan did tensions and the Reagan–Costa Rican alliance subside.

Throughout this period, the stance of the official Costa Rican Church either directly or indirectly bolstered the government's position vis-à-vis Nicaragua. Thus, during the Monge administration, the Church declared its support for the government's proclamation of neutrality.[63] But, simultaneously, the Church worked against the Sandinistas on several levels. The Church hierarchy, for example, persisted in "satanizing" the Sandinista state as a "Marxist regime,"[64] and Monseñor Arrieta was particularly incensed over the fact that priests occupied several key positions in the revolutionary government.[65] The archbishop also harshly chastised the newspaper *Eco Católico* for running an editorial that criticized U.S. President Reagan's policies toward Nicaragua and praised the early accomplishments of the revolutionary government.[66] In addition, the Costa Rican bishops clearly sided with the Sandinistas' archenemy, Cardinal Miguel Obando y Bravo. In Nicaragua, the "popular church" had publicly split with Cardinal Obando shortly after the revolution; the Costa Rican Church hierarchy's attack on the "popular church" was one form of support for the embattled cardinal. The bishops also openly pledged their solidarity with the leader of the "persecuted" Nicaraguan Church and invited him to join Monseñor Arrieta to celebrate the annual public mass in honour of Costa Rica's patron saint.[67] Significantly, the Costa Rican hierarchy was silent regarding the channelling of U.S. military aid to the *contras*, in contrast to many other Latin American religious leaders at the time.[68] Finally, when the time came, the Church also threw its weight behind President Arias's peace plan, asking the faithful to pray for its acceptance and celebrating its success with a thanksgiving mass.[69]

In the end, and as I will indicate, the Costa Rican bishops' stance on Nicaragua was not merely an opinion on Costa Rican foreign policy: its anti-Sandinista position can also be linked to the Church's institutional need for self-preservation. For now, however, suffice it to say that the Costa Rican Church hierarchy's public statements on Nicaragua were, like so many of its actions during this time, another form of support for the Costa Rican government struggling with an economic crisis at home and a political crisis next door.

◆ A Change in the Church's Direction? (1990–96)

The final period under investigation was marked by numerous official Church statements of import from a social justice perspective, including two major pastoral letters. Monseñor Arrieta released *New Evangelization and Human Promotion* in 1993,[70] and the Costa Rican bishops collectively published *Mother Earth* in 1994.[71] While in many respects the bishops simply presented more of the same socio-political convictions during this period, there appeared to be some significant shifts to the left in their positions around the time *Mother Earth* was released. These new and ostensibly liberationist notes in the Church hierarchy's message deserve closer analysis.

To begin, however, it is notable that the archbishop and the rest of the hierarchy did not waver on their definitions of core socio-religious concepts. In fact, Monseñor Arrieta's 1980 four-point discussion of Christian liberation was republished, almost verbatim, in 1990 and in 1996.[72] The option for the poor was once again carefully cast—this time as a "commitment to the poor"[73] or, in the words of the CELAM bishops at the Santo Domingo conference, as an "authentic preferential option for the poor"[74] and an "effective preoccupation for the poorest"[75] alongside a "preferential option for youth."[76] The wording of each of these phrases clearly represents a weakening of the originally bold and unequivocal liberationist option for the poor at Medellín. As in previous years, there is also an emphasis on maintaining social peace and on the unity of all Costa Ricans as a means to overcome social problems.[77]

Monseñor Arrieta's political partisanship, so evident in the period 1982-89, resurfaced in the early 1990s. It can be detected, for instance, in his cool and critical attitude toward the newly elected PUSC government. Hence, in marked contrast to his supportive behaviour following the elections of PLN presidents Monge and Arias, Arrieta did not offer a thanksgiving service following the electoral victory of Rafael Angel Calderón Fournier (much, reportedly, to the resentment of the incoming president).[78] Even more obvious were the archbishop's harsh comments directed against the government's policies during his public homily to celebrate the feast of the Virgin of Los Angeles (Costa Rica's patron saint) later that same year.[79] Tellingly, Arrieta's position provoked heated complaints and rebuttals from PUSC party members, while PLN representatives responded with support for the archbishop's remarks.[80]

Monseñor Arrieta's 1993 pastoral letter continued in the same vein, with several pointed references to the incapacity of the state to fulfil its duties and the failure of government policies to alleviate socio-economic problems in the country.[81] Not surprisingly, Arrieta's position once again triggered displays of public outrage from PUSC officials.[82] In fact, the charges of political bias were justified in many respects, especially given that the document was released less than three months before the 1994 presidential elections and that parallels could be drawn between Arrieta's critique of neo-liberal policies and the campaign platform of PLN candidate José Figueres (Jr.).[83]

▶ *Social Change and the CEBs*   Despite these obvious similarities in the Costa Rican Church's position during the 1980s and the first half of the 1990s, however, it also appears that the Church hierarchy began to shift its position significantly toward the end of this period. In this respect, in 1994 there is the strong denunciation in *Mother Earth* of the conditions suffered by Costa Rica's *campesinos* and indigenous peoples, and of the government's role in creating and sustaining these conditions. The bishops critique, among other things, the inequitable distribution of land in Costa Rica, the negative effects of transnational corporations' influence in the social, cultural, economic, and ecological realms, and the flaws in an economic model excessively oriented toward exports.[84] The fact that one of the harshest condemnations of Costa Rica's socio-economic crisis in Church history came during the administration of a PLN president, José Figueres, makes this pastoral letter all the more remarkable.

Also noteworthy is the fact that, in this pastoral letter, the bishops appear to move away from a strictly top-down model of responsibility for social change. They do emphasize that the state, its institutions, and Church bodies should be reforming their policies and programs for the benefit of the poor. But they also chastise such organizations for the often insensitive and paternalistic manner in which they treat the poor and dis-

respect their cultures.[85] They stress that it is the *campesinos* and indigenous peoples themselves who are the "subjects of their own development."[86]
As such, those at the base of society are also urged to undertake actions
to organize themselves to defend their rights and find solutions for their
needs.[87]

The bishops' move toward encouraging the empowerment of the poor
is reinforced by the increasing efforts of the Church to incorporate CEBs
into its pastoral strategy. Sporadic allusions had been made to promoting
base communities ever since the Archdiocesan Synod of 1984,[88] but it was
not until 1995 that the hierarchy made a concerted attempt to develop a
coherent and official position on the topic. In that year, the bishops asked
the Comisión Nacional Episcopal de Laicos (CONEL, National Episcopal
Commission of Laity) to develop definitions and criteria to guide parishes
as they incorporated CEBs into their pastoral planning. The resulting document, entitled *Base Ecclesial Communities in the Costa Rican Church*,
was fully endorsed by CECOR, which recommended its guidelines to all
priests and laity in the country.[89] With this initiative and the statements
in *Mother Earth*, it appeared that the Costa Rican bishops were taking
some important steps to democratize the exceedingly hierarchical Costa
Rican Church structure.

Nonetheless, a closer investigation of the type of CEBs being promoted, along with the contents and context for the 1994 pastoral letter,
reveals that the hierarchy's conservative bias remained largely intact. For
instance, the role envisioned for CEBs in the Costa Rican Church is far
more pastoral than political. Hence in the CONEL document there is a
marked emphasis on the spiritual aspects of CEBs. The base communities
are portrayed primarily as a new Church structure that can respond to
peoples' "hunger for the Word of God" and function as a way to motivate
people "to sample the joy of Christian coexistence."[90] CEBs are seen as
having their origin and sustenance in the Holy Spirit, as being centred on
the Bible, as working to overcome religious ignorance, and as fostering fraternal love.[91] Granted, there are references to the communities making a
"preferential option for the poor" and to their social pastoral work.[92] Still,
the option for the poor is once again cautioned to be "neither excluding nor
exclusive."[93] Further, instead of a clear call for political activism, there are
vague references to the base community operating as a "community of
service and charity" in which "assistential, promotional, and liberative"
efforts are expressed.[94] Echoes can be heard of Pope Paul VI's *Evangelii
Nuntiandi* warnings that CEBs should not be identified with political ideologies or positions; these echoes underscore the Costa Rican Church's
teaching that the base communities in Costa Rica are not intended to
transform society.[95]

Nor are such communities intended to transform the Church. While
lay animators are said to fulfil an important ministry within CEBs, much

emphasis is placed on the appropriate role of bishops and priests in accompanying the work of the communities.[96] And both Monseñor Arrieta's earlier comments and the CONEL document stress — also in line with Pope Paul VI's admonitions in *Evangelii Nuntiandi* — that CEBs are to develop firmly within the local and the universal Church and in communion with her legitimate pastors.[97] With this focus on the CEBs as an extension of the Church's hierarchical structure and as subsumed under it, it is clear that neither pastoral independence nor pastoral creativity is desired by the Costa Rican bishops. Far from Leonardo Boff's suggestion that CEBs could be the means to reinvent and democratize the Church, then, for the Costa Rican hierarchy, these new ecclesial units are simply a further elaboration of the already deeply entrenched authoritarian institutional pattern.

In addition, and despite the appearances given by the language of the text, in *Mother Earth* the bishops do not entirely embrace the liberationist Catholic social teaching perspectives on social change. Hence, although they mention the right of the poor to be agents of their own development, the bishops clearly advocate state-directed developmentalism, not the liberation of those who have been largely excluded from the benefits of the established socio-economic structure. The particular responsibilities accorded to *campesinos* and indigenous peoples in the document are vague and largely overshadowed by those assigned to the government (and, to a lesser extent, the Church). Granted, dictating a number of specific actions for *campesinos* and indigenous peoples to follow would be inconsistent with a true respect for their agency and independence. Yet, advice such as "coordinate plans and actions among different organizations," "know Catholic social teaching more deeply," or "safeguard the environment while undertaking productive activities"[98] glosses over the issues of who holds power and how they use it to maintain an unjust distribution of privileges; these are necessary elements to consider if grassroots-inspired social transformation is to be successful. In fact, almost all the recommendations to the poor in the letter guide them to transform relations among themselves (e.g., to overcome individualism and rivalries), or to retrieve what they have lost (e.g., cultural traditions). While this admittedly paternalistic advice may be valuable, actions for social change must also be directed beyond the individuals and groups that make up the impoverished communities themselves, to challenge some of the larger societal structures that generate inequality. The statist bias of the letter, in contrast, conforms to the top-down approach to social responsibility that has been embodied in generations of conservative Catholic social teaching.

Although there is one recommendation in *Mother Earth* to "maintain a dialogue" with the relevant organizations to ensure that just prices are paid for agricultural products,[99] there are no calls to work for liberation or struggle for justice in the letter. The bishops make absolutely no allowance for conflict or confrontation; the only struggle alluded to is the one needed to overcome tensions within and among *campesino* and indigenous peoples' groups. This omission becomes problematic because, as I have outlined, in the face of dire conditions hopes for significant social change through consensus can be naive: confrontation is often an inescapable companion to the significant redistribution of societal privileges. Yet in the end, no matter how harsh the bishops' critique of the established system in *Mother Earth* may be, it is clear that reform, and not revolution, is their goal. After all, the bishops' position that "the market is the opportunity to live in solidarity with all" reveals their implicit faith in the capitalist system — albeit once the necessary adjustments are made and fairer prices are instituted.[100] The bishops' reluctance to look beyond the existing socio-economic structure for solutions to its inequities is one further way in which they place themselves closer to the conservative, as opposed to the liberationist, end of the Catholic social teaching spectrum.

▶ *Still Standing with the Government*   Finally, in *Mother Earth* the bishops reveal that there is no true split between the Church and its favourite political party — its publication during Figueres's term notwithstanding. Coming as it did only a few months into the term of the new president, this pastoral letter is not a condemnation of the newly elected PLN government; rather, it is an indictment of the programs of the PUSC government under Calderón (who, as I have indicated, was also subjected to direct criticism from the Church when he was in power). In fact, the bishops explicitly point to the "state policies of the past years" when they lay blame for the predicament of Costa Rica's poor.[101] Further, while the letter attacks the neo-liberal programming that defined Calderón's presidency, it can also be read as a reaffirmation of the state-led reformism that Figueres, appealing to his father's legacy (Figueres, Sr., led the country from 1953–58 and from 1970–74), had himself tried to promote during his election campaign. The bishops' emphasis in *Mother Earth*, on state responsibilities toward the poor and on reforming and expanding government programming in areas such as the environment, coincides with certain classic social democratic principles of the PLN. Significantly, the recently elected PLN deputies were not upset with the bishops' letter but, instead, publicly praised its contents as "on the mark," "laudable," and "timely." These declarations are further proof of the perseverance of the PLN-Church alliance during this period.[102]

After 1994, President Figueres reneged on his election promises and began to embrace a neo-liberal program. He signed another stabilization agreement with the IMF in 1995 and, among other things, cut thousands of public-sector jobs and benefits while pushing for privatization in banking and the state electrical utility.[103] Crucially, the Church did not mention the government's hypocrisy or repeat its attack on neo-liberalism. Instead, Church leaders reverted to calls for unity among Costa Ricans as a means to overcome the economic crisis. Importantly, a repeated variation on this theme was that of political unity: the idea that no group or political party acting alone could save Costa Rica, and that reconciliation had to take place among elected representatives in the country's legislative assembly.[104]

This plea for unity takes on its full meaning when one considers the position into which Figueres had been forced: having failed to achieve a parliamentary majority in 1994, the PLN leader was dependent on the cooperation of PUSC members in order to pass the legislation necessary to appease the IMF. When the recalcitrance of PUSC members began to cause costly stalemates almost immediately, Figueres sought an agreement with PUSC ex-president Calderón. The so-called Figueres-Calderón Pact[105] was signed in 1995. Although Figueres was then able to pass several pieces of critical legislation expediently, the agreement remained controversial and Figueres's popularity began to plummet. The widely held perception that he was a liar who went back on his election promises soon made him the most unpopular president in the history of Costa Rican polling.[106] Within this context, then, the Church's calls for unity provided an important means of support for Costa Rica's struggling president and his new bipartisanism. While this type of political intervention was certainly more indirect than it had been, for example, during Monge's rule, the hierarchy's comments can be construed as once again calling on Costa Ricans to close ranks around a PLN government.

Despite some of the superficial changes in the Costa Rican Church's position during the 1990s, then, its socio-political standpoints remained remarkably stable after Monseñor Arrieta's 1979 appointment as archbishop. In many ways, the archbishop and the rest of the hierarchy adopted several of the standard conservative principles found in post-Vatican II Catholic social teaching. They did so, moreover, in a manner uniquely responsive to the Costa Rican historical context and the particular political options presented there. While it will be necessary to investigate the bishops' religious expressions and political alliances from a more theoretical perspective, the teachings of the hierarchy that focus more particularly on the rights of workers first deserve a closer consideration.

The Costa Rican Bishops and Workers' Rights

Costa Rican Church officials have in general paid a considerable amount of attention to specific workers' issues. The Church hierarchy overall, but especially Monseñor Arrieta in his annual May 1st addresses to workers,[107] has consistently promoted the rights of workers as they are usually defined in Western democracies and in the Catholic social teaching tradition. Repeated references can be seen in CECOR documents and in Arrieta's homilies to the right of individuals to employment, to free association, to strike, to fair remuneration, to work in a healthy environment, to weekly periods of rest, to vacation time, and to social security and unemployment benefits.[108] And while an affirmation of these standard rights may be predictable, three particular emphases come to the fore in the discussion of these issues by Costa Rican Church officials.

First, the Costa Rican bishops express concern for social harmony, much as was the case in their more general treatments of socio-economic problems. Here, the corollary to the bishops' call to respect workers' rights is often the warning that, if such rights are disregarded, social peace will be endangered. Arrieta's motto that "where there is work there is bread, and where there is bread there is peace"[109] is but the most subtle of these warnings. Frequently, the more direct message is that workers' rights are essential to maintaining social peace.[110]

Second, the bishops are clearly using the major papal encyclicals on workers' issues (most notably *Rerum Novarum*, *Quadragesimo Anno*, and *Laborem Exercens*) as a frame of reference when it comes to defining workers' rights. They impart, however, a distinctly nationalistic flavour to the discussion, as can be seen in the priority given to the concept of a just salary or, more accurately, a "just family salary" (the notion that a salary should be sufficient to satisfy the basic needs of the worker and those of his or her dependants). The bishops do acknowledge that the concept of a just salary was elaborated in *Rerum Novarum* and *Quadragesimo Anno*, but they also strive to ensure that the faithful are aware that two early and illustrious Costa Rican Church leaders issued *cartas pastorales* on this very theme. They do so by frequently invoking the 1893 letter of Monseñor Thiel and the 1941 letter of Monseñor Sanabria, both of which are entitled *On the Just Salary*.[111] Moreover, the bishops are demonstrably proud of Sanabria's role in the instituting of the Social Guarantees and the Labour Code in 1940s Costa Rica, the story of which they cite often.[112] With their repeated references to the accomplishments of Thiel and Sanabria, the bishops demonstrate that they consider the lobby for workers' rights to be a cornerstone of Costa Rican Church history.

Third, and perhaps most interestingly, the CECOR bishops have worked to emulate the legacy of Sanabria through their own involvement in efforts to reform long-standing Costa Rican social legislation. In 1988, Church leaders were invited by the PLN minister of labour and social security to submit their advice on proposed revisions to the decades-old Labour Code. In response, the hierarchy issued a lengthy pastoral letter, *Comments on the New Labour Code Project*,[113] which reviewed past Church teachings from the Vatican as well as from Thiel and Sanabria on the rights of workers. In addition, both before and since that time, Monseñor Arrieta has lobbied—unsuccessfully—for a thorough revision of both the Labour Code and the Social Guarantees, arguing that this legislation is inadequate to respond to the conditions faced by present-day workers.[114]

The actual social teaching perspectives outlined in the letter and subsequent statements on the issue are discussed below; what is important to note here is that this is an attempt by the Church to foster social justice through the endorsement of legislative reforms. The hierarchy's support for revisions to the Labour Code and the Social Guarantees underscores their belief that one of the best ways to ensure that workers' rights are respected is through state-sponsored change.

♦ The Right to Strike

Of all the rights to which workers are entitled, it is the right to strike and the right to form unions that have the most relevance in the Costa Rican context. Importantly, the Costa Rican hierarchy has developed clear and detailed positions on both of these issues. The attitude of CECOR toward strikes, for example, closely follows the perspective historically espoused by the Vatican, a stance that finds its most recent expression in John Paul II's *Laborem Exercens*. That is, the Costa Rican bishops view the strike as a last resort, an extreme means to be employed only once all other avenues of negotiation have been exhausted.[115] Like Pope John Paul and several of his predecessors, the Costa Rican bishops also focus on the negative effects of strikes (particularly losses in production and the loss of social peace)[116] and warn that strikes are not to be abused in the pursuit of "political" ends.[117]

The attitude of the bishops on the topic is perhaps best revealed through comments found in their pastoral letter on the Labour Code:

> The exercise of [the strike] cannot be unconditional, which would cause serious damages to the general interests of the community. The strike should be seen as an instrument of conciliation, of an ultimate and temporal character, but one that should improve the condition of the workers and one that must be accepted as socially just whenever the demands made are reasonable, economically possible, and would not cause serious public harm.[118]

This passage reinforces the notion of the strike as a sometimes necessary evil, one that is subject to a number of restrictions. Yet some of these restrictions raise important questions. Who, for instance, determines what demands are "reasonable"? What criteria are used to decide whether workers' demands are "economically possible"? Would strikes for employment stability be deemed less reasonable in the eyes of a government beholden to neo-liberal policies that dictate the downsizing of the state and the elimination of public-sector jobs? Would calls for higher wages be labelled economically impossible in light of campaigns for austerity in times of economic crisis? Recall too that Costa Rican law already severely restricts the conditions under which a strike can be legally declared. The bishops, by focusing on the negatives of most strikes and the limits of legitimate ones, thereby contribute to what is a fairly unfavourable attitude toward labour activism in Costa Rica.

After all, in the eyes of the bishops, the ideal is that strikes would not need to occur at all. They maintain that workers and employers should attempt to resolve their differences through dialogue and negotiation, good-will and mutual co-operation—not through strikes and lockouts.[119] The hierarchy even labels the building of harmonious relations by business owners and union leaders a "patriotic" duty.[120] The bishops' general empha-sis on social harmony in Costa Rica thus resurfaces in their particular position on workers' right to strike.

Consistent with the bishops' disfavour of strikes and emphasis on harmony has been Monseñor Arrieta's role as a mediator in more than ten strikes since his appointment as archbishop.[121] Basically, Arrieta facil-itates communication between both sides in the dispute with the aim of bringing an end to the strike as quickly as possible. He also acts as a guar-antor to ensure that the promises made during negotiations are kept. According to the archbishop, impartiality is a key element of this media-tion: he will act in this capacity only if both parties in the dispute request his services, and he will focus solely on what is asked for and the merits of the demands—not on who is doing the asking. The result, Arrieta has declared, is a limit to the material losses incurred, an overcoming of the climate of confrontation, and the fulfilment of the workers' just demands.[122]

There is no doubt that the intervention of the archbishop can mean a faster resolution to a strike: every strike in which Arrieta has mediated has ended relatively soon after his involvement began.[123] Yet, while a speedy end to a strike may limit the amount of labour time lost, it does not nec-essarily mean that workers' "just demands" are met. In 1995, for exam-ple, Arrieta helped to bring an end to the teachers' strike by getting the government to agree to discuss its proposed changes to the educators' pen-sion program with the teachers' representatives themselves.[124] Teachers went back to their classes, and negotiations resumed between union lead-ers and the government. In the end, however, the strike was deemed a fail-ure, as the teachers were unable to win most of their demands.[125] Arrieta did help to end the strike and he did help to put the teachers' concerns on the negotiating agenda; but, he did not function as an advocate for the teachers' actual demands. As a self-declared "impartial" mediator he would only clarify issues—not come out in favour of one side or another.

The problem with such disinterested mediation is that, in cases where a power differential exists between the two parties involved, not making a clear option for one side is the same as supporting those who already hold the most power. In the case of strikes by public-sector work-ers—whose unions have suffered from a decline in membership, frag-mentation, and discriminatory legislation in Costa Rica—a professed neutrality on the part of Monseñor Arrieta is akin to an option for the government, the power holder in this situation. His averred neutrality is also a form of abandonment of the workers, those who need Arrieta's clear advocacy most of all in the context of the government's neo-liberal agenda.

Monseñor Arrieta's mediation in strikes was not emulated by Monseñor Ulloa in Limón. Ulloa refused to mediate in the 1996 Limón en Lucha strikes; he chose instead to support the protestors and pressure the government on their behalf. One can only imagine how much greater influence the archbishop of San José could have had on behalf of strikers, *if* he had made known his unequivocal support for the workers and their demands. Instead, Arrieta's mediation appears to have functioned primarily to end strikes expediently and thereby to contain their disruptive social consequences. While this may do much to bolster those in power, the archbishop's actions have not necessarily served social justice.

♦ The Right to Association

As on the issue of strikes, the Costa Rican Church hierarchy clearly affirms the standard Vatican position on workers' right to freedom of association. According to the bishops, workers have the inalienable right, which should be protected by law, to organize in unions to defend their legitimate interests.[126] This right to unionize signifies for workers the duty to represent their fellow workers, to collaborate in the economic progress of society, and to share in the responsibility for the realization of the common good.[127]

Beyond this theoretical support for the workers' right to unionize, the bishops' statements have, on occasion, explicitly coincided with the practical demands of the union movement. For example, when the government revealed its proposed changes to the Labour Code in 1988, union leaders were particularly concerned about the clauses that would give employers more power to terminate employment contracts at will and that would strengthen the juridical scope of direct agreements (i.e., as promoted by *solidarismo*) at the expense of collective conventions.[128] The bishops, in their pastoral letter on this Labour Code revision, explicitly addressed these two issues; they argued for limits on the cases in which employers could unilaterally terminate an employment contract and affirmed the need to protect the collective bargaining process as the primary tool for workers to lobby for their rights.[129] Significantly, the position taken by the bishops in the letter was publicly and enthusiastically applauded by the Confederación Unitaria de Trabajadores (CUT), one of the most important union confederations in Costa Rica.[130]

The bishops' promotion of freedom of association, however, is not limited to the workers in unions. The Costa Rican hierarchy has also consistently supported the right of workers to join the solidarity associations promoted by owners and employers. In fact, almost every reference to *sindicalismo* in Costa Rican Church documents is accompanied by an affirmation that *solidarismo* is also a legitimate option for workers to pursue. According to Monseñor Arrieta, the Church looks with "great affection" on the development of *solidarismo* in Costa Rica, since it seeks "the integral and permanent improvement of workers" through the "most harmonious relations possible" between workers and owners.[131] Not surprisingly, then, the bishops stress that solidarity associations are entitled to the same protection under the law as are unions.[132]

These pronouncements bring about the question, of course, of whether the bishops display any preferences for one form of labour organization over another. The archbishop, who has addressed this question most frequently, insists that "it is the right of workers to seek association in the form of organization that they are most attracted to or are sympathetic to" — whether that be *sindicalismo*, *solidarismo*, or another form of labour organization (such as co-operativism).[133] Arrieta further asserts that the Church defends, promotes, and supports both *sindicalismo* and *solidarismo* equally.[134] Perhaps the strongest proof for the impartiality of the Church in this regard is the fact that organizations allied with both of these major labour movements are represented within the Archdiocese's Vicaría de Pastoral Social (Vicariate for the Social Pastorate), founded in 1985. Here, CECODERS caters to unionized workers, while the ESJ23 is clearly supportive of the solidarity movement. And, since both of these Church organizations fit into the institutional structure of the archdiocese at exactly the same level, in theory there is no difference in ecclesial support between the two.[135]

Still, it is possible to detect a certain bias toward *solidarismo*, above all in the archbishop's statements. This is perhaps not very surprising, since the solidarity movement's emphasis on harmony and dialogue is consistent with the Church hierarchy's concentration on the same themes. Thus, *solidarismo*'s fostering of harmonious relations between capital and labour is praised and ultimately given legitimacy by Monseñor Arrieta as "congruent with Christ's supreme commandment of fraternal love."[136] At another point, the archbishop suggests that *solidarismo*'s means of solving labour conflicts can perhaps have "greater advantages" than what workers can obtain through a "costly and painful" strike.[137] In general, *sindicalismo* is treated with a far more critical tone than is *solidarismo*; at times, union leaders are chastised for allowing class struggle and confrontation to be their instruments for the vindication of workers' rights.[138] The bishops also repeat the papal proviso that unions should not "play politics." They further warn against union leaders falling into a "exaggerated politicization," or "ideologicalization," arguing that workers instead expect their leaders to be inspired by Christian and democratic values.[139] Although the bishops are careful not to offer any blatant endorsement of one form of labour organization over the other, their preference for *solidarismo* appears evident.

This bias for *solidarismo* is reinforced by the hierarchy's failure to forthrightly condemn the violation of union liberties by *solidarista* promoters.[140] As I discussed in chapter 3, the development of *solidarismo* in Costa Rica is closely related to various coercive tactics used by *solidarista* promoters on newly hired workers and against union members. The bishops do allude to this issue in their commentary on the Labour Code, stipulating that "workers' committees" should be constituted by the free decision of workers and cautioning that such committees should not be used as an instrument to weaken unions.[141] The bishops' overall treatment of the subject, however, is vague and *solidarismo* is not mentioned by name. In light of the very public and very grave accusations against the solidarity movement in this regard, it is astonishing that there are no other CECOR pronouncements on the issue from a Church hierarchy that claims to protect and promote the rights of workers.

The bishops' reluctance to adopt a critical perspective regarding *solidarismo* — much as they have done with *sindicalismo* — amounts to more than a case of bias. It can also run the risk of contributing to an anti-worker climate in Costa Rica. Added to the restrictive attitude the bishops hold in regard to strikes, the hierarchy's supposedly pro-worker stance is further called into question. Although the needs of the state (in crisis or not) may be best met by discouraging strikes and protests while promoting collaboration and conciliation, the needs of the workers may very well fall by the wayside.

Conclusion

The words and actions of Monseñor Arrieta and the rest of the Costa Rican hierarchy after 1979 constitute a form of conservative Catholic social teaching. Not only in relation to workers' issues most narrowly defined, but also in matters of social structure and social change, the Costa Rican bishops' positions coincide in several respects with the conservative Vatican tradition. Hence, beyond their maintenance of a relatively restrictive attitude toward unions and strikes, the bishops consistently avoid any overtly political interpretation of "liberation" or any unequivocal option for the poor. While the bishops do recognize the serious social problems and inequities that plague Costa Rica, their concerns for maintaining social peace and for fostering class collaboration take priority over calls for significant structural change. The bishops never question the dynamics of capitalism itself, as they seek remedies for social problems in the state's neo-liberal reforms, not grassroots innovation. While the Church hierarchy under Arrieta may have broken the long silence on social justice, it did not break away from the conservative tradition of Catholic social teaching that has long predominated in the worldwide Church.

In many respects, the bishops' positions from 1979 to 1996 could be interpreted as a reaction to the economic crisis. More precisely, however, they were also the reaction of a Church itself in crisis. Because of the close relationship that has developed over the decades between the state and the Church in Costa Rica, when the stability of the former is threatened, so are the privileges of the latter.[142] On this theme, consider the favourable position the Catholic Church has occupied in Costa Rica. The enshrinement of Roman Catholicism as the state religion in Article 75 of the constitution, aside from providing the symbolic legitimation of the faith by the political power structure, has also been used to justify a host of tangible benefits for the Church as an institution. Among the most significant of these are tax exemptions on Church properties, financial grants for Church projects and buildings, and state support for a variety of Church educational endeavours, such as Catholic private schools and mandatory religion classes in public schools. These educational efforts are important as a means for the propagation of the faith and, since classes are typically taught by priests, a source of income for the clergy. Given this high degree of Church association with — and even dependence on — the state, a crisis that affects the state would also constitute a crisis for the Church. On this level, then, it is not surprising that the Church's words and actions during the nation's crisis were aimed at preserving the social order on which both the Church institution and the threatened governments depended.

Certainly, the bishops' positions (particularly those related to protecting and promoting social peace and class collaboration) would have functioned to support the established order, regardless of its leaders' particular political persuasion. Nonetheless, as I have argued, many of the bishops' statements during this period reveal a clear preference for the PLN. The Church's political partisanship makes sense in the light of Costa Rican history, since the traditionally reformist policies of the PLN represent the recuperation of the social Christian political principles from the era of the revered Monseñor Sanabria.[143] More generally, the classic emphasis of the PLN on state-directed developmentalism is consistent with the bishops' conservative Catholic social teaching, in which top-down and gradual social change is promoted. Beyond this partisanship, it is noteworthy that the PLN program meant prestigious positions for several members of the clergy in the autonomous institutions that comprised the expanding welfare state in the 1960s and 1970s. The PLN was also the party that launched the Church's important role in administering the social assistance programs necessary to help those left behind by the government's development schemes.[144] In addition, personal friendships have developed between officials from the party and the Church: the close relationship between Monseñor Arrieta and President Monge has been frequently commented on.[145] In light of this history, the Church's traditional support for the PLN government appears fairly predictable.

Still, such alliances and the need to maintain privileges linked to the established political order can provide just part of the explanation for the Church's positions from 1979 to 1996. The Church's crisis cannot be reduced to the crisis as experienced by the Costa Rican state. After 1979 the Church was facing its own unique problems in Costa Rica, as it began to see its long-held dominance in the religious realm slip in the face of the triple threat of Protestantism, secularism, and communism.

Costa Rican Catholic Church leaders have been keenly aware of the growth in the number of evangelical Protestant churches in the country since the 1970s. As such, the bishops have released numerous public statements warning Catholics about the "fanaticism, proselytization, and aggression against the Catholic Church" characteristic of what they pejoratively refer to as the *sectas*.[146] Monseñor Arrieta has been particularly vocal in this regard and has campaigned vigorously to prevent as many people as possible from making the "grave error" of leaving the Catholic faith.[147] On this theme, it is also important to note that the Costa Rican Church has more to lose than just the souls of the faithful to Protestant churches. As the Catholic Church's hold on the majority of Costa Ricans begins to slip, so does the validity of one of its leaders' favourite justifications for the Church's constitutional privileges and for its right to assert its moral authority on questions of national importance. Monseñor Arrieta has repeatedly countered accusations of meddling in politics or preferential treatment for the Church with the argument that such behaviour is legitimate because the Church represents almost all citizens.[148] If this is no longer the case, exclusive exemptions and special treatment for the Church may become less defensible.

The threat of secularism also weighs heavily on the Church, with Monseñor Arrieta once labelling the trend "the most pernicious heresy of the contemporary world."[149] Certainly, over the past few decades, factors such as urbanization have taken their toll on the traditional religiosity of Costa Ricans; in the mid-1990s, for example, less than half (41.9 percent) of all Costa Ricans were attending Mass on a weekly basis.[150] Most often, Church leaders cast the problem of secularism as one of "religious indifference" or "religious ignorance" — the latter being declared doubly dangerous, as such ignorance has been identified by the bishops as a main cause for Catholic defection to the *sectas*.[151] In the end, combatting religious ignorance among the faithful remains one of biggest challenges the present-day Church in Costa Rica has set for itself.[152]

No less serious is the threat that communism poses to the Costa Rican Church. The decline of the Catholic Church in Castro's Cuba, and the communists' presumed atheism and endorsement of class struggle, have long fuelled fear and condemnation in Costa Rican Church circles. Even though the formal left in Costa Rica has been relatively weak (the communist party is only supported by a very small proportion of the population and, since the 1980s, has also been plagued by infighting and schism), the triumph and persistence of the Sandinista revolution next door in Nicaragua could not be ignored by the Church.

Even more threatening than the political model enacted by the Sandinistas, however, was the particular ecclesiological model associated with the revolution—that of the "popular church."[153] In the ideal Church of the hierarchy (in Nicaragua as in Costa Rica), unity is assured by obedience to the bishops and pope, and by submission to the one authentic teaching they express. The popular church, in contrast, was an exercise in the democratization of sacred power and the decentralization of theological production. In effect, it was no less than a rejection of the hierarchy's traditional authoritarianism and orthodoxy. The popular church in Nicaragua was organized into CEBs and inspired by liberation theology; thus, it threatened the Church's internal power structure from which the hierarchy had traditionally benefitted. Therefore, even if the Costa Rican bishops could be assured that the Sandinistas were not going to export their political revolution across the border, they were understandably frightened of the spread of the popular church and its accompanying ecclesiological reinvention.

The institutional vulnerability created by these threats to the Costa Rican Church places the bishops' positions in a different context. Take the case of the CEBs as promoted by the hierarchy, for example. The incorporation of these small religious education groups into the pastoral strategy of the archdiocese provides the clergy with the ideal tools for combatting religious ignorance and, by extension (in the logic of the hierarchy at least), the *sectas*. Monseñor Arrieta himself has openly declared as much.[154] As such, the prescribed episcopal accompaniment for the base communities takes on additional relevance as a preventative measure against the development of "parallel magisteria" (as was deemed to have happened in Nicaragua)—the ultimate affront to Church unity. Monseñor Arrieta is reluctant even to call these groups CEBs; he often labels them "small Christian communities," "family assemblies," or "authentic CEBs."[155] These reidentifications, along with his directly disparaging remarks against the popular church, are indications of his desire to distance his Church from the Nicaraguan phenomenon.

The hierarchy's tightly controlled definitions of important socio-religious concepts are also significant here. Liberation is explained in such a way (i.e., faith-based, individual, non-violent) that it would be impossible to link it to the left-wing political movements associated with liberation theology in Central America. The liberationist option for the poor is also diluted and defined—as neither excluding nor exclusive—with an eye to preserving the integrity of an ecclesiological model based on the traditional Catholic hallmarks of unity and universality. Certainly, one can detect in these definitions clear echoes of the most recent CELAM and Vatican positions on the same topics.

But the Costa Rican bishops' expressions here are not just a function of their obedience to orthodoxy; they are also conditioned by a further institutional imperative, one that helps to account for the fact that such potentially dangerous concepts have not been anathematized in the Church altogether. Much like the pope within the context of the worldwide Church, the leaders of a national Church must make an effort to appear responsive and relevant to the majority of their constituents, regardless of their personal agreement or disagreement with the latter's positions. In fact, beyond being one of the implications of the magisterium's emphasis on unity and universality, this attitude can be seen as one of the standard requisites for any elite group seeking to maintain its dominance. Leaders must take into account the various tendencies and interests of the subordinate groups in society and must on occasion make concessions to these groups for their leadership to be accepted as legitimate. The key for leaders, of course, is to make only compromises that will not jeopardize established relations of power. Within the Church, for example, this means that, while the most revolutionary or blatantly heretical concepts of the liberationists will be rejected by leaders outright, the concept of liberation (or the option for the poor) itself will be recovered, reworked, and resubmitted to the laity in a form that projects the priorities and protects the interests of the hierarchy. Ultimately, the aim of this process, as Maduro once summarized it, is "to preserve the unity of the Church by gaining possession of factors threatening that unity."[156]

It is on a similar plane that Monseñor Arrieta's insistence on unbiased mediation, or the bishops' claim to equal treatment for both *solidarismo* and *sindicalismo*, is best interpreted. The Church as an institution, especially as it is rendered vulnerable by the crises and threats outlined above, simply cannot afford to rebuff any large sector of its constituency directly. In light of the circumstances, the neutral position is the most prudent to assume, even if true biases and alliances remain intact. Thus, while a close examination of the archbishop's homilies or the bishops' pastoral letters can reveal their theological principles and political preferences, their overall message remains universal enough for both those on the left and the right—or for both unionists and solidarity association members—to find some legitimacy in the words. The attempt of the hierarchy to reflect some of the inner pluralism of the Church community is one of the keys to maintaining its position of power within the institution.

Crucially, in so far as this authority is to be maintained by consent and not coercion, Church leaders must relinquish some of their control at lower levels of the institution. Therefore, the archdiocese can provide space under the auspices of its Vicaría de Pastoral Social for the representatives of both *sindicalismo* and *solidarismo* to operate within the Church. And it can define the mandates of CECODERS and the ESJ23 as these groups minister to workers on behalf of the Church. Yet Church leaders must, at some point, cede some authority to the priests and lay people involved in these organizations. This, in turn, provides the possibility for representatives of these organizations to develop pastoral and political positions that go beyond those expected of the archbishop or CECOR bishops themselves. Even a bishop acting with the clergy in his own diocese, and apart from his responsibilities to represent the national Church as a member of CECOR, may develop a perspective on workers' issues at odds with those of the Costa Rican hierarchy in general. I examine just such possibilities in the following three case studies that focus on CECODERS, the ESJ23, and the official Church in Limón.

CECODERS, hand-in-hand with the worker.
—Banner carried by CECODERS representatives
in Labour Day parade (May 1, 1996)

The poor peoples make a dramatic accusation against the rich peoples.
—Pope Paul VI, *Populorum Progressio* (quoted on a poster in the CECODERS office)

The Centro Coordinador de Evangelización y Realidad Social—better known in Costa Rica by its acronym, CECODERS—was created in 1984 by a decree of the Fifth Archdiocesan Synod.[1] The centre was part of the archdiocese's Vicaría de Pastoral Social, itself formed by synodal decree to co-ordinate the efforts of all of the Church's social pastoral agencies based in the Archdiocese of San José. CECODERS officially began its work in October 1985. From the very start of its existence, Padre Orlando Navarro Rojas has acted as director of the centre and has been instrumental in shaping its mandate to include a number of programs aimed specifically at workers in Costa Rica. In this chapter, I describe CECODERS, its structure, and the wide array of activities that it has organized over the years as part of the Church's *pastoral social*. Then, focusing particularly on the centre's education, training, and accompaniment programming, I examine the complex manner in which CECODERS' pastoral options are related to the archdiocese's conservative positions on social justice and workers.

The Centre's Structure and Programming

CECODERS, Cáritas, the ESJ23, and Hermandades de Trabajo are the key agencies that have been brought under the co-ordination of the Vicaría de Pastoral Social.[2] CECODERS is not only the youngest of these organizations, but, with the exception of the nearly defunct Hermandades de Trabajo, is also the smallest. As of 1996, CECODERS maintained only eight people on its permanent staff, while the ESJ23, the closest counterpart to the centre within the Vicaría, employed more than one hundred. Moreover, and in contrast to the impressive facilities housing the ESJ23 in several locations throughout the country, CECODERS operates from a cramped complex of offices and meeting rooms on the grounds of the Church of Santa Marta Y Griega in San José.

Despite such modest appearances, however, CECODERS is a stable Church organization that has long provided an impressive range of programs and services to its constituents. Part of this is owing to the fact that, while staff size is kept low, members are able to draw on the support of others in the Church and the community at large. Thus, while Padre Navarro is the only member of the clergy formally employed at the centre, he can count on a long-standing network of approximately ten other priests who voluntarily help him with fundraising and organizing activities.[3] The core staff (consisting of administrators, a statistician, a theologian, and sociologists, of which Padre Navarro himself is one) frequently collaborate with members of a broader pool of social scientists and journalists. These latter individuals will either donate their services to CECODERS or work for the centre on a contract basis as the need for their expertise arises.[4] Taken together, this interdisciplinary network of professionals provides CECODERS with resources and labour power far beyond what the organization's low operating budget would suggest.

Over the years, the centre's staff has come to concentrate their energies in three main areas: social scientific research; support for small scale productive projects among disadvantaged sectors of the population; and education, training, and accompaniment programs. Examining each of these areas in turn can reveal the depth and breadth of activities encompassed in the *pastoral social* of the centre.

♦ Social Scientific Research

Even before CECODERS was an official Church entity, Padre Navarro recognized that the first step in effective social pastoral planning must be an accurate understanding of the socio-economic reality experienced by Church members. He believed that providing Church leaders with sociological *diagnosticos* (diagnoses) of their target populations would be the key to organizing pastoral strategies that truly responded to their needs.[5] The delegates to the Archdiocesan Synod agreed that the Church's social assistance and human promotion programming should be informed by socio-religious research, and they translated this conviction into the mission assigned at the synod to CECODERS.[6] With this, CECODERS was on its way to becoming the main social scientific research centre in the Costa Rican Catholic Church.

In the beginning, the *diagnosticos* were carried out only within the archdiocese, with Navarro and his assistants collecting and analyzing all the data themselves. Before long, however, the need for the centre's services became obvious in other dioceses in the country; staff members then began to visit parishes to train individuals there to gather information by means of a "parish family census."[7] The data from the detailed census, which asked questions on such topics as family composition, health, assets, employment, and religious practices, were then processed and analyzed at the centre in San José. Once the statistics were compiled and basic analyses performed, they would be returned to the original parishes where the priest, interviewers, and other pastoral agents would meet to discuss the results. The idea was that together these individuals could compare the census results with their own interpretations and experiences, and could analyze the trends uncovered in terms of Catholic social teaching. From this process of interaction and consultation, future priorities for the parishes' pastoral programming could, ideally, take shape.

Moreover, while early research was carried out primarily at the parish level in Costa Rica, CECODERS soon began to provide services to entire dioceses and, eventually, to international Church and development organizations. Within Costa Rica, most noteworthy has been the collaboration between CECODERS and the bishop and social pastoral commission of the Church in the Limón region. In particular, the socio-economic *diagnosticos* co-ordinated by CECODERS in Limón in 1987–88 and 1993 formed the basis of what were to become the Limón Church's groundbreaking and liberationist pastoral plans. Beyond this, CECODERS has provided research for various Costa Rican dioceses that were considering building new parishes, and has prepared reports for the Vatican as it has investigated the creation of new dioceses in the country.

Internationally, the bishops of CELAM and SEDAC have also requested studies from the staff of CECODERS, as have various Central American university organizations and UNICEF in the United States and Latin America.[8] These international contracts not only indicate the impressive and far-reaching reputation that the centre has built up over time; they also represent a significant source of income for the small Church organization.

In addition, it is important to recognize that CECODERS carries out both what it terms "socio-religious" research, which is intended primarily for use in parish and diocesan pastoral planning, and more traditional sociological studies. In this latter area, the centre maintains a data bank of economic, social, and political information, from which it can generate thematic studies on such topics as neo-liberalism, structural adjustment, AIDS, or the informal economy in Costa Rica. These data and studies are always at the disposal of bishops, other Church representatives, academics, and activists who wish to consult them; many have been translated into popular education materials that are more widely distributed among the population. Further, CECODERS members themselves use the insights gained from this research to decide on priorities for the centre's programming areas.

◆ The Productive Projects Program

Over the years, CECODERS has evolved into an agency that provides counselling and credit to poor individuals, families, and small groups who seek to set up productive projects, sometimes called *microempresas*, in city slums. Research performed by CECODERS in various Costa Rican communities had indicated that small-scale enterprises, based on skills that individuals already possessed or could easily learn, would be effective tools for social and economic development. The simple products and services sold in the *microempresas* are the means to generate desperately needed income for the urban poor.[9] Originally, the centre was not intended to develop these types of activities itself; within the Vicaría, the responsibility for so-called "human promotion" projects was delegated more directly to Cáritas. However, productive projects have come to constitute a significant part of the centre's programming. By the mid-1990s, CECODERS was shepherding approximately 150 different productive projects in such marginalized urban areas as Aserrí, Desamparado, and Tibas. Centre staff members solicit funding for this programming from various national and international development agencies, usually on a project-by-project basis.[10]

In terms of the projects themselves, CECODERS focuses primarily (although not exclusively) on developing *microempresas* with women. This is due to the large number of female-headed households in Costa Rican cities, and the difficulty that single mothers often have in finding child care when they work outside the home. In response to this situation, CECODERS has generated projects revolving around dressmaking and *artesanía* that allow women to earn an income while they stay at home with their children. The centre provides training in the practical skill involved as well as in basic accounting and administration and, once such training is completed, it provides access to a rotating microcredit fund to help with start-up or expansion costs. While CECODERS offers ongoing technical and administrative advice for everyone involved in the productive projects, the long-term goal is for the micro businesses to detach from the centre and learn to manage on their own.

◆ Education, Training, and Accompaniment Programs

Education, training, and accompaniment efforts represent the centre's largest and, at least in terms of this investigation, most important programming area. Here, in the context of its more general mission "to spread (*divulgar*) the Social Doctrine of the Church, applying it to the Costa Rican reality through adequate programs,"[11] CECODERS offers specialized services to three particular groups. As an expression of what the centre's leaders label "their option for the poor,"[12] CECODERS works most closely with members of San José's burgeoning informal economy, with individuals diagnosed as HIV-positive and their families, and with unionized workers.

In recent years, the informal sector of the Costa Rican economy has grown considerably. Ambulatory vendors now populate many of the streets of central San José, selling their wares from sacks slung over their shoulders, or displaying their inventories on small wooden tables or sheets of plastic spread on the sidewalk. Many of these vendors are immigrants from other Central American countries and their merchandise is sometimes imported illegally. As such, they may not have the licence required by the local government and are subject to harassment and persecution by the police.

The centre has conducted detailed studies on this phenomenon for the municipal government, comparing the situation of the San José vendors with that of vendors in other Latin American cities and illustrating how the difficulties surrounding the sector cannot be dealt with in isolation from larger social and economic problems. The centre also works directly with the merchants by helping them to attain their licences whenever possible. Even more importantly, CECODERS has set up workshops and projects that encourage street vendors to organize among themselves, both as a means of protection against harassment and as a way to take advantage of economies of scale. Perhaps the most successful CECODERS project in this area to date has involved the setting up of an artisan's alley in the Plaza de la Democracia, a main tourist site in San José's central core. There, the vendors can count on a permanent, safe, and legally sanctioned market for their goods, along with a steady flow of customers and continual access to small business advice from the centre. Altogether, CECODERS works with over 1,500 street merchants in San José and has begun to branch out and consult with vendors employed by larger private corporations (e.g., selling newspapers or ice cream), educating them about their rights and the benefits of labour organization.[13]

The centre's programming for HIV-positive individuals and their families takes place on a much smaller scale than its work with street vendors. The Pastoral de la Esperanza (Pastorate of Hope) was created by CECODERS in 1992 as a response to the alarming growth in the rate of HIV infection in Costa Rica and the prejudice, fear, and isolation that those sick with AIDS often face. This arm of CECODERS, which operates in conjunction with the parish of Santa Marta Y Griega, distributes popular education materials aimed at teaching the public about the disease.[14] It also helps to provide spiritual support to people with AIDS, along with material assistance in terms of doctors' fees, prescriptions, food, and clothing. Weekly meetings are held for those diagnosed as HIV-positive and for those interested in volunteering with the program. Activities are financed through such informal means as raffles, food sales, teas, bingo nights, or voluntary contributions.[15] With this pastorate, CECODERS has come to play a vital role in the Costa Rican Church's growing ministry to people with AIDS.[16]

The centre's programming in the informal economy and in its AIDS ministry is undoubtedly significant in terms of its overall contribution to the Church and Costa Rican society. More relevant to this study, however, is the centre's workers' pastorate. The remainder of this chapter is thus devoted to an analysis of the approach that CECODERS takes to Catholic social teaching and of the Centre's relationship with Costa Rican workers' movements.

The Controversial 1986 *Folleto*

In general, CECODERS carries out its mandate to divulge Catholic social teaching to Costa Rican society by means of workshops and publications. The centre's occasional workshops are typically built around a particular papal encyclical or theme suggested by the encyclicals and are held at the CECODERS installations in San José. Popular education materials, small working groups, and participatory methodologies are the norm at these sessions, with discussion and interaction among seminar participants being stressed. A much wider audience, however, has been reached by means of the centre's publications. From 1986 to 1991 (the year of Pope John Paul II's last major social encyclical), CECODERS released a number of popular education *folletos* (pamphlets) and articles in *Eco Católico* that served to raise awareness about Costa Rican social history and about the Catholic Church's social teaching.[17]

One of the earliest examples of the centre's work in this regard — and undoubtedly the most notorious — is a popular education *folleto* entitled *The History of Costa Rica? And of Our Community!*[18] Published in conjunction with Cáritas in January 1986, this pamphlet illustrates a hypothetical discussion by men and women meeting at a local school. The members of this Church group express the belief that helping one's neighbour is the best form of evangelization and acknowledge that this is only possible once the historical causes of the community's problems are understood.[19] Having gathered to teach one another about their country's history, they divide the material into three time periods (1940–48, 1948–73, and 1973–85). Through the presentations, questions, and reflections that follow, a relatively detailed picture of Costa Rican political history emerges.

The class-based analysis of the *folleto* is apparent almost immediately. The period leading up to the 1940s is portrayed in terms of a conflict between the powerful privileged classes (i.e., coffee oligarchs and bankers in control of the government) and the majority of the people, who are suffering and hungry.[20] The shifting alliances and confrontations immediately preceding the 1948 civil war are also illustrated in terms of class location. Hence the *folleto* describes the conflicting interests of three main groups: the privileged or "rich" classes, the reformist bourgeoisie and working classes allied behind Rafael Angel Calderón Guardia, and the disaffected *cafetaleros*, middle classes, and popular sectors supporting the eventual victor of the civil war, José Figueres, Sr.[21] The Church's involvement in the union movement, as well as Monseñor Sanabria's alliance with Calderón and the communists to promote the Social Guarantees, is also highlighted here.[22]

The bulk of the *folleto* is devoted to a critical analysis of the development model proposed by Figueres and his successors in the PLN. Here, the pamphlet outlines the characteristics of the interventionist and benefactor state that emerged in the 1950s and 1960s, and also explains the government's import substitution industrialization strategy and growing external debt load. The *folleto*'s evaluation of government policies during this period is harsh. Although some benefits of this development model are noted, the cartoon characters that illustrate the pamphlet emphasize that targeted social problems were not solved and that, overall, such phenomena as poverty, landlessness, and unemployment grew.[23] Popular organizations and government associations operating during this time are caricatured as puppets of the state that acted on behalf of communities in name only.[24] Transnational corporations from rich and powerful countries are blamed for their economic, political, and cultural oppression, and for transforming Costa Rica into a dependent and consumerist society.[25] One of the characters summarizes the situation under this model of industrialization by quoting the Latin American bishops at their 1979 Puebla conference that the "rich get richer and the poor, poorer."[26] Significantly, even the Church itself does not escape criticism in the *folleto*'s analysis, as it is accused of attaching itself to PLN policies and—while some exceptions are noted—of failing to provide an effective response to the most poor.[27]

The final section of the *folleto* discusses the economic crisis in Costa Rica and the rise in power of the neo-liberals, who are defined as "those who want the freedom to produce in order to sell, and of course to earn more, and to exploit the workers more."[28] The structural adjustment programs of the IMF and the World Bank, and the self-interested involvement of the United States in these institutions, are explained and attacked. Once again, the *folleto* notes, it is the poor who must carry the burden (*pagar los platos rotos*). No mention is made of the Costa Rican Church here, but the bishops from the Puebla conference are cited once more, this time in their condemnation of the "idols" of wealth and capitalist liberalism.[29] Significantly, moreover, even the widespread image of Costa Rica as the "Central American Switzerland" is discredited with statistics, then directly dismissed as a myth propagated by politicians.[30] A priest concludes the hypothetical meeting in the *folleto* with a list of discussion questions for readers about Costa Rican history and the responsibilities of Christians and the Church in the face of the crisis.[31]

This *folleto* is noteworthy in several respects. It provides a clearly liberationist analysis of Costa Rica's history and the crisis of the 1980s.

Through the *folleto*, CECODERS demonstrates the reality and effects of class conflict and social inequality in Costa Rican society. In so doing, the centre revises the predominant version of history that has been taught to generations of children and their parents by teachers and politicians. The *folleto* unmasks the myth of Costa Rica as the *suiza centroamericana*, just as it challenges the equally pervasive, but equally false, belief that the nation is free from conflict. The problems in society are not portrayed as stemming from sinful attitudes or faulty morals but, rather, are diagnosed as linked to an inequitable development model. In contrast to the style of analysis in which poverty is blamed on vague "excesses" of capitalism (a common approach in the Catholic social teaching tradition), the *folleto* explains the processes involved and names the parties, politicians, and policies responsible. The critique of reality found in this *folleto* thus fits squarely into the standard liberationist line of thought, but does so within the Costa Rican historical context.

Naturally, this perspective placed CECODERS in an antagonistic relationship vis-à-vis Costa Rica's neo-liberal leaders. After all, the pamphlet not only criticizes the economic and political bases of their dominance but also, through its work of demythologization, undermines the ideological support for their rule. Given this, it is not surprising that heated debate over the publication eventually broke out.

♦ Public Responses to the *Folleto*

In March 1987, news of the "Marxist-Leninist vision" in the *folleto* surfaced in the right-wing daily *La Nación*.[32] Over the following weeks, more than seventy articles on the *folleto* appeared as the debate raged in the national press.[33] In one corner were *La Nación* and its editorialists, including Julio Rodríguez, the paper's resident theologian and one-time advisor to the ESJ23. Editorials in *La Nación* portrayed the paper as a defender of Costa Rican democracy that was serving the *patria* by alerting its readers to the dangers of communist infiltration in the Church.[34] As proof of such infiltration, the paper cited the comments of two Costa Rican bishops, Monseñor Trejos and Monseñor Morera, who had expressed concern over support for the popular church and liberation theology within official Church organizations.[35] The paper highlighted the *pugna* (clash) among the clergy that had emerged over such issues and blamed Monseñor Arrieta for not doing enough himself to stop the spread of Marxism within the Church.[36]

In the other corner were Monseñor Arrieta and the Church hierarchy. Arrieta's responses to the newspaper revealed his indignation over its attack; he stated that the first articles were published while he was out of the country and, therefore, could not immediately respond to the accusations.[37] The archbishop acknowledged that there were some problems with the *folleto* but denied that as a whole the publication was communist. In fact, he attempted to minimize the presence of Marxism in the Church overall and argued that none of the clergy or hierarchy should be accused of Marxism when they were simply collaborating, in obedience to the pope and Church magisterium, in social pastoral work.[38] The archbishop likewise took exception to the portrayal of disunity among the bishops within the Church, claiming that *La Nación*'s interpretation of Monseñors Trejos and Morera's remarks was "absolutely false."[39] Writing as a collective, the CECOR bishops supported the archbishop's position and railed against *La Nación*'s "insidious campaign" and "malevolent attempts" to portray the episcopate as divided. The reality, the bishops wrote, was that they acted "with only one soul and only one spirit, in the name of Christ."[40] Arrieta also reported in his own defence that, when complaints about the CECODERS publication began to surface, he did convene meetings and take actions to correct the errors in the *folleto*. Perhaps most importantly, the archbishop announced that he, along with a recently formed archdiocesan commission, would personally review all future writings of CECODERS and of the ESJ23 prior to publication.[41]

Throughout this furor, CECODERS itself kept a relatively low profile. Although *La Nación* reported that the centre's director, Padre Navarro, originally disagreed with Arrieta's assessment of the *folleto* as problematic, the paper also noted that Navarro was willing to amend its contents if necessary.[42] Eventually, Navarro issued a public response to Arrieta explaining the centre's position on the issue. In this letter, Navarro emphasized that CECODERS was "united with our Bishop in dialogue, obedience, and love" and repeated that the centre would rectify any errors indicated by the leader of the Church.[43] Moreover, Navarro repudiated *La Nación*'s charges of Marxist-Leninist infiltration in the Church. To underscore his point, he demonstrated, by citing passages from CELAM's Puebla conference document and CECOR's 1979 *carta pastoral*, that the Church's "preferential option for the poor" and its responsibility to collaborate in social transformation were fully justifiable in terms of the Church's social teachings.[44]

Some supporters of CECODERS also took pains to illustrate, with numerous and lengthy quotations from Pope John Paul II's encyclicals, that the centre's positions were acceptable in light of Catholic social teaching.[45] Much was also made of *La Nación*'s unprofessional behaviour in the whole affair. Highlighted here was the accusation that the newspaper's journalists decided to create news about the *folleto* over a year after it was published solely in order to make editorial comments about it. Critics also claimed that the paper distorted the words of Monseñors Trejos and Morera by implying that they were commenting on the *folleto* when they were actually making remarks about other Church organizations. Most commentators further emphasized the conservative political agenda driving *La Nación* throughout the controversy; essentially, they argued that the paper's charges of communism in the Church served the interests of those wishing to maintain the unjust status quo in Costa Rica and block the Church's work on behalf of the poor.[46]

Certainly, much of this commentary about *La Nación*'s perspective and tactics is accurate. As I have noted, the liberationist analysis of the *folleto* would quite understandably prove threatening to the elite segments of society represented by *La Nación*. Capitalizing on Costa Ricans' fear of communism would thus be one way to undermine support for progressive Church positions. Further, the newspaper's manipulation of fact is an inexcusable abuse of journalistic licence. The commentators, in their efforts to discredit *La Nación* and defend CECODERS, however, miss something significant. As reprehensible or distasteful as *La Nación*'s rightwing rhetoric and redbaiting may have been in this debate, the paper's editorialists have nonetheless highlighted a truth about the Church as an institution in Costa Rica. They have detected the split that exists within the Church and the fact that the Church, like Costa Rican society itself, is not immune to conflict.

♦ Division within the Costa Rican Church

The CECODERS *folleto*, although it does not indicate all the characteristics of the conflict, highlights certain important facets of this intra-Church split. To begin with, the *folleto* demonstrates that CECODERS and the Costa Rican Church hierarchy have dramatically different perceptions of their country's reality. The centre's revelation of inequality and conflict in Costa Rica presents a challenge to the Church hierarchy's persistent belief in social peace and Christian unity. Beyond this, the *folleto* openly contradicts the claim of Church leaders that they are politically neutral (as in Monseñor Arrieta's long-standing refrain "neither Liberationist nor Social Christian") by pointing to the Church's political alliances, first with Calderón in the 1940s and then more recently with the PLN. The *folleto*'s attack on the traditional reformist project of the PLN is thereby also an attack on Church leaders whose words and actions, as I have shown, have long helped to bolster this party's particular political options. In addition, the centre's harsh critique of the neo-liberal policies that had been embraced by PLN leaders contrasts with the symbolic support for structural adjustment programs that the Church hierarchy had begun to display (Arrieta's original *Ten Commandments of Austerity*, for example, was released the year prior to the *folleto*'s publication). And, questions of political partisanship aside, the pamphlet directly charges the Church with failing to respond effectively to the poor. The *folleto*, then, reveals a conservative-liberationist clash in the Church: whereas the Church hierarchy speaks and acts for the nation's neo-liberal leaders and their political agenda, CECODERS formulates an unmasking of and opposition to these positions on behalf of the poor.

The proclamations of unity made by the various Church parties during the debate—proclamations made in spite of the polemics crystallized by the *folleto*—are likewise significant. Clearly, the hierarchy's affirmation of Church unity on social pastoral matters is consonant with its promotion of harmony and collaboration (i.e., unity) within society. But it is also consistent with the Costa Rican bishops' more general conservative ecclesiological perspective, one that emphasizes overall Church unity and obedience to the bishops who are said to guarantee it. Thus, even though some of the bishops themselves originally, if unwittingly, pointed to a split within the Church (by voicing their fears about the influence of liberation theology and the popular church over some of the clergy), their eventual reassertion of Church unity is not surprising. Further, Monseñor Arrieta's move to place CECODERS under more direct supervision is at once an admission that there is an unacceptable level of diversity or disunity within the Church, and a safeguard to ensure that such diversity would not be replicated in the future. In the end, the institutional imperative to preserve Church unity is strong. Just as it was necessary for the Costa Rican bishops to react against the threat of the popular church in Nicaragua, it was also necessary for it to deny any sort of polarization or left-wing penetration into their own Church.

Interestingly, and perhaps contrary to what one would expect given the overtly liberationist reading of reality in the CECODERS publication, the centre's director, Padre Navarro, appeared to cede relatively quickly to the Church hierarchy's pressure for unity. He did so not only by agreeing to change the *folleto* and submit future writings to Monseñor Arrieta but also by directly reiterating the centre's obedience and unity to the archbishop. These statements do not seem so unlikely, however, if we regard them simply as an expression of the novice and subordinate status of the centre within the archdiocese. In other words, in so far as CECODERS had been recently created by, and was still officially subsumed under, the very Church body now pressuring it to modify its course, Padre Navarro and the centre's staff would have had little choice but to change. To remain defiant could have meant the end of their sociological research centre—or at least their employment therein—and their valuable social pastoral work in parishes and with the poor of San José. In any case, whatever the motivations for the centre's pledge of solidarity with the archbishop, one thing remains certain: since the controversy over the *folleto* died down, no differences of opinion in the Church regarding the centre's positions or publications have surfaced for public scrutiny.

CECODERS and Catholic Social Teaching

Reflecting on the debate over the 1986 *folleto*, one must not forget that CECODERS and its supporters appealed to Catholic social teaching as proof of the validity of the centre's positions. Pointing to its use of the standard teachings of the Church magisterium, in other words, was another attempt by the centre to demonstrate Church unity. Since the centre continued to publish documents and articles related to Catholic social teaching even after the *folleto* controversy, the forms of social teaching used and the roles that these play in CECODERS materials deserve a closer investigation.

First, however, it should be stressed that CECODERS does not actually create Catholic social teaching in its writings. Instead, the organization concentrates on disseminating fragments of an already existing tradition. Strictly speaking, this is in line with the mission assigned to CECODERS by the Archdiocesan Synod, as well as with the traditional ecclesiastical division of labour in which the members of the hierarchy are seen as the only progenitors of the Church's teachings. Still, one could reasonably expect (as in the case of the liberation theologians, for example) that other Church bodies would generate their own forms of unofficial Catholic social teaching by means of their interpretation of, dialogue with, or reaction to, the larger tradition. Nonetheless, this is not the case with CECODERS: in the centre's materials, there is little original theological reflection that is not directly derived from the major papal encyclicals or the CELAM documents.

Instead, the CECODERS materials contain lengthy quotations taken straight from Catholic social teaching sources themselves. Sometimes, various paragraphs (or paraphrases) are selected from the original documents and strung together to provide a representative sampling of papal thought on, for example, the state,[47] spirituality,[48] or the common good and solidarity.[49] Or an article will show the evolution of an idea over time; it may demonstrate, for instance, how the notion of human dignity first surfaced in *Rerum Novarum*, and then was clarified and expanded on in *Laborem Exercens*.[50] In some cases, one can read a section-by-section summary of the contents of an encyclical.[51] Elsewhere is a chronology of the major Catholic social teaching documents from the Vatican and Latin America, a detailing of the names and themes of encyclicals and conferences from the time of Leo XIII onward.[52] As simple lessons about Catholic social teaching, these are competently compiled and well written. But at no point is the reader convinced that CECODERS has made a contribution to Catholic social teaching on its own.

This is not to imply, however, that there is absolutely no analysis or evaluation in this material. On the contrary, several of the CECODERS pieces contain opinions regarding issues commonly debated in relation to Catholic social teaching. Still, in these cases the judgments are often predictable and are consistently laudatory. Thus, for example, a CECODERS document asserts that, even though the earliest encyclicals remain relevant in the present day,[53] there is a clear split between pre- and post-conciliar

Catholic social teaching.[54] The centre also echoes the commonplace belief that the conference outcomes at Puebla affirmed those of the conference at Medellín.[55] Further, the centre posits that Pope John Paul II's social writings are original and innovative,[56] and that this pope supports liberation theology and has adopted its methods and objectives.[57] These positions are contained in columns for *Eco Católico* penned by CECODERS representatives as well as in more lengthy and scholarly articles written by the centre's directors for journals and books.

Significantly, and especially in the commentaries related to liberation theology, certain key points are ignored in the centre's writings. For example, on what basis can these assessments of the pope's writings be made? Whose definition of "liberation" and what form of this theology has the pope adopted? The CECODERS material asserts that, with the 1986 Vatican Instruction on liberation theology, the controversy over this theology has been straightened out. Yet this interpretation is based on a superficial reading of the texts themselves, and it also does not take into consideration the Vatican's persecution and censorship of liberationists and their allies in Latin America. The treatment of the option for the poor by Padre Navarro also leaves certain questions unanswered. While he notes that Pope John Paul II has "redefined" this option as a "preferential option for the poor,"[58] the centre's director does not examine the reasons behind, or the implications of, this redefinition. Such investigations are especially warranted because, as I have shown, using the language of the liberationists does not necessarily imply a corresponding abandonment of fundamentally conservative perspectives. In fact, the centre's uncritical presentation of the key elements of the Catholic social teaching tradition coincides with the needs of the conservatives in the Church. By not delving into the controversies and conflicts, by not asking difficult questions or even acknowledging the existence of some of the debates involved here, CECODERS is allowing the dominant — and predominantly conservative — visions of Catholic social teaching in the Church to be transmitted unchallenged.

Nonetheless, even if the centre's writings do not constitute original responses to Catholic social teaching or facilitate deep reflection on the tradition, they do fulfil certain functions crucial to liberationist aspirations. These are primarily related to the readings of the "signs of the times" found in many CECODERS articles on Catholic social teaching. Significantly, alongside the standard and uncritical presentations of Catholic social teaching in the centre's publications, one finds alternative and critical readings of Costa Rican and Latin American history. A short description of Pope John Paul II's subject matter in *Sollicitudo Rei Socialis*, for instance, is followed by the comment that "the preceding invites us to reflect on the Costa Rican economic sphere, especially when we find ourselves on the verge of the approval of the Second Structural Adjustment Loan."[59] The succeeding reflection, in turn, is a lengthy and unflinchingly negative portrayal of structural adjustment and its effects. Also inserted among the paragraphs and paraphrases taken directly from Catholic social teaching are explanations of the indicators of the socio-economic crisis throughout Latin America,[60] revelations of Latin American militarism and human rights violations in the 1970s,[61] and analyses of the causes and consequences of Costa Rica's huge external debt.[62] Particularly noteworthy is the centre's discussion of poverty in which the poor are defined primarily as members of classes: classes in conflict with and made poor by the dominant classes, and classes who demand justice by means of an alternative social project involving structural changes in society.[63] Taken together, these articles provide an incisive look at socio-economic conditions in Costa Rica and reveal elements that are frequently ignored or strategically obfuscated by the mainstream press and political leaders. Catholic social teaching presented relatively objectively in this way serves as the link to, and legitimation for, CEDODERS' subjective version of history. In this consciousness-raising process, the concepts, vocabulary, and tools of political critique are disseminated to a wider audience in the Church.

Regardless of the liberationist implications of such a use of Catholic social teaching, however, the fact remains that CECODERS employs an uncritical method of citing social teaching. This practice leaves very little room for accusations that the centre is disloyal to, or in conflict with, the message of Church leaders. Moreover, CECODERS allows the division of labour implied by the Archdiocesan Synod and consistent with the hierarchical structure of the Catholic Church to prevail. The centre concentrates on studying and presenting factual sociological data, while leaving the production of theological judgments to the Church magisterium itself.

CECODERS and the Union Movement

Padre Orlando Navarro and his staff have devoted themselves to promoting the well being of unionized workers since the very inception of CECODERS. In this section, therefore, I turn finally to examine the alliances and activities that constitute the centre's accompaniment of the Costa Rican union movement.

♦ CECODERS and ASEPROLA

The work of the centre with the union movement can best be understood from the starting point of Padre Navarro's long-standing interests in the *solidarismo* phenomenon. In the early 1980s, he and Gustavo Blanco, a fellow student of sociology and a committed lay Catholic, began to perceive certain practical and philosophical contradictions between the union movement and the solidarity movement in Costa Rica. Navarro and Blanco collaborated on a joint thesis on the history, development, and doctrine of *solidarismo*, which was published in 1984 as one of the first large-scale critiques of *solidarismo* in Costa Rica.[64] Shortly after, when Navarro as a priest was organizing the newly founded CECODERS, he and Blanco created a lay organization to operate alongside the centre. Soon to be known as the Asociación Servicios de Promoción Laboral (ASEPROLA, Association for Labour Promotion Services), this latter organization focused primarily on educating workers and union leaders about the dangers posed by the rapidly expanding solidarity movement.[65]

In the early days, there was much collaboration and overlap in the work of CECODERS and ASEPROLA. The association was never officially designated as part of the archdiocese's Vicaría de Pastoral Social, but the two organizations shared office space and resources. Padre Navarro also spent much time working directly on the programs for workers that Blanco was developing for ASEPROLA. Activities carried out jointly by the two were sometimes attributed to CECODERS and sometimes to ASEPROLA, depending on which organization's mandate the work most closely matched. Also at this time, under the auspices of ASEPROLA, Blanco and Navarro began to question Church leaders' apparent favouritism toward *solidarismo* and their distant relationship with the country's union movement.[66]

Before long, Navarro and Blanco's critiques caught the attention of Monseñor Arrieta. Their campaign against *solidarismo* also angered Padre Claudio Solano, the director of the ESJ23 and one of the country's leading proponents of *solidarismo*. In 1987, as a result of Solano's lobbying and the archbishop's own discomfort with the direction that ASEPROLA's activities were taking, Monseñor Arrieta pressured Padre Navarro to disassociate CECODERS and ASEPROLA.[67] Accordingly, ASEPROLA moved out of the CECODERS office space and the day-to-day collaboration between the two groups ceased. Navarro and the centre moved their attention away from the solidarity movement and focused more exclusively on accompanying the union movement as representatives of the official Church.

After the split, Gustavo Blanco and his association continued to concentrate on providing training and consulting services to unions in the battle against *solidarismo*. According to Blanco, this arrangement was useful because it allowed ASEPROLA to operate with a great deal of autonomy as it went about the "dirty work" of denouncing *solidarismo* in Costa Rica. Since it was no longer closely associated with the Church, the organization could not be censored as it carried out its political critique and its questioning of the Church's relationship to workers' organizations. Navarro and CECODERS, by contrast, were subject to more restrictions; as Blanco readily concedes, they had to be more cautious and compromise more with the Church hierarchy in order to maintain their status within the official institution.[68]

This division of labour persists until this day. Occasionally, material from CECODERS will refer to the growth of the solidarity movement in Costa Rica or the fact that *solidarismo* serves the interests of owners as opposed to workers,[69] but the centre generally avoids this controversial subject.[70] ASEPROLA, by contrast, has maintained its strong position against *solidarismo*: studying the phenomenon, holding workshops for union members on the dangers of *solidarismo*, and publishing extensively (i.e., written and audio-visual popular education materials, union training manuals, scholarly works) on the solidarity movement as a whole. In recent years, moreover, ASEPROLA has grown considerably in size and in the scope of its activities. The organization now includes several Protestants and non-Christians on its staff, with its Christian Program representing the remains of the group's lay Catholic origins. In particular, it is the staff of this program that work most closely with representatives from the social pastoral commission of the Limón Church. (I deal with the specific nature of ASEPROLA's involvement in Limón in chapter 9.) In its direct work with unions, the association has developed programming in the areas of occupational health (particularly in relation to banana plantations through-out Central America) and women's rights within the union movement. Through its Woman Worker Program, the association has also undertaken a popular education campaign aimed at increasing awareness of labour rights for *maquila* workers.

Throughout, relations between ASEPROLA and CECODERS remain friendly. While the two groups occasionally collaborate on specific projects, they still regard their work as separate although complementary.[71]

♦ CECODERS and Labour Struggles

CECODERS, since its split with ASEPROLA, has concentrated on foster-ing a rapprochement between the union movement and the Church. On one hand, the centre offers workshops on Catholic social teaching for union leaders and, on the other, Padre Navarro and his staff work to edu-cate bishops about the theory of unionism and the actual state of *sindical-ismo* in Costa Rica. Perhaps most importantly, the centre also sponsors monthly meetings between interested Church members and union repre-sentatives. Further, although it does carry out some projects with *campesino* organizations and continues to provide research support to the Limón Church, most CECODERS activities are centred in San José.

As might be expected, the Catholic social teaching used to define the centre's position on work is drawn from standard magisterial sources. For example, Padre Navarro and the centre's documents cite Leo XIII, Paul VI, and John Paul II in support of the right of workers to unionize to defend their interests.[72] Moreover, referring to the tradition of Monseñor Sanabria and to John Paul II's writings in *Laborem Exercens*, Navarro has called for "substantial changes" in the Costa Rican wage structure to make the "just salary" a reality for all workers.[73] A particular focus in CECODERS writings and statements also comes from Pope John Paul II's encyclical on work—the notion that the human being is the subject of work and that it is through work that one realizes one's humanity.[74] Importantly, on this point CECODERS emphasizes the pope's notion of the priority of labour over capital.[75] Still, in place of an acknowledgment that, within capitalism, the interests of labour and capital are by definition opposed (an assertion more in line with liberationist thought), the centre adopts the patently conservative position from John Paul II's *Centesimus Annus* that work naturally unites people.[76] At one point in a discussion of strikes, CECODERS even quotes a passage from Leo XIII's *Rerum Novarum* that highlights the damages to workers, commerce, and society that strikes can cause.[77] Given such reference points, it would be easy to presume that the centre's position merely echoes the dominant and conservative Catholic social teaching tradition, a tradition that I have shown to be propagated by the pope in the Vatican and the hierarchy in the Costa Rican Church.

Nonetheless, a closer look at the work of the centre reveals certain marked differences in the positions of CECODERS and the Church magisterium. Many of these can be seen in the attitude of CECODERS toward strikes, both past and present, in Costa Rica. Publications meant to educate workers about the history of the labour movement, for example, tell the story of several path-breaking strikes from the early 1900s to the late 1930s involving banana workers, shoemakers, bakers, and tailors. The articles explain the conditions suffered by the workers at the time and describe how they organized to demand improvements in their workplaces and salaries. Importantly, the message conveyed in these pieces is twofold: that there is strength in a unified workers' movement and that workers' persistence in striking is ultimately rewarded with concessions from employers.[78] Considering this context, one can see that the quotation from *Rerum Novarum* (cited above) about strikes causing damage is used neither to stigmatize labour militancy nor to dissuade workers from striking. Rather, CECODERS here is illustrating that the disruption caused by strikes is enough to pressure the state and business owners to respond to workers' demands.[79] It appears that the centre is not so much focused on the drawbacks to strike activity as it is concerned with providing examples of the success of strikes. CECODERS is therefore adopting a position at odds with that of the Costa Rican Church hierarchy which, as seen in the previous chapter, tends to dwell on the extremity, dangers, and limits of strikes.

The actions of CECODERS during the 1995 teachers' strike reinforce this interpretation. In comparison to the efforts of Monseñor Arrieta to function as an impartial mediator between the teachers and the government, Padre Navarro and CECODERS assumed a more partisan position, primarily by organizing a fax campaign on behalf of the striking teachers.

The centre composed a document and circulated it to parishes throughout the country, eventually gaining the support of sixty-seven priests in their public declaration and petition to the government.[80] In the strongly worded document, the workers' right to strike is affirmed and the government's use of propaganda to sway public opinion is denounced.[81] CECODERS points out that the teachers' protests are not only a reaction to the proposed reforms of the pension law, but that they are also a manifestation of the broader popular discontent with the effects of the latest structural adjustment program. The document also singles out the undemocratic means through which the reform of the state has been carried out in the country and the detrimental effects that this reform has had on the majority of the population. Significantly, the CECODERS fax asks the government to initiate negotiations with the teachers and to do so without demanding that the teachers end their strike first. A quotation from Vatican II's *Gaudium et Spes*, regarding the legitimacy of the strike as a necessary means to defend workers' rights, is used to reinforce this request.[82] Again, the position taken by CECODERS directly contrasts with that of the archbishop. Monseñor Arrieta attempted to minimize the disruption caused by the strike and tried to return teachers to their classrooms as a precedent for beginning negotiations. But CECODERS recognizes the value of the persistent strike as a weapon in the struggle against both an unjust pension law and the neo-liberal state.

This broader opposition to neo-liberalism informs most of CECODERS' work with unions in Costa Rica. Recognizing that the pressure to privatize is one of the most pernicious elements of structural adjustment policy, the centre has made it a priority to accompany unions in the very sectors targeted for privatization.[83] In this regard, CECODERS' most notable work has been with various unions in the health care sector. While the state has gradually been reducing its funding to health care since the 1980s, the structural adjustment agreement signed by the government in 1993 contained a particularly ambitious Health Care Sector Reform Project. With this project, the government began to transfer responsibility for a wide array of medical services from the Costa Rican Social Security Bureau to private hands. In response to this situation, CECODERS has tried to raise awareness about how budget cuts have created a crisis in health care and about why privatization, based as it is on the logic of profitability, will only make matters worse.[84] The centre also works to forge unity among the exceedingly fragmented unions in the health care sector.[85] In 1995, for example, CECODERS was instrumental in the co-ordination of fourteen unions to form the Frente de Organizaciones Sindicales del Sector Salud (FOSSS, Front of Health Sector Union Organizations). This coalition seeks to organize and mobilize its constituents to defend the interests of both workers and patients affected by the changes in the Costa Rican health care system. According to the Frente's working plan, which was elaborated by CECODERS, FOSSS will become the operations base for future pressure on and negotiations with the government regarding health care reform.[86] The ongoing support CECODERS provides to health care workers through this coalition thus makes the centre an important ally in the campaign to reverse the trend toward privatization in Costa Rica.

The regular meetings that CECODERS sponsors between priests and union representatives also take place within the larger context of Costa Rican neo-liberalism. These meetings, then, are not only designed to foster closer ties between two groups that were frequently estranged in the past. They are also meant to pool resources, develop strategies, and unite these agents together in protest against the profound social changes and increasing poverty that have accompanied the restructuring of the Costa Rican state. As the working plans for the meetings confirm, CECODERS sees itself as provoking conscientization about the situation in Costa Rica. The centre also seeks to provide a space for dialogue and co-ordination among unions, and between unions and the Church, so that they can come to be "strong interlocutors in the face of the government."[87] Ultimately, the centre's goal with this project is to unite the popular sectors of the country, to arrive at alternative economic policies and at development options that respond to the needs of the poorest, and to create a Costa Rica where everyone has access to the wealth.[88]

The proceedings of one these meetings, held in mid-1996, reveal the combination of strategic and theoretical concerns involved with such tasks.[89] The meeting began with a survey of the latest restructuring and layoffs in the Costa Rican civil service and the continued inability of the fragmented union movement to mobilize workers effectively against the government's policies. Some of the discussion revolved around choosing one issue (e.g., rising gasoline prices, inadequate salary increases, layoffs) around which to rally the population and garner support for the protest movement. Further, there was the recognition that the opposition to the government should not be merely conjunctural, but that it should also be based on a defined ideological and political base in order to sustain the unity of the movement. Perhaps most significantly, the delegates justified class struggle and confrontation, as opposed simply to dialogue and negotiation, as the instruments needed to reclaim workers' rights:

> The union movement has always made room for dialogue, negotiation, and solidarity, but we believe, contrary to Monseñor Arrieta, that these elements have given way to class struggle and confrontation, owing to the great abuse of power of the present government and all its allies, such as the businessmen and the Catholic Church itself, who have forgotten their commitment to the Costa Rican people and have thrown them into poverty, unemployment, and indignity, and who have taken advantage of the present situation to make the rich richer and the poor poorer.[90]

Significantly, the priests and union leaders here point to both the reality of class conflict in society and the real need for struggle to transform the current state of social relations. Thus, they acknowledge a pre-existing social conflict between the government and its allies on one hand, and the poor on the other. But, they also indicate that, in light of government's intransigence, social change will necessarily involve an element of conflict. In addition, the meeting delegates provide further evidence, by means of their overt disagreement with the archbishop and their accusations regarding the Church's alliance with an unjust government, of the internal conflict within the Costa Rican Church. As was the case with CECODERS' 1986 *folleto*, these meetings are a tangible illustration of the theoretical assertion that the Church functions as an interclass social space — the conflicts and confrontations present in the larger society are reproduced within the Church institution itself.

Conclusion

CECODERS falls near the liberationist end of the ideological spectrum within the Church. This can be seen particularly in relation to the centre's perspectives on social reality and its programming for workers and the poor in the Archdiocese of San José. The centre's controversial *folleto*, its history of Costa Rican strikes, and its analyses of neo-liberalism work to discredit the myth that Costa Rica is the "Central American Switzerland" and to expose the structural bases of the inequality and injustice in Costa Rican society. The centre points to conflict within society without reserve and likewise acknowledges that the movement for social change may involve the element of confrontation. In the centre's support for striking workers or its accompaniment of unions struggling against structural adjustment, this theoretical acknowledgment is transformed into a concrete commitment on behalf of the poor and workers, and against the state. In many of these practical alliances, moreover, CECODERS adopts positions that are in direct conflict with those held by Monseñor Arrieta and the Costa Rican hierarchy. In so doing, CECODERS challenges the established orders within and outside of the Church.

This liberationist stance of CECODERS can only be fully understood in the context of Costa Rica's socio-economic crisis and threatened state. CECODERS was founded in the mid-1980s, a time when the increase in popular protests was evidence not only of growing economic hardship for Costa Ricans but also of Costa Ricans' growing discontent with the government's neo-liberal solutions to their problems. At one level, CECODERS simply ministered to those most affected by the changes in the country: workers and women, the poor and the sick. Beyond this, while the words and actions of the Church hierarchy helped to legitimate the government's policies and to generally fortify the basis of its rule, CECODERS came to adopt a distinctly opposing role. CECODERS staff members, through their studies of and programming for the poor in Costa Rica, were converted into spokespersons for the cause of the popular classes. Sometimes these centre intellectuals, with their various retellings of history or their analyses of the economic crisis, themselves articulated the concepts and categories critical to the challenge to neo-liberalism. At other points, through their actions of accompaniment and co-ordination, they provided crucial logistical support to the unions and union coalitions in their struggles with the government. Importantly, through their appeals to the relevance of Catholic social teaching in these situations and as members of the official Church themselves, these centre members also conferred a degree of religious legitimacy to the efforts of those working against the government's political agenda. Overall, then, through CECODERS these Church agents played a significant role in helping to express and direct the complaints and aspirations of Costa Rican workers as they moved toward the construction of an alternate socio-economic order.

The words and actions of CECODERS do not, however, constitute a completely or consistently liberationist project, as this would necessarily involve a critical questioning and re-reading of *all* the ideological elements buttressing the current order. Granted, CECODERS does effectively challenge the myth of Costa Rica as a Switzerland and the myth of structural adjustment as a cure for the crisis. But, because the centre does not go on to question the validity of the Catholic social teaching tradition as it has been transmitted via the Church hierarchy, the centre may ultimately fail in its liberationist task. The reluctance of CECODERS to investigate the links between the dominant ideas of Church leaders and the dominant ideas of government leaders threatens its ability to contribute to a truly thorough social transformation. By automatically assuming the relevance of Catholic social teaching for its liberationist agenda, then, CECODERS may unwittingly be sabotaging its own efforts.

The concept of the hermeneutic circle, taken from the work of liberation theologian Juan Luis Segundo, can be profitably employed here.[91] Segundo uses this concept as a means to explain how a truly liberative theology can be generated. In this dialectical circle, the reality of historical contradiction and injustice is first experienced and exposed, leading to a rereading and reinterpretation of scripture and a further movement to alter reality, which then is followed by a fresh reinterpretation of scripture. In this neverending cycle, reality is not judged in light of the precepts of theology but, rather, theology itself arises from the changing conditions of reality. Only as part of this radically inductive process can theology be an effective tool in the transformation of the social order. Otherwise, once cast as an unquestionable orthodoxy, theology's own role in processes of domination and subordination will remain unchallenged, if not completely undetected.

Segundo is referring to the creation of a liberative theology through the critical and continual rereading of scripture. One can, however, apply the same principles to the creation of a liberative *pastoral social* or *pastoral obrera*, this time through the critical and continual rereading of Catholic social teaching.[92] When viewed from this perspective, the work of CECODERS clearly falls short. Despite its members' obvious commitment to workers and their struggles, the organization's pastoral approach cannot be truly liberative as long as it is based on an uncritical adoption of Catholic social teaching. While CECODERS' mission may intersect with the hermeneutic circle at various points, it is never drawn completely into the spiralling dialectic of critique and re-creation. Thus, even though CECODERS appears in many respects to be drastically different from its sponsors in the Costa Rican Church and in the Vatican, the centre never fully escapes from this conservative lineage because it treats Catholic social teaching as orthodox.

Disappointing as it may be from a liberationist perspective, this reluctance to question orthodoxy makes sense in the context of the patently subordinate position that CECODERS occupies within the Church's organizational structure. As Monseñor Arrieta's responses to the 1986 *folleto* and to the centre's collaboration with ASEPROLA demonstrate, the Archdiocese maintains a close watch on CECODERS. The archbishop will not hesitate to step in and dictate changes if the centre's positions prove threatening to the interests of the Church as a whole. Given such precedents, it is unlikely that the centre will undertake any serious critique of the doctrinal positions held by the hierarchy. In fact, the centre's uncritical acceptance and citation of the standard Catholic social teaching sources, and the unity in the Church that this acceptance implies, may even afford the centre a measure of symbolic protection as it develops political alliances that otherwise may prove problematic in the eyes of Church leaders. Regardless of whether or to what degree these appeals to Catholic social teaching are deliberate or sincere, they are one means by which CECODERS can survive as a relatively liberationist entity within a larger, more powerful, and more conservative Church institution.

Limón Province 7

Although geographically and politically Costa Rica is one, in the people's mind, Limón is still considered as another Costa Rica.
—Miguel Picado, *La Iglesia costarricense entre el pueblo y el estado*

I f one word were to describe both the Costa Rican province of Limón and the Catholic Church in Limón, that word would be "marginalized." Limón province is the country's poorest region; located on Costa Rica's Atlantic coast, it stands apart from San José and the central valley politically and culturally as well as economically. The Church in Limón, for its part, was long classified as an immature ecclesiastical unit and was only upgraded from its status as an apostolic vicariate to a diocese in its own right at the end of 1994. A decade later, it is still considered by many to be a younger sibling of the more powerful Archdiocese of San José.

It calls one's attention, then, that Limón is precisely where *una nueva forma de ser iglesia* (a new church character) is developing in Costa Rica. It is in Limón where the CEB phenomenon is the strongest, where the Church agents are most active on behalf of the poor, and where the most emphasis has been placed on the development of a *pastoral social* in line with a liberationist socio-religious perspective. Moreover, in all of Costa Rica, it is the Limón Church that has acted and spoken out most strongly in favour of workers' rights, and that has made the greatest progress in developing a formal *pastoral obrera* with its members.

On the other hand, Limón province is also where one finds the most outstanding example of a conservative *pastoral social* in Costa Rica—that espoused by the ESJ23. Formally, the school falls under the jurisdiction of the Archdiocese of San José; in recent decades, however, it has carried out most of its work in the Limón region. There, school representatives have campaigned against the "violent" and "communist" unions and have laboured tirelessly to promote the solidarity movement on the banana plantations. As the next chapter indicates, several of the school's practices and its particular interpretation of Catholic social teaching place it in direct conflict with the liberationist agenda of the official Church in the area.

To understand fully the unique liberationist and conservative expressions of the Church in Limón, however, one must first grasp the unique character of the region and of the Limón Church itself. This chapter, therefore, illustrates the socio-economic and religious-institutional contexts for the final two cases to be examined in this study.

Socio-Economic Conditions in Limón

In any contemporary survey of Costa Rica, the characteristics of Limón province stand out. The region is the most ethnically diverse in the country, with Afro-Caribbean, Chinese, and indigenous peoples comprising a substantial proportion of the population. The Limonense dialect is heavily infused with English. In addition, Limón plays a crucial role in generating revenue for Costa Rica, as it produces 95 percent of the country's number one export—bananas.[1] It has been estimated that up to 80 percent of Costa Rica's imports and exports pass through two large ports in Limón,[2] further underscoring the province's importance to the nation.

Limón's cultural richness and income generating activities, however, contrast with its endemic poverty. Despite the wealth the region generates, many Limonenses do not have access to adequate education, health care, housing, and employment.[3] On top of this, Limón has been the site of some of Costa Rica's most violent strikes and popular protests, up to and including the Limón en Lucha protests against deteriorating living standards and the proposed privatization of the stevedore industry. Tourist guidebooks warn of the crime and drug use in the capital city, Puerto Limón: one notes that it is becoming known as "Piedropolis" (Crack City);[4] many Costa Ricans themselves are wary of travel to this city on the coast.

Many of Limón's distinctive characteristics and many of its problems can be traced to its history as an economic enclave built on the banana and railway industries from the late nineteenth century.[5] Tens of thousands of immigrants (mostly from the Caribbean and in particular from Jamaica) were solicited to work on building the railways and on the banana plantations. From the beginning, working conditions in the region were inhumane: back-breaking labour in the tropical lowlands was exacerbated by the blatant racism and exploitation visited on workers by company officials.[6] The Costa Rican government, moreover, did little to improve this situation. Not only was there not adequate labour legislation in effect at that time, but the government had racist policies of its own and had granted many operating privileges to the international companies setting up in Costa Rica. For most of the century, Limón remained a wet and mosquito-ridden foreign territory, out of sight from the rest of the country and accessible only by a long and slow rail ride.[7]

The boom and bust economy of the banana industry continued to drive Limón's economy through the mid-1900s. Increases in world demand for bananas and expansions in production would attract more workers and generate spin-off employment; decreases in market demand, surges in agricultural diseases, or the rising frequency of labour conflicts would result in the transnational companies abandoning the area and the consequent unemployment and further displacement of workers. The unstable nature of employment on plantations contributed to a poor and precarious existence for many Limonenses. For its part, the government continued to neglect its citizens in Limón and was slow to provide them with the welfare state benefits and infrastructural development from which the rest of the country was benefitting.[8] Regardless of the growth and development that Costa Rica as a whole was said to be experiencing at this time, Limón was still being left behind.

This situation largely persisted into the time period covered by this study, with a few important changes. In the mid-1980s, for example, the construction of the Braulio-Carillo Highway provided the first direct access to and from Limón by road. Once connected to the capital city and beyond, Limón began to attract even more agricultural job seekers from the rest of Costa Rica. The highway thus boosted population growth and contributed even more to the infrastructural and industrial development that the latest banana boom had brought to Limón. Nonetheless, during the 1980s Limón continued to lag behind most of the rest of Costa Rica in terms of social and economic indicators.

Matters were not helped, to say the least, by the disasters that beset Limón in the 1990s. The lowlands on the coast have always been susceptible to damage by storms and flooding, but little could compare to the earthquake that struck the region on April 22, 1991.[9] Measuring 7.4 on the Richter scale, the quake left dozens dead, hundreds injured, and 13,000 homeless. It also destroyed more than 3,000 buildings in the province and severely damaged Costa Rica's only oil refinery and a crucial port; the port's shutdown was responsible for a temporary but expensive halt to the export of bananas. In addition, the earthquake induced landslides that stripped the Talamanca Mountains of vegetation, contributing to severe flooding when heavy rains fell a few months later. All told, the region's basic infrastructure suffered greatly. Years later, not all the bridges, roads, and sources of potable water in Limón have been repaired. In February 1996, a second major disaster hit the province in the form of destructive flooding. According to some estimates, the people affected by the floods numbered at least 27,000, with damage to housing and roads correspondingly severe.[10] With events such as these dragging them down, it is hardly surprising that, by the start of this millennium, the people of Limón had not been able to attain acceptable living conditions.

The problem with such disasters is that they are not entirely "natural." It is true that no one can control seismic activity nor rainfall; yet it is also true that what constitutes a problem—however serious—in a northern industrialized nation can take on truly catastrophic proportions in an area that is already economically disadvantaged. In this sense, such disasters are often just as much a product of humankind as they are of nature.

The human hand behind much of the suffering in Limón in the 1980s and 1990s has been related to the neo-liberal economic policies enforced under the nation's various structural adjustment programs. As I have explained, government leaders, in conjunction with international financial institutions, attempted to combat Costa Rica's economic crisis in part by promoting the agricultural export sector and by instituting regulations that would make it as easy as possible for Costa Rica to become integrated into world markets.

Of particular relevance for Limón was the Plan de Fomento Bananero (Banana Promotion Plan) established in 1985. This plan aimed to increase the total amount of bananas exported, extend the area devoted to banana cultivation, generate new jobs in the industry, and re-establish the participation in the world banana market that the country had lost in previous years.[11] These goals were to be accomplished through legislative changes and through various financial incentives granted to international banana companies.[12]

As with many structural adjustment programs, however, while the effects of this plan have been impressive from the point of view of the market, in human and ecological terms they have been dismal and destructive. Since 1985, for example, the total area in Costa Rica devoted to the cultivation of bananas has increased from 35,000 to 51,000 hectares.[13] Such expansion came largely, however, from the transnational companies' displacement of small and medium-sized farmers;[14] this process was often coercive and aided by such government actions as the withholding of credit to smaller-scale producers. Extra land for banana production has also come from the clearing of thousands of hectares of primary rainforest, a process with serious consequences for Costa Rican ecosystems.[15] In addition, the excessive use of pesticides and the huge amount of waste produced during banana production have caused extensive ecological damage to the rivers and soil in the Limón region.[16]

The Banana Promotion Plan has also appeared to be impressive in terms of increased employment, with close to 52,000 people working on banana plantations in 1997.[17] Still, only a small proportion of such workers are permanently employed, with the majority left to wander from plantation to plantation, competing with one another for short-term work (usually less than three months in duration). Salaries and benefits for workers on banana plantations have also decreased since the institution of the plan and migrant workers (generally illegal immigrants from Nicaragua who comprise up to 60 percent of the *bananero* labour force) are often denied even the most basic labour benefits.[18] Moreover, as I have discussed, the infiltration of *solidarismo* and the decline of the union movement on banana plantations in Limón has done much to counteract the workers' legal rights to freedom of association and to collective bargaining.

Living and working conditions on the plantations are also, as one might expect, a threat to human health. By its very nature, plantation work is extremely arduous and performed in sweltering heat. Those who work on plantations—as well as people who live on or near them—are regularly exposed to dangerously high levels of pesticides.[19] Some observers estimate that approximately 13,000 Costa Rican workers have been rendered sterile as a result of their contact with agro-chemicals;[20] thousands more citizens have been affected by diseases of the skin and central nervous system, digestive problems, and congenital birth defects.[21] Moreover, while foreign workers and women appear to be the ones most adversely affected by the poor working conditions,[22] everyone suffers from the high levels of poverty, crime, prostitution, alcoholism, and drug abuse that are reported on the plantations. Costa Rica's increased participation in the world market has come at the expense of the health and well being of its citizens and natural resources.

This social and economic context is the arena in which the ESJ23 operates and in which the official Church in Limón has developed its *pastoral social*. Yet social and economic factors alone are not the only variables important for understanding the positions of the ESJ23 and the Limón Church on social justice and the rights of workers. As I have already shown in the cases of Monseñor Arrieta, CECOR, and CECODERS, the institutional characteristics and necessities of a Church body can also have an effect on the type of social pastorate that is developed.

The Institutional Insecurity of the Limón Church

The social and economic marginalization of Limón within Costa Rica is paralleled by the institutional weakness of its local Church within the Costa Rican Church as a whole. Historically, three main factors—both internal and external to the Church—have contributed to the institutional insecurity of the Church in the region: the weak organizational character of the Limón Church itself; union activity in the region; and threats arising from the religious diversity in Limón.

♦ Organizational Weakness

In 1921, the Costa Rican Diocese of San José was divided into three and the Vicariato Apostólico de Limón was born. The very fact that Limón was designated an apostolic vicariate instead of a diocese is noteworthy. In the Catholic Church, an apostolic vicariate is regarded as an ecclesiastical unit that is not yet mature enough to "stand on its own two feet." Owing to its limited human, economic, and pastoral resources, an apostolic vicariate receives special attention and assistance, including financial aid, from the Roman Congregation for the Evangelization of Peoples. In fact, a vicariate falls under the direct responsibility of this congregation and its prefect, who is appointed by the pope. The bishop of an apostolic vicariate, therefore, carries out his functions in the name of the Holy See.[23]

In its early days, the Apostolic Vicariate of Limón suffered from a material poverty consistent with that in the region as a whole, as well as from a shortage of pastoral agents. Instead of Costa Rican clergy, priests from Germany performed the bulk of the Church's labours in the area. Further, the Limón Church was greatly affected by its character as a "missionary" Church. This was a different case than in the rest of Costa Rica where, by the twentieth century, the Catholic Church had long been installed as the church of the majority. By contrast, Limón, with its large numbers of indigenous peoples and Afro-Caribbean and Chinese immigrants—almost none of whom were Catholic to begin with—remained "a land of missions."[24] As such, the status that the Church enjoyed in the rest of the country was never definitively achieved in Limón. The continual pressure to preserve and increase the influence of the Catholic Church in face of many other faiths, as I elaborate below, has constituted an added measure of insecurity for an institution that already had a limited number of official representatives. Moreover, because of the relatively small size of their constituency, the pastoral agents in Limón concentrated more on going to the corners of the land and seeking converts than on developing the centralized administrative apparatus and organizational infrastructure common elsewhere in Costa Rica.[25] These internal circumstances contributed to the relatively weak institutional presence of the Catholic Church in Limón in the first half of the twentieth century.

The situation did not improve much in the decades that followed. By the late 1960s, many of the German priests were leaving for home to help compensate for the lack of vocations there.[26] And, because they did not approve of the pastoral changes that certain of the younger Costa Rican clergy were trying to implement in the wake of Vatican II and the Medellín conference, some of the older priests began to defect.[27] By the time Monseñor Alfonso Coto Monge was appointed bishop in 1980, there were only fifteen priests and two seminarians in the area, clearly an insufficient number to minister adequately to the needs of the vicariate.[28] When one also considers the material poverty of the institution throughout this time, it is not surprising that the Limón Church was known as an "underage minor" or as the "younger sibling" of the dioceses in the country.[29]

The Limón Church did not lose these monikers even after it became a diocese in 1994. Since that time, the Limón Church has existed in a particularly subordinate relationship vis-à-vis the Archdiocese of San José. The archdiocese's strength and status have long been bolstered by its leaders' long-standing ties to the secular centres of Costa Rican power. Yet it is also worth noting that the immense influence of the *sede metropolitana* is perceived, by those outside and inside the Church, to extend beyond the archdiocese's limits. Although within the Catholic Church generally, each local diocese has the right to determine for itself its own identity and characteristics without interference from another diocese or bishop or even archbishop, this practice has not prevented a two-tiered system of Church power from developing in Costa Rica. There, a pattern has developed in which the archdiocese has tended to dominate the affairs of the Church in the country as a whole, with the other dioceses and their leaders treated as a secondary or subordinate stratum.[30] In this schema, the Limón Church is commonly considered to rank quite low, if not lowest, among the peripheral churches. However unsanctioned in terms of canon law Limón's subordination to San José may be, in actuality this relationship has threatened the Limón Church's rightful autonomy. This situation represents a further way in which the institutional strength of the Limón Church has been compromised.

♦ Unions in Limón

While several challenges to the institutional security of the Limón Church are related to factors internal to the Church itself, the external political context in Limón provides other potential threats to the local Church institution. Of particular importance here is the challenge that the union movement in Limón poses — or is perceived to pose — to the Church.

In the past, the union movement in Limón was the strongest in the country, with labour activism on banana plantations being particularly militant. Even today the memory of the Atlantic Banana Plantation Strike of 1934 remains alive and infamous in the popular imagination.[31] Since that time, the fortunes of the union movement in Limón have waned somewhat. Still, although it is true that, since the 1980s, *solidarismo* has largely replaced *sindicalismo* on the banana plantations, unions have not completely disappeared from either the coastal region as a whole or even from the plantations themselves. The participation of labour in the Limón en Lucha movement in 1996 could even be taken to suggest that union activism in the area is on the upswing once again.

A particularly important period of labour activism in Limón took place in the late 1970s and early 1980s. At that time, Limón was described as "the belligerent vanguard of social organization and mobilization in the country."[32] Apart from the struggles by *campesinos* and members of the more general community, union-led strikes were a particularly noticeable facet of life in Limón. Of these, the most outstanding were the prolonged strikes that took place on the banana plantations. From December 1979 to January 1980, for example, a massive strike against the Standard Fruit Company (at that time the company responsible for half of all banana production in the region) lasted for twenty-eight days and involved the participation of four major unions.[33] Another major strike against the company lasted well over a month (from December 1981 to January 1982).[34] While there were other large-scale strike actions in the Limón region during this time, the banana strikes were particularly noteworthy because of the central importance of the industry to the region and because of the huge losses typically incurred during work stoppages on the plantations.[35] In any case, by the 1980s, the level of organization and the combativeness of the unions in Limón could not be missed.

This very visible and very volatile union activity in Limón was seen as a threat by the Church in the region. Church leaders viewed union leaders and communists to be drawing dangerously close together and commonly diagnosed the unions as being infected with a *tinta comunista*.[36] Further, they were of the opinion that people—especially in the context of the inequality and injustice in the area—were attracted to the unions and their communist ranks out of sheer necessity, as opposed to ideological discernment.[37] By the early 1980s, Catholic leaders in Latin America had witnessed the experience of the Church in revolutionary Cuba, and the Sandinista government in neighbouring Nicaragua had already begun to clash with the Catholic hierarchy there. The prospect of a communist resurgence in Costa Rica would not have been appealing to Church representatives. At the very least, the communists would have been seen as competing with the Limón Church for constituents, thereby threatening the institution and its need to preserve its presence within a competitive ideological atmosphere.

◆ Religious Diversity

The greatest threat to the Limón Church and its institutional self-preservation comes not from its internal organizational weaknesses nor external political competition but, rather, from specifically religious competition. Because of the religious diversity in the area, Limón is probably the only region in Costa Rica where the word "church" is not automatically assumed to signify "Catholic Church." While the Catholic Church remains the church of the majority of people in the area, Limón is the province in Costa Rica with the highest density of Protestant churches. The Afro-Caribbean peoples in Limón, who comprise up to 40 percent of the area's total population, are predominantly Protestant. This fact is not surprising, given that the original Jamaican and other Caribbean immigrants brought their colonizers' religions with them when they arrived at the turn of the century.

The mainline Protestant churches in Costa Rica—also known as "historical" Protestant churches—are considered to be the Anglican, Baptist, Methodist, Lutheran, and Moravian churches and the Salvation Army. In general, relations between the Catholic and mainline Protestant churches in Limón are quite positive. An attitude of mutual respect has developed among them and practical collaboration has become fairly frequent. For example, some of the Catholic and Protestant leaders have formed a pastors' association that meets monthly to discuss issues of relevance to the churches and to the region as a whole. Joint activities for youth and ecumenical conferences for lay people have also taken place. In addition, Catholic and Protestant representatives have worked together to secure financial support for corn farmers in the area, to respond to the effects of natural disasters, and to demand improvements in the living and working conditions in Limón both during and apart from the Limón en Lucha protests.[38]

In contrast to the good working relationship between the Catholic and mainline Protestant churches in Limón, the relationship between the official Catholic Church and the Pentecostal churches is characterized by fear, distrust, and even hostility. As in other areas of Central America, these small evangelical Protestant churches have been spreading quickly in Costa Rica. Limón province has one of the highest rates of Pentecostal growth and the highest density of Pentecostal churches in the country.[39] Catholic Church representatives take great care to distinguish the historical Protestant churches in Limón from what they disparagingly refer to as *sectas*. They negatively characterize these groups as "fanatical," "hostile," and "fundamentalist," and they view them as a threat to the Catholic Church.[40] The attitude of some of the Pentecostal leaders is no more open. As one Assemblies of God pastor has explained, the Catholic Church and his church could not mix, since they are "like water and oil."[41] As perhaps can be expected from such descriptions and comments, formal relations or ecumenical efforts between Catholic and Pentecostal leaders do not exist.

Importantly, however, some Catholics and Pentecostals do appear to be drawn together through their support for *solidarismo*. Jaime Valverde has observed that, in the banana zones of Limón, Pentecostals generally do not participate in popular political organizations, union activities, or strikes. As such, they are seen as *empleados de confianza* (trustworthy employees) valued by the management of the banana companies. Further, when they do become involved in organized activities, Valverde notes, Pentecostals become involved in the solidarity movement and often occupy executive posts in solidarity associations.[42]

In fact, there is a significant convergence between the Pentecostal world view and the *solidarismo* doctrine. As Valverde affirms, Pentecostals emphasize social peace as a Christian value and characterize movements of political rebellion as sinful.[43] As the Assemblies of God pastor quoted above also mentioned in a discussion of recent labour and political conflicts in Limón: "*sindicalismo* and strike movements, what they are doing is seeking conflict with the authorities. The Bible says that we should subject ourselves to the authorities."[44] He also noted that "the Christian is a pacifist, not a fighter," and that "*solidarismo* is good ... it seeks agreement between the manager and the employee."[45] These attitudes fit well with the emphasis on collaboration and harmony that is characteristic of the doctrine of the ESJ23.

Banana company officials have apparently recognized the implications of Pentecostalism for labour relations. Valverde reports, for example, that companies have preferentially hired Pentecostal workers. Companies have also attempted to facilitate the growth of Pentecostal churches in the area by providing them with financial and material aid when they are getting established on the plantations.[46] The advantage that this assistance confers on the Pentecostal churches is that much greater in light of the loss of access to Vatican funds that the Limón Church experienced when it became a diocese in 1994.

Overall, the threat that the Protestant denominations pose to the Catholic Church in Limón is complex. On the one hand, while the Church seems to coexist peacefully and even collaborates with the historical Protestant churches in the region, the traditional influence of Protestantism in Limón means that the Catholic Church still cannot take for granted its status as the Church of the majority in the area. On the other hand, Catholic leaders are quite open about their distress over the growing numbers of Limonense Catholics who are leaving the Church for the *sectas*. The advantages that the transnational companies confer on the Pentecostal churches, and these churches' links to the powerful *solidarismo* movement on the plantations, make the growing Pentecostal phenomenon in Limón all the more threatening. In the end, whether Church leaders view the Protestant churches positively or not, the fact remains that the Catholic representatives do have to work harder to maintain and increase their constituency in such a religiously diverse area.

Conclusion

The typical plantation or dock worker in contemporary Limón does not have an easy life. Workers' rights are frequently ignored, labour is hard and often hazardous, wages are low. Workers must subsist in a region polluted by chemicals, ravaged by nature, and dominated by transnational companies with priorities far from their own. High rates of crime, poverty, and substance abuse complete the picture of this province on the periphery, a land where the idealized image of Costa Rican development and stability is even more of a fable than elsewhere.

The precarious position of the Church as an institution in Limón further complicates the context, at least for Church agents. Beyond dealing with the socio-economic forces that affect workers, Church officials must contend with an occasionally overbearing archdiocese, the purportedly communist unions, and the burgeoning *secta* phenomenon. In the next two chapters, I detail how Church pastoral programming for workers in Limón has developed sometimes in direct reponse to, and always in the context of, these trying conditions.

The solution of worker-employer conflicts by means of conciliation, harmony and dialogue is the most important fruit of the Escuela Social Juan XXIII.
—Monseñor Román Arrieta Villalobos (statement frequently quoted in ESJ23 literature)

The harmony of *solidarismo* is that of the dictator: everyone shuts up, nothing more. The harmony is that nobody complains.
—Padre Jesús Doncel, priest in the banana plantation town of Río Frío

The Escuela Social Juan XXIII (ESJ23, John XXIII Social School) was established in 1963 by Monseñor Rodríguez (1960-79) as an official Church agency charged with the responsibility to "teach, defend and diffuse Catholic social doctrine and to coordinate all the works of Catholic Social Action in the Archdiocese [of San José]."[1] The school floundered under its early directors and was plagued by funding shortages and internal ideological division until the appointment in 1971 of Padre Claudio Maria Solano Cerdas as director.[2] Solano, who has continued as the school's leader since then, revitalized the organization and transformed it into an affluent and influential wing of the Costa Rican Catholic Church.

In this chapter, I discuss the expansion of the school under Padre Solano and document how the promotion of *solidarismo* came to be the raison d'être of the organization itself. Next, I analyze Solano's statements and school materials to show how the particular expression of Catholic social teaching found within them is related to the web of economic, political, and Church alliances to which the ESJ23 belongs.

Padre Solano and the Expansion of the ESJ23

Padre Solano began his work at the ESJ23 as a relatively well-educated but inexperienced young priest. Solano received his theological training in Costa Rica and France, earned a degree in philosophy from the Pontifical Gregorian University in Rome, and completed postgraduate studies at the International Sociological Institute, also in Rome. He was ordained to the priesthood in 1969. Prior to arriving at the ESJ23 in August of 1971, Padre

Solano served briefly as an assistant priest in parishes in San Ignacio de Acosta and Heredia, Costa Rica, and also worked as an advisor to the National Scout Movement.[3] Three decades later, however, this former Boy Scout leader is a powerful and controversial public figure whose name has become synonymous with the ESJ23 in Costa Rican society.

Under Solano, the school's mission and objectives have expanded considerably. No longer content with the 1963 mandate to "teach, defend, and diffuse" Catholic social teaching, the school's mission is now to "promote, impel, coordinate, teach, diffuse, defend and apply the principles of Catholic Social Doctrine in the social, community, family and institutional realms and especially to develop action in the fields of labour and education."[4] Chief among the school's objectives — and most relevant to the theme of this study — is the fostering of social peace, harmony, and good relations between workers and employers.[5]

For more than a quarter of a century, Padre Solano has sought to achieve these goals through the energetic promotion of *solidarismo*. A form of labour organization that renounces collective agreements and the right to strike, *solidarismo* emphasizes the common interests and collaboration of workers and owners. According to school lore, Solano began his term as the ESJ23's director by attempting to find an appropriate channel through which to translate the theory of Catholic social teaching into practice. After considering and rejecting both *cooperativismo* and *sindicalismo*, he discovered *solidarismo*. Although the solidarity movement was strictly a secular phenomenon, Solano judged it to be fundamentally compatible with Christian principles of social justice. He felt that, once enriched by these same principles, the solidarity movement would be the ideal means to spread Catholic social teaching among Costa Rican workers.[6] Thus, in the words of one school administrator, Solano began to use the solidarity movement as a "Trojan horse" to bring Catholic social teaching to the people.[7] Since 1971, then, Solano and his staff have devoted most of their attention and resources to furthering the *solidarista* cause. For the first several years, the school concentrated its efforts in urban commercial and industrial sectors. However, after 1978, members began to focus more intensively on the country's Atlantic banana plantations where, as I have noted, union organizing and deleterious working conditions had combined to make the workers particularly combative.

In the Atlantic region, school outreach workers, called *promotores solidaristas*, travel to factories, public offices, and plantations to hold workshops and give speeches on Catholic social teaching and the benefits of *solidarismo*. Workers are also brought by bus to the school's Solidarista Training Centre in Tres Ríos, Cartago, to attend seminars on the same topics. Padre Solano himself sometimes speaks to groups of workers but more frequently promotes the benefits of *solidarismo* to company owners and managers. When a group decides to form a solidarity association, the school is there to supply the necessary guidance and registration materials; it can provide both association members and their employers with ongoing training and administrative support in the legal aspects of *solidarismo*, as well as in the areas of accounting, human resources, and labour relations. At each step, the school distributes copious amounts of printed material in the form of pamphlets, training manuals, and study guides, all approved by Solano and produced by the school's education department.

Beyond the activities directly related to the promotion of *solidarismo*, the ESJ23 has developed a number of other training, spiritual assistance, and education programs over the years.[8] In 1975, for example, Solano established the Instituto de Formación Integral Mixto (IFIM, Co-ed Institute for Integrated Training) as an artisanal and technical training centre. The IFIM is run from the school's headquarters in Curridabat, but also has offices in marginal urban communities and the Atlantic region. The training centre offers courses in such areas as sewing, nutrition, flower arranging, toy making, confectionery, hairdressing, and aesthetics. Many of these classes are directed specifically at women, as are the seminars in self-esteem, household budgeting, and leadership offered to *damas solidaristas* (wives and daughters of male *solidarista* workers) at the school's Tres Ríos installation. Finally, the school runs Voz Amiga (Friendly Voice), a service that offers free psychological counselling and spiritual guidance over the telephone.

Over time, as one might expect, the ESJ23 has developed a considerable infrastructure to support this programming. The school headquarters, located across from the church in the centre of the San José suburb of Curridabat, is an airy complex of classrooms and offices equipped with the latest in modern technology. Padre Solano has always maintained his office there. Apart from the director, the school's *sede central* employs approximately thirty-five staff members who function as the administrative core of the organization. In contrast to the urban setting of the Curridabat installation, the ESJ23 training centre in Tres Ríos (fifteen minutes outside the city of Cartago) is an isolated and sprawling property filled with green and open spaces. Located at the centre, which opened in 1987, are offices, classrooms, conference facilities, cabins, sports and recreation facilities, a dining hall, and a print shop. Approximately forty people work in the departments of education and administration at this site, where between four and five thousand workers receive courses every year.[9] Finally, close to forty people also work in the school's *solidarista* promotion offices. One of these offices is located in San José; the other six are scattered throughout the banana-producing zones of the country in Guapiles, Siquirres, Buenos Aires, Valle de la Estrella, Río Frío, and Sixaola. This thriving organization is certainly a far cry from the small, cash-strapped, and struggling school that existed during the 1960s.

Perhaps the most striking indication of the school's accomplishments under Padre Solano, however, can be seen in the phenomenal growth of the *solidarismo* movement. The number of solidarity associations in Costa Rica has increased by more than sixtyfold since Solano took up the cause. Prior to 1972, there were only thirty associations in the entire country; today there are between 1,800 and 2,000 associations in Costa Rica, with up to 250,000 registered affiliates.[10] On the banana plantations of Limón province, where *solidarismo* has become the dominant form of labour organization, the effects of the movement's growth are particularly noteworthy. According to school officials, "labour peace" has reigned on many plantations for well over a decade because of *solidarismo*.[11] School supporters claim that the resultant absence of strikes and the favourable working environment have translated into increases in banana production and savings of millions of dollars for Costa Rica.[12] Judging by the numbers, at least, the success of the school appears undeniable.

School representatives, not surprisingly, have ready explanations to account for such accomplishments, in particular for the remarkable spread of *solidarismo* in recent years. They claim that, aside from the tireless efforts of Padre Solano, the "basic reason" for the expansion of *solidarismo* in Costa Rica "rests in the close links between *solidarismo* and the fundamental principles of Christianity: fraternity, respect, harmony, liberty, [and] justice in the relations between the workers and the company, characteristics of the economic and social development of Costa Rica."[13] According to this interpretation, once workers themselves are given the right to choose, most opt "naturally" for *solidarismo* and its attendant benefits.[14]

The ESJ23 and Catholic Social Teaching

Given the school's claims of the congruency of the Church's message with the nature of *solidarismo*, the formulation of Catholic social teaching propagated by the ESJ23 deserves close scrutiny. Through such an examination, one can see precisely how the fundamental principles of Christianity are expressed in the school's teachings, and where the doctrine of the school falls along the conservative-liberationist continuum.

♦ The School and Pre-Conciliar Catholic Social Teaching

The first thing to note about the ESJ23's use of Catholic social teaching is the school's heavy reliance on pre-Vatican II papal statements and encyclicals. School representatives and instructional materials repeatedly cite the words of Leo XIII in *Rerum Novarum* and Pius XI in *Quadragesimo Anno* on social issues.[15] Even the teachings of Pope Pius XII (1939-58), whose statements are overlooked in many analyses of Catholic social teaching, receive heavy emphasis in the school's literature.[16] From justifications for the Church's social magisterium to evaluations of principles of social organization, to pronouncements about appropriate relations between employers and their workers or between the state and its citizens: the pre-conciliar papal social statements are clearly a touchstone for the school's teachings.

On labour issues as they are most narrowly defined, for example, school materials explicitly draw on pre-Vatican II social teaching documents. Thus, despite the school's links to and promotion of the solidarity movement, its Catholic social teaching manual (*Manual para el estudio de la Doctrina Social de la Iglesia*) still cites Leo XIII, Pius XI, and Pius XII in its affirmation that workers do have the right to form unions.[17] Moreover, while the ESJ23 does on occasion refer to Vatican II's position on the right to strike (the classification of a strike in *Gaudium et Spes* as an extreme, although sometimes necessary, means to resolve worker oppression),[18] by far the greater emphasis is on strikes as an "evil," as well as on the costs and losses, and hatred and violence that school officials claim strikes almost inevitably involve.[19] In this way the ESJ23, with its emphasis on what makes strikes wrong (as opposed to what may justify them), clearly echoes the earliest Catholic social teaching and the opposition of popes Leo XIII and Pius XI to any form of labour militancy.

An overt anti-communism also played a role in Leo XIII and Pius XI's distrust of union pressure tactics. Products of their time and cognisant that left-wing movements might well draw the working class out of the pews and into the streets, these popes were fearful of the threat communists and other "crafty agitators" posed to social order and to the souls of the faithful.[20] While many decades have passed since these popes gave voice to their fears in *Rerum Novarum* and *Quadragesimo Anno*, the anti-communism of early Catholic social teaching resurfaces in a particularly virulent, and often surprisingly facile, form in the teachings of the ESJ23.

Particularly revealing in this regard is one of the school's main Catholic social teaching textbooks, *La Doctrina Social de la Iglesia* (*introducción a su estudio*) (*The Social Doctrine of the Church* [*Introduction to Its Study*]). This study guide, complete with fill-in-the-blank and matching-column exercises, was originally published in 1985 and is still a staple in school seminars for workers. It emphasizes the many dangers associated with communism, most often referred to as the "Communist Dictatorship" and represented in drawings as a hammer and sickle or a silhouette of the Soviet Union with the city of Moscow marked. In the lessons preceding the one devoted exclusively to communism, students learn to equate communism with, among other things, atheism, the treatment of humans as soul-less animals, poverty, enslavement, divorce, and ignorance (because communists do not let parents properly educate their children).[21] In the introductory remarks for the lesson on communism itself, students are "alerted" to the "trick" of the communists and are told that the following pages will "unmask" communism for what it truly is. This is important, according to the workbook, because communists triumphed in Cuba among the "good" Cubans precisely because they disguised themselves and their intentions until after they had grasped power. The workbook then warns that: "In Costa Rica [communism] can triumph, if we let ourselves be fooled by this group of masked men."[22] The chapter continues to show students communism as it "really" is: a doctrine of hate and class struggle in which the rich and the poor aim to annihilate one another, a strategy for revolution based on deceit and false promises, and a system of power based on terror and torture. Finally, the lesson concludes with the call to prevent communism from seizing power in the "free world."[23] Regardless of what has actually happened since the crumbling of the Soviet Union and the Berlin Wall, the continued use of this workbook at the school and the persistence of Fidel Castro's government in Cuba means that, for the EJS23, the enemy is alive and well and living in Latin America.

Both the school's attack on communism and its promotion of *solidarismo* are clearly rooted in a particular conception of what society is and what it should be. In the school's material, unity, harmony, and solidarity are core concepts in both an analysis of present-day society and in the remedies for any social problems that may arise—much as they were in the Catholic social teaching documents issued many decades before. Although these concepts are not found exclusively in pre-conciliar Catholic social teaching, the school's linking of these principles to their earlier formulations bears some comment here.

According to the school's analyses, *solidarismo* as a movement is based on, and tries to apply, *solidaridad* (solidarity) as a concept: "Solidarity presents the idea of close or strong cohesion, of unity, of integration. Therefore, solidarity is not selfishness, nor imposition, nor hatred, nor struggle or conflicts, but the union of various parts, the collaboration of different persons, to achieve a common objective."[24] The school further explains that solidarity is a fact; it is the normal and normative state of affairs in nature and in society—from the parts of the human body functioning together in unity, to the members of a soccer team whose triumph depends on the collaboration of all the players, to the stars and planets of the universe that move together as do the parts of a watch. In this schema, the positing of a unity among humans in society stems from the argument that all have a common Father in God, all are human beings with immortal souls and material bodies occupying the same world, and all have the same final end in God. Whether at home, in the workplace, or in society in general, then, humans are called to behave in a manner consistent with such principles; solidarity is both a fact (*hecho*) of life, and an obligation (*deber*) in life.[25]

According to the teachings of the school, these lessons trace their origins to Jesus' command to love one another and to the Pauline notion of various Christians forming only one body in Christ.[26] They are also, however, expressed repeatedly in the Catholic social teaching tradition. On the topic of solidarity in the world of work, for example, school materials cite quotations from Leo XIII and Pius XI on the necessary alliance and the mutual agreement between capital and labour.[27] The more general doctrinal analysis of the concept, meanwhile, concentrates more closely on the words of Pius XII, whose *Summi Pontificatus* (1939) appears to have provided a veritable template for the school's explanation of the nature and causes of solidarity.[28] In both the conceptions of the pre-conciliar popes and of the ESJ23, a largely functionalist conception of society and human relations—with people of various classes and callings all working together to contribute to the good of the whole—prevails.

The school's adoption of this doctrine, however, does not imply that school representatives believe there are no social problems at all in Costa Rica. In fact, apart from the threat of the communists, the school does point to poverty and labour strife as threats to the country's social peace. Although school documents contain almost no explanations for how such problems arose, they repeatedly and emphatically indicate the appropriate solution for ills at any level in society: changes in behaviour and attitudes. Selfishness, corruption, consumerist habits, a "tribal" conception of human relations, and any classist mentality of confrontation must be overcome. Instead, all Costa Ricans, including workers and employers, must develop a "mentality of solidarity," which is described in one school pamphlet as "a necessary attitude, the only solution in the face of current circumstances."[29]

Given the school's focus on this "profound transformation of mentality," the solutions to social problems are necessarily found on the individual and interpersonal levels. So when the Catholic social teaching workbook asks, for example, How can the poverty among the Costa Rican people be remedied? the answer does not involve suggestions regarding anything related to economic restructuring or government programming. Rather, the answer lies in the "mutual comprehension" of the parties involved:

> That the worker understands the *empresario* [business owner] and the *empresario* understands the worker…. When there is mutual comprehension, both owners and workers benefit, because justice will reign; a true community of mutual interests will be created: in large part, the conflicts that hold up or diminish production will disappear.[30]

This mutual comprehension and collaboration are, of course, fostered by the solidarity association to which workers should belong.

The errors in such a perspective begin with its superficial analysis of social relations. The dire poverty in Limón, the problems on the banana plantations, and the denial of basic workplace liberties are all neglected in the face of an emphasis on unity as the organizing principle of human affairs. School materials do not even include detailed descriptions or moral condemnations of the conditions in the region. Moreover, the problems in Limón are not traced to the economic logic of international capitalism or the distorted priorities of a neo-liberal government, but they are implied to be the products of the greed and selfishness of individual actors. The school's focus on the individual and the interpersonal effectively excludes any broader understanding of the causes and consequences of the structural flaws in the agro-export industry. Only in this schema can divorce be defined as a serious social problem, while the spraying of pesticides from banana company airplanes onto workers (and children in nearby schoolyards) is not. In this sense, even the encyclicals of the pre-conciliar popes revealed more of a sensitivity to the suffering and working conditions of people in their time than do the materials of ESJ23 representatives—many of whom, ironically, spend their days in direct contact with workers and their families.

The ESJ23's lack of attention to anything but interpersonal dynamics and the need for attitudinal change renders its key educational materials little more than pop psychology manuals from the Church. Far from being resources in the struggle for social justice or primers for conscientization and empowerment, the school's workbooks and pamphlets perpetuate the false impression among workers that problems between workers and employers can be "talked out," provided that both sides are willing. According to the school's logic, the dynamics of exploitation and the drastic differences in political and economic power between the parties involved do not matter once both parties assume the correct "Christian" demeanour of trust and understanding. Yet this assumption, in the context of Limón, ultimately functions to keeps workers as docile employees instead of empowered agents who demand the wages, job security, and poison-free environment that is rightfully theirs.

The school's vehement anti-communism also works to demonize anyone who dares to challenge this status quo. Hence, even though the school's director admits that Catholic social teaching dictates that workers do have the right to form unions, the unions in Limón, and throughout Costa Rica generally, must be stopped because—according, at least, to Padre Solano—they are controlled by the communists.[31] Even though strikes as a last resort are also accepted in theory in the school's teachings, in practice they are condemned as the preferred weapon of communists and as vehicles for the hatred and violence that communism embodies.[32] In this simplistic world view, any analysis of reality that contradicts the school's assumption of the unity underlying social relations, and any protest that occurs outside the boardroom, can be painted red. In Costa Rica, where the national mythology also incorporates elements of anti-communism, this message from the school is particularly powerful: the good Christian—the good Costa Rican—is one who loves peace and compromise, not conflict and struggle. Unfortunately, this means that work to combat inequities and exploitation can thereby be precluded if it potentially involves an element of struggle or confrontation.

The school's teachings as they have been described to this point certainly contain many of the hallmarks of conservative pre-conciliar Catholic social teaching: a blunt anti-communism, a functionalist view of the social order, and a focus on solving social problems through reformed attitudes, dialogue, and collaboration. The references in school documents, moreover, also make it clear that the pre-conciliar popes are the primary sources of doctrinal inspiration for these perspectives. Some commentators argue that this firm grounding in pre-conciliar Catholic social teaching means that the positions of the school stand in opposition to the Catholic social teaching tradition of the post-Vatican II Church. They suggest that the Catholic social teaching espoused by the school is based on outdated principles that have been replaced or superseded by more contemporary Catholic social teaching.[33] As I will argue, however, these assertions do not take into account the more recent teachings of the school. Such assertions are also based on certain unwarranted assumptions about Catholic social teaching and about the differences between pre- and post-conciliar forms of this teaching.

♦ The School and Post-Conciliar Catholic Social Teaching

At the most obvious level, it should be pointed out that, far from relying solely on the teachings from the pre-conciliar era, publications and representatives of the ESJ23 do refer to more recent Catholic social teaching documents of the Church magisterium. Encyclicals from John XXIII (*Mater et Magistra* and *Pacem in Terris*) are cited in school documents, as are documents from Paul VI (*Populorum Progressio* and *Octogesima Adveniens*) and even CELAM (the 1968 Medellín conference documents). Perhaps not surprisingly, the most common references in school materials are to Pope John Paul II's comments on the importance of solidarity, including the notions that solidarity is a Christian virtue and that solidarity is a necessary component of social justice.[34] In other cases, the school's statements on collaboration between workers and owners, and on the need for dialogue and the peaceful resolution of conflicts in the world of work, are supported by further references to John Paul II's encyclicals.[35] These school teachings may have a pre-conciliar ring to them, but nonetheless they are readily supported by the words of Pope John Paul II.

The relationship between the school's teachings and other themes found in post-conciliar Catholic social teaching is less straightforward. Interestingly, although concepts such as liberation and the option for the poor—in both their liberationist and conservative interpretations—are found in the Catholic social teaching of the past few decades, the use of these concepts is either studiously avoided or critiqued by ESJ23 representatives. The word "liberation," for example, is almost never used in any of the school's promotional pamphlets or instructional literature. One of the very few references to the term, found in a description of the Medellín conference documents, touches only briefly and vaguely on Christ's "message of liberation for the poor."[36] It certainly does not describe liberation as involving socio-economic empowerment for the popular classes or the structural transformation of society. In other materials, instead of the language of the liberationists, one finds references to the "integral development" of human beings and to "development in solidarity," phrases that were given prominence in Pope Paul VI's encyclical *Populorum Progressio*.[37] The emphasis here is on a collaborative and gradual process of development in society, not on the deep-rooted social change promoted by the liberationists. Thus, neither the actual word "liberation," nor the potentially radical concept behind it, is given attention in school documents.

The school's director, Padre Solano, has also made it clear that he wants to avoid making any sort of option for the poor:

> It is necessary to demythologize the option for the poor. Each time that we help to form the conscience of the *empresarios* [business owners] we realize this option. I do not want to belong to a Church that understands the "poor" as an economic term, at least not exclusively. It would be a hypocritical and outdated Church that would go against God's universal and saving will. Be afraid of this option for the poor.[38]

For Solano, the role of the Church is not to opt for one group over another; the Church and the social school are never to exclude anyone on the basis of his or her social, political, or economic status. Rather, the Church needs to promote dialogue, collaboration, and mutual responsibilities among all her "children."[39]

As I have noted, an emphasis on Church unity and universality and a reluctance to commit to the partiality necessary for an efficacious option for the poor are defining features of post-conciliar Catholic conservatism. By attempting to cater to all groups in society at once and by refusing to support the poor and their rights unequivocally, the attempt at a non-partisan position in fact becomes an anti-poor position, because it carries no direct critique of or challenge to those who help to perpetuate the sources of injustice in society. Padre Solano's reluctance to characterize "the poor" as an economic entity further compounds the issue because it implies that everyone, regardless of their socio-economic circumstances, can be viewed as poor. Refusing to acknowledge and define the poor as the economically disadvantaged people they are is another way of denying that serious inequities exist in Costa Rica. This denial is not only an affront to the thousands of workers toiling under harsh conditions on Limón plantations; it is also a Church-sanctioned excuse for those who control those plantations to do nothing about such conditions. Regardless of the inequality legitimated and perpetuated by this refusal to take sides, regardless of the fact that sometimes the only way to act for justice is to act against the interests of a particular group, and regardless of the consequences that an "option for everyone" allows, Padre Solano and the ESJ23 maintain a fear of an option for the poor.

This fear, along with the school's emphasis on Pope John Paul II's teachings on solidarity, has led some commentators to suggest that the pope's social teachings are being distorted by school promoters eager to lend legitimacy to *solidarismo*. They argue that the ESJ23 is wrong to overemphasize John Paul II's comments on labour-capital harmony and that it is ignoring the pope's teachings on the preferential option for the poor and liberation, teachings they presume would contradict the anti-liberationist bias of *solidarismo*.[40]

In response, I reiterate that, despite the appearance that terms like "liberation" and "preferential option for the poor" lend to the pope's statements, John Paul II is still promoting a conservative message of interclass collaboration. This persistent conservatism can be seen in the pope's attacks on Marxism and class struggle, in his teachings on unity in the Church and society, as well as in his spiritualistic (as opposed to political) interpretation of the term liberation and in his promotion of a preferential option for the poor that excludes no one. Despite the surface differences in language, then, the pope's conservative Catholic social teaching and that of the ESJ23 are extremely similar. Solidarity and harmony are hallmarks not only of pre-conciliar Catholic social teaching but also of John Paul II's social teachings, and the campaign of the ESJ23 falls squarely within this persistent doctrinal tradition. As the comments of one plantation worker and solidarity association member underscore, "the solidarity movement is the same as the Church. Both teach the way of Jesus: peace, tranquillity, and bearing the burden."[41]

Another Side to the School's Success

If one were to believe the assertions of the ESJ23's *solidarista* promoters, the story of the school presented here could end after the biography of its leader, the description of its programming and facilities, and the exposition of its Catholic social teaching. According to them, no additional information would be necessary to understand the expansion of the school and the spread of *solidarismo* in Costa Rica. Others, however, would offer at least two further factors to explain the apparent success of the school and the content of the *solidarista* message. One is the nature of the ESJ23's activities on the banana plantations; the other is its alliances with the country's business, political, and religious elites.

♦ School Activities on the Plantations

In stark contrast to the school's explanations for the popularity of *solidarismo*, numerous reports have indicated that there are other—sometimes shocking—factors behind the predominance of this form of labour organization. In Costa Rica's Limón region, the ESJ23 and its *solidarista* promoters have been implicated in the outright coercion of workers on banana plantations. These charges not only tarnish the school's reputation, but they qualify its claims for the success of *solidarismo* and lead many to question the form of Catholic social teaching to which the school claims to adhere.

I have already made some general references to the unethical tactics that have been used to persuade workers to join solidarity associations. In particular, the pressure to join a solidarity association can begin as soon as potential workers arrive on a plantation. Often, when workers seek jobs on the *fincas*, they are asked to sign association membership cards before they are shown a contract with the banana company. Those who affiliate with the solidarity movement are granted employment; those who refuse to sign may be told that there are no jobs available.[42] In other efforts to convince existing employees to affiliate with *solidarismo*, company supervisors may promise workers better postings and housing, more overtime hours, or secure jobs for their children. Further, workers who are members of solidarity associations have few problems passing the three-month probationary period, after which a worker's job is more secure and benefits begin to accrue; unaffiliated workers run a greater risk of losing their jobs or being transferred while on probation, hence losing the coveted three-month record of employment.[43] Perhaps most notoriously, workers who complain about the company or the solidarity association, workers who become union members, or workers who are otherwise sympathetic to *sindicalismo* risk being named on a company's *lista negra* (blacklist). Workers who are listed are intimidated, harassed, or fired, and, since the names contained on the list are shared among banana company officials on plantations throughout the region, these workers have difficulty finding jobs once they have left the *finca* where their problematic behaviour is said to have originated.[44] Thus, although in Costa Rica workers are legally guaranteed the right of freedom of association, on the plantations and in practice many are not truly free to choose the type of workers' organization with which to associate.

Some banana company officials are certainly involved in such unscrupulous behaviour. There can also be no doubt that these individuals operate with the knowledge, consent, and, in some cases, outright assistance of the ESJ23's leaders and *solidarista* promoters. On one level, the sheer amount of time that Padre Solano and his *solidarista* promoters spend on the plantations and in consultation with company workers and officials makes it inconceivable that school representatives would be unaware of the dirty dealings taking place on behalf of *solidarismo*. Eyewitnesses have also reported that Solano and other school officials have actively participated in the rooting out and firing of workers whose actions are deemed to be contrary to the solidarity movement's ideals.[45] Moreover, copies of the photographs taken of plantation workers for school identification cards are routinely forwarded to banana company managers. These pictures, accompanied by reports from school instructors about which workers ask questions deemed to be unsupportive of company and *solidarista* aims during training sessions, allow the companies to detect and eliminate troublemakers in the ranks much more efficiently.[46] Such actions may have helped to swell the numbers of *solidaristas* and to silence the solidarity movement's critics on plantations. However, they also challenge the veracity of the ESJ23's claims to be based on Catholic social teaching principles.

In the first place, and as I have indicated, the Catholic social teaching tradition has long accorded workers the freedom to unionize. Even the school itself does not deny this fact and claims to respect such rights. Yet the reality is that ESJ23 representatives go to considerable lengths to *prevent* workers from affiliating with the union movement. Thereby, they directly violate the rights of workers that are supposed to be guaranteed by both Costa Rican law and the Church's social teaching tradition. Even if school officials are not direct participants in the persecution of unionists but merely stand by and fail to object to such unethical practices, they still have an obligation to speak out on behalf of workers who are targeted by anti-union discrimination and who suffer from its effects. The commitment to truth and justice throughout the Catholic social teaching tradition demands no less.

Yet, ironically, one suspects that it is precisely a commitment to the "Truth" that lies behind the apparently hypocritical behaviour of Padre Solano and other school members. In this case, the truth that justifies the persecution of *sindicalistas* derives from the definition of the solidarity movement as good on the one hand, and the union movement as evil on the other. While Solano claims that he has no aversion to unionism per se and even that unions can play an important role in clarifying and defending the rights of workers, he also reveals his conviction that, in Costa Rica in general and in Limón in particular, unions have strayed from their true democratic origins and betrayed the support that the Church once gave them.[47] He then portrays *solidarismo* as an "instrument to save the Atlantic Zone" from the "exploitation," "attack on human dignity," and "perversion of democracy" fomented by communist unionism.[48] Once the school's campaign is thus outlined in terms of good versus evil and right versus wrong, the promotion of *solidarismo* by whatever means necessary is not so much seen as a matter of denying workers the right to unionize as it is denying the communists a foothold in Costa Rica.

This stance is reminiscent of the Vatican treatment of certain liberation theologians. While Pope John Paul II and his supporters claim, for example, to have no problem with the promotion of liberation or the preferential option for the poor (when these are "correctly" defined), they have silenced those liberationists, such as Leonardo Boff, whom they see as guilty of perverting the Church's authentic message. Here too the silencing of Boff is not so much seen as a matter of repressing dissent in the Church as it is preserving the Vatican's interpretation of doctrine. In both the case of the ESJ23 and the Vatican, then, the rights of those at the base of the Church can be sacrificed in the attempt to protect and propagate the Church's or the ESJ23's perception of the "Truth." This practice of granting privilege to the Church's "Truth" over the need to enact justice in the historical realm is, of course, another characteristic of conservative Catholic social teaching. In concrete terms for Limón's *bananeros*, however, Padre Solano's perception of the truth about labour organization also means that they will continue to suffer from poverty, violence, and disease without much control over how to react to them.

Unscrupulous activities aside, other keys to understanding the influence of the ESJ23 in Costa Rica can be found in an analysis of the support that the school receives from segments of the broader Costa Rican society. An examination of the school's sources of corporate funding, its practical and symbolic alliances with the state, and its forms of approval from the archdiocese provides the additional context and information needed for a complete analysis of the school's Catholic social teaching.

♦ Sources of Corporate Funding

Since Padre Solano took charge of the ESJ23, the organization has operated without any direct financial assistance from the archdiocese.[49] This is not meant to imply that the Costa Rican Church hierarchy has been indifferent to Solano and the school; in fact, rather, the archdiocese has given the ESJ23 its concerted support, as I discuss below. What it does mean, however, is that Solano has long had to solicit funds from outside the Church for the school's ever-growing roster of activities.

After his 1971 appointment, Padre Solano wasted little time in lining up the necessary financiers for the school's mission. In 1972, for example, he initiated the formation of the Asociación de Empresarios Pro-Justicia Social y Paz (Association of Businessmen for Social Justice and Peace). Composed of prominent Costa Rican business leaders, this association functioned as a powerful lobby for the solidarity movement in the country and also provided a financial lifeline for the ESJ23 for many years. According to Gustavo Blanco and Orlando Navarro, the ESJ23 was almost completely economically dependent on this association from 1972 to 1980. During this time, the association donated substantial amounts of money to the school in the form of outright grants, but it also covered many of the school's basic operating costs, including its utility bills and officials' travel expenses. Crucially, for at least part of this time, the association directly paid the salaries of Padre Solano and most of the ESJ23's administrative staff.[50] In this sense, school representatives were effectively treated as employees of the Asociación de Empresarios Pro-Justicia Social y Paz and the school could be viewed as a subsidiary of the association.

The association was dissolved in 1980, but this did not spell the end of corporate financing for the ESJ23. Over the years, national and international companies, particularly in the banana industry, have donated large sums of the money to the ESJ23 through the Fundación Juan XXIII, the fundraising organization set up by Padre Solano to support school programs. Reports indicate that substantial amounts have been donated by the Asociación de Bananeros Nacionales (ASBANA), the Banana Development Corporation (BANDECO), the Standard Fruit Company, the United Fruit Company, and Piñas de Costa Rica (PINDECO), a pineapple producer.[51] Beyond these large-scale donations, it should also be noted that, when workers from banana plantations attend courses at the school's training centre in Tres Ríos, it is the banana companies themselves who select the workers and pay for their course fees.[52] Conversely, when school promoters hold meetings on company plantations, it is generally the company that covers such costs associated with holding the meetings and printing pamphlets.[53] Through these means, large companies in Costa Rica with an interest in perpetuating *solidarismo* have underwritten many of the ESJ23's expenses.

A final important source of private funding for the ESJ23 comes from the revenue generated by the school's provision of services to the business community at large. Apart from hosting its *solidarista* training activities at the Tres Ríos installation, the school also generates income from renting out parts of this facility as a convention centre. Companies can host their own private retreats, meetings, and conferences on the school grounds, and pay the school for the use of such facilities as meeting rooms, auditoria, and lodging and dining space.[54] Although this is a more indirect source of financing for school activities, it nevertheless serves to reinforce the already strong ties between the school and Costa Rica's business elite.

The relationship that has developed between the ESJ23 and the corporate class in Costa Rica can best be described as symbiotic. The school does rely heavily on income from private-sector funding—so much so that, without such funding, the very ability of the school to maintain its staff and programming would be doubtful. Yet, the school offers business leaders much in return: the practical promotion and the religious legitimation of a form of labour association that is ideally suited to corporate needs. Solidarismo's insistent doctrine of class unity functions to obfuscate the conflict between labourers on and owners of Costa Rican plantations, thereby hampering the development of a class consciousness among workers and hindering their efforts to transform the inequitable structures under which they labour. The anti-*sindicalismo* and anti-communist bias of *solidarismo* and the school also helps to pre-empt labour activism on plantations. This is particularly important in a region, such as Limón, where historically unions have been combative and strikes have been costly to business. The investment that certain corporate leaders have made in the ESJ23 has thus paid handsome dividends in the form of developing a docile labour force whose members are encouraged only to cultivate the right attitudes, not left-wing activism.

♦ Alliances with the State

Apart from the symbiotic relationship that the ESJ23 engages in with Costa Rica's business elite, Padre Solano as its director has himself long maintained several noteworthy alliances with the country's political powerbrokers. In the past, Solano served as chaplain for the Costa Rican Public Forces (1978–95) and spent more than a decade (1984–95) on the board of directors of the Costa Rican Social Security Bureau.[56] He maintains close ties with government officials and, for example, is reported to have weekly meetings with the Costa Rican president and regular sessions with the minister of labour.[57] Both in his role as director of the ESJ23 and in extradirectorial endeavours, Padre Solano has become a notable player in Costa Rican political life, thereby securing privileges and prestige for the school and for himself.

Even though whatever occurs during Solano's meetings with political leaders cannot be known, the esteem that government leaders hold for *solidarismo* and the ESJ23 is no secret. Government officials, for example, frequently attend and speak at special events at the school.[58] That *solidarismo* is highly regarded by the government is also evident in a two-page newspaper item that appeared in January 1990 in *El Diario Extra*. This article heralds *solidarismo* as a "national pride" and features pictures of, and lengthy quotations from, key Costa Rican political leaders, including then-president Oscar Arias as well as nine former presidents and presidential candidates from both major political parties.[59] The politicians in this article pay tribute to the wonders of *solidarismo* and, often, to the importance of the school's work; with their references to *solidarismo* as a "brilliant idea," the "best labour formula," and the "essence of democracy," these politicians' enthusiasm for the *solidarista* model is unmistakable. Interestingly, as well, at least one of these politicians, former president Monge, once wrote to President Reagan in the United States in similarly glowing terms about the contributions the solidarity movement has made to peace and democracy in Costa Rica.[60]

With such friends and admirers in high places, it is not surprising that Padre Solano has been able to secure domestic and international government funding for the school. In the past, the ESJ23 has received financial assistance from the Costa Rican government and from the embassies of the United States, Guatemala, Chile, and Israel. Such organizations as the Pan American Development Foundation, USAID, and the Canadian International Development Agency (CIDA) have also contributed funds to the ESJ23.[61] Within Costa Rica, Solano has been feted with honours on various occasions, having received the Freedom Prize from the National Association for Economic Advancement (1983), and having been named "Costa Rican of the Year" (1981) and "Forger of Democracy" (1988).[62] With the exception of Monseñor Arrieta, no other Church leader in recent Costa Rican history has attained such close connections with the government and such a high public profile.

The reasons government representatives look upon Padre Solano and the ESJ23 with such favour are no mystery. The doctrine and *solidarista* labour model associated with the school fit well with the needs of a state attempting to respond to socio-economic crises through neo-liberalism.[63] The school's emphasis on co-operation and class collaboration corresponds to the government's pleas for everyone to tighten their belts and adhere to the austerity measures demanded by international lending institutions. The ideals of solidarity and social peace emphasized by the ESJ23 are consistent with the state's appeals, in the face of escalating popular protests, to the pacific and democratic character of the Costa Rican people. *Solidarismo* itself can help the country to offer the lower wages, weak union presence, and generally undemanding workforce so attractive to the foreign investors on whose capital Costa Rica is dependent to help service its heavy debt. The school has thus functioned as an important ideological ally in the government's attempts to impose neo-liberal demands on its citizens.

In return, Padre Solano and the school have benefitted immensely and far beyond the tangible rewards such as government funding. Solano's good relations and ideological similarities with Costa Rican politicians undoubtedly played a role in his successful efforts to gain legal recognition for the *solidarista* phenomenon. In 1979, Solano and the ESJ23 presented the Costa Rican legislative assembly with a draft of proposed legislation defining the scope and functions of solidarity associations. This law, which was passed in 1984, accords *solidarismo* juridical status and legal protection under the state. In 1991, also under the initiative and advice of Solano and the ESJ23, President Calderón promulgated a series of supplementary regulations to the law, further entrenching the solidarity movement's position in the structure of Costa Rican society.[64]

Padre Solano and school materials cite this law repeatedly, treating it almost as if it were a badge of honour. They also make frequent mention of the fact that both the constitution and the Labour Code contain articles explicitly based upon the "Christian principles of social justice,"[65] thereby establishing a further link between the school—which, of course, is also emphasized to be based on Catholic social teaching—and Costa Rican political institutions. On prominent display in the courtyard of the school's headquarters is a firm reminder of this link: a fountain has been constructed in part from railings taken from the site of the country's first legislative assembly. The accolades heaped upon the work of Solano and the ESJ23 by past and present politicians work to reinforce this image of the school as closely tied to the political infrastructure of the nation.

From the point of view of the ESJ23, all this is highly advantageous in a country where, regardless of public favour or disfavour toward the actual holders of political office, the citizenry in general looks on Costa Rica's democratic heritage and its legislative foundations with a great deal of pride. Hence, beyond the legitimacy conferred on the ESJ23 and its message through the use of Catholic social teaching, the credibility of the institution is also enhanced by its apparently close relationship with the Costa Rican democratic tradition. In Costa Rica, any organization that can thus imply the support of both the Catholic Church and the state is powerful indeed.

♦ Archdiocesan Support

Importantly, when it comes to the Archdiocese of San José and the figure of Monseñor Arrieta, Padre Solano and the ESJ23 can do more than just imply the support of the Church. While the archdiocese does not provide any direct financing for school activities, Monseñor Arrieta does supply other forms of backing that have been essential in bolstering the school's position in Costa Rica and within the Costa Rican Church institution. In terms of material assistance, the archdiocese has donated buildings and land to the school. In 1987, for example, Arrieta oversaw the transfer of the archdiocesan seminary in Tres Ríos to the ESJ23.[66] This gift of the seminary, which now serves as the base for many of the ESJ23's training and educational activities, was crucial in helping the school to increase the reach of its *solidarista* message. In addition, owning the Tres Ríos property has also allowed the school to rent space and sell services to corporate Costa Rica, which itself provides funding for the school and further cements the ties school leaders maintain with the business sector. None of these endeavours would have been possible had the school been restricted to operating out of the relatively modest Curridabat offices; the donation of the seminary has made a decisive contribution to the growth and financial stability of the ESJ23.

In non-material terms, Monseñor Arrieta's accolades for *solidarismo* and the labours of the school have been public and unequivocal. On several occasions, Arrieta has praised *solidarismo* as an effective means for resolving social problems between workers and employers harmoniously. Referring to it as a "very Costa Rican instrument," he has also called *solidarismo* the "best option" for workers, and the form of labour association that "preserves the most faithful relation to the supreme commandment that Jesus left us, that of love."[67] Consistent with such an evaluation, he has contested charges that *solidarismo* benefits the owners only. Moreover, and despite the evidence to the contrary cited above, Arrieta insists that the expansion of the movement has not been reached to the detriment of social justice.[68] He has thus lauded the ESJ23 for its "faithful devotion to the irrenunciable principles of justice," and has given thanks for the work of both Padre Solano and the school in spreading Catholic social teaching and putting its principles into practice in Costa Rica.[69]

Monseñor Arrieta's support for *solidarismo* is not surprising, given that he shares Padre Solano's conviction that dialogue and collaboration are preferable to confrontation and conflict when it comes to dealing with social problems. It is also consistent with the archbishop's own ties to Costa Rica's political and economic leaders. A photograph taken in 1987 at the archbishop's palace, featuring Arrieta receiving a hefty donation for the ESJ23 from BANDECO and PINDECO officials, symbolizes the importance of the archbishop's allegiances for the school.[70] That the archbishop has chosen to ignore and even deny charges of unjust practices on the plantations is a further indication of his approval for the mission of the school and its *solidarista* promoters. Such sanction from the leader of the Costa Rican Church provides a valuable form of legitimation for a movement that has faced condemnation from national and international unions for its actions.

Finally, archdiocesan support for the ESJ23 functions to reinforce the position of the school over and against the official Church in Limón. As I shall discuss in the next chapter, Limón Church representatives not only enact a *pastoral obrera* that falls at the opposite end of the ideological spectrum from the ESJ23, its officials have also publicly criticized the tactics used by school promoters in the region. Perhaps more importantly, several members of the Limón clergy (including the former bishop himself) have complained that, as an archdiocesan institution, the school has no right to operate in the Diocese of Limón.[71] Padre Solano, for his part, proclaims that he "does not need a passport" to enter into any diocese and work in the field of labour relations.[72] Yet, even though the Church's established jurisdictional guidelines indicate that Solano is mistaken and that Limón Church officials have every right to determine the parameters for pastoral activity in their own diocese, the archbishop persists in offering Solano and the school his blessings. That Monseñor Arrieta would side with the ESJ23 in this way provides a noteworthy example of the archdiocese's subordination of the official Church in Limón. And while the Limonense clergy are forced to contend with this significant threat to the institutional strength of their local Church, the ESJ23 continues to operate with impunity in their diocese.

Conclusion

The ESJ23 provides a second example of a conservative *pastoral obrera* in the Costa Rican Catholic Church. As was the case with Monseñor Arrieta and CECOR, the ESJ23 promotes a workers' pastorate consistent with the stream of Catholic social teaching that emphasizes unity over conflict, and collaboration over confrontation. From this perspective, problems in society are attributable to faulty attitudes and flawed mentalities; by extension, they can be resolved through a renovation of the spiritual, not a transformation of the structural. In fact, the idea of societal restructuring raises for the ESJ23 the dreaded spectre of communism, with the violence and hatred that threatens to infect workers and other good Costa Ricans through the union movement charged with bearing this godless ideology. That the well-being of workers is ultimately sacrificed in the battle against *sindicalismo*, however, appears of little consequence in light of the ESJ23's overriding mandate to promote *solidarismo*, the form of labour organization legitimated by the conservative Catholic social teaching of the school.

While the primary components of the ESJ23's socio-religious doctrine are drawn from the social teaching tradition of the Catholic Church, the precise form this doctrine takes is clearly influenced by variables external to the Church. The close alliances that school officials have formed with Costa Rica's business and political leaders have no doubt affected the shape of the organization's *pastoral obrera*. In other terms, one can say that the ESJ23's pastoral discourse expresses the interests and the agenda of the social sectors on whom its survival depends. In the words of a popular Costa Rican saying: *quien paga la orquestra, manda el baile* (whoever pays the orchestra, controls the dance).[73] Consistent with the case of the archbishop as I have described it, the close relationship that the ESJ23 maintains with Costa Rica's political and economic elites affects the organization's ideological production at a deep level.

Still, a further question remains. Although the ESJ23 is an archdiocesan organization fully sanctioned by Monseñor Arrieta himself, although both the archbishop and the school share the same basic political-economic perspective, and although the school's interpretation and employment of Church teachings clearly resonate with that emanating from the archdiocese, there is one crucial difference between these two expressions of Catholic social teaching. Whereas Monseñor Arrieta has made frequent use of the language associated with the liberationists — to advance an agenda that is nonetheless conservative—ESJ23 representatives are loath to employ any liberationist terminology themselves in pursuit of goals that are essentially the same as the archbishop's. Why is it, therefore, that the archbishop clearly finds it advantageous to co-opt the concepts of the liberationists, while Padre Solano, whose position is so similar to that of archbishop in so many other respects, clearly does not?

The answer lies in the differing institutional characteristics and needs of the two parties. As I have argued, Monseñor Arrieta, as archbishop of San José, sees himself as head of the Church in Costa Rica and therefore must appear to be responsive, whatever his true alliances and agenda may be, to all factions within his Church. By adopting the terms of the liberationists yet adapting them to serve a conservative message, he can demonstrate his institution's relevance to both the left and right within the Church. Arrieta's official support of both the ESJ23 (which leans vehemently to the right) and CECODERS (which leans cautiously to the left) is another way to cover two disparate ideological bases in terms of pastoral programming.[74]

Padre Solano, by contrast, as head of a relatively small and specialized organization, need not appear to be responsive to the same range of Catholic social teaching perspectives. Since his school is technically independent of the archdiocese, at least in terms of funding, Solano is not bound to replicate the breadth of the archbishop's appeal. Further, workers themselves do not ultimately determine the success or failure of the organization: most attend ESJ23 classes because their managers tell them to, many join solidarity associations because their jobs may depend on it. Thus, there is little motivation for the ESJ23 to affect the liberationist discourse that may be more attuned to workers' life experiences and needs. In fact, an appeal to liberationist concepts could potentially alienate the very groups on which the school does depend—the owners and representatives of the large agro-export companies. Given the ESJ23's position within the Church and within Costa Rican society, the gain to be achieved by appearing to adopt elements of the liberationist world view would be relatively small compared to the risk entailed.

Taken altogether, what I argue in this chapter indicates that, contrary to the assertions of school representatives, Solano does not use *solidarismo* as a "Trojan horse" to spread Catholic social teaching among the people. While the analogy is an apt one to describe the tactics and effect of the ESJ23's work, the elements are reversed. In Limón, it is Catholic social teaching and religious representatives that are used as the vehicles importing the solidarity movement into the banana plantations. Legitimated by its association with the Church, *solidarismo* is implanted among the workers by the Trojan horse that is the ESJ23. In place of the peace and harmony promised by Padre Solano and the solidarity movement, however, is a misrepresentation of reality, a suppression of dissent, and a disrespect for workers' rights. Far from bringing socio-economic salvation to Limonense banana workers and their families, the ESJ23 instead contributes to their continued exploitation.

The Official Church in Limón 9

We are in solidarity with those who suffer,
not with those who take advantage of this pain.
—Monseñor Coto and Limón priests (on behalf
of protesters occupying the Limón cathedral)

The case of the official Church in Limón can be considered the opposite of that presented in the previous chapter. Where the *pastoral obrera* of the ESJ23 is conservative, that of the Limón Church is liberationist. In this chapter, I explore the forms that this official workers' pastorate takes in Limón and seek to uncover the reasons for their progressivism. Of particular significance here is the discussion of the pastoral letter issued in 1989 by the Limón Church under the leadership of Monseñor Coto. This important document, the effects of which were felt well into the episcopate of Coto's successor, Monseñor Ulloa, constitutes the Limón Church's unique contribution to the corpus of Costa Rican Catholic social teaching. Yet as we shall see, the *carta pastoral* is also one of the key texts that can serve to reveal the fascinating manner in which the worldwide body of Catholic social teaching, that emanating chiefly from the Vatican, can be employed to advance particularly Limonense local needs.

The Limón Church under Monseñor Coto

Monseñor Alfonso Coto Monge was made a bishop and named apostolic vicar of Limón on March 7, 1980. This appointment was unique and noteworthy for several reasons. To begin with, Coto had the honour of being the first Costa Rican priest elevated to the role, as the four bishops in Limón prior to him were all German. Second, although the standard practice in the Catholic Church is to entrust the leadership of an apostolic vicariate to a member of a religious order (in Limón, the tradition had been to appoint a Vincentian priest to the role), Monseñor Coto was a diocesan priest.[1] Even more important than Coto's nationality or clerical designation, however, was his personality. Tellingly, one of Coto's first acts as bishop was to donate his episcopal ring to the community of Corales so that they could use the funds generated from its sale to construct a communal chapel.[2] At the time, this was seen as a sign of poverty and of solidarity with the poor; in the following years, it became clear that this gesture was not merely for show but was in fact a sincere symbol of the bishop's commitment to the people of Limón. Indeed, Monseñor Coto was to go on to become one of the foremost liberationists within the Costa Rican Catholic Church—a true advocate for the poor in Limón.

After he was named bishop, Coto spent the first few months of his appointment travelling and visiting the parishes and CEBs in the vicariate; in this way, he witnessed the problems and concerns faced by members of the Church throughout Limón province. Later in 1980 he issued his first pastoral letter, the bulk of which was devoted to routine administrative matters (e.g., the appropriate amounts to charge for baptisms and marriages).[3] In this exhortation, Monseñor Coto also commented that on his tour he had become aware of the scarcity of priests in the area and had "encountered communities that are like 'sheep without a pastor' exposed to the danger of losing their faith in the face of the constant, insidious and bold propaganda of certain Protestant sects or social agitators."[4] It is significant to note that, in light of such threats, Coto proposed the strengthening of the CEBs in the vicariate. He treated them much as the bishops at Puebla had done in the previous year—as groups focused primarily on spiritual enrichment and not necessarily on social action.[5] In fact, Monseñor Coto made no direct mention of social justice issues in this document.

Nonetheless, the new bishop was given the chance to demonstrate his practical concern for the poor in the same month that this statement was released. While the members of Costa Rica's legislative assembly were meeting in Limón, a group of *campesinos* occupied the Limón cathedral to try to pressure the government to listen to their concerns regarding land distribution. On hearing this news, Monseñor Coto left his seat of honour in the gymnasium where the assembly was meeting and went to listen to the *campesinos*. The following day, the bishop, along with three priests from the area, published a strongly worded communiqué supporting the *campesinos* and petitioning the government to meet their demands. In this statement, the bishop and priests explicitly announced their "preferential option for the poor" and their solidarity and identification with the poor *campesinos*.[6] Even before the end of his first year as bishop, then, Coto was already beginning to demonstrate his concern for social justice in Limón.

In 1981, Monseñor Coto convened an assembly of clergy, religious, and lay people from the vicariate. The conclusions of the six-day meeting emphasized a "pastoral option" for CEBs and, this time, mention was made of the commitment of such groups to working for social justice.[7] From this point, Coto organized such meetings in the vicariate at least once a year; they became a crucial arena for discussing social problems in Limón province and for involving lay people in the decision-making process of the Church in Limón. Over the years, the meetings became an important means for the clergy and other concerned Catholics to collaborate in evaluating the previous year's pastoral work and charting future plans of the Limón Church. By the late 1980s, the two characteristic features of these assemblies—pastoral planning based on an awareness of the social reality in the region and significant participation by lay persons—had been incorporated more formally into the overall pastoral work of the vicariate.[8]

The dual emphasis, which is unique in the Costa Rican Church, was evident in several projects and aspects of the vicariate's work. First, Church officials made a concerted effort to obtain a more accurate indication of the pastoral problems and socio-economic context of the vicariate. To this end, a detailed social scientific study, somewhat like a census, was conducted in 1987-88.[9] This diagnostic study was co-ordinated by CECODERS, but the real labour power came from hundreds of pastoral agents located in the vicariate. Working in small teams, Church members spread throughout Limón province, going door-to-door to collect data on such subjects as household composition and income, occupations, and health; they also gathered information on people's religious affiliation and solicited opinions about the Church's work.

The eventual analysis of the thousands of information forms completed indicated, with statistical formality, the extremity of the problems in Limón that delegates to the bishop's annual meetings had long been reporting. But, and perhaps more importantly, the process of conducting the survey had had—to use Paulo Freire's concept—a conscientizing effect on the participants.[10] The pastoral agents who went into the field saw with their own eyes the poverty and problems experienced by their neighbours; they heard at first hand the difficulties that many were facing in their struggles to survive. Some of the CEBs were able to reinforce this consciousness-raising experience by sponsoring meetings at which the pastoral workers could share their impressions and attempt to discuss the preliminary results in the light of scripture and Catholic social teaching. Through such activities, members at all levels of the Church in Limón became more sensitized to the socio-economic injustices in the province and more committed to overcoming them.

At about the same time that the diagnostic surveys and discussions were being carried out in Limón, more resources and attention were being devoted to developing the formal structure of the vicariate's *pastoral social*. In 1988, Padre Gerardo Vargas assumed responsibility for what came to be known as the Comisión Diocesana de Pastoral Social (Diocesan Social Pastoral Commission). Vargas notes that, when he took over from Padre Esquivel (who had co-ordinated the *pastoral social* work in the region to this point), Esquivel handed him one box of papers and a bank book show-ing the equivalent of a few hundred dollars in the Church's *pastoral social* account. From this modest start Vargas, drawing on the interest and sup-port of Monseñor Coto, was able to procure office space and equipment, an archive, a small support staff and, eventually, two vehicles for the com-mission's work. In the following years, the commission grew to co-ordi-nate five main areas: production (securing credit for microenterprises, such as small agricultural or artisanal projects); popular housing (rebuilding housing after natural disasters); human rights (conscientization and legal advocacy work, mainly involving migrant workers in the Atlantic coastal region); education and training (arranging workshops and seminars, and producing popular education materials); and the *pastoral de la tierra* (land pastorate, dealing with issues of land distribution and organic farming).[11]

Decision making and projects related to each of these five areas are han-dled by one of a series of democratically appointed and accountable com-mittees. At the most basic level, each parish in Limón elects a Parish Social Pastoral Commission. From this local committee, two people are elected to represent their community in one of the three Vicarial Social Pastoral Commissions in the region. Finally, each of these vicarial commissions elects two of its members to the co-ordinating body for the region, the Diocesan Social Pastoral Commission. Padre Vargas works most closely with this latter commission, which ultimately defines the mission and programs for the Church in the region as a whole. Crucially, however, information, suggestions, and concerns flow both ways up and down this three-tiered structure, thereby involving members from all levels and loca-tions in the Limón Church. This structure is important because it helps to democratize power in the region's Church by encouraging lay participa-tion in *pastoral social* work and by formalizing channels for this partici-pation. Although it is true that Padre Vargas, the diocesan commission, and Monseñor Coto are the chief official figures in the *pastoral social* of the Limón Church, and although they function as its representatives to the world outside the region, internally, the power structure of the local Church has become relatively horizontal.[12]

The diagnostic census and the democratic organizational structure that developed within the Church in Limón were both essential to the production of its *Plan Global de Pastoral (Overall Pastoral Plan)*.[13] The plan, the first of its kind in Costa Rica, grew out of the discussions of the census that took place in the vicariate's assemblies of 1988 and 1989; it was formulated with the help of a pastoral advisor from CELAM. The introduction to the plan states that it was meant to "stimulate lines of pastoral action that will help [all members of the Church in Limón] dis-cover paths toward a new kind of Church, incarnate in and committed to the realities of the vicariate, in order to achieve an integral transforma-tion of people and of structures."[14] This emphasis on both personal and social transformation, which is found in other points of the document as well, is a key element in the liberationist tradition.[15]

Tellingly, the plan also reveals some of the worries of the pastoral agents in Limón regarding, for example, injustices in the world of work (especially in relation to *solidarismo*),[16] Protestant sects,[17] and the insufficient number of pastoral workers in the Church.[18] These passages, it should be stressed, were included in a document that was to serve as the guide for future pastoral work in the vicariate. As such, they helped to reinforce the perception that the Church as an institution, and its members who were workers, were threatened.

Finally, the document spells out the main areas for pastoral action: the family, training of laity, CEBs, *pastoral social*, and youth.[19] These areas were accorded priority in part, the plan states, because they open up more spaces for lay participation in the Church and because they favour the poor. Of the five priorities listed, the area of *pastoral social* is the most relevant to this study. It is said to be a "liberating" pastorate, one that operates from a "preferential option for the poor," "attacks" all forms of poverty, and continually analyzes and reflects on the socio-economic reality of the vicariate. Interestingly, the Church here also states its intent to "develop and promote a *pastoral social* with the workers of the banana plantations."[20] In fact, Church agents began this task immediately after the *Overall Pastoral Plan* was formulated and, as I show below, they continued to work on it throughout the 1990s.

By the end of the 1980s, then, Monseñor Coto and members from all levels of the Church in Limón were tackling the problems of the Church and of the world around them. The structure of the *pastoral social* had been formalized and a variety of programs for conscientization were in place. Nonetheless, at this point, these activities were all largely contained within the vicariate itself, and they attracted relatively little attention and commentary from Church and secular representatives outside Limón. All this was to change suddenly, however, with the release of a certain *carta pastoral* in 1989.

The 1989 *Carta Pastoral*

On December 25, 1989, a pastoral letter was released in the Apostolic Vicariate of Limón.[21] Interestingly, Monseñor Coto and the clergy of Limón issued the document. This collaboration was quite unusual because, in general in the Catholic Church, pastoral letters are signed by a bishop alone or, in the case of a collective episcopal letter, by a conference of bishops. The only other exceptions to this rule in Latin America have been some of the documents issued by certain bishops in Brazil and by the late Monseñor Oscar Romero of El Salvador.[22] That the authorship of the Limón letter is attributed to the bishop and the priests collectively is significant because it reflects the process of participatory communication and document formulation that had occurred prior to the release of the letter.[23]

As I have noted, representatives of the Church in Limón did have a tradition of meeting to discuss social concerns, and they did have access to the results of the detailed survey of problems in the area compiled by CECODERS. These consultations and the study had confirmed the impression that the living and working conditions on the banana plantations in particular needed to be addressed. Hence, in October 1989, a three-day workshop was held in which the bishop, priests, and some lay representatives from the region examined the conditions on banana plantations and the nature of *sindicalismo* and *solidarismo* in the Limón region. Initially, the delegates at this workshop wrote only a brief pronouncement on the proposed government plan to convert 21,000 additional hectares of Costa Rican land to banana cultivation. At the behest of Monseñor Coto, however, they revised and expanded this document and released it as the pastoral letter in December.[24] While by all accounts the bishop was instrumental in the formulation and publication of the *carta pastoral*, as the letter's byline indicates, the final document was a product of genuine collaboration.

If the authorship of this pastoral letter was unusual, then its contents were extraordinary—at least in the context of the contemporary Costa Rican Church. As I have discussed, many recent Costa Rican pastoral letters have been rather moderate documents, full of vague suggestions and indirect criticism. In the Limón letter, by contrast, the bishop and priests condemn and denounce the uncontrolled expansion of the banana industry in the country. Further, they link this expansion to a variety of socio-economic problems, arguing, for example, that the conditions of banana production compromise human dignity and foment alcoholism, drug addiction, prostitution, and violence.[25] The family structure and children's education are also said to suffer as a result of the continual migration and employment instability in the industry.[26] More broadly, Coto and the priests attack the dependency on transnational corporations and monocropping (the production of a single crop),[27] the concentration of land ownership in the hands of a few companies,[28] and the widespread environmental degradation that characterize the Limón region.[29]

Specifically in reference to labour issues, the *carta pastoral* discusses the activities of the ESJ23 and broaches the controversial topic of the conflict between *sindicalismo* and *solidarismo* in Limón. The ESJ23, as I have discussed, receives a great deal of its funding from the banana companies and devotes itself largely to spreading *solidarismo* throughout Limón. Further, school representatives have been accused of helping banana company officials to root out and fire union sympathizers on plantations, and there is widespread evidence that workers are pressured by plantation officials to join solidarity associations in order to secure their jobs. Commenting on these situations, the pastoral letter criticizes the imposition of one model of labour organization to the exclusion of others and denounces the resulting violation of such workers' rights as the right of freedom of association and the right to strike.[30] Although the pastoral letter does not mention *solidarismo* by name at this point, it makes the link clear from further references to unjustified firings and to the denial of employment to workers affiliated with the "opposing" form of labour organization.[31] There is also a plea in the letter for adequate legal protection for the union movement.[32] In the final section of the *carta pastoral*, the work of the ESJ23 is declared to have no relation to the Church in Limón or to its pastoral goals, and the danger of identifying Catholic social teaching with the *solidarismo* movement is underscored.[33] With these statements, the Church in Limón places itself in direct opposition to the banana industry and its influential religious supporters based in the Archdiocese of San José.

The bishop and priests outline the pastoral tasks for the Church in Limón in the conclusion to their pastoral letter. These include a concentration on the Church's social pastorate in the region and the promotion of CEBs as a means of both deepening the people's faith and their commitment to societal transformation.[34] This focus on CEBs is consistent with the Limón Church's decision to produce a popular version of the pastoral letter, rather bluntly entitled *La expansión bananera incontrolada (The Uncontrolled Expansion of the Banana Industry)*.[35]

The significance of this popular pastoral document deserves some comment. In Costa Rica, many important Church documents are published in the daily national newspapers or the weekly Catholic periodical *Eco Católico;* they are generally reproduced verbatim and, hence, may not be entirely comprehensible to significant segments of the population. By contrast, the popular version of the 1989 *carta pastoral*, with its simplified language and humorous illustrations, was much more widely accessible. In fact, this version was produced with the intent that it be used as a basis for reflection in the parishes and CEBs of the region. This ensured that the letter did not remain a wordy text full of references to unfamiliar theological concepts and papal encyclicals, but was instead transformed into a tool for popular conscientization. The production of a popular version of the document, along with the collaboration that went into writing it, reflects the growing democratization of the Church in Limón: not only the bishop issues the letter, and not only the literate elite are privy to its contents.

In addition, the popular version of the *carta pastoral* most clearly displays the Limón Church's commitment to an inductive liberationist methodology (one already implied by the formal version of the letter). The popular text first divides the original document into eight central themes for study and discussion, among them "Human Dignity," "Current Economic Policies," "The Sphere of Labour," and "Environmental Health and Ecological Imbalance." Each theme is then subdivided into the three categories of "seeing," "judging," and "acting." Seeing involves stating, and illustrating with cartoons, the conditions and problems in the region; judging takes the form of brief quotations from Catholic social teaching (drawn from both papal and CELAM documents); and the acting sections contain themes for further discussion, along with suggestions for demanding legislative changes and for community and pastoral activities. Through this format, the popular version of the 1989 *carta pastoral* contributes to the recognition of and challenge to the socio-economic situation in Limón, and does so for the benefit of those most affected by that situation: poor workers and their families. Importantly, the popular letter offers those with few economic resources and little concrete power immediate and specific suggestions for actions that can contribute to the overcoming of their unjust socio-economic positions. Taken together, then, the official *carta pastoral* and its popular incarnation represent the liberationist wing of official Costa Rican Catholic social teaching.

♦ The Aftermath of the Pastoral Letter

In the months following its Christmas release, the *carta pastoral* generated widespread media attention and controversy. A flurry of articles and editorials related to the letter were published in early 1990, and they revealed quickly polarizing opinions. Representatives of banana companies, the government, the solidarity movement, and much of the mainstream press attacked the document variously as inflammatory, inaccurate, counter-productive, and tainted with extremist or communist views.[36] On the other hand, the editor of *Eco Católico* and certain contributors to *La Nación* backed Monseñor Coto and the Limón clergy. Arnoldo Mora in *La Nación*, for example, remarked that the letter was a "great Christmas gift" for Costa Ricans.[37]

Opinions were also divided in the official Costa Rican Church. Monseñor Coto and his priests stood firmly behind their document, releasing in January of 1990 their own press declaration that sought to clarify the intent and content of the letter in response to what they labelled the "distortions" of the truth that were "venomously launched" against them by those with "vested interests."[38] A group of priests from the neighbouring Diocese of Tilarán took out a half-page signed advertisement in the Catholic press to declare their support for the Church in Limón;[39] these priests were rumoured to have done so, however, against the wishes of their own bishop.[40] In fact, the official Costa Rican Church showed no support for the Limón bishop and clergy: not even a telegram was sent to Coto from his colleagues in the episcopate. As one priest from Limón remarked (with a certain bitterness), given the wave of criticism and pressures that the Church in Limón had to tolerate, some minimal show of solidarity could have been offered.[41] Thus, while the Limón Church was united throughout this process, the bishop and priests were also quite isolated from the rest of the Costa Rican Church.

The effects of this very public debate should not be underestimated. The controversy surrounding the document had the effect of arousing interest outside of Limón and beyond the original audience of the letter. It thus played an important role in raising the awareness of Costa Ricans who otherwise may have remained fairly isolated from, or indifferent to, the situation on the coast. Significantly, the letter and the discussion it generated served to break the silence about the conditions in the banana industry and, as such, they were crucial steps in dispelling some of the myths that Costa Ricans had long been taught about the relative prosperity and stability of their country. In sharp contrast to Monseñor Arrieta's role in supporting the neo-liberal program of the government during this period, the bishop and clergy in Limón, with their demythologizing letter, helped to undermine the key ideological propositions of this same program.

Moreover, the release of the letter and the ensuing debate took place in the weeks leading up to the 1990 presidential elections in Costa Rica. This forced the incumbent leader, Arias, and the eventual election winner, Calderón, to address the problems in Limón. This is remarkable in that, in the past, such issues were largely absent from the political agenda. Erick Thompson, President Calderón's minister of labour, took a special interest in the issues raised by the *carta pastoral*. He organized meetings between representatives from the Limón Church and the banana companies to discuss the poor conditions on the plantations. Unfortunately, this dialogue ended when Thompson resigned from his post; some believe he was forced to do so because of pressures from some of the banana companies.[42] Nonetheless, as a result of these meetings — and, no doubt, the damaging allegations about the banana companies made public during and after the letter's release — some of the companies began to reform their behaviour. In particular, certain efforts were made to build better housing for workers and their families, housing that was located outside of the plantations and with access to potable water and sanitation services. Some companies also tried to limit the amount of environmental contamination resulting from the cultivation and processing of bananas.[43] While the conditions in the banana industry are still far from acceptable, at least the letter instigated some improvements.

Also of importance were the closer relations that the pastoral letter fomented between the local Church and certain secular social movements in Limón. Certainly, there had been a fair amount of activism and popular mobilization in Limón in the decade preceding the release of the *carta pastoral*. During this period, however, the unions and popular organizations generally did not have much of a relationship with the Church in Limón, in large part because they perceived it to be *"dormida, bendita, sometida"* ("asleep, blessed, and submissive").[44] The 1989 *carta pastoral* served to dispel this perception and draw these parties closer together in a variety of ways.

▶ *The Limón Church and the Union Movement*

The change in the relationship between the Limón Church and the union movement was noticeable soon after the letter's release in December 1989. For example, approximately one month following the letter's publication, when the public controversy over the document was in full swing, the Consejo Permanente de los Trabajadores (CPT, Permanent Workers' Council) — a coalition of the largest union centrals in the country — issued a public statement defending Monseñor Coto and the priests.[45] The coalition's statement applauded the Limón Church and affirmed that its own members shared the letter's perspective; further, it linked those who attacked the pastoral letter to economic interests and practices incompatible with the social teaching of the Church. In July 1990, at about the time the popular version of the pastoral letter was released, the CPT held a workshop, along with ASEPROLA and the Apostolic Vicariate of Limón, for fifty union representatives and twenty members of the Limón Church.[46] This Church/Unionism Forum, as it was called, provided an opportunity to discuss the challenges to *sindicalismo* in the banana sector, the *solidarismo* phenomenon, and the Church's position on unionism. Although primarily an arena for reflection and the exchange of information, practically speaking the workshop served to promote more contact between Church and union representatives and to reinforce the goodwill between the two groups that had been generated by the *carta pastoral*.

In the years since then, the Church in Limón has provided a variety of services and resources to the union movement. Many parishes, for instance, have offered their meeting halls as a safe space for union meetings and organizing, a necessity in a region where the persecution of unions is common.[47] In addition, members of the Diocesan Social Pastoral Commission have co-ordinated educational workshops for union members on Catholic social teaching and have attended union meetings as guest speakers. Together, union and Church members work on community service projects and continue to meet to discuss social problems in Limón. In such activities, the relationship between the Church and the banana unions has been especially strong.[48] As a result, unions of banana plantation workers in Limón now consider the Church to be "a guiding friend who always has an open door for the banana worker."[49]

Perhaps most significant, however, has been the role that the local Church has played in labour conflicts in Limón. Formally, the bishop is routinely called on to be a mediator during strikes; in these instances, the bishop's main task is to facilitate communication between the workers and the employer, or the workers and the government, whichever is the case.[50] As mediator, the bishop must remain as impartial as possible and work to seek an expedient end to the strike (this is similar to Monseñor Arrieta's usual role as a mediator). In other cases, however, the Church will do more to side with the unions. According to Monseñor Coto, the

Church will officially support union strike action and demands if the unions have exhausted all channels of dialogue in search of solutions, and if they agree to renounce all violence. Only if such conditions are met, stresses Coto, will the Church step in and support the unions in their struggle.[51]

At a less formal level, and at lower strata of the Church, assistance to the unions in times of conflict appears to be less conditional. While such support has not always been publicly declared, Padre Vargas reports that: "We have always been in favour of the strike. Because the strikes here have been in defence of the workers, we have supported the struggles."[52] Members of the Diocesan Social Pastoral Commission, for example, have provided food and information for striking workers and have lent strikers office support (e.g., access to telephones) and vehicles. Padre Vargas is firm: "We have a very clear position on this. Here [in Limón], we first of all support the worker."[53]

▶ *Foro Emaús*

At about the same time as the Church/Unionism Forum was developing and the popular version of the *carta pastoral* was released, Church agents in Limón began to organize and participate in workshops to discuss the themes of the pastoral letter and the controversy surrounding it. These workshops continued on an occasional basis over the next two years and drew a variety of participants, at times including journalists, environmentalists, academics, development activists, representatives from other Christian churches, indigenous peoples' representatives, members of *campesino* movements, and unionists. In June 1992, a large forum of this kind met in Casa Emaús, a pastoral centre in Puerto Limón, to discuss the uncontrolled banana expansion in Limón and Sarapiquí. There, they made a decision to build a formal coalition, "Foro Emaús," to work together to protect human rights and the environment in the Atlantic banana region.

Soon after its formation, the coalition decided to move from intragroup dialogue to externally directed activism. Their first formal activity was the elaboration of the public declaration entitled "Stop the Uncontrolled Banana Expansion," which was published in half-page advertisements in Costa Rican national newspapers. A few months later, in September 1992, Foro Emaús co-ordinated a well-attended "March for Life and Human Rights" in the capital city, San José, to protest the destructive nature of the banana industry. The following month another march was co-ordinated in San José, this time to demonstrate solidarity with the indigenous peoples in Limón, whose land had been invaded by the banana companies and whose way of life had thereby been disrupted. Foro Emaús also began to petition the government with various proposals for revisions to the laws related to the banana industry. In addition, the coalition built an international network of support among European development and environmental organizations; through this network, Foro Emaús began to raise awareness and promote activism in countries that import Costa Rican bananas. As of 1997, Foro Emaús had thirty-five member organizations, including the Church in Limón and several public and private sector union organizations. It had also built an impressive national and international profile.[54]

Significantly, publications by Foro Emaús still refer to the 1989 *carta pastoral* and the mission of the coalition remains "to halt the uncontrolled expansion of the banana industry" in Costa Rica. With this in mind, I would suggest that, in many respects, the 1989 *carta pastoral* from Limón was to the Costa Rican Church what the documents from the 1968 Medellín conference were to the Latin American Church as a whole. These controversial texts all expressed some of the emerging political currents within the Church under their jurisdictions, and they all instigated and sanctioned further activism by religious agents in the political arena. And—as is still the case with the Medellín documents in Latin America today—the Limón *carta pastoral* can serve as the liberationist touchstone against which to compare other Church statements and social activism in Costa Rica.

A New Bishop in a New Diocese

In the time that has passed since the release of the *carta pastoral*, much has changed in the Church in Limón. Monseñor Coto, for example, is no longer bishop of Limón,[55] having been replaced in January 1995 by Monseñor José Francisco Ulloa Rojas. Further, at about that time, the Vatican declared the Apostolic Vicariate of Limón to be a diocese in its own right. This shift meant that the Church in Limón gained a greater degree of independence from Rome, but it also meant that it was no longer eligible to receive the financial assistance that the Holy See provides for vicariates. As a diocese, the Limón Church has had to rely on contributions from its faithful to finance its operation.[56] Given these new factors, then, it is legitimate to examine what has happened in recent years to the progressive paths originally pursued by Monseñor Coto and the pastoral agents of the Limón Church. How have the impulses sparked by the 1989 *carta pastoral* fared over these years?

In general, Monseñor Ulloa and other Church members in Limón have maintained and broadened the social and pastoral commitments developed during the 1980s and early 1990s. Immediately after his appointment, when he received a congratulatory telephone call from President José Maria Figueres, Ulloa petitioned the president for more government attention and resources to be devoted to remedying social problems in Limón. Further, Ulloa had personal meetings with Limón's representatives in the legislative assembly and with key players in the region's public institutions, with a view to achieving their collaboration in the social and economic development of Limón.[57] At about that time, the new bishop also met with union representatives from the banana industry and the port sector in Limón. These were all clear attempts by Monseñor Ulloa to indicate that he intended to continue and build on Monseñor Coto's social involvement and advocacy. Importantly, Monseñor Ulloa reported that, during the union encounters in particular, his overtures were received with "much goodwill" and openness.[58]

In the period that followed, Monseñor Ulloa proved himself a strong supporter of workers and social activists in Limón. In early 1996, for example, he came to the defence of the region's distressed dockworkers. Hundreds of labourers in the stevedore industry had been illegally dismissed and were unable to find alternate employment; many others were receiving pay below the legal minimum wage and below the level needed for subsistence. On top of this, irregularities had been reported in the managing of workers' funds by leaders of a key union in the industry, the Sindicato de Trabajadores Portuarios y Ferrocarrileros de Limón. In response, Ulloa and the other members of the ecumenical Ministerial Association of Limón (which included all of the non-Catholic churches that are considered the "historical" Protestant churches) issued a public communiqué directed to President Figueres. This letter, to which Ulloa was the first signatory, denounced the injustice of the situation, asked that the government investigate the accusations against the stevedore companies and the union, and called for the government to create more job opportunities for the unemployed dockworkers.[59] It is important to note that, although in this case Ulloa clearly acted on behalf of the dockworkers, he also did not shy away from criticizing unions when it appeared necessary.

Later that same year, nonetheless, Monseñor Ulloa and his pastoral agents did unequivocally support the unions that were involved in the Limón en Lucha movement. Ulloa refused to play the role of mediator between the government and the protesters, choosing instead to support Limón en Lucha's members and to act as the movement's chief negotiator with the government. Padre Gerardo Vargas, himself a central player in the negotiation process, explained that it was impossible for members of the Church in Limón to act as mediators in the case of Limón en Lucha because this would have imposed on them a neutrality that did not exist. From the beginning of the struggle, he averred, they had maintained a clear position in support of those who were protesting against the government and its policies.[60] Months after an agreement between the parties was reached and the protests died down, the Church continued to pressure the government to fulfil the promises made during the negotiations.[61] Much as Monseñor Coto and the Limón clergy had done with their 1989 carta pastoral, Monseñor Ulloa and the Limón Church were making a strong option for the poor in the case of Limón en Lucha.

This option was also evident in the pastoral lines pursued by Monseñor Ulloa from the beginning of his episcopate. Ulloa began his appointment with a vow to continue the pastoral programs of his predecessor; the co-ordinator of the Diocesan Social Pastoral Commission confirms that, in terms of material and moral support, the bishop has fulfilled this promise.[62] Also important in this respect is the Limón Church's second diocesan pastoral plan, intended to cover the years 1996 through 2000.[63] The first plan was meant to be in effect only until 1993, but several factors caused a delay in the writing and release of the second plan. The disruptions caused by the Church's transition from vicariate to diocese and by the change in bishops were partly responsible for the late publication of the document. In addition, however, Church representatives deemed it necessary to make revisions to the plan based on the changed historical conditions in Limón, and on the reflections and recommendations that arose out of consultations with the faithful from all levels of the Church. This meant that a further comprehensive socio-religious survey of Limón was undertaken by CECODERS, and that the laity, religious, and clergy had a chance to participate in the revision of the plan during a general pastoral assembly. The plan and the Church's pastoral priorities were then updated accordingly.[64]

The six main areas of pastoral concern in the revised diocesan plan include a mixture of traditional and newer targets of Church activity in Latin America: women, *pastoral social*, the family, CEBs, youth, education, and culture. Also, importantly, the plan indicates that in the *pastoral social*, as well as in several of the other target areas, promoting a change of both people (or "mentalities") *and* structures is a key objective of the Church's work. Finally, it is clear from the specific policies and strategies advocated that it is the laity—a trained, conscientized, and organized laity—who are intended to be the central agents in such pastoral efforts.[65]

This emphasis on a well-prepared and active laity can be seen in numerous programs and activities in the diocese. The CEBs, for example, have come to occupy an even greater role in the Church in Limón than their inclusion as only one of six pastoral priorities would suggest. In fact, the co-ordinator of the Diocesan Social Pastoral Commission indicates that the Church is working toward grounding all of the work in the diocese in the CEBs;[66] the bishop affirms that these small communities constitute the new way of "being Church" in Limón.[67] Along these lines, the commission hosts approximately fifty workshops per year for animators and other lay people within these base communities. These seminars aim to deepen lay knowledge of Catholic social teaching and other Church doctrine, and to involve lay people concretely in the execution of the diocese's pastoral plan. The Church in Limón also organizes annual assemblies at the parish and vicarial (or zonal) levels that, in addition to the yearly diocese-wide meeting, are meant to involve lay people in the process of evaluating past work and constructing future pastoral programming.[68] These assemblies are an important way to incorporate the laity into the decision-making process in the Limón Church. Hence, not only has Monseñor Ulloa vowed to consult with the clergy and committed lay people before making any changes to the pastoral orientations of the Church,[69] but these meetings at all levels of the diocese have helped to turn his rhetoric into reality.

As a result of all these efforts—which, by and large, are continuations of the programs, priorities, and structures developed during the episcopacy of Monseñor Coto—the Church in Limón has evolved into a relatively democratic institution with a fairly horizontal structure. By the estimation of the priests who have been involved in the *pastoral social*, the participation of lay people in pastoral activities and commissions has been "simply incredible" and "phenomenal"—to the point where it is considered normal that, in certain cases, a layperson will even assume the coordination of a pastoral program.[70] While the priests of course remain important religious figures in their respective parishes, in terms of the *pastoral social* of the Limón Church, the laity are responsible for the bulk of the activities, with priests playing a lesser but supportive role. In general, this grassroots orientation of the Church in Limón corresponds with one of the hallmarks of the liberationist tradition: instead of the clergy monopolizing religious production and decision making, such responsibilities are shared out among the People of God.

♦ A Developing *Pastoral Obrera* in Limón

The programs, activities, and attitudes described above clearly reveal the commitment of Limón Church agents to democracy within the Church and to justice in society. Moreover, the role played by Church representatives in the face of the exploitation of workers on the plantations and during actual labour conflicts constitutes a *pastoral obrera* in practical terms. Yet, this study still has not broached the subject of an explicit or formal *pastoral obrera* in Limón, one that is on par, for example, with that espoused in the EJS23's documents and educational materials. In fact, it has only been during the past few years that the Limón Church has made an effort to develop certain systematic guidelines for a *pastoral obrera*. As I shall indicate, however, even in its rudimentary stages the Limonense *pastoral obrera* has exhibited a character that is distinct in Costa Rica.

As early as the first pastoral plan, representatives of the Church in Limón acknowledged the need "to organize a *pastoral obrera* capable of accompanying workers in their needs and conflicts and able to offer them Christian education."[71] Few formal efforts were subsequently devoted to fulfilling this need, however, and the second pastoral plan confessed that the Church in Limón had not developed a specific pastorate in this area.[72] Once again, the creation of a *pastoral obrera* was proposed. Its outline was specific: the *pastoral obrera* was to study the condition of workers in Limón, support and promote the organization of workers in defence of their rights, educate people about workers' right to unionize and right to collective bargaining, provide for relevant training for workers in Catholic social teaching, and critically analyze the theory and practice of the solidarity movement.[73] This time, the Church followed through with its plan and concrete steps were taken to develop and promote the new pastorate.

The first phase in this process was co-ordinated by the Diocesan Social Pastoral Commission in Limón in conjunction with representatives from ASEPROLA. Together, they commissioned Dr. Jorge Arturo Chaves, a priest and economist with the Universidad Nacional de Costa Rica, to write a document that presented in a straightforward manner the fundamental principles of Catholic social teaching as they relate to the world of work. The book-length result, entitled *Magisterio social y pastoral de los trabajadores* (*The Social Magisterium and the Workers' Pastorate*), was published in 1996.

Chaves's book is meant to be an educational resource for pastoral animators and for leaders of popular organizations and unions in Limón. As such, it is written at an intermediate level of sophistication.[74] Hence, although the book aims to popularize the principles of Catholic social teaching, it is not in itself a popular educational material. In this way, it is different from, for example, the ESJ23's *The Social Doctrine of the Church*, which is a very basic workbook. Nonetheless, Chaves's work can still be classified in the same category as the ESJ23's textbook because both claim to treat Catholic social teaching in a fundamentally expository, as opposed to interpretative, manner. While the presentation of Catholic social teaching by the ESJ23 displays many of the hallmark characteristics of Catholic conservatism, however, that in *Magisterial social y pastoral de los trabajadores* contains several elements consistent with the liberationist model.

Nowhere does this become clearer than in an examination of Chaves's methodology. As with the 1989 *carta pastoral*, Chaves's book exemplifies the see/judge/act methodology of the liberationists. Hence, Chaves first analyzes the socio-economic situation in Limón and the general condition of labour in contemporary society. He then elaborates on relevant themes in Catholic social teaching, and, finally, discusses the directions for action that the reading of the historical situation and the papal and episcopal documents suggest. Throughout, Chaves's vision is sophisticated. He understands, for example, that an analysis of labour struggles must go beyond the local market, employment, and salary issues to discuss the broader trends and neo-liberal policies that dominate the global economy.[75] Moreover, Chaves's directions for action are transparently left of centre: he calls for social and economic transformation, and underscores the importance of unions in the process of social change.[76]

Still, most revealing are Chaves's comments in the judgment phase of his assessment, for it is there that he explicitly broaches the topic of how to read Catholic social teaching. For Chaves, the point is not to read Catholic social teaching, but to *reread* it—repeatedly. For him, changes to historical circumstances—be they new technologies or relationships in the labour market, new political norms in the national or international community, or the emergence of new social movements in a society—necessitate a rereading of the teachings of the magisterium. Chaves argues that the papal and episcopal texts of the past century are not to be repeated literally but, rather, are to be reinterpreted according to the demands of the changed economic and social situation.[77]

It is important to note that Chaves does not view this process as a task of the Church hierarchy or clergy alone; instead, for him, the primary responsibility rests with the members of the local communities themselves—the laity. For Chaves, Catholic social teaching must be read from the perspective of those at the base of the Church, those who themselves experience oppression and who struggle to overcome it.[78] In the end, writes Chaves, the goal of rereading Catholic social teaching is not to become more "cultured" nor to augment one's knowledge but, rather, to equip oneself to transform reality.[79] Thus, Chaves sees the Limón Church's *pastoral obrera* developing as Church representatives and the poor collaborate to analyze their social and economic reality, to reread Catholic social teaching, and to struggle to alter reality and overcome injustice.

Consistent with such convictions, representatives of the Limón Church have developed a Catholic social teaching school for laity.[80] Church agents have started to meet with a group of about twenty lay people (including some parish and union leaders) in the town of Siquirres on the fourth Sunday of every month. These meetings treat Catholic social teaching in a more systematic and long-term manner than the workshops and seminars on the topic already held at various places in the diocese. Inspired by the material and methodology outlined in Chaves's book, moreover, this study is not meant to be mere book learning. Instead, participants approach Catholic social teaching in the context of their own experiences and discussions of the social, economic, and ecological problems prevalent in Limón. They also learn about their human and legal rights, with the idea that, through such discussions and collaboration, concrete strategies for social change can be developed. Eventually, the plan is to reach more people directly through the monthly Sunday sessions and indirectly through, for example, popular education kits to be used by CEB animators, radio programs for distance education, and a bulletin that expresses the experiences and opinions of workers in the region.[81] For now, however, although this Catholic social teaching school is still in its infancy, the philosophy behind it is well defined. Significantly, one Church agent explained that Catholic social doctrine "does not make any sense if it is not meant to transform.

And injustice or, better yet, the search for justice, is the guide [*norte*] of this doctrine."[82] The approach to Catholic social teaching employed by this school is therefore consistent with the methodology exemplified in Chaves's book and that embedded in the 1989 *carta pastoral*.

The *pastoral obrera* that emerges from these processes in the Limón Church is—to adapt an important insight of Alfredo Fierro—historically and politically mediated. This is because it "incorporates social and political realities into its discourse as judgmental elements for interpreting [Catholic social teaching] and also as realities that must be evaluated in terms of [Catholic social teaching]."[83] Moreover, the *pastoral obrera* is mediated because it also involves "a practical movement that will alter the existing social situation."[84] It is clearly liberationist, then, since it is intimately linked to the experiences and struggles of the poor in Limón, as opposed to being deduced from a predetermined and inflexible doctrine that is invested with truth and authority apart from the current historical situation. In other words, this emerging *pastoral obrera* and the process that developed it are further ways in which the Church in Limón pursues an option for the poor.

The Limón Church and Catholic Social Teaching

Given the practical programs and stances on behalf of workers emerging from the Church in Limón, and given its leaders' liberationist approach to Catholic social teaching, one might expect the Limón Church's documents to draw heavily or even exclusively from those texts that represent the liberationist stream in Catholic social teaching. In other words, one might anticipate references to the Medellín conference documents to be relatively common, while expecting citation and quotation from Pope John Paul II's conservative encyclicals, such as *Sollicitudo Rei Socialis* or *Centesimus Annus*, to be minimal or perhaps even absent from the Limón texts. This would indicate a certain consistency between the actions urged or taken and the documents used to inspire or justify them.

Yet the matter is not so simple. In fact, Limón Church documents draw passages from the whole of the Catholic social teaching tradition. The infamous *carta pastoral* (both in its original form and in the popular version derived from it), for example, cites a variety of post-conciliar sources, including the Puebla conference final document and Pope John Paul II's *Laborem Exercens* and *Sollicitudo Rei Socialis*. Chaves's book goes even further, as he employs most of the major Catholic social teaching documents ranging from such pre-conciliar texts as *Rerum Novarum* and *Quadragesimo Anno*, through to the papal and conciliar documents of the 1960s and 1970s, to Pope John Paul II's *Laborem Exercens*, *Sollicitudo Rei Socialis*, and *Centesimus Annus*. Therefore, it appears that the Church in Limón is employing conservative Catholic social teaching documents to lend legitimacy to practical positions that are liberationist in nature.

What is going on here? Some indication can be taken from the particular quotations selected by the authors of the Limón Church documents. The Church members who collaboratively composed the *carta pastoral*, for instance, have indeed chosen several passages from magisterial documents that bespeak a liberationist stance. Yet they have often done so regardless of the conservative context of the original quotation. Hence, the letter reflects an insistence on the priority of labour over capital (a liberationist concept) as outlined in *Laborem Exercens*, but without mention of the closely related (but conservative) notion from the same encyclical that work unites all people—labour and capital.[85] When listing the rights of workers, the *carta pastoral* does cite papal support for the right to free association and the right to strike;[86] however, unlike the source documents for these passages, the *carta pastoral* does not emphasize the supposed dangers of union activism and strikes (e.g., that they stray into the realm of politics or may cause socio-economic burdens). While the treatment of such issues by popes Paul VI and John Paul II tends to dwell on what would make unions and strikes wrong (as opposed to what makes them a workers' right), the *carta pastoral* goes in the opposite direction and urges legislative changes and the creation of a new Labour Code that can protect the interests of workers more adequately.[87] Instead of just employing quotations from the patently liberationist documents of the Catholic social teaching tradition, the authors of the *carta pastoral* have surveyed even the conservative papal encyclicals of the tradition, and then have extracted liberationist passages from them. In short, it could be said that members of the Church in Limón are using Catholic social teaching out of context.

To be more precise, I would argue that, in the *carta pastoral*, Catholic social teaching is used out of context only in so far as this context is defined by the Vatican or by the pope. However, the social teaching employed in the pastoral letter *is* consistent within the immediate context of the Church in Limón. Given the conflictual socio-economic reality of Limón and the alliance of the official Church there with workers, it is not surprising that the presentation of Catholic social teaching in the *carta pastoral* resonates with a liberationist message. As I have discussed, Church members in Limón have witnessed and even participated themselves in some of the popular struggles in the region; such experiences are reflected in their selective appropriation of papal teachings. The religious message presented by the *carta pastoral* is thus not a simple translation or objective application of the magisterium's teachings to the situation in Limón (nor can such a process be expected). Rather, the *carta's* message is a both a product of and a weapon in the efforts by the Limón Church to make an option for the poor.

A further example of the strategic employment of papal teachings in the *carta pastoral* relates not only to political and economic conditions and positions but also to institutional considerations. Toward the end of the letter, the authors refer to a passage in the Puebla conference document to affirm that the bishop has the responsibility to watch over his flock, to safeguard the unity of the Church, and to guide all those who teach within the Church in order to prevent the formation of parallel ministries/magisteria.[88] On the surface, this passage does not appear to be liberationist at all but, instead, evokes images of traditional Catholic conservatism: a top-down power structure, doctrinal rigidity, and an ecclesiological model in which unity and universality are privileged over theological creativity and committed solidarity with the poor. Certainly, such a reading makes sense in light of the campaign by CELAM and the Vatican to discredit liberation theology and to defuse the threat presented by the CEB movement. But the reality of the Church in Limón, and the way in which these teachings from Puebla are used in the *carta pastoral*, suggest a different interpretation.

In the letter from Limón, the comments on the role of the bishop and Church unity occur in the midst of a broader discussion of the ESJ23, its interference in the training of lay people, and its false identification of Catholic social teaching with the solidarity movement.[89] Indeed, as I have already discussed, the ESJ23 propagates a conservative version of Catholic social teaching, and the school's presence in the Diocese of Limón constitutes a threat to the position of the official Church there. Hence, whereas the original references in the Puebla document to unity and to the danger of parallel magisteria refer to liberation theology and the CEBs, the Church in Limón uses the same concepts as a means to bolster its defences against its own ideological and ecclesiastical rival, the ESJ23. The fact that the *carta pastoral* also stresses that the ESJ23's work does not have an ecclesial character, and that it bears no relation to the pastoral plan of the Church in Limón, reinforces the notion that opting for the poor in the Limón Church implies a unity that excludes the ESJ23. In this way, members of the Church in Limón are not echoing the meaning of the original CELAM texts but, rather, are reading these texts in accordance with their own particular social and ecclesiastical needs. Taking the historical and institutional reality of the Diocese of Limón into consideration can thereby explain the Limón Church's use of otherwise conservative Catholic social teachings.

It should be noted at this point that Chaves himself would likely disagree with parts of this argument. In *Magisterio social y pastoral de los trabajadores*, it is clear that Chaves does not share my assessment of the Catholic social teaching tradition as a largely conservative one. Instead, he views it as one that has consistently promoted the interests and the liberation of the poor (which would, by implication, render inapplicable my points about the conflict between a conservative document and its liberationist appropriation). His presentation of Catholic social teaching, for instance, emphasizes the magisterium's central preoccupation with conflict and socio-economic inequality in society,[90] its enduring see/judge/act methodology,[91] its repeated critique of capitalism,[92] its origin in the option for the poor,[93] and its overall orientation toward social and economic transformation.[94] These characteristics, of course, are hallmarks of what I have referred to as the liberationist expression of Catholic social teaching. Yet such characteristics only predominate in a minority of Catholic social teaching texts, and certainly do not define the tradition as a whole from *Rerum Novarum* to *Laborem Exercens*, as Chaves suggests. Chaves's argument does appear plausible, though, because he focuses in his book on the above-listed liberationist indicators in papal and episcopal texts, while neglecting the conservative counterparts to such principles that are in fact more dominant in the tradition, such as the focus on unity and consensus in society, a deductive methodology that accords privilege to Truth and Authority, a critique of the personal sins and attitudinal weaknesses of capitalists, and an emphasis on the spiritual components of liberation.

Interestingly, Chaves claims that he is not providing an interpretative reading of Catholic social teaching but, rather, that he is presenting only the fundamentals of the tradition.[95] In doing so, moreover, he sees himself as "helping to rescue the pontifical and episcopal documents from the hands of the defenders of the status quo, who have taken advantage of generalized ignorance to strengthen, with a fragmentary use of Social Doctrine, their conservative positions."[96] What Chaves does not acknowledge, however, is that what he purports to be his "correct reading" of magisterial documents is in itself a selective presentation of principles that reflects his own political sympathies and practical alliances: in fact, he uses papal and episcopal documents to bolster his own liberationist positions. Chaves may be an academic expert on Catholic social teaching, but he cannot be expected to present his analyses in a strictly unbiased fashion. Every exposition is in reality a form of interpretation; in Chaves's case, his interpretation is necessarily related to his position as a priest conscious of and sympathetic to the struggles of workers and the marginalized poor in Limón. Chaves's interpretation is also related to his collaboration with the Diocesan Social Pastoral Commission in Limón and his staunch support of the Limón Church during the controversy over the *carta pastoral*.[97] The liberationist reading of Catholic social teaching that Chaves provides is hence not strictly a product of the original texts themselves.

Conclusion

The characteristics of the official Church in Limón and its emerging *pastoral obrera* fit readily into the template of the liberationist stream of the Catholic social teaching tradition. The Church's portrayals of society and prescriptions for social change take into account the structural as well as the spiritual. Pastoral planners derive priorities not directly from papal or episcopal decree but, rather, from the demands of social reality, as documented by the tools of social science and as experienced by those at the base of the Church. Pastoral agents emphasize and facilitate informed lay participation both within the CEBs and in the Limón Church as a whole. Church leaders, in their written statements and in their collaboration with popular movements, do not shy away from conflict or controversy. It is through such words and actions that representatives of this Church make their option for the poor clear.

Yet how did this option arise? Certainly, the progressive pastoral stance in Limón is, in part, a response to the socio-economic situation in the region. Limón is a poor and conflict-ridden province. Importantly, Church leaders know this: whether through pastoral visits, first-person reports, Church assemblies, or the CECODERS diagnostic census, Church officials have been made aware of the economic hardships suffered by the majority of their constituents. Through their experiences, the clergy in Limón have undergone a process of conscientization, which has had the effect of deepening their commitment to work for justice as part of their pastoral mission. As Monseñor Coto has remarked, once Church agents experienced first hand the tremendous injustices faced by labourers in Limón, they simply could not remain indifferent.[98]

The experience of poverty in itself, however, is usually not enough to inspire and sustain such solidarity with the poor. After all, Padre Solano and the staff of the ESJ23 are also well aware of the living conditions in the region. Additional factors are often involved. In this case, the insecure institutional position of the Catholic Church in Limón reinforced the impetus to develop a *pastoral obrera* that assumed forms consistent with the liberationist model. A shortage of vocations to the priesthood in Limón, for example, meant that the survival and development of pastoral programming was dependent on lay people assuming positions of responsibility within the Church. Monseñor Coto, in fact, proposed strengthening the CEBs as a way to counter the difficulties faced by the communities in his vicariate (e.g., the scarcity of priests, the expansion of Protestant sects, the "social agitators"). Monseñor Ulloa, for his part, sees the "intensification" of lay doctrinal formation as a way to prevent "emigration" to non-Catholic creeds;[99] like his predecessor, he also views the CEBs as the best form for the Church, given the large number of *sectas* and other churches in Limón.[100] Religious competition, therefore, appears to figure significantly as a motive for the move to democratize the Church via the base communities. Further, one could treat the Church's increased political activism and support for unions as a means to ensure that, if Catholics were drawn to participate in certain political activities of a leftist bent, they would not feel forced to leave the Church to do so.

None of these factors is meant to imply that the development of a liberationist *pastoral social* in the Limón Church was a merely strategic move by its leaders, one absent of personal conviction or genuine conversion to the cause of the poor. The actual mixture of true belief and tactical manoeu-vring would be impossible to discern in this or any other case. It does indi-cate, however, that institutional necessities can provide additional motivation for Church officials to adopt positions or implement program-ming that, under other circumstances, might be viewed as too radical for the organization. The perceived existence of serious threats to the Church's survival will, in effect, mitigate the potential threat represented by pas-toral innovation. In some situations, moreover, a move that may have been born primarily of organizational need (and hence is more liberationist in appearance than in motivation) can itself contribute to a true shift in perspective further down the line. Therefore, whatever the original rea-soning behind incorporating more lay people into the decision-making bodies of the Church in Limón, once they claimed more of a voice in the running of the organization, the pastoral work of the Church naturally came to reflect their needs, experiences, and demands. Overall, then, it would be accurate to speak of a confluence of class and institutional inter-ests that contributed to the emergence of the option for the poor in Limón.

Throughout such a process, Catholic social teaching plays a crucial role. Regardless of its largely conservative character and previous use in the worldwide Church and in Costa Rica, Catholic social teaching provides an essential framework for the liberationist pastorate of the Limón Church. Employing Catholic social teaching allows Church agents in Limón to identify themselves with the universal institution, to place themselves in the line of the tradition to which Catholics look for guidance. Moreover, while the form of the Limonense *pastoral obrera* suggests that Church agents may have adopted only the letter of Catholic social teaching to serve their own spirit, such an adaptation can serve to legitimate the positions of the Church in Limón. This ability to cite the texts of the Church mag-isterium, to declare itself a local Church within the bounds of the univer-sal body, is particularly valuable given the controversial nature of the Limón Church's political positions vis-à-vis those of the ESJ23, of the Archdio-cese of San José, and, ultimately, of the Vatican itself.

In this context, what has changed is not Catholic social teaching per se, but its use. The socio-economic situation in Limón and the organiza-tional needs of the vicariate, and now diocese, can go far to explain why Monseñor Coto and others adopted Catholic social teaching in the liber-ationist manner they did. Yet, there are further questions surrounding the liberationist use of what is fundamentally a conservative doctrine: are there limits, for instance, to the political actions that Vatican and CELAM social teachings can legitimate? At what point will the needs and charac-teristics of the worldwide Church as an institution override the relatively autonomous interpretation of Catholic social teaching by liberationist bod-ies such as the Church in Limón? A discussion of these and related mat-ters follows in the concluding chapter.

Liberationist and Conservative Catholicisms in Costa Rica and Beyond 10

> The same ideas can point to different conclusions
> for different classes at the same time.
> —Christopher Hill, *Change and Continuity in*
> *Seventeenth-Century England*

In this study, I have analyzed the Catholic Church in Costa Rica and the variety of positions its representatives have produced on social justice and workers' issues between 1979 and 1996. Against a background of contemporary Costa Rican social history, the institutional exigencies of the Church organization, and Vatican and Latin American Catholic social teaching, I have examined four Costa Rican Church entities—CECOR, the ESJ23, CECODERS and the Church in Limón—and have characterized them as either primarily conservative or liberationist in orientation. In this conclusion, I highlight some of the more important points in my argument and suggest implications from my analysis for broader questions in the study of Costa Rican and Latin American Catholicism.

The Conservative-Liberationist Struggle within the Costa Rican Church

The four case studies presented here are a concrete illustration of the theoretical proposition that the Church is an interclass social space.[1] Church agents representing competing social classes and political options in Costa Rica meet within the Church and attempt to use the material and symbolic resources of this institution to further their respective causes. Regardless of the wishes and assertions of the Church hierarchy, conflicts prevalent in the larger society are not negated or superseded by a common denominator of faith. Instead of revealing the Costa Rican Catholic Church to be a completely coherent and unified entity, the four Church organizations studied here represent four different Costa Rican Catholicisms[2]—divided into two basic ideological camps. The perspectives they promote on social justice and workers' rights express either a conservative or liberationist variation of Catholicism.

♦ Conservative Catholicisms: CECOR and the ESJ23

In certain respects, the two entities that inhabit the conservative corner in the Costa Rican Church appear to have little in common. The members of CECOR are bishops, high-ranking representatives of the world-wide Church in Costa Rica, while the ESJ23 is led by a priest and is otherwise staffed entirely by lay people. Monseñor Arrieta, archbishop of San José and CECOR spokesperson, is widely respected in international Church circles and is affectionately revered as *Manzanita* (the little apple) by many Costa Ricans. The ESJ23's director, Padre Claudio Solano, on the other hand, is a controversial figure whose work, while admired by many, has drawn scorn and allegations of illegality from labour activists in Costa Rica and beyond. In terms of Catholic social teaching, the CECOR bishops rely almost exclusively on the post-conciliar Vatican and CELAM sources, occasionally even adopting some of the language of the Latin American liberationists. Representatives of the ESJ23, by contrast, make heavy use of both pre- and post-conciliar magisterial documents, and carefully distance themselves from the concepts and terminology most often associated with liberation theology. Finally, while Monseñor Arrieta and the Church hierarchy strive to appear neutral in their approach to workers' issues, Padre Solano and the ESJ23 *promotores* are unabashedly partisan in their praise and promotion of *solidarismo*. Considering these factors, it seems unlikely that CECOR and the ESJ23 could share a similar political or social pastoral outlook.

Nonetheless, these two parties do coincide in their promotion of a fundamentally conservative message. Key to the discourse of both CECOR and the ESJ23 is a predominantly functionalist perspective on social reality in which peace and harmony are idealized, often while serious inequities are overlooked and struggles for justice neglected. Social change for these conservatives implies reform instead of revolution, and the renovation of attitudes instead of the transformation of structures. Not only are collaboration and consensus the tools for social reform here, but, especially in the case of the Costa Rican Church hierarchy, the architects of the process are the government, the rich, and the powerful — not the grassroots, the marginalized, or the meek. Even the apparent differences in the ESJ23's and CECOR's approaches to workers' issues fade considerably once the purportedly non-partisan positions of the hierarchy are revealed to hold a bias for *solidarismo* and a relatively negative evaluation of the strike as a political pressure tactic. Ultimately, the positions of both CECOR and the ESJ23 function to reinforce the power of a state facing a serious economic crisis, as well as to respond to the needs of those who seek solutions to this crisis in the neo-liberal capitalist model.

Contrary to the assumptions and assertions of many academic observers of the Catholic Church, these positions do not represent a reversion to a strictly pre-conciliar Catholic social teaching model nor a corresponding affront to latter-day Vatican teachings on social justice. Rather, the words and actions of CECOR and the ESJ23 resonate with pre-Vatican II papal encyclicals *and* many of the documents of the post-conciliar era. There is a remarkable consistency throughout much of the magisterial social teaching over the decades, a consistency that is best expressed in the enduring centrality of the concepts of unity and solidarity as the organizing principles for both the Church and society. Moreover, although this consistent conservatism may sometimes be concealed, it is never truly contradicted by the borrowing of liberationist language by Pope John Paul II or the CELAM bishops in their conferences at Puebla and Santo Domingo. In Costa Rica, in turn, this conservatism surfaces in the proclamations and practices of CECOR and the ESJ23.

Admittedly, CECOR and the ESJ23 are not identical entities. Of the two, the ESJ23 is clearly closer to the right-wing extreme. But, since this variation is not based on two different Catholic social teaching traditions, CECOR's and the ESJ23's differing needs, positions, and alliances within and outside of the Church necessarily come into play. Monseñor Arrieta and the CECOR bishops must respond to the variety of demands placed on them as they function as both institutional and spiritual leaders in a fragile socio-economic order and competitive cultural milieu. For example, the hierarchy's need to protect its alliances with the nation's political power brokers, and thereby also protect the Church's secular privileges, must be balanced with the bishops' religious mission to serve as pastors who represent and unite all constituents within the Church. In addition, the bishops' moves to retain and impose their authority within the institution must be tempered by the consideration that the Catholic Church no longer monopolizes the expression of religious sentiment in Costa Rica. The complex interplay of these and other factors ensures that any partisan and conservative political or pastoral options are carefully presented in a neutral and moderate manner.

Padre Solano and the ESJ23, by contrast, are far less affected by such considerations, in part because the school has a narrower range of responsibilities within the Church, but also because it is less vulnerable in terms of the overall social order. Since Solano is in charge of an organization meant to represent only a fraction of the Church's constituency, his need to present an inclusive message or to appear to cater to conservatives and liberationists alike is correspondingly diminished. The alliances of school officials with Costa Rica's business elite — and the material security ensured by those relationships — also indicate that the ESJ23 would have little to gain, and potentially much to lose, by broadening its conservative message to address the concerns and demands of more progressive elements in the Church and beyond. Moreover, even the relatively subordinate status of the ESJ23 within the Church has not meant that the school has been subject to ecclesial sanction or censure for its extreme propaganda and sometimes illegal activities. On the contrary, the underlying doctrinal affinities between the Church hierarchy and the school, along with the tacit approval the archbishop provides for Solano's crusade on behalf of *solidarismo*, mean that the ESJ23 has been able to survive and even thrive in spite of the controversy it generates. Ultimately, then, CECOR and the ESJ23 are highly compatible exemplars of Costa Rican Catholic conservatism.

◆ Liberationist Catholicisms: The Official Church in Limón and CECODERS

The official Church in Limón and CECODERS have much in common as representatives of the liberationist wing of the Costa Rican Catholic Church. In general terms, both can be said to carry out the principles and priorities embodied in the documents from the 1968 CELAM conference at Medellín. This means that both approach the social order with a critical eye, using the tools of the social sciences to uncover and analyze the conflicts and inequality in society. By doing so, they help to discredit and delegitimate the predominant myths that obfuscate — and thereby perpetuate — injustice in Costa Rica. For these Church entities, moreover, the struggle against injustice is not merely a matter of academic analysis; it also incorporates a variety of practical efforts directed at contesting and transforming the unjust socio-economic structures of society. Essentially, the model for social change employed here illustrates several of the features of the original liberationist option for the poor. Hence, these Church organizations foster the conscientization and empowerment of those at the base of society through a variety of popular education efforts and, in the case of the Church in Limón, through CEBs. Further, representatives of the Church in Limón and CECODERS acknowledge the partisanship that this option implies, even when this partiality leads to a conflict or confrontation with some of the more powerful elites in society or in the Church. Finally, these Church agents accord workers and union organizations a central role in this bottom-up movement for change. Through their support of union coalitions in San José or the Limón en Lucha protests on the coast, CECODERS and the Limón Church help to encourage and direct popular challenges to the neo-liberal state.

One significant variation between CECODERS and the Church in Limón, however, is related to the Catholic social teaching that each uses to legitimate its liberationist practical agenda. More precisely, it is not the Catholic social teaching documents cited by these Church representatives that are in themselves different, as both draw heavily on what I have cast as the conservative doctrinal tradition in the Church. Rather, it is how they approach this Catholic social teaching that is the crucial difference. CECODERS is reluctant to apprehend Catholic social teaching in a critical manner and, instead, accepts the orthodox presentation of this social teaching as the reference point for its *pastoral social*. In this way, CECODERS jeopardizes the efficacy of its liberationist project because it closes itself off from seeing how elements of this orthodoxy can in themselves contribute to the inequities that it is struggling to overcome. The Church in Limón, on the other hand, rereads Catholic social teaching from the vantage point of the conflicts in which it is embroiled and re-creates the meaning of the tradition accordingly. The Church in Limón thereby sets historical action as a priority over authoritative doctrine, a process that is paralleled and reinforced by the movements toward democratization within the Limón Church structure. Thus, Limón Church agents can potentially go further than those from CECODERS in transforming the quest for social justice from rhetoric into reality.

Some of these differences in approach to Catholic social teaching can be attributed to the differing institutional locations and alliances of these two entities within the Costa Rican Church. Only the Limón Church, under and because of its bishop, has the ecclesiastical authority and autonomy that can allow it to make a creative re-evaluation of and contribution to the Catholic social teaching corpus. Strictly speaking, and within the traditional top-down authority structure of the Catholic Church, only the members of its hierarchy produce Catholic social teaching. Bodies such as CECODERS, as revealed by the centre's assigned mandate, are restricted to reproducing and spreading these received teachings to others. Monseñor Arrieta's different responses to the controversies involving documents from CECODERS and the Limón Church are one illustration of this principle. After the public outcry in reaction to the CECODERS *folleto* on the history of Costa Rica, the archbishop brought the centre back into the archdiocesan line; the equally provocative 1989 *carta pastoral* from the Church in Limón, however, was essentially ignored by the archbishop (recall that Monseñor Arrieta has no actual jurisdiction in Limón). Put another way, only the official Church in Limón has had the hierarchical sponsorship—through Monseñor Coto and Monseñor Ulloa—needed for it to be able to develop a liberationist approach to Catholic social teaching. Despite its practical collaboration with the Limón Church, CECODERS operates within the Archdiocese of San José and, there, unlike the ESJ23, it has not had a highly placed Church leader to support, sponsor, or sanction a rereading of Catholic social teaching more in line with its class alliances and commitment to social change.

This situation should not suggest that intermediate-level Church organizations will simply reproduce the positions of their bishops on all pastoral and doctrinal levels; rather, it only implies that there is a limit to how far progressive positions can be developed without support from at least part of the Church hierarchy. The more important issues in terms of the liberationist wing in the Costa Rican Church, then, may be related to how Church leaders within the Diocese of Limón arrived at their progressive positions. Among the salient factors were Church agents' direct encounters with the poor of Limón, which provoked a process of conscientization. Also important was the institutional insecurity of the Church in the region, including its perceived vulnerability to the rapidly spreading Protestant *sectas*, which encouraged it to move toward democratization. Perhaps most crucial, however, was the willingness of the bishop and the clergy in Limón to struggle alongside workers and the poor at the base of the Church, and to allow their perspectives and priorities to be reflected in pastoral planning and the production of Church documents. Through the interaction of these variables the Limón Church agents, much like the CELAM bishops at Medellín decades earlier, have come to represent a liberationist minority within the dominant conservative Catholic social teaching tradition of the Church hierarchy.

Final Reflections

Keeping in mind the content and the comparisons of the case studies presented above, I wish to consider some of the broader implications of the material examined in this study for other work on the Costa Rican and Latin American Church. By now, it should be clear that any strict separation among the three levels of analysis outlined in the introduction is artificial. In order to understand the various positions of Costa Rican Church organizations, examining the Church's socio-economic context is as crucial as assessing the Church as an institution and evaluating Catholic social teaching. These categories do, however, provide a convenient means to elaborate some brief and concluding reflections.

♦ Religion and Socio-Economic Context

The Costa Rican socio-economic crisis and the neo-liberal responses to this crisis opened up new opportunities for Church agents to become involved in the political realm. Although the Church hierarchy had long been allied with the state and had played an important role in the articulation and consolidation of the reformist political model in Costa Rica, the onset of the crisis provoked a level of commentary on social issues from CECOR that had not been heard for decades. When, after the early 1980s, structural adjustment became state leaders' preferred means of responding to Costa Rica's problems, Monseñor Arrieta and the CECOR bishops adapted the nature of their traditional alliances accordingly and provided the symbolic support needed by the government as it imposed its highly contested neo-liberal policies. At the same time and under the same conditions, entities such as the Church in Limón and CECODERS developed and enacted their liberationist option for the poor. In these latter cases, the structural contradictions in Costa Rican society exposed by the crisis, and the inequities perpetuated and worsened by the supposed solution to the crisis, served to inspire and validate the liberationists' perspectives as well as their practical actions on behalf of workers and the poor.

The emergence of the liberationist faction in the Costa Rican Church provides an interesting contrast to the development of the progressive Church in much of the rest of Latin America. There, particularly in such countries as Brazil, Peru, Nicaragua, and El Salvador, the liberationist wing of the Church either surfaced or expanded substantially under conditions of military dictatorship.[3] In Costa Rica, however, the progressive Church developed within a relatively open civilian political system. The experience in Costa Rica thereby suggests that it may be appropriate to re-evaluate the commonly held notion that dictatorship is a necessary (although not sufficient) condition to bring the progressive Church into existence.[4]

Studying the Costa Rican liberationists may also help to qualify the related and more recent hypothesis that the increased democratization in Latin America is linked to the decline and/or fragmentation of the popular Church (because, presumably, the more democratic a society is, the less need there is for Church agents to speak out and demand social changes).[5] On the one hand, the increased formal democratization that has persisted in Costa Rica since the 1948 civil war did not preclude the eventual emergence of a progressive Church there. On the other hand, if one characterizes the negative effects that various neo-liberal state policies have had on the majority of Costa Ricans as a diminution in actual democracy, then the notion that there is a relationship between the level of democracy and the level of Church activism might receive some support.

At the heart of the matter here is how one defines democracy, a debate that has surfaced with renewed intensity in the recent literature on Latin America. In a challenge to the traditional assumption that democracy is strictly a political order in which people have the right to elect their government representatives on a regular basis, some have argued that democracy is also a social condition in which the principle and practice of equality prevail. According to scholars such as Atilio Boron, for a society to be truly democratic, there must exist both formal mechanisms to allow for popular participation in government and a citizenry physically, socially, intellectually, and economically capable of effective political participation.[6] The neo-liberal capitalist order, because of its exclusionary and inegalitarian nature, can therefore be said to function as a detriment to democracy in countries such as Costa Rica.

Significantly, liberationist Church agents in Costa Rica have attempted to provoke a similar debate within their country for some time. Their implicit and explicit challenges to the various myths about Costa Rican democracy (including the myths related to the country's exceptionalism, pacifism, and likeness to Switzerland) parallel Boron's argument. And, while the liberationists' priority with these challenges has undoubtedly been a practical one—the conscientization and mobilization of Costa Ricans—the lessons of their demythologizing work should not be lost on scholars of other Latin American countries. Quite simply, the Costa Rican case shows that an absence of dictatorship should not be equated with the presence of a true democracy.

◆ The Church as an Institution

The four case studies presented here have focused on entities that are indisputably part of the official Church institution. I have shown how Church leaders' reactions to institutional insecurity can be an important factor in provoking pastoral innovations, such as encouraging the formation of CEBs, that in turn can have implications that are liberationist (as demonstrated by the Church in Limón) or conservative (as reflected by the Archdiocese of San José). Beyond these, other elements related to the structure of the Church organization may also suggest whether liberationist or conservative tendencies will predominate in the Costa Rican Church in the future.

In general, the Church structure in Costa Rica is relatively authoritarian in nature. Though there has been a belated effort by CECOR to incorporate CEBs into pastoral planning for the Church as a whole, only in the Diocese of Limón has the CEB phenomenon truly taken root and indicated a movement toward Church decentralization and democratization. The relatively tight control that Monseñor Arrieta and CECOR seek to retain over those at lower levels of the institution (i.e., the CEBs and intermediate organizations such as CECODERS) indicates the hierarchical and centralized ecclesiological pattern that predominates in the Costa Rican Church.

This top-down authority pattern in itself suggests that the national Church is likely to continue to support the socio-economic status quo in Costa Rica. Even apart from the political predilections or economic alliances of the individuals in control of the Church organization, the very fact that such authoritarian relations prevail within the institution is problematic from the viewpoint of those wishing to transform society. The logic of hierarchical and centralized organization dictated by the Church encourages the faithful to maintain a respectful attitude toward hierarchy, authority, and centralized power in general. Thus, this inculcation of hierarchical logic within the Church facilitates the submission of the faithful to other forms of social hierarchy, including those of capitalist economic dominance.[7] By extension, only once the Church's internal power relations are transformed can the institution be an effective symbol and force for the transformation of power relations in the broader society. Judging by the relatively traditional and hierarchical structure of the Church as it is led by Monseñor Arrieta, this will not happen soon in Costa Rica.

Regardless of the conservatism and authoritarianism that dominates the Church, however, the liberationists in Costa Rica, as elsewhere in Latin America, have generally chosen to remain within the institution. Apart from what, presumably, are the liberationists' personal beliefs about the legitimacy of the Church as an institution, there are also genuine benefits that working from inside the Catholic Church can bring.[8] For example, Church membership can provide access to material resources in the form of money or office space. Affiliation with the official Church can also bolster one's credibility and respect, especially given that, in Costa Rica, bishops are widely admired and the Church as a whole has consistently remained one of the most trusted institutions in society.[9] Finally, because the Catholic Church still provides ordinary Costa Ricans with much of their world view, values, and even vocabulary, a liberationist movement that seeks to incorporate and influence these people would logically be better situated within, as opposed to outside, the Church's institutional orbit. Ultimately, then, the goal of the liberationists is not to leave or abolish the institution, but to work from inside to transform it.

Moreover, for as long as the institutional nature of liberationist activism persists, the actions and opinions of those who hold key offices in the Church hierarchy will remain extremely important. In this work, I have focused on the positions of various Costa Rican bishops and have indicated the importance of episcopal support for the success of both liberationist and conservative endeavours at lower levels of the Church. Indeed, researchers have established that a similar phenomenon routinely occurs in other Latin American countries.[10] Yet, given the structure of the Church, one must move beyond the national level of analysis to recognize that other Latin American bishops as members of CELAM, and the bishop of Rome himself as head of the worldwide Church, will also have an influence on the Costa Rican Church. Since this influence stems largely from the doctrinal directions of the pope and CELAM, a final consideration of the Catholic social teaching tradition is warranted.

◆ Catholic Social Teaching

CELAM is active and publishes documents throughout Latin America on a regular basis. Costa Rican Church representatives, however, have typically considered its general conference documents — those from Medellín, Puebla, and Santo Domingo — to be the primary sources for Catholic social teaching inspiration. Whether the conservatism of the Puebla and Santo Domingo documents will be reaffirmed at the next CELAM general conference remains to be seen, but the chances are slight that this continental episcopal body will produce another liberationist manifesto. While the infamous and ultraconservative Monseñor Alfonso López Trujillo no longer runs CELAM, there are few indications that the episcopal council has adopted a drastically new course since his departure (now a cardinal, he

serves as head of the Pontifical Council for the Family). In any case, regardless of who is president of CELAM, the pope in the past has had no qualms
about sending conservative Curial representatives to oversee its meetings
on his behalf. Moreover, the restrictions the pope has placed on progressive Latin American bishops over the years may well have depleted any
remaining liberationist fervour in the organization. Beyond this, the conservative new bishops whom John Paul II has been appointing in Latin
America since the mid-1980s may also help to keep CELAM on his preferred path.[11]

As for the pope's own statements regarding Catholic social teaching,
it does appear that he has devoted less energy to attacking liberationists
directly in recent years. In fact, in a 1996 statement to Latin American
journalists, John Paul II even indicated that liberation theology was no
longer a great problem on the continent, commenting that: "Liberation
theology was somewhat a Marxist ideology. Today, following the fall of
communism, liberation theology has fallen a little too."[12] Generally speaking, in this post-communist era, the pope seems more interested in defining the Church's stance on issues related to gender, sexuality, and
ecumenism than in expanding the Catholic social teaching corpus.

Nonetheless, this does not mean that John Paul II has changed his
mind about the liberationists. The pope certainly has not changed—and
has even taken steps to reinforce—his position on the nature of Church
authority, which, as discussed, is closely related to his reaction against the
liberationist movement. The heavy-handed approaches to bishops and
priests who run afoul of Vatican policy continue in the form of excommu-
nications, forced resignations, retirements, and transfers.[13] Major statements from national bishops' conferences, if they are not unanimous, are
now subject to Vatican approval.[14] And the oath obliging theologians working at Catholic universities to submit without dissent to magisterial teaching on key doctrinal matters has recently been written into the Code of
Canon Law.[15] Pope John Paul II is, perhaps now more than ever, a "cen-
tralizing, power-collecting prelate," to quote Michael Budde.[16]

Of course, the pope's advanced age and physical frailty suggest that he
will not remain at the helm of the Vatican much longer. This means that
the positions and persuasions of his successor will soon provide a new
subject for analysis. Yet, regardless of the forms that the next Catholic
social teaching statements from CELAM and a new pope take, only with
time and careful scrutiny should they be declared "liberationist" or "conservative." One cannot assume that the use of liberationist terms, be they
related to the right to strike or the responsibility to change society, always
correspond to authentically liberationist practical positions. Similarly, conservative Catholic social teaching concepts cannot be expected to function only to legitimate actions that are acceptable from the conservative
point of view. Catholic social teaching does not stand isolated from the

intentions and institutions of those who produce it or use it, and the continual interplay among these Church representatives and their ecclesial and social environments indicates that the conservative-liberationist struggle may never be settled once and for all. Past, present, and future Catholic social teaching documents must therefore always be appraised within their specific contexts and with a critical eye.

Finally, I would suggest that this critical stance is not only an academic imperative: it is also a crucial element for the survival and success of Church agents' efforts to bring about justice in the world. Waiting for another conference like the one at Medellín or for the next pope to provide the definitive justification for a liberationist social justice agenda may well prove fruitless, as would accepting Catholic social teaching and the magisterial interpretations of it at face value. The hope for change in the Church and in society does not rest as much in the Church's doctrinal tradition as it does in those individuals who, through their committed rereading and reclaiming of Catholic social teaching, dare to react to it and struggle to enact it for themselves.

Notes

Notes to Chapter 1 : Introduction

1 While there are several Christian churches in Latin America, for the purposes of this work, "Church" refers to the Roman Catholic Church.

2 J. Lloyd Mecham, *Church and State in Latin America: A History of Politico-Ecclesiastical Relations*, rev. ed. (Chapel Hill, NC: University of North Carolina Press, 1966).

3 Ivan Vallier, *Catholicism, Social Control, and Modernization in Latin America* (Englewood Cliffs, NJ: Prentice-Hall, 1970).

4 Ivan Vallier, "Extraction, Insulation, and Re-entry: Toward a Theory of Religious Change," in *The Church and Social Change in Latin America*, ed. Henry A. Landsberger (Notre Dame, IN: University of Notre Dame Press, 1970), 9–35.

5 Daniel Levine, for example, notes that Vallier's model, based as it is on a structural-functionalist understanding of society, wrongly implies that religion and politics are distinguishable and separable spheres of activity: *Religion and Politics in Latin America: The Catholic Church in Venezuela and Colombia* (Princeton, NJ: Princeton University Press, 1981), 24 and 135–36. This argument is echoed in Philip J. Williams, *The Catholic Church and Politics in Nicaragua and Costa Rica* (London: Macmillan, with St. Anthony's College, Oxford, 1989), 6–8.

6 Frederick C. Turner, *Catholicism and Political Development in Latin America* (Chapel Hill, NC: University of North Carolina Press, 1971).

7 Emanuel de Kadt, *Catholic Radicals in Brazil* (Oxford, UK: Oxford University Press, 1970).

8 Levine, *Religion and Politics in Latin America*; Daniel H. Levine, Continuities in Colombia, *Journal of Latin American Studies* 17, Pt. II (1985): 295–317; Brian H. Smith, *The Church and Politics in Chile: Challenges to Modern Catholicism* (Princeton, NJ: Princeton University Press, 1982); and Michael Fleet and Brian H. Smith, *The Catholic Church and Democracy in Chile and Peru* (Notre Dame, IN: University of Notre Dame Press, 1997).

9 This is not very surprising, given the leading role sectors of the Brazilian Church played in the 1950s, 1960s, and 1970s in the development of CEBs and, more generally, of progressive Catholic social teaching.

10 Thomas C. Bruneau, *The Political Transformation of the Brazilian Catholic Church* (London: Cambridge University Press, 1974) and *The Church in Brazil: The Politics of Religion* (Austin, TX: University of Texas Press, 1982).

11 Madeleine Adriance, *Opting for the Poor: Brazilian Catholicism in Transition* (Kansas City, MS: Sheed and Ward, 1986); and Scott Mainwaring, *The Catholic Church and Politics in Brazil, 1916–1985* (Stanford, CA: Stanford University Press, 1986).

12 Madeleine Cousineau Adriance, *Promised Land: Base Christian Communities and the Struggle for the Amazon* (Albany, NY: State University of New York Press, 1995); Warren Edward Hewitt, *Base Christian Communities and Social Change in Brazil* (Lincoln, NB: University of Nebraska Press, 1991); and Manuel A. Vásquez, *The Brazilian Popular Church and the Crisis of Modernity*, Cambridge

Studies in Ideology and Religion (Cambridge, UK: Cambridge University Press, 1998). CEBs are small, neighbourhood-based Church groups that engage in Bible study and/or social activism. They are frequently led by lay people.

13 See, for example, Daniel H. Levine, "Religion, the Poor, and Politics in Latin America Today," in *Religion and Political Conflict in Latin America*, ed. Daniel H. Levine (Chapel Hill, NC: University of North Carolina Press, 1986), 3–23; "Colombia: The Institutional Church and the Popular," in *Religion and Political Conflict*, 187–217; "Conflict and Renewal," in *Religion and Political Conflict*, 236–55; and *Popular Voices in Latin America Catholicism* (Princeton, NJ: Princeton University Press, 1992).

14 Phillip Berryman, *The Religious Roots of Rebellion: Christians in Central American Revolutions* (Maryknoll, NY: Orbis Books, 1984), and *Stubborn Hope: Religion, Politics, and Revolution in Central America* (New York: New Press and Maryknoll, NY: Orbis Books, 1994).

15 Many of these can be found in Edward T. Brett, "The Impact of Religion in Central America: A Bibliographical Essay," *The Americas* 49, 3 (January 1993): 297–341.

16 Víctor Sanabria Martínez, *Anselmo Llorente y Lafuente, primer obispo de Costa Rica: Apuntamientos históricos* (San José, CR: Editorial Costa Rica, 1972), *Bernardo Augusto Thiel, segundo obispo de Costa Rica: Apuntamientos históricos y primeros* (San José, CR: Editorial Costa Rica, 1982), *La primera vacante de la diócesis de San José, 1871–1880* (San José, CR: Editorial Costa Rica, 1973), and *Reseña histórica de la Iglesia en Costa Rica desde 1502 hasta 1850* (San José, CR: DEI, 1984).

17 See the essays collected in Víctor Hugo Brenes Leiva, *40 años de la muerte de Monseñor Sanabria* (San José, CR: Ediciones CECOR, 1992); and Arnoldo Mora, *Las fuentes del cristianismo social en Costa Rica* (San José, CR: DEI, 1989), 95–115.

18 Miguel Picado, *La Iglesia costarricense: Entre Dios y el César*, 2nd ed. (San José, CR: DEI, 1989), 117–37.

19 Javier Solís, *La herencia de Sanabria: Análisis político de la Iglesia costarricense* (San José, CR: DEI, 1983).

20 Williams, *Catholic Church and Politics*, 121–34.

21 José Miguel Rodríguez, "Política y religión: La función política de la Iglesia Católica en Costa Rica," *Revista de Ciencias Sociales* 13 (April 1977): 77–101; and Williams, *Catholic Church and Politics*, 121.

22 See Williams, *Catholic Church and Politics*, 147–57; Rodolfo Cardenal, "The Rise and Fall of Social Catholicism in Costa Rica," in *Church and Politics in Latin America*, ed. Dermot Keogh (London: Macmillan, 1990), 176–86; and the work with the most detailed material regarding these themes, including primary source documents from the various players involved: Solís, *La herencia de Sanabria*.

23 Conferencia Episcopal de Costa Rica (CECOR), "Evangelización y realidad social de Costa Rica: Carta pastoral colectiva," in *La palabra social de los obispos costarricenses: Selección de documentos de la Iglesia Católica costarricense 1893–1981*, ed. Miguel Picado (San José, CR: DEI, n.d.), 159–81.

24 Miguel Picado, *La Iglesia costarricense entre el pueblo y el estado (de 1949 a nuestros días)* (San José, CR: Ediciones Guayacán, 1989).

25 Andrés Opazo Bernales, *Costa Rica: La Iglesia católica y el orden social* (San José, CR: DEI, 1987).

26 Williams, *Catholic Church and Politics*.

27 Mons. Bernardo Augusto Thiel, "Trigésima carta pastoral sobre el justo salario," in *La palabra social de los obispos costarricenses: Selección de documentos de*

la Iglesia Católica costarricense 1893-1981, ed. Miguel Picado (San José, CR: DEI, n.d.), 27-36. In this letter, Thiel was following the teachings of Pope Leo XIII's encyclical *Rerum Novarum*, which was issued two years prior. For a discussion of this encyclical and subsequent papal teaching on labour issues, see chapter 4.

28 Eugene D. Miller, *A Holy Alliance? The Church and the Left in Costa Rica, 1932-1948* (Armonk, NY: M.E. Sharpe, 1996).

29 Lawrence Kent, "The Social Pastoral Work of the Catholic Church in Costa Rica," *Michigan Journal of Political Science* 6 (1985): 8-37.

30 James Backer, *La Iglesia y el sindicalismo en Costa Rica*, 3rd ed. (San José, CR: Editorial Costa Rica, 1978).

31 Gramsci (1891-1937), a founding leader of the Italian Communist Party, was jailed by Mussolini in 1928. In 1929, he began writing his famous *Quaderni del carcere*, better known in English as the *Prison Notebooks*. The notebooks, numbering thirty-three in total, consist of fragmentary notes and organized essays on topics such as Italian history, Marxism, philosophy, politics, and religion. They are known for their sophisticated analyses of superstructural phenomena. One of the best translations of the *Quaderni* remains *Selections from the Prison Notebooks of Antonio Gramsci*, ed. and trans. Quintin Hoare and Geoffrey Nowell Smith (London: Lawrence and Wishart, 1971).

32 Born in Venezuela, Otto Maduro studied at the Catholic University of Louvain in Belgium and now lives and works in the United States. Among his key works are "Marxist Analysis and the Sociology of Religion: An Introduction," *Social Compass* 22, 3-4 (1975): 305-22, "New Marxist Approaches to the Relative Autonomy of Religion," *Sociological Analysis* 38, 4 (1977): 359-67, and *Religion and Social Conflicts*, trans. Robert R. Barr (Maryknoll, NY: Orbis Books, 1982).

33 Madeleine Adriance, "Opting for the Poor: A Social-Historical Analysis of the Changing Brazilian Catholic Church," *Sociological Analysis* 46, 2 (1985): 131-46; Mario Caceres, "Gramsci, la religion et les systèmes socio-économiques," *Social Compass* 35, 2-3 (1988): 279-96; Andrés Opazo Bernales, "La fonction de l'Eglise dans la lutte pour l'hégémonie," *Social Compass* 26, 2-3 (1979): 237-60; and Carlos Alberto Torres, *The Church, Society, and Hegemony: A Critical Sociology of Religion in Latin America*, trans. Richard A. Young (Westport, CT: Praeger, 1992).

34 See, for example, the comments in John Burdick, "The Progressive Church in Latin America: Giving Voice or Listening to Voices?" *Latin American Research Review* 29, 1 (1994): 184-97.

35 See, for example, Rowan Ireland, *Kingdoms Come: Religion and Politics in Brazil* (Pittsburg, PA: University of Pittsburgh Press, 1991).

36 See, for example, Hewitt, *Base Christian Communities*, 4-5. For a broader critique of the neo-Marxist perspective as it is embraced by some Latin American liberation theologians, see also Warren Edward Hewitt, "Liberation Theology as Social Science: Contributions and Limitations," in Roger O'Toole, ed., *Sociological Studies in Roman Catholicism: Historical and Contemporary Perspectives*, Studies in Religion and Society, vol. 24 (Lewiston, NY: Edwin Mellen Press, 1989), 143-65.

37 Levine, *Religion and Politics in Latin America*, 12-13.

38 Levine, *Popular Voices*, 140, 178, 323-24, and 337.

39 Michael L. Budde, *The Two Churches: Catholicism and Capitalism in the World System* (Durham, NC: Duke University Press, 1992), 31; Hewitt, *Base Christian Communities*, 5-6; Levine, *Popular Voices*, 178; and Levine, "Religion, the Poor, and Politics," 15.

40   See, for example, Irving M. Zeitlin, *Ideology and the Development of Sociological Theory*, 3rd ed. (Englewood Cliffs, NJ: Prentice-Hall, 1987), 111.

41   Maduro, "New Marxist Approaches," 364–67; and Maduro, *Religion and Social Conflicts*, 79–109.

42   See Roger O'Toole, *Religion: Classic Sociological Approaches* (Toronto, ON: McGraw-Hill Ryerson, 1984), 32–33 and 190–92.

43   The passage reads: "*Religious* distress is at the same time the *expression* of real distress and the *protest* against real distress. Religion is the sigh of the oppressed creature, the heart of a heartless world, just as it is the spirit of a spiritless situation. It is the *opium* of the people" (emphases in original): Karl Marx, "Contribution to the Critique of Hegel's Philosophy of Right," in Karl Marx and Friedrich Engels, *On Religion*, 2nd impr. (Moscow: Foreign Languages Publishing House, 1964), 42. Further evidence that Marx—and particularly Engels— recognized the protest potential of religion, under certain circumstances, is amassed by O'Toole in *Religion*, 68.

44   Gramsci, *Prison Notebooks*, 366; Maduro, "Marxist Analysis," 312–14; and Maduro, *Religion and Social Conflicts*, 19 and 41–46.

45   Friedrich Engels, "Engels to Bloch," letter dated September 21–22, 1890, in Marx and Engels, *On Religion*, 274–77. For an investigation of Marx's writings that convincingly shows that charges of economic determinism cannot be applied to his work, see José Porfirio Miranda, *Marx against the Marxists: The Christian Humanism of Karl Marx*, trans. John Drury (Maryknoll, NY: Orbis Books, 1980).

46   Gramsci, *Prison Notebooks*, 407.

47   Maduro, *Religion and Social Conflicts*, 87. The militant writings of Lenin on religion are the best example of the crudely reductionist position: see, for example, the essays entitled "Socialism and Religion," and "The Attitude of the Workers' Party towards Religion," in *On Socialist Ideology and Culture*, 2nd ed. (Moscow: Foreign Languages Publishing House, 1962).

48   One Latin Americanist who has clearly grasped the significance of this point is Daniel Levine, who asserts that "the Church is not *primarily* an agent of social, economic, or political action. As an intermediary between people and God, its central mission remains the diffusion of the message of salvation and service" (emphasis in original): *Religion and Politics in Latin America*, 13.

49   See Vásquez's comments on non-reductive materialism: *Brazilian Popular Church*, 12.

50   Opazo, "La fonction de l'Eglise," 254.

51   I borrow this phrase from Hugo Villela, "The Church and the Process of Democratization in Latin America," *Social Compass* 26, 2–3 (1979): 267.

52   Fleet and Smith note that: "Catholics...come in all shapes and sizes" (*Catholic Church and Democracy*, 15–16). Gramsci too writes not of Catholicism but of Catholicisms: "there is one Catholicism for the peasants, one for the *petits-bourgeois* and town workers, one for women, one for intellectuals" (*Prison Notebooks*, 420). The continuing relevance of Gramsci's observation is also confirmed in Roger O'Toole, "Introduction," in *Sociological Studies in Roman Catholicism*, xv.

53   Villela, "The Church," 267; Opazo, *Costa Rica*, 196.

54   Gramsci, *Prison Notebooks*, 5–6; and Maduro, *Religion and Social Conflicts*, 72–74, 122–35.

55   Gramsci, *Prison Notebooks*, 408.

56   For a history of changes in the Costa Rican Catholic Church's legal status, see Mecham, *Church and State in Latin America*, 332–35.

57   *Constitución política de la República de Costa Rica* (7 de noviembre de 1949), rev. Marco Castillo Rojas (Cartago, CR: Uruk Ediciones, 1996), 17.

58 See a description and discussion of these benefits in Picado, *La Iglesia costarri-cense entre el pueblo y el estado*, 46-47, 67-75; and Williams, *Catholic Church and Politics*, 126-27.

59 Costa Rican pollsters recently estimated that people constituting 78.8 percent of the population consider themselves to be Catholic. While this is a substantial majority, it is significantly lower than the popularly cited figure of 95 percent: Larissa Minsky Acosta, "¿Somos lo que creemos?" *La Nación (Revista Dominical)*, March 17, 1997, 9.

60 The best analysis of the rise of Pentecostalism in Costa Rica remains Jaime Valverde, *Las sectas en Costa Rica: Pentecostalismo y conflicto social* (San José, CR: DEI, 1990). More recent data on this phenomenon can be found in Timothy J. Steigenga, *The Politics of the Spirit: The Political Implications of Pentecostalized Religion in Costa Rica and Guatemala* (Lanham, MD: Lexington Books, 2001).

61 Maduro, *Religion and Social Conflicts*, 92-94.

62 Michael Schuck does note, however, that some commentaries on social issues are found in the papal documents of the pre-Leonine period (1740-1877): see *That They Be One: The Social Teaching of the Papal Encyclicals, 1740-1989* (Washington, DC: Georgetown University Press, 1991).

63 Although well-known liberation theologians Victorio Araya and Elsa Tamez are based in Costa Rica, they work from within the Protestant tradition. The prolific Costa Rican publishing house Departamento Ecuménico de Investigaciones (DEI, Ecumenical Research Department) has also released a number of books dealing with liberation theology.

64 Readers specifically interested in the liberation theology phenomenon are directed to two of the seminal primary texts on the topic: Gustavo Gutiérrez, *A Theology of Liberation: History, Politics and Salvation*, trans. and ed. Sister Caridad Inda and John Eagelson (Maryknoll, NY: Orbis Books, 1973); and Juan Luis Segundo, *The Liberation of Theology*, trans. John Drury (Maryknoll, NY: Orbis Books, 1976).

65 Backer, *La Iglesia*, 39-40.

66 The most overt statement of this position is found in Kent, "Social Pastoral Work," 21-22.

67 One of the most frequent and, as I discuss in chapter 4, serious errors in this regard is the conflation of the teachings of the CELAM conferences at Medellín and Puebla: see, for example, Kent, "Social Pastoral Work," 30; Opazo, *Costa Rica*, 183; and Picado, *La Iglesia costarricense entre el pueblo y el estado*, 200.

68 Gramsci, *Prison Notebooks*, 366.

69 Maduro, *Religion and Social Conflicts*, 113.

Notes to Chapter 2 : Crisis in Costa Rica

1 The war erupted after the government overturned the results of the 1948 presidential elections in Costa Rica—elections that had been won by the opposition candidate Otilio Ulate Blanco. Ulate's supporters launched an armed rebellion that defeated the government's army and established a *junta* that ruled Costa Rica for eighteen months, after which Ulate stepped in as president. For detailed accounts of the war that include analyses of the broader political and economic factors contributing to the conflict, see Oscar Aguilar Bulgarelli, *Costa Rica y sus hechos políticos de 1948: Problemática de una década*, 2nd ed. (San José, CR: EDUCA, 1974); John Patrick Bell, *Crisis in Costa Rica: The 1948 Revolution* (Austin, TX: University of Texas Press, 1971); and Manuel Rojas Bolaños, *Luchas sociales y guerra civil en Costa Rica, 1940-1948*, 4th ed. (San José, CR: Editorial Porvenir, 1989).

2 Rodolfo Cerdas Cruz, "Costa Rica since 1930," trans. Elizabeth Ladd, in *Central America since Independence*, ed. Leslie Bethell (Cambridge, UK: Cambridge University Press, 1991), 303.

3 James Dunkerley, "Costa Rica: Stability at a Price," in *Power in the Isthmus: A Political History of Modern Central America* (London: Verso, 1988), 609-10.

4 Cerdas, "Costa Rica since 1930," 311.

5 Mylena Vega, "CODESA, Autonomous Institutions, and the Growth of the Public Sector," in *The Costa Rica Reader*, ed. Marc Edelman and Joanne Kenen (New York: Grove Weidenfeld, 1989), 140-44. Subsequent references to works in this collection are cited as *The Costa Rica Reader*.

6 Dunkerley, "Stability at a Price," 605-06.

7 Alicia Korten, *Ajuste estructural en Costa Rica: Una medicina amarga* (San José, CR: DEI, 1997), 28.

8 Cerdas, "Costa Rica since 1930," 318.

9 Korten, *Ajuste estructural*, 30-32; and Juan Manuel Villasuso Etomba, "The Impact of the Economic Crisis on Income Distribution," in *The Costa Rica Reader*, 199-200.

10 Marc Edelman, "Back from the Brink," *NACLA Report on the Americas* 19, 6 (1985): 39.

11 Korten, *Ajuste estructural*, 33 and 38; and Villasuso Etomba, "The Impact of the Economic Crisis," 200-201.

12 John A. Booth, *Costa Rica: Quest for Democracy* (Boulder, CO: Westview Press, 1998), 161.

13 Marc Edelman and Jayne Hutchcroft, "Costa Rica: Resisting Austerity," *NACLA Report on the Americas* 18,1 (1984): 38; Marc Edelman and Joanne Kenen, "The 1980s Economic Crisis: Editors' Introduction," in *The Costa Rica Reader*, 188-89; and Marc Edelman, *Peasants against Globalization: Rural Social Movements in Costa Rica* (Stanford, CA: Stanford University Press, 1999), 74.

14 Villasuso, "Impact of the Economic Crisis," 198 and 204.

15 Lynn M. Morgan, "Health Effects of the Costa Rican Economic Crisis," in *The Costa Rica Reader*, 213-16.

16 Villasuso, "Impact of the Economic Crisis," 201-203.

17 Edelman and Hutchcroft, "Resisting Austerity," 38.

18 Manuel Rojas Bolaños, *Los años ochenta y el futuro incierto*, Nuestra Historia Series, no. 20 (San José, CR: EUNED, 1992), 13-14.

19 For particular details on each program, see Korten, *Ajuste estructural*, 38-44; and José Manuel Valverde R., *Proceso de privatización en Costa Rica...¿ Y la respuesta sindical?*, 2nd ed. (San José, CR: ASEPROLA, 1994), 30-33.

20 Edelman and Kenen, "The 1980s Economic Crisis," 192, and Tim Golden, "After the Bitter Pill, Costa Rica Improves," both in *The Costa Rica Reader*, 218-19; and Korten, *Ajuste estructural*, 48-51.

21 Morris J. Blachman and Ronald G. Hellman, "Costa Rica," in *Confronting Revolution: Security through Diplomacy in Central America*, ed. Morris J. Blachman, William M. Leogrande, and Kenneth Sharpe (New York: Pantheon Books, 1986), 168 (as cited in Dunkerley, "Stability at a Price," 636, n.108); see also Edelman, "Back from the Brink," 40-43; and Edelman and Kenen, "The 1980s Economic Crisis," 189.

22 Rojas, *Los años ochenta*, 16.

23 Jean Hopfensperger, "Costa Rica's Right-Wing Paramilitary Groups," in *The Costa Rica Reader*, 313-20.

24 Korten, *Ajuste estructural*, 65-76.

25 Korten, *Ajuste estructural*, 78-80.

26 Korten, *Ajuste estructural*, 70-71 and 93-102.

27 Booth, *Quest for Democracy*, 161 and 167-68; and Proyecto Estado de la Nación, *Estado de la nación en desarrollo humano sostenible: Un análisis amplio y objetivo sobre la Costa Rica que tenemos a partir de los indicadores más actuales* (San José, CR: Impr. Lara Segura, 1996), 256.

28 Proyecto Estado de la Nación, *Estado de la nación*, 95.

29 Booth, *Quest for Democracy*, 167-68; and Proyecto Estado de la Nación, *Estado de la nación*, 47-48, 86, and 106.

30 Proyecto Estado de la Nación, *Estado de la nación*, 87-88.

31 Edelman, *Peasants Against Globalization*, 84-87.

32 Administración Figueres Olsen, *Plan nacional de combate a la pobreza: Hacia una Costa Rica integrada de oportunidades* (San José, CR: Consejo Social, Segunda Vicepresidencia de la República, 1996), 9 (as cited in Proyecto Estado de la Nación, *Estado de la nación*, 100). Also, see the discussions regarding conflicting Costa Rican poverty rates and their interpretation in Edelman, *Peasants Against Globalization*, 87-88; and José Itzigsohn, *Developing Poverty: The State, Labor Market Deregulation, and the Informal Economy in Costa Rica and the Dominican Republic* (Philadelphia, PA: Pennsylvania State University Press, 2000), 54-55.

33 My summary of these protests is taken from Revista Aportes, "Electricity Rates: From Discontent to Organized Resistance," in *The Costa Rica Reader*, 204-08; and Rojas, *Los años ochenta*, 25-29.

34 For a detailed chronicling and analysis of the *precarista* movement, from which my comments are adapted, see Sandra Cartín and Isabel Román, *Echando raices: la lucha por la tierra en Costa Rica* (San José, CR: Centro de Estudios para la Acción Social, 1991; and Opazo, *Costa Rica*, 69-71. For a more recent, theoretically sophisticated, and broader view of peasant struggles and rural activism in response to Costa Rica's neo-liberal reforms of the 1980s, see Edelman, *Peasants Against Globalization*.

35 Cartín and Román, *Echando raices*, 69-85.

36 The quintessential expression of this traditional view is summarized in Carlos Monge Alfaro, "The Development of the Central Valley," in *The Costa Rica Reader*, 9-12.

37 See, for example, Carlos Meléndez Chaverri, "Land Tenure in Colonial Costa Rica," 13-19, Samuel Z. Stone, "Aspects of Power Distribution in Costa Rica," 20-28, and Lowell Gudmundson, "Costa Rica before Coffee: The Village Economy of the Late 1840s," all in *The Costa Rica Reader*, 28-32.

38 Marc Edelman and Joanne Kenen, "The Origins of Costa Rican Exceptionalism—Colonial Period and the Nineteenth Century: Editors' Introduction," in *The Costa Rica Reader*, 2-3.

39 Opazo, *Costa Rica*, 14 and 176-78.

40 Opazo, *Costa Rica*, 171; and Diego Palma, "The State and Social Co-optation in Costa Rica," in *The Costa Rica Reader*, 134.

41 Palma, "The State," 135; for more details on this agrarian reform, see Mitchell A. Seligson, "Agrarian Reform in Costa Rica," in *The Costa Rica Reader*, 169-75.

42 Opazo, *Costa Rica*, 175-78.

43 It has been publicized that Costa Rica's armed *guardia de seguridad* has more than 40,000 troops. See: "Honduras critica "militarismo" costarricense," *La Nación*, October 7, 1996, 24A.

Notes to Chapter 3 : The Unions in the Face of the Crisis

1 Marielos Aguilar and Victoria Ramírez, "Crisis económica y acción sindical en Costa Rica (1980-1987)," *Revista de Ciencias Sociales* 44 (June 1989): 57-58. Many fine studies exist on the history of the Costa Rican labour movement prior to the period of concern in this book. For an overview of the labour movement from its nineteenth century origins onward, see Vladimir de la Cruz, "Características y rasgos históricos del movimiento sindical en Costa Rica," in *El sindicalismo frente al cambio: Entre la pasividad y el protagonismo*, ed. Jorge Nowalski (San José, CR: DEI and Fundación Friedrich Ebert, 1997), 17-42. For studies that treat more recent periods in considerable detail, see Marielos Aguilar, *Clase trabajadora y organización sindical en Costa Rica, 1943-1971* (San José, CR: Editorial Porvenir, FLASCO, and ICES, 1989); and Elisa Donato Monge and Manuel Rojas Bolaños, *Sindicatos, política y economía: 1972-1986* (San José, CR: Editorial Alma Mater, 1987).

2 Union involvement has generally remained below 18 percent of the work force, with levels as low as 15 percent as recently as 1993: Aguilar and Ramírez, "Crisis económica," 57; and Rodrigo Aguilar Arce, *Actualidad del movimiento sindical en Costa Rica* (San José, CR: Fundación Friedrich Ebert, 1993), 15.

3 José Manuel Valverde R., *Proceso de privatización en Costa Rica … ¿ Y la respuesta sindical?*, 2nd ed. (San José, CR: ASEPROLA, 1994), 64-66.

4 Rodrigo Aguilar, secretary of the Confederación de Trabajadores Rerum Novarum, interview by Dana Sawchuk, San José, Costa Rica, July 16, 1997.

5 Aguilar, *Actualidad*, 15.

6 Jorge Nowalski, "El sindicalismo: ¿Actor pasivo en el proceso de desarrollo de Costa Rica?" in *El sindicalismo frente al cambio: Entre la pasividad y el protagonismo*, ed. Jorge Nowalski (San José, CR: DEI and Fundación Friedrich Ebert, 1997), 52.

7 Aguilar interview.

8 de la Cruz, "Características y rasgos históricos," 32.

9 Eduardo Díaz Alemán, *Sindicatos: Naturaleza, características, problemática y cifras, setiembre 1993* (San José, CR: Ministerio de Trabajo y Seguridad Social, Dirección General de Planificación, 1995), 25; and Nowalski, "El sindicalismo: ¿actor pasivo," 51.

10 Martén was an influential Costa Rican lawyer and politician who served for a brief period as minister of finance in the Figueres *junta* following the 1948 civil war. For a more detailed analysis of Martén's thought and of the creation of the solidarity movement, see Gustavo Blanco and Orlando Navarro, *El solidarismo: Pensamiento y dinámica social de un movimiento obrero patronal* (San José, CR: Editorial Costa Rica, 1984), 25-58.

11 Escuela Social Juan XXIII (ESJ23), ed., *Ley de asociaciones solidaristas: Su reglamento y otros documentos afines*, 4th ed. (Curridabat, CR: Escuela Social Juan XXIII, 1993), 13; and José Mairena, "Gigante de ₡50 mil millones," *Rumbo*, June 3, 1996, 15.

12 Mairena, "Gigante," 14 and 17; and Proyecto Estado de la Nación, *Estado de la nación en desarrollo humano sostenible: Un análisis amplio y objetivo sobre la Costa Rica que tenemos a partir de los indicadores más actuales* (San José, CR: Impr. Lara Segura, 1996), 140.

13 Centro Nacional de Trabajadores, *Denuncia sindical sobre el solidarismo en Costa Rica* (San José, CR: ASEPROLA, 1989), 3.

14 Gustavo Leonel Blanco B., "La paz del silencio obrero," *Revista Aportes* 7, 32-33 (January–April 1987): 21; Centro Nacional de Trabajadores, *Denuncia sindical*, 6-11; Juan José Flores Madrigal, *El solidarismo desde adentro: Testimonio de*

Juan José Flores (San José, CR: ASEPROLA, 1989), 52-72; Gabriela Hernández, "Bananeros denuncian arreglos directos con La Standard," *Revista Aportes* 7, 37 (September 1987): 14-15; and Lawrence Kent, "The Social Pastoral Work of the Catholic Church in Costa Rica," *Michigan Journal of Political Science* 6 (1985): 18-19.

15 For more details on the companies' tracking of problematic employees, see Philippe I. Bourgois, *Banano, etnia y lucha social en Centro América* (San José, CR; DEI, 1994), 40.

16 *Constitución política de la República de Costa Rica* (7 de noviembre de 1949), rev. Marco Castillo Rojas (Cartago, CR: Uruk Ediciones, 1996), 15; and República de Costa Rica, *Código de Trabajo*, 12th ed. (San José, CR: Editorial Porvenir, 1997), 147-49.

17 Costa Rica, *Ley de asociaciones solidaristas*, Art. 8, in ESJ23, ed., *Ley de asociaciones solidaristas*, 20-21.

18 "Agrupación internacional condena solidarismo tico," *La Nación* June 19, 1989, 4A; and CIOSL, ORIT, CATD, CCTD, and CNT, "Fallo de la OIT favorece al movimiento sindical," paid advertisement in *Eco Católico*, June 16, 1991, 13.

19 *Constitución Política de la República de Costa Rica*, 15.

20 de la Cruz, "Características y rasgos históricos," 33.

21 República de Costa Rica, *Código de trabajo*, 151-52.

22 Laura Martínez, "Solo 22 huelgas legales en los últimos 50 años," *La Nación*, October 15, 1993, 4A.

23 Martínez, "Solo 22 huelgas legales," 4A.

24 Guillermo García-Huidobro, *Política económica de ajuste y mercado de trabajo: el caso de Costa Rica, 1982-86* (Santiago, Chile: OIT-PREALC, 1987), 11.

25 John A. Booth, *Costa Rica: Quest for Democracy* (Boulder CO: Westview Press, 1998), 167.

26 García-Huidobro, *Política económica de ajuste*, 11.

27 Aguilar and Ramírez, "Crisis económica," 53.

28 García-Huidobro, *Política económica de ajuste*, 10; and Juan Diego Trejos S., *Costa Rica: Economic Crisis and Public Policy, 1978-1984*, Latin American and Caribbean Center, Occasional Paper Series, no. 11 (Miami: Florida International University, 1985), 6.

29 García-Huidobro, *Política económica de ajuste*, 10-11.

30 *La Tribuna Económica* (San José, Costa Rica) 5, 5 (May 1987): 50 (as cited in Aguilar and Ramírez, "Crisis económica," 52).

31 Marc Edelman, *Peasants Against Globalization: Rural Social Movements in Costa Rica* (Stanford, CA: Stanford University Press, 1999), 86.

32 MIDEPLAN data are cited by Edelman, *Peasants Against Globalization*, 87.

33 Edelman, *Peasants Against Globalization*, 86-87.

34 Centro de Estudios para la Acción Social, *Costa Rica en el umbral de los años 90: deterioro y auge de lo social en el marco del ajuste* (San José, CR: CEPAS, 1992), 49.

35 García-Huidobro, *Política económica de ajuste*, 12.

36 See the detailed discussion of this phenomenon in José Itzigsohn, *Developing Poverty: The State, Labor Market Deregulation, and the Informal Economy in Costa Rica and the Dominican Republic* (Philadelphia, PA: Pennsylvania State University Press, 2000), 61-85.

37 Centro de Estudios para la Acción Social, *Costa Rica en el umbral*, 41 & 49; Edelman, *Peasants Against Globalization*, 88; and Itzigsohn, *Developing Poverty*, 79-81.

38 Manuel Rojas Bolaños, "El movimiento obrero y popular en los años setenta," *Anuario de Estudios Centroamericanos* 6 (1980): 77.

39 Marielos Campos, "Gobierno intenta frenar huelgas," *Al Día*, July 27, 1993, 4.
40 William Mendez, "Despenalizan participación en huelgas," *La Nación*, June 16, 1993, 6A.
41 de la Cruz, "Características y rasgos históricos," 32–33.
42 Aguilar interview.
43 Sileny Rivera Chang, "'Limón en Lucha' … interna," *Al Día*, August 20, 1996, 4; and Angela Orozco, "Negociaciones de Limón en punto muerto," *La República*, August 25, 1996, 4A.
44 José David Guevara, "Arduas negociaciones en Limón," *La Nación*, September 3, 1996, 8A; José David Guevara and Marvin Barquero, "Comité declara huelga en Limón," *La Nación*, August 23, 1996, 4A; and José David Guevara and Marvin Barquero, "Pulso entre gobierno y muelleros," *La Nación*, August 15, 1996, 4A.
45 José D. Guevara and Carlos Villalobos, "Paralizan muelles de Limón," *La Nación*, August 14, 1996, 4A.
46 José David Guevara, "Brote de violencia en Limón," *La Nación*, August 16, 1996, 4A; and Angela Orozco, "Limón es un infierno," *La República*, August 28, 1996, 4A.
47 By February 1997, the government was claiming that it had fulfilled approximately 77 percent of the commitments it had made; Limón en Lucha leaders were accusing the government of misrepresentation and charging that much had remained unchanged in the region: Marco Leandro, "Gobierno asegura que ya cumplió con Limón," *El Diario Extra*, February 15, 1997, 2; and Angela Orozco, "Tambores de guerra en Limón," *La República*, February 15, 1997, 5A.

Notes to Chapter 4 : Official Catholic Social Teaching on Workers' Issues

1 Pope Leo XIII, "Rerum Novarum," in *Catholic Social Thought: The Documentary Heritage*, ed. David J. O'Brien and Thomas A. Shannon (Maryknoll, NY: Orbis Books, 1992), 14–39. Subsequent references to works in this collection are cited as *Catholic Social Thought*.
2 I have elected to use the term "Catholic social *teaching*," as opposed to "Catholic social doctrine" or "Catholic social thought" in this study. Catholic social teaching refers, literally, to the documents issued by the bearers of the Church's ecclesial magisterium (i.e., the Church's teaching authority)—the pope and bishops. Catholic social doctrine is often considered to be an outdated phrase with dogmatic overtones; Catholic social thought is a relatively loose term that refers to texts issued by the Church hierarchy and by other Catholic theologians.
3 Second Vatican Council, "Gaudium et Spes," in *Catholic Social Thought*, no. 67; Pope John Paul II, "Laborem Exercens," in *Catholic Social Thought*, no. 16.
4 Pope Leo XIII, *Rerum Novarum*, nos. 22, 27, and 34; Second Vatican Council, *Gaudium et Spes*, no. 34; and Pope John Paul II, *Laborem Exercens*, no. 10.
5 Pope Leo XIII, *Rerum Novarum*, no. 16; Pope Pius XI, "Quadragesimo Anno," in *Catholic Social Thought*, no. 83; Second Vatican Council, *Gaudium et Spes*, no. 67; and Pope John Paul II, *Laborem Exercens*, nos. 6–7 and 9.
6 Pope John Paul II, *Laborem Exercens*, nos. 6 and 16.
7 Second Vatican Council, *Gaudium et Spes*, nos. 34 and 67; and Pope John Paul II, *Laborem Exercens*, no. 25.
8 Pope John Paul II, *Laborem Exercens*, no. 27.
9 Pope John Paul II, *Laborem Exercens*, no. 26.
10 Donal Dorr, *Option for the Poor: A Hundred Years of Vatican Social Teaching*, rev. ed. (Maryknoll, NY: Orbis Books, 1992), 25.
11 Pope Leo XIII, *Rerum Novarum*, no. 31.

12   Pope Leo XIII, *Rerum Novarum*, no. 16.

13   Pope Leo XIII, *Rerum Novarum*, nos. 36–37.

14   Pope Leo XIII, *Rerum Novarum*, no. 43.

15   Jean-Yves Calvez and Jacques Perrin, *The Church and Social Justice: The Social Teaching of the Popes from Leo XIII to Pius XII (1878–1958)* (Chicago, IL: Henry Regnery, 1961), 381–83; and Dorr, *Option for the Poor*, 30–31.

16   Pope Leo XIII, *Rerum Novarum*, nos. 40 and 44.

17   Pope Pius XI, *Quadragesimo Anno*, nos. 30–36.

18   Pope Pius XI, *Quadragesimo Anno*, nos. 82–87. It should be noted that, although the corporatist society Pius advocates in *Quadragesimo Anno* is not based on a fascist model, Pius's overall relation vis-à-vis Italian fascism has its ambiguities. For a discussion of this complex issue, see John Coleman, "Development of Church Social Teaching," in *Official Catholic Social Teaching*, Readings in Moral Theology, no. 5, ed. Charles E. Curran and Richard A. McCormick (New York: Paulist Press, 1986), 174–85 (subsequently cited as *Official Catholic Social Teaching*); and Marie J. Giblin, "Corporatism," in *The New Dictionary of Catholic Social Thought*, ed. Judith A. Dwyer (Collegeville, MN: The Liturgical Press, 1994), 245–46 (subsequently cited as *New Dictionary of Catholic Social Thought*).

19   Pope Pius XI, *Quadragesimo Anno*, nos. 91–95.

20   Pope John XXIII, "Mater et Magistra," in *Catholic Social Thought*, 84–128.

21   Pope John XXIII, *Mater et Magistra*, no. 97.

22   Pope John XXIII, *Mater et Magistra*, no. 100.

23   Pope John XXIII, *Mater et Magistra*, no. 103.

24   Second Vatican Council, *Gaudium et Spes*, no. 68.

25   Second Vatican Council, *Gaudium et Spes*, no. 68.

26   Pope Paul VI, "Populorum Progressio," in *Catholic Social Thought*, nos. 26 and 39.

27   Pope Paul VI, "Octogesima Adveniens," in *Catholic Social Thought*, nos. 265–86.

28   Pope Paul VI, *Octogesima Adveniens*, no. 14.

29   Pope Paul VI, *Octogesima Adveniens*, no. 14.

30   For a more detailed examination of this point, see Dorr, *Option for the Poor*, 220–23.

31   Pope John Paul II, "Sollicitudo Rei Socialis," in *Catholic Social Thought*, no. 15.

32   Pope John Paul II, "Centesimus Annus," in *Catholic Social Thought*, nos. 7, 15–16, 19, 26, 35, and 43.

33   Pope John Paul II, *Laborem Exercens*, no. 20.

34   Thomas R. Donahue, "From Rerum Novarum to Laborem Exercens: A United States Labor Perspective," 404, and Richard A. McCormick, "Laborem Exercens and Social Morality," 222, both in *Official Catholic Social Teaching*.

35   Peter Hebblethwaite, "The Popes and Politics: Shifting Patterns in Catholic Social Doctrine," in *Official Catholic Social Teaching*, 281.

36   Histories of CELAM include: Juan Botero Restrepo, *El CELAM: Elementos para su historia* (Medellín, Colombia: Consejo Episcopal Latinoamericano, 1982); François Houtart, "L'histoire du CELAM ou l'oubli des origines," *Archives de Sciences Sociales des Religions*, 62,1 (Jul.–Sep. 1986): 93–105; and Cecilio de Lora Soria, "History, Structure, and Present Activities of CELAM," in *The Church and Social Change in Latin America*, ed. Henry A. Landsberger (Notre Dame, IN: University of Notre Dame Press, 1970), 173–90.

37   II Conferencia General del Episcopado Latinoamericano, *Medellín conclusiones: La Iglesia en la actual transformación de América Latina a la luz del concilio* (Bogotá, Colombia: Secretariado General del Consejo Episcopal Latinoamericano, 1990). Subsequent Medellín documents are cited as: CELAM, "Document name," in *Medellín*.

38 CELAM, "Justicia," in *Medellín*, no. 7; and CELAM, "Pastoral de élites," in *Medellín*, nos. 1–2 and 19.

39 CELAM, "Justicia," in *Medellín*, no. 12.

40 III Conferencia General del Episcopado Latinoamericano, *Puebla: La evangelización en el presente y en el futuro de América Latina* (Bogotá, Colombia: Secretariado General del Consejo Episcopal Latinoamericano, 1990) (subsequently cited as CELAM, *Puebla*).

41 CELAM, *Puebla*, nos. 44, 1162–63, and 1244.

42 CELAM, *Puebla*, nos. 36, 44, and 442.

43 CELAM, *Puebla*, no. 1244. In the former quotation, the bishops are adopting the words of Pope John Paul II in his January 31, 1979 address to workers in Monterrey.

44 CELAM, *Puebla*, no. 45.

45 IV Conferencia General del Episcopado Latinoamericano, *Santo Domingo conclusiones: Nueva evangelización, promoción humana, cultura cristiana* (Santafé de Bogotá, Colombia: CELAM, 1992) (subsequently cited as CELAM, *Santo Domingo*).

46 CELAM, *Santo Domingo*, no. 182.

47 CELAM, *Santo Domingo*, nos. 183 and 185.

48 CELAM, *Santo Domingo*, no. 183.

49 CELAM, *Santo Domingo*, no. 185.

50 CELAM, *Santo Domingo*, no. 183.

51 This thinking is similar to that found in the failed "trickle-down" development schemes of the 1960s (in which benefits for the wealthy were supposed to trickle down to aid the poor) and in the current neo-liberal programs in Latin America.

52 Pope Leo XIII, *Rerum Novarum*, no. 14.

53 Pope Pius XI, *Quadragesimo Anno*, no. 114.

54 Pope Leo XIII, *Rerum Novarum*, no. 2.

55 Pope Pius XI, *Quadragesimo Anno*, no. 83.

56 Pope Pius XI, *Quadragesimo Anno*, no. 101.

57 Pope Leo XIII, *Rerum Novarum*, nos. 1 and 35.

58 Pope Pius XI, *Quadragesimo Anno*, no. 105.

59 Pope Pius XI, *Quadragesimo Anno*, no. 109.

60 Pope Leo XIII, *Rerum Novarum*, nos. 1–3, 14, 16, and 20.

61 Pope Pius XI, *Quadragesimo Anno*, no. 131.

62 Pope Pius XI, *Quadragesimo Anno*, nos. 132–35.

63 Pope Pius XI, *Quadragesimo Anno*, nos. 112–17.

64 Pope Pius XI, *Quadragesimo Anno*, no. 127.

65 Pope Leo XIII, *Rerum Novarum*, no. 18.

66 Pope Leo XIII, *Rerum Novarum*, no. 15; and Pope Pius XI, *Quadragesimo Anno*, nos. 53 and 100.

67 Pope Leo XIII, *Rerum Novarum*, nos. 19, 24, and 45; and Pope Pius XI, *Quadragesimo Anno*, nos. 88, 110, and 137.

68 Pope Leo XIII, *Rerum Novarum*, nos. 27 and 29–30; and Pope Pius XI, *Quadragesimo Anno*, nos. 25 and 88.

69 Dorr, *Option for the Poor*, 222.

70 Dorr, *Option for the Poor*, 23 and 27.

71 Pope Leo XIII, *Rerum Novarum*, no. 20.

72 Pope Leo XIII, *Rerum Novarum*, no. 14.

73 Pope Leo XIII, *Rerum Novarum*, no. 20.

74 See, for example, Gutiérrez, *A Theology of Liberation: History, Politics and Salvation*, trans. and ed. Sister Caridad Inda and John Eagelson (Maryknoll, NY: Orbis Books, 1973).

75 CELAM, "Justicia," in *Medellín*, nos. 1–2; and CELAM, "Paz," in *Medellín*, nos. 2–7.

76 CELAM, "Paz," in *Medellín*, nos. 8–10.

77 CELAM, "Paz," in *Medellín*, nos. 1 and 14.

78 CELAM, "Paz," in *Medellín*, no. 16.

79 CELAM, "Paz," in *Medellín*, nos. 6, 14, and 17.

80 CELAM, "Justicia," in *Medellín*, no. 1; CELAM, "Paz," in *Medellín*, nos. 7, 16–17, and 19; and CELAM, "Juventud," in *Medellín*, no. 3.

81 CELAM, "Justicia," in *Medellín*, nos. 3, 10, 14, and 16; CELAM, "Paz," in *Medellín*, no. 16; and CELAM, "Educación," in *Medellín*, nos. 7–8.

82 CELAM, "Justicia," in *Medellín*, nos. 3–5; CELAM, "Juventud," in *Medellín*, no. 16; CELAM, "Pastoral de élites," in *Medellín*, no. 13; CELAM, "Catequesis," in *Medellín*, no. 4; CELAM, "Movimientos de laicos," in *Medellín*, nos. 9–11; and CELAM, "Religiosos," in *Medellín*, no. 8.

83 Details of the bishops' recommendations for change are found in: CELAM, "Justicia," in *Medellín*, nos. 6–23; CELAM, "Paz," in *Medellín*, nos. 20–33; and CELAM, "Educación," in *Medellín*, nos. 10–31.

84 CELAM, "Pastoral de élites," in *Medellín*, no. 8; the bishops' three-fold classification system is spelled out in CELAM, "Pastoral de élites," in *Medellín*, nos. 5–8.

85 CELAM, "Justicia," in *Medellín*, no. 7.

86 The bishops refer to these small Church groups in more than one document. According to them, the CEBs are a focal point for evangelization and are essential factors in development, the consolidation of rights, and the search for justice.

87 The bishops here are clearly influenced by the work of the Brazilian popular educator Paulo Freire, who defines "conscientization" as "learning to perceive social, political, and economic contradictions, and to take action against the oppressive elements of reality" (*Pedagogy of the Oppressed*, trans. Myra Bergman Ramos (New York: The Seabury Press, 1970), 19. Freire originally used the Portuguese form of the word, *conscientização*; in Spanish, the term is *conscientización*.

88 CELAM, "Justicia," in *Medellín*, nos. 17 and 20; CELAM, "Paz," in *Medellín*, nos. 18 and 27; CELAM, "Educación," in *Medellín*, nos. 3–8 and 16; CELAM, "Formación del clero," in *Medellín*, no. 21; CELAM, "Pastoral de conjunto," in *Medellín*, no. 10; and CELAM, "Medios de comunicación social," in *Medellín*, nos. 2, 5–6, and 15.

89 These ideas can be found in Leonardo Boff, *Church: Charism and Power. Liberation Theology and the Institutional Church*, trans. John W. Diercksmeier (New York: Crossroad, 1985), chap. 1, 9, and 10; and Leonardo Boff, *Ecclesiogenesis: The Base Communities Reinvent the Church*, trans. Robert R. Barr (Maryknoll, NY: Orbis Books, 1986), chap. 1 and 3.

90 CELAM, "Paz," in *Medellín*, no. 19.

91 The original passage reads: "We know, however, that a revolutionary uprising— save where there is manifest, long-standing tyranny which would do great damage to fundamental personal rights and dangerous harm to the common good of the country—produces new injustices, throws more elements out of balance and brings on new disasters. A real evil should not be fought against at the cost of greater misery" (Pope Paul VI, *Populorum Progressio*, no. 31). For a more detailed discussion of this issue, see Dorr, *Option for the Poor*, 210–11.

92 See Dean Peerman, "CELAM III: Measured Steps Forward," *The Christian Century* 96, 12 (April 1979): 378; Pablo Richard, "Puebla: Hope of the Poor," trans. Robert Lazear, *Missiology: An International Review* 7, 3 (July 1979): 292; and Ser

gio Torres, *Puebla 1979: The III Conference of the Latin American Bishops*, Theology in the Americas Documentation Series, no. 7 (New York: Theology in the Americas, 1979), 9 and 14.

93 See, for example: Pope John XXIII, *Mater et Magistra*, no. 92; Pope John XXIII, "Pacem in Terris," in *Catholic Social Thought*, nos. 31, 33–35, 98, 100, and 129; Second Vatican Council, *Gaudium et Spes*, nos. 26 and 78; Pope Paul VI, *Octogesima Adveniens*, no. 50; and Pope John Paul II, *Sollicitudo Rei Socialis*, no. 31.

94 Pope John XXIII, *Mater et Magistra*, no. 155; Pope John XXIII, *Pacem in Terris*, no. 171; Second Vatican Council, *Gaudium et Spes*, nos. 24, 32, 38, 40, 42, 56, and 92; Pope Paul VI, *Populorum Progressio*, nos. 62, 67, 73, and 75; Pope Paul VI, *Octogesima Adveniens*, nos. 12, 17 and 23; and Pope Paul VI, "Evangelii Nuntiandi," in *Catholic Social Thought*, no. 28.

95 CELAM, *Santo Domingo*, no. 122.

96 Pope John Paul II, *Centesimus Annus*, no. 51.

97 Pope John Paul II, *Sollicitudo Rei Socialis*, no. 48. Other examples include: Second Vatican Council, *Gaudium et Spes*, nos. 24, 32, and 42; and Pope Paul VI, *Evangelii Nuntiandi*, no. 77.

98 Jon Sobrino, "Bearing with One Another in Faith," in *Theology of Christian Solidarity*, trans. Phillip Berryman (Maryknoll, NY: Orbis Books, 1985), 9.

99 Otto Maduro, *Religion and Social Conflicts*, trans. Robert R. Barr (Maryknoll, NY: Orbis Books, 1982), 133–34.

100 The most notable examples of such praise are found in Gregory Baum, *The Priority of Labor: A Commentary on Laborem Exercens, Encyclical Letter of Pope John Paul II* (New York and Ramsey, NJ: Paulist Press, 1982).

101 Pope John Paul II, *Laborem Exercens*, no. 20.

102 Pope John Paul II, *Laborem Exercens*, no. 9. For further comments on the notion of all people as workers, see Dorr, *Option for the Poor*, 309.

103 Pope John Paul II, *Laborem Exercens*, nos. 12–15.

104 A visit to a *maquiladora* or banana plantation and a view of the working conditions suffered there will provide graphic evidence of some of the other outcomes of this exploitive relationship.

105 Pope John Paul II, *Laborem Exercens*, nos. 11–15.

106 Pope John Paul II, *Laborem Exercens*, no. 13.

107 Pope John Paul II, *Laborem Exercens*, nos. 8, 11, and 13.

108 Pope John Paul II, *Laborem Exercens*, no. 13.

109 While I have made particular mention of Antonio Gramsci and Otto Maduro in this regard, one could also discuss here the work of such individuals as George Lukács or Mihailo Markovic, or the work of such "critical theorists" as Herbert Marcuse or Max Horkheimer. See also the discussion of the development of various Marxisms after Marx in Arthur F. McGovern, *Marxism: An American Christian Perspective* (Maryknoll, NY: Orbis Books, 1980), 49–89.

110 José Porfirio Miranda, *Marx against the Marxists: The Christian Humanism of Karl Marx*, trans. John Drury (Maryknoll, NY: Orbis Books, 1980), 57.

111 Karl Marx, *Theories of Surplus Value*, vol. 1 (Moscow: Progress Publishers, 1963), 288 (as cited in Miranda, *Marx against the Marxists*, 37–38).

112 The Church's hostility toward communism (and hence, Marxism) has historically been tied to its need to condemn anything that threatens its ability to survive and freely proclaim its message of salvation. Given the persecution the Church has suffered under certain communist regimes in the past, it is not surprising that the pope does not present a nuanced view of the Marxist tradition.

113 Mary E. Hobgood, "Conflicting Paradigms in Social Analysis," in *The Logic of Solidarity: Commentaries on Pope John Paul II's Encyclical "On Social Concern,"* ed. Gregory Baum and Robert Ellsberg (Maryknoll, NY: Orbis Books, 1989), 178.

114 See, for example, Pope John XXIII, *Mater et Magistra*, nos. 6, 92, and 257; and Pope John XXIII, *Pacem in Terris*, nos. 31, 107, and 129.

115 Pope Paul VI, *Populorum Progressio*, nos. 32, 43–44, 46–50, 53–54, 70–73, and 83–84.

116 Pope Paul VI, "Honoring Christ in His Poor," address in San José, Colombia, on August 23, 1968, in *The Pope Speaks* 13,3 (1968): 236; Pope Paul VI, "Changing Social Structures: A Time of Crisis," address in Bogotá, Colombia, on August 23, 1968, in *The Pope Speaks* 13,3 (1968): 240; and Pope Paul VI, "Discurso de S.S. Pablo VI en la apertura de la segunda conferencia," in CELAM, *Medellín*, 24–25.

117 Pope Paul VI, *Evangelii Nuntiandi*, no. 37.

118 CELAM, *Puebla*, nos. 486, 531–34, and 1259.

119 Pope John Paul II, *Centesimus Annus*, nos. 23–25. See also Kenneth R. Himes, "War," in *New Dictionary of Catholic Social Thought*, 979–80.

120 Pope John Paul II, *Laborem Exercens*, no. 8.

121 Dorr, *Option for the Poor*, 303–08.

122 Pope John Paul II, *Laborem Exercens*, no. 8; and Dorr, *Option for the Poor*, 305.

123 Pope John Paul II, *Laborem Exercens*, no. 20.

124 Karol Wojtyla, "The Self and the Act," in *Karol Wojtyla (Pope John Paul II): An Anthology*, ed. Alfred Bloch and George T. Czuczka (New York: Crossroad, 1981), 30–56.

125 Pope John Paul II, *Sollicitudo Rei Socialis*, no. 38.

126 Pope John Paul II, *Sollicitudo Rei Socialis*, no. 39.

127 Pope John Paul II, *Sollicitudo Rei Socialis*, no. 37.

128 Pope John Paul II, *Sollicitudo Rei Socialis*, no. 39; and Pope John Paul II, *Centesimus Annus*, no. 22.

129 Pope John Paul II, *Sollicitudo Rei Socialis*, nos. 40 and 42; Pope John Paul II, *Centesimus Annus*, nos. 10–11.

130 Pope John Paul II, *Sollicitudo Rei Socialis*, nos. 8–9, 35, 37, and 41.

131 Pope John Paul II, *Sollicitudo Rei Socialis*, no. 36.

132 Pope John Paul II, *Sollicitudo Rei Socialis*, nos. 14, 26, and 36.

133 Pope John Paul II, *Sollicitudo Rei Socialis*, no. 47.

134 Pope John Paul II, *Reconciliatio et Paenitentia*, no. 16 (as cited in Pope John Paul II, *Sollicitudo Rei Socialis*, no. 36, n.65).

135 Pope John Paul II, *Sollicitudo Rei Socialis*, no. 38.

136 Pope John Paul II, *Centesimus Annus*, nos. 15, 19, 33–39, and 42.

137 Pope John Paul II, *Sollicitudo Rei Socialis*, no. 7.

138 Pope John Paul II, *Sollicitudo Rei Socialis*, no. 39; Pope John Paul II, *Centesimus Annus*, no. 23.

139 The pope does, however, remark on the Polish workers' protests against "Marxism." Still, he notes the efficacy of these protests, based as they were not on violence, but "on trying every avenue of negotiation, dialogue and witness to the truth, appealing to the conscience of the adversary" (Pope John Paul II, *Centesimus Annus*, no. 23).

140 Pope John Paul II, *Centesimus Annus*, no. 10.

141 CELAM, "Justicia," in *Medellín*, nos. 3–5.

142 Cited in Juan Luis Segundo, *Theology and the Church: A Response to Cardinal Ratzinger and a Warning to the Whole Church*, rev. ed., trans. John W. Diercksmeier (San Francisco, CA: Harper and Row, 1987), 71. A detailed summary of the development of this idea in the Church is found at pages 66–77.

143 Pope Paul VI, *Octogesima Adveniens*, no. 45.

144 Pope Paul VI, *Evangelii Nuntiandi*, nos. 29–34.

145 Donal Dorr, *Option for the Poor: A Hundred Years of Vatican Social Teaching* (Maryknoll, NY: Orbis Books, 1983): 194.

146 Pope Paul VI, *Octogesima Adveniens*, nos. 28 and 45.

147 Pope Paul VI, *Evangelii Nuntiandi*, no. 35.

148 CELAM, *Puebla*, nos. 327-39.

149 CELAM, *Puebla*, nos. 187-97 and 475.

150 CELAM, *Puebla*, nos. 348-55.

151 CELAM, *Puebla*, no. 519.

152 CELAM, *Puebla*, nos. 96-98 and 640-43.

153 Pope John Paul II, *Sollicitudo Rei Socialis*, no. 46; Pope John Paul II, *Centesimus Annus*, no. 26; and Sacred Congregation for the Doctrine of the Faith, *Instruction on Christian Freedom and Liberation* (Washington, DC: United States Catholic Conference, 1986).

154 Sacred Congregation for the Doctrine of the Faith, *Instruction on Certain Aspects of the "Theology of Liberation"* (Washington, DC: United States Catholic Conference, 1984).

155 Marsha Hewitt, *From Theology to Social Theory: Juan Luis Segundo and the Theology of Liberation* (New York: Peter Lang, 1990), 135-36; Sacred Congregation for the Doctrine of the Faith, *Instruction* (*1984*), 31-32, and *Instruction* (*1986*), 21-24 and 44-46.

156 Sacred Congregation for the Doctrine of the Faith, *Instruction* (*1984*), 3; and Segundo, *Theology and the Church*, 27-29 and 34.

157 CELAM, *Santo Domingo*, no. 123.

158 Pope John Paul II, *Redemptoris Missio*, no. 59 (as cited in CELAM, *Santo Domingo*, no. 157).

159 Pope John Paul II, *Redemptoris Missio*, no. 20 (as cited in CELAM, *Santo Domingo*, no. 157).

160 See especially Gutiérrez, *A Theology of Liberation*, 287-306. Significantly, Gutiérrez was one of the theological advisors at the Medellín conference.

161 CELAM, *Puebla*, nos. 382, 733, and 1134-45; and CELAM, *Santo Domingo*, no. 180.

162 Pope John Paul II, *Sollicitudo Rei Socialis*, no. 42. See also Pope John Paul II, *Centesimus Annus*, no. 11.

163 Segundo, *Theology and the Church*, 41.

164 Segundo, *Theology and the Church*, 41-43.

165 Second Vatican Council, *Lumen Gentium*, in *Vatican Council II: The Conciliar and Post Conciliar Documents*, ed. Austin Flannery (Northport, NY: Costello Publishing, 1987), no. 1-4; and Pope John Paul II, "Unity of the Church," *The Pope Speaks* 28,3 (1983): 206-10.

166 Second Vatican Council, *Lumen Gentium*, nos. 12-13; and Pope Paul VI, *Evangelii Nuntiandi*, nos. 61-65.

167 Gutiérrez, *A Theology of Liberation*, 301.

168 Richard, "The Latin American Church," 42-43.

169 CELAM, *Puebla*, nos. 733, 1145, and 1165; see also Pope John Paul II, "Preferential Option for the Poor Must Be Gospel-Based," *The Pope Speaks* 32 (1987): 241.

170 Pope John Paul II, "Unity of the Church," 207.

171 Richard, "The Latin American Church," 41-43.

172 Pope John Paul II, "Veritatis Splendor: The Splendor of Truth," *The Pope Speaks* 39, 1 (1993), no. 113.

173 Pope John XXIII, *Humanae Salutis, The Encyclicals and Other Messages of John XXIII*, ed. staff (Washington, D.C.: The Pope Speaks Press, 1964), 387 (as cited in Thomas L. Schubeck, *Liberation Ethics: Sources, Models, and Norms* (Minneapolis, MN: Fortress Press, 1993), 48, n.44).

174   Pope John Paul II, *Centesimus Annus*, no. 3.

175   Pope John Paul II, *Centesimus Annus*, no. 3.

176   Richard McCormick, "The Teaching Office as a Guarantor of Unity in Morality," in *Christian Ethics: Uniformity, Universality, Pluralism*, Concilium no. 150, ed. Jacques Pohier and Dietmar Mieth (Edinburgh: T. & T. Clark, 1981), 73–74.

177   Pope Pius XI, *Quadragesimo Anno*, no. 18.

178   Sacred Congregation for the Doctrine of the Faith, *Instruction* (1986), 5; see also *Instruction* (1984), 14 and 30.

179   For a more detailed discussion of the repercussions of a theology that is "homiletic" rather than historically mediated, see Alfredo Fierro, *The Militant Gospel: A Critical Introduction to Political Theologies*, trans. John Drury (Maryknoll, NY: Orbis Books, 1977), 72–74 and 328–39.

180   Pope Paul VI, *Evangelii Nuntiandi*, no. 58.

181   CELAM, *Puebla*, no. 263.

182   CELAM, *Puebla*, no. 262.

183   Edward L. Cleary, "The Journey to Santo Domingo," in *Santo Domingo and Beyond: Documents and Commentaries from the Fourth General Conference of Latin American Bishops*, ed. Alfred T. Hennelly (Maryknoll, NY: Orbis Books, 1993), 15; and Leslie Wirpsa, "Vatican Clampdown on CLAR Continues," *National Catholic Reporter*, May 24, 1991, 9.

184   Arthur F. McGovern, *Liberation Theology and Its Critics: Toward an Assessment* (Maryknoll, NY: Orbis Books, 1989), 231–32; and Brady Tyson, "Brazil: End of an Era?" *Christianity and Crisis*, June 12, 1989, 193–94.

185   The best discussion of this case remains Harvey Cox, *The Silencing of Leonardo Boff: The Vatican and the Future of World Christianity* (London, UK: Collins, 1989).

186   Pope John Paul II, *Laborem Exercens*, no. 2.

Notes to Chapter 5 : Monseñor Arrieta and CECOR

1   Pablo Richard and Guillermo Meléndez, "La Iglesia de los pobres en Costa Rica," in *La Iglesia de los pobres en América Central: Un análisis socio-político y teológico de la Iglesia centroamericana (1960-1982)*, ed. Pablo Richard and Guillermo Meléndez (San José, CR: DEI, 1982), 271.

2   Jorge Mario Salazar Mora, *La Iglesia rebelde en América Latina: El caso de Costa Rica* (San José, CR: Universidad de Costa Rica, 1978), 17–18.

3   For a more detailed description of this controversy, see Philip J. Williams, *The Catholic Church and Politics in Nicaragua and Costa Rica* (London: Macmillan, with St. Anthony's College, Oxford, 1989), 133–34.

4   Richard and Meléndez, "La Iglesia de los pobres," 292–94.

5   "Curriculum vitae de Mons. Román Arrieta Villalobos, Arzobispo de San José," *Eco Católico*, September 21, 1986, 5.

6   See, for example, "Popularidad que es aceptación," *El Mensajero del Clero* 23 (November 1987): 16.

7   Conferencia Episcopal de Costa Rica (CECOR), "Evangelización y realidad social de Costa Rica: Carta pastoral colectiva," in *La palabra social de los obispos costarricenses: Selección de documentos de la Iglesia Católica costarricense 1893-1981*, ed. Miguel Picado (San José, CR: DEI, n.d.), 159–81. Subsequent references to Conferencia Episcopal de Costa Rica documents are cited as CECOR, and to the Picado collection as *La palabra social*.

8   CECOR, "Iglesia y momento actual: Carta pastoral del episcopado costarricense sobre la actual situación del país y la campaña electoral (1981)," in *La palabra social*, 183–94.

9   CECOR, "Navidad 1981—Unidos en la Esperanza: Carta pastoral del episco-
    pado sobre la crítica situación que vive el país," in *La palabra social*, 195–200.
10 CECOR, *Evangelización y realidad social*, no. 2.4.
11 CECOR, *Evangelización y realidad social*, no. 2.4.
12 CECOR, *Evangelización y realidad social*, no. 2.5.
13 CECOR, *Evangelización y realidad social*, no. 2.5.
14 CECOR, *Evangelización y realidad social*, no. 5.12.
15 CECOR, *Evangelización y realidad social*, nos. 5.4 and 5.6.
16 CECOR, *Evangelización y realidad social*, no. 5.8.
17 CECOR, *Evangelización y realidad social*, no. 2.6.
18 CECOR, *Evangelización y realidad social*, no. 3.5; see also nos. 2.1 and 8.1.
19 CECOR, *Evangelización y realidad social*, no. 6.2; see also no. 3.2.
20 Richard and Meléndez, *La Iglesia de los pobres*, 296–97; and Williams, *Catholic
    Church and Politics*, 138–39.
21 CECOR, *Evangelización y realidad social*, no. 3.4.
22 CECOR, *Evangelización y realidad social*, no. 3.5.
23 CECOR, *Evangelización y realidad social*, no. 3.2; see also nos. 2.3, 5.11, and 6.4.
24 CECOR, *Evangelización y realidad social*, no. 3.2.
25 CECOR, *Iglesia y momento actual*, no. 2.2.3.
26 CECOR, *Unidos en la esperanza*, no. 3.6.
27 CECOR, *Iglesia y momento actual*, no. 2.2.2.
28 CECOR, *Unidos en la esperanza*, conclusion.
29 CECOR, *Unidos en la esperanza*, nos. 3.6 and 3.10; and CECOR, *Iglesia y
    momento actual*, nos. 2.1.8 and 2.2.2.
30 CECOR, *Unidos en la esperanza*, no. 1; and CECOR, *Iglesia y momento actual*,
    nos. 2.1 and 2.1.7.
31 CECOR, *Unidos en la esperanza*, no. 3.6.
32 CECOR, *Unidos en la esperanza*, no. 3.10.
33 CECOR, *Iglesia y momento actual*, nos. 1.3, 2, 2.1.8, and 2.2.2.
34 CECOR, *Iglesia y momento actual*, no. 2.2.3.
35 CECOR, *Iglesia y momento actual*, no. 2.2.3.
36 CECOR, *Evangelización y realidad social*, no. 6.2.
37 CECOR, *Evangelización y realidad social*, no. 3.2.
38 Mons. Román Arrieta, "La Iglesia de Cristo siempre se ha preocupado por los
    pobres," *Eco Católico*, November 22, 1981, 2.
39 Mons. Román Arrieta, "Liberación cristiana opta sólo por Cristo," *Eco Católico*,
    September 28, 1980, 2.
40 CECOR, *Bendito el que viene en el nombre del Señor: Exhortación de los obis-
    pos de Costa Rica ante la próxima venida de S.S. Juan Pablo II* (San José, CR:
    Ediciones CECOR, 1983).
41 CECOR, "La iglesia ante el proceso electoral: Exhortación pastoral de la Confer-
    encia Episcopal de Costa Rica," *Eco Católico*, September 15, 1985, 2–3.
42 CECOR, *Una llamada de los obispos de Costa Rica a la conciencia del país* (San
    José, CR: Ediciones CECOR[?], 1988).
43 CECOR, *Una llamada de los obispos*, no. 1.
44 CECOR, *Bendito el que viene*, III: nos. 4.1–4.3.
45 CECOR, *Bendito el que viene*, III: no. 4.3.
46 CECOR, *La Iglesia ante el proceso electoral*, no. 16.
47 Mons. Román Arrieta, "Festividad de Nuestra Señora de los Angeles–Cartago, 2
    de agosto de 1984: Homilía," *El Mensajero del Clero* 15 (September 1984): 19;
    see also his "Solemnidad de nuestra Señora de los Angeles," *Eco Católico*,
    August 9, 1987, 2.

48 CECOR, *La Iglesia ante el proceso electoral*, nos. 21-22.

49 CECOR, *Bendito el que viene*, I: no. 2.

50 CECOR, *Bendito el que viene*, II: no. 2.

51 CECOR, *Bendito el que viene*, I: no. 2.1.

52 CECOR, *Bendito el que viene*, I: no. 2.2; see the similar repudiation of the popular church in Mons. Arrieta, "Solemnidad de nuestra Señora de los Angeles (1987)," 2; and Armando Mayorga, "Conferencia Episcopal de Costa Rica: Desautorizado folleto de 'iglesia popular,'" *La Nación*, November 30, 1988, 12A.

53 CECOR, *Bendito el que viene*, II: no. 1.3.

54 Mons. Román Arrieta, "Declaración sobre la Instrucción de la Sagrada Congregación para la Doctrina de la Fe, con relación a algunos aspectos de la teología de la liberación," *El Mensajero del Clero* 15 (September 1984): 29-30.

55 Mons. Román Arrieta, "Alocución de Mons. Román Arrieta Villalobos, Arzobispo de San José, con motivo de la elección de don Luis Alberto Monge, como Presidente de la República," *El Mensajero del Clero* 8 (December 1982): 4-5.

56 Luis Alberto Monge, "Necesito solidaridad entre los costarricenses," *Betania*, May 9, 1982, 2.

57 Andrés Opazo Bernales, *Costa Rica: La Iglesia católica y el orden social* (San José, CR: DEI, 1987), 74-79.

58 CECOR, *Una llamada de los obispos*, preambulo.

59 CECOR, *Una llamada de los obispos*, no. 1.

60 Mons. Román Arrieta, "Decálogo de la austeridad," *Eco Católico*, January 15, 1984, 3.

61 Opazo, *Costa Rica*, 77; and Williams, *Catholic Church and Politics*, 142.

62 The context for the Costa Rican government's shifting policies on Nicaragua is explained in Marc Edelman and Joanne Kenen, "Costa Rica and the Nicaraguan Revolution: Editors' Introduction," in *The Costa Rica Reader*, ed. Marc Edelman and Joanne Kenen (New York: Grove Weidenfeld, 1989), 269-78.

63 Mons. Román Arrieta, "Segundo aniversario de la proclama de neutralidad," *Eco Católico*, November 24, 1985, 2.

64 Miguel Picado G., "La Iglesia Católica costarricense en la crisis centroamericana," *Cristianismo y Sociedad* 89 (1986): 88.

65 Mons. Román Arrieta, "Reacción del Arzobispo de San José frente a declaraciones del comandante Daniel Ortega," *Eco Católico*, July 29, 1994, 2.

66 "El Plan Reagan: Una trampa moral," *Eco Católico*, March 21, 1982, 2; and Mons. Román Arrieta, "Comunicado del Arzobispo de San José sobre un editorial del Eco Católico," *Eco Católico* (*Suplemento Campesino*), April 11, 1982, 1.

67 CECOR, "Acuerdos importantes tomados por la CECOR, en su primera reunión extraordinaria de 1986," *El Mensajero del Clero* 19 (October 1986): 5-6.

68 Picado, "La Iglesia Católica costarricense en la crisis centroamericana," 88.

69 Mons. Arrieta, "Solemnidad de nuestra Señora de los Angeles (1987)," 2; and his "Misa de acción de gracias por el Acuerdo de Paz," *El Mensajero del Clero* 23 (November 1987): 20-21.

70 Mons. Arrieta, *Nueva evangelización y promoción humana* (Curridabat, CR: Escuela Social Juan XXIII, 1993).

71 CECOR, *Madre Tierra: Mensaje de los obispos de Costa Rica sobre le situación de los campesinos y los indígenas* (San José, CR: Ediciones CECOR[?], 1994).

72 Mons. Arrieta, "Como debe ser la liberación cristiana," *Eco Católico*, May 19, 1996, 4, and his "Liberación cristiana: Características que la distinguen," *Eco Católico*, June 17, 1990, 3.

73 Mons. Román Arrieta, "La Iglesia tiene un compromiso con los más pobres," *Eco Católico*, April 8, 1990, 3.

74 Mons. Arrieta, *Nueva Evangelización*, IV: no. 6.
75 Mons. Arrieta, *Nueva Evangelización*, IV: no. 37.
76 Mons. Arrieta, *Nueva Evangelización*, IV: no. 24.
77 Mons. Arrieta, *Nueva Evangelización*, II: nos. 19 and 21, and IV: no. 34, "Pacíficos, trabajadores, y honrados por la patria," *Eco Católico*, September 15, 1991, 4, and "Reflexiones de Año Nuevo," *Eco Católico*, January 13, 1991, 3.
78 Alvaro Fernández González, "Iglesia católica y ajuste estructural: Dilemas y conflictos," *Ciencias Sociales* 61 (September 1993): 94.
79 Mons. Arrieta, "Homilía de Mons. Román Arrieta Villalobos, Arzobispo de San José, en la fiesta de María Reina de Los Angeles," *Eco Católico*, August 12, 1990, 2.
80 Alfredo Chacon V., "Socialcristianos critican a Monseñor," *La Prensa Libre*, August 3, 1990, 6; and Dino Starcevic, "Arzobispo condena a Ministro," *La República*, August 6, 1990, 2A.
81 Mons. Arrieta, *Nueva Evangelización*, II: nos. 18, 19, 41, and 61.
82 José Alberto Briceño, "Calderón rechaza críticas de Arzobispo," *La República*, November 19, 1993, 5A; Marielos Campos and Fernando Lopez G., "Ministros alegan desconocimiento de Arzobispo," *Al Día*, November 24,1993, 6; and Luis Cartin S., "Monseñor debe buscar mejor información," *La Prensa Libre*, November 22, 1993, 6.
83 Rosa Brenes S., "Alejandro Soto: Pastoral confirma nuestra tesis," *La Prensa Libre*, November 23, 1993, 11.
84 CECOR, *Madre Tierra*, primera parte, I: nos. 1–31, and II: nos. 32–54.
85 CECOR, *Madre Tierra*, primera parte, II: nos. 50–53.
86 CECOR, *Madre Tierra*, tercera parte, III: no. 73.
87 CECOR, *Madre Tierra*, tercera parte, III: nos. 73.1–73.11.
88 A brief treatment of early references to the CEB phenomenon in Costa Rican Church documents can be found in Carlos Castro Calzada, "Las comunidades eclesiales de base: ¿Una opción pastoral de la Arquidiocesis de San José?" *Senderos* 52 (January–April 1996): 113–17.
89 Comisión Nacional Episcopal de Laicos (CONEL), *Las comunidades eclesiales de base en la Iglesia costarricense* (San José, CR: Ediciones CECOR[?], 1995).
90 CONEL, *Las comunidades eclesiales de base*, 9.
91 CONEL, *Las comunidades eclesiales de base*, 20–23.
92 CONEL, *Las comunidades eclesiales de base*, 25.
93 CONEL, *Las comunidades eclesiales de base*, 36.
94 CONEL, *Las comunidades eclesiales de base*, 24–25.
95 CONEL, *Las comunidades eclesiales de base*, 19 and 22.
96 Mons. Arrieta, *Nueva evangelización*, IV: no. 12; and CONEL, *Las comunidades eclesiales de base*, 28–33.
97 Mons. Arrieta, *Nueva evangelización*, IV: no. 12; and CONEL, *Las comunidades eclesiales de base*, 17 and 19.
98 CECOR, *Madre Tierra*, tercera parte, III: nos. 73.4, 73.6, and 73.10.
99 CECOR, *Madre Tierra*, tercera parte, III: no. 73.7.
100 CECOR, *Madre Tierra*, segunda parte, I: no. 64.
101 CECOR, *Madre Tierra*, primera parte, I: no. 30; see also primera parte, I: no. 16.
102 Carlos Arguedas C., "Gobierno acepta críticas de obispos," *Al Día*, August 19, 1994, 4.
103 John A. Booth, *Costa Rica: Quest for Democracy* (Boulder CO: Westview Press, 1998), 165. For an examination of the contradictions between the PLN's social democratic electoral promises and its neo-liberal policies once in government, see Bruce M. Wilson, "Leftist Parties, Neoliberal Policies, and Re-election Strate-

gies: The Case of the PLN in Costa Rica," *Comparative Political Studies* 32 (September 1999): 752–79.

104   Mons. Arrieta, "Unidad para solucionar problemas del país," *Eco Católico*, August 6, 1995, 4, and his "Solemnidad de nuestra Señora de los Angeles, Cartago, agosto 2 de 1996: Homilía" (CECOR archives, photocopy).

105   The text announcing the accord, interestingly, uses language similar to that used by Arrieta in his appeals to place the good of the *patria* above factional political interests. See Gerardo Hernández Naranjo, "El discurso del pacto Figueres-Calderón," *Revista de Ciencias Sociales* 72 (June 1996): 32–33.

106   Wilson, "Leftist parties," 763.

107   Since 1961, the archbishop of San José has celebrated a public mass every year in honour of the Feast of Saint Joseph the Worker.

108   See, for example, Mons. Arrieta, "Decálogo de los derechos de los trabajadores," *Eco Católico*, September 26, 1993, 4, and his "Los trabajadores, con el auxilio divino, son los artífices de la justicia, la paz y el amor en el mundo," *Eco Católico*, May 10, 1992, 4; see also CECOR, *Evangelización y realidad social*, nos. 6.3 and 6.9–6.10.

109   See, for example, Mons. Arrieta, "Los trabajadores," 4.

110   Mons. Arrieta, "El 1º de mayo," *Eco Católico*, May 8, 1988, 5.

111   See, for example, Mons. Arrieta, *Nueva Evangelización*, I: nos. 1–4 and 11.

112   See, for example, Mons. Arrieta, "Las conquistas del Código del Trabajo son derechos del trabajador, no dádivas," *Eco Católico*, October 3, 1993, 4; and his "En los cuarenta años de la promulgación del Código de Trabajo," *El Mensajero del Clero* 14 (June 1984): 18–19.

113   CECOR, "Comentarios sobre el Proyecto de Nuevo Código de Trabajo," in *Iglesia Católica, crisis y democratización en Centro América (Documentos seleccionados de las conferencias episcopales y del SEDAC, 1979–1990)* (Guatemala City: INCEP, 1990).

114   Mons. Arrieta, "Fiesta de San José Obrero: Homilía (1996)" (CECOR archives, photocopy).

115   Mons. Arrieta, "En los cuarenta años," 19, and his "El 1º de mayo," 5.

116   Mons. Arrieta, archbishop of San José, interview by Dana Sawchuk, San José, Costa Rica, July 4, 1997; and his "El 1º de mayo," 5.

117   CECOR, "Comentarios sobre el Proyecto," no. 8.

118   CECOR, "Comentarios sobre el Proyecto," no. 8.

119   Mons. Arrieta, "Reflexión de Mons. Román Arrieta en la Asamblea Legislativa, sobre la Rerum Novarum," *Eco Católico*, June 23, 1991, 2; and CECOR, *Evangelización y realidad social*, no. 6.7.

120   CECOR, *Unidos en la esperanza*, no. 2.5.

121   The most noteworthy of these included a 1984 strike by government social service workers and strikes by teachers in 1988 and 1993.

122   Mons. Arrieta interview.

123   Mons. Arrieta interview.

124   Mon. Román Arrieta, "Iglesia sí intervino por solución a huelga," *Eco Católico*, September 10, 1995, 4.

125   Booth, *Costa Rica*, 165.

126   CECOR, "Comentarios sobre el Proyecto," no. 7; CECOR, *Evangelización y realidad social*, nos. 6.8–6.10; and Mons. Arrieta, "En los cuarenta años," 19.

127   CECOR, *Evangelización y realidad social*, no. 6.10.

128   Alvaro Fernández González, "Iglesia católica y conflicto social en Costa Rica, 1979–1989," *Cristianismo y Sociedad* 103 (1990): 76–77.

129   CECOR, "Comentarios sobre el Proyecto," nos. 6–7.

130 Fernández, "Iglesia católica y conflicto social," 77.
131 Mons. Arrieta, "En los cuarenta años," 19.
132 CECOR, "Comentarios sobre el Proyecto," no. 7.
133 Mons. Arrieta interview.
134 Mons. Arrieta, "Discurso de Mons. Román Arrieta a los trabajadores el primero de mayo," *Eco Católico*, May 11, 1986, 2.
135 The practical relationships between the archbishop and CECODERS, and between the archbishop and ESJ23, are discussed in chapters 6 and 8, respectively.
136 Mons. Arrieta, "En los cuarenta años," 19.
137 Mons. Arrieta, "Alocución de Mons. Román Arrieta en el desayuno de amistad cristiana," *El Mensajero del Clero* 4 (August 1981): 12.
138 Mons. Arrieta, "Fiesta de San José Obrero: Homilía."
139 Mons. Arrieta, "Discurso a los trabajadores el primero de mayo," 2; *Nueva Evangelización*, II: no. 54; and his "Los trabajadores," 4; see also CECOR, "Comentarios sobre el Proyecto," no. 7.
140 While the hierarchy as a collective sidesteps this issue, as I discuss in chapter 9, Mons. Coto and the official Church in Limón have publicly denounced the unscrupulous practices of *solidarista* representatives on banana plantations.
141 CECOR, "Comentarios sobre el Proyecto," no. 7.
142 Several analysts of the Costa Rican Church have advanced similar arguments: see, for example, Opazo, *Costa Rica*, 208; and Miguel Picado, *La Iglesia costarricense entre el pueblo y el estado (de 1949 a nuestros días)* (San José, CR: Ediciones Guayacán, 1989), 46–47 and 67–75.
143 Opazo, *Costa Rica*, 24–25.
144 Williams, *Catholic Church and Politics*, 126.
145 Picado, *La Iglesia costarricense entre el pueblo y el estado*, 125.
146 CECOR, "Carta circular de la conferencia episcopal," *Eco Católico*, August 26, 1979, 3.
147 Mons. Arrieta, "La penetración protestante," *Eco Católico*, December 18, 1988, 3; see also his "Sobre sectas protestantes," *Eco Católico*, April 14, 1991, 4.
148 Mons. Arrieta usually cites the inflated figure of 90 percent: see, for example, "Dios nos llama a la vigencia y la práctica de la justicia," *Gente*, April 20, 1987, 6. In contrast, polls have shown that the number of Catholics is fewer than 80 percent: Larissa Minsky Acosta, "¿Somos lo que creemos?" *La Nación (Revista Dominical)*, March 17, 1997, 9.
149 Mons. Arrieta, "La penetración protestante," 3.
150 Minsky, "¿Somos lo que creemos?" 12.
151 Mons. Arrieta, "Sobre sectas," 4; and CECOR, "Carta circular," 3.
152 Mons. Arrieta interview.
153 See Dana Sawchuk, "The Catholic Church in the Nicaraguan Revolution: A Gramscian Analysis," *Sociology of Religion* 58, 1 (Spring 1997): 48.
154 Mons. Arrieta, "Homilía en la fiesta de María Reina de Los Angeles," 2.
155 Mons. Arrieta, "Homilía en la fiesta de María Reina de Los Angeles," 2.
156 Otto Maduro, "New Marxist Approaches to the Relative Autonomy of Religion," *Sociological Analysis* 38, 4 (1977): 363.

Notes to Chapter 6 : CECODERS

1 See V Sínodo Arquidiocesano, *Decretos sinodales* (Curridabat, CR: Ludovico, 1985), no. 203.
2 I deal with the ESJ23 in chapter 8; for more information on Cáritas, see V Sínodo Arquidiocesano, *Decretos sinodales*, no. 204; for Hermandades de Trabajo, see J. Amando Robles Robles, "Movimientos eclesiales de la Iglesia católica en Costa Rica," *Mensajero del Clero*, extra. iss. (September 1983): 38–40.

3   Mario Solis, CECODERS theologian, interview by Dana Sawchuk, San José, Costa Rica, July 24, 1996.

4   Yadira Bonilla, assistant director of CECODERS, interview by Dana Sawchuk, San José, Costa Rica, July 26, 1997.

5   Bonilla interview; and Padre Orlando Navarro Rojas, director of CECODERS, interview by Dana Sawchuk, San José, Costa Rica, July 18, 1996.

6   V Sínodo Arquidiocesano, *Decretos sinodales*, no. 203c.

7   CECODERS, *Censo parroquial familiar* (San José, CR: CECODERS, n.d.)

8   Bonilla interview.

9   Bonilla interview.

10 Bonilla interview.

11 V Sínodo Arquidiocesano, *Decretos sinodales*, no. 203a.

12 Bonilla interview and Navarro interview.

13 Bonilla interview and Solis interview.

14 In this regard it is interesting to note that the Church-sponsored pamphlets openly promote the use of condoms as a way to prevent the transmission of the virus.

15 Pastoral de la Esperanza–CECODERS, *SIDA y VIDA* (Curridabat, CR: Ludovico, n.d.)

16 The archdiocese itself has recently constructed a small palliative care home for those dying of AIDS.

17 Many of the *Eco Católico* articles are simply excerpts taken from the longer booklets used in CECODERS seminars.

18 CECODERS and Cáritas, *¿La historia de Costa Rica? Y la de nuestra Comunidad!!!* Cuadernos para la pastoral social no. 1 (San José, CR: CECODERS–Cáritas, 1986).

19 CECODERS and Cáritas, *¿La historia de Costa Rica?*, 2–3.

20 CECODERS and Cáritas, *¿La historia de Costa Rica?*, 3–5.

21 CECODERS and Cáritas, *¿La historia de Costa Rica?*, 5–8.

22 CECODERS and Cáritas, *¿La historia de Costa Rica?*, 6.

23 CECODERS and Cáritas, *¿La historia de Costa Rica?*, 15.

24 CECODERS and Cáritas, *¿La historia de Costa Rica?*, 16.

25 CECODERS and Cáritas, *¿La historia de Costa Rica?*, 18–19.

26 CECODERS and Cáritas, *¿La historia de Costa Rica?*, 21.

27 CECODERS and Cáritas, *¿La historia de Costa Rica?*, 14, 20, and 24.

28 CECODERS and Cáritas, *¿La historia de Costa Rica?*, 27.

29 CECODERS and Cáritas, *¿La historia de Costa Rica?*, 28.

30 CECODERS and Cáritas, *¿La historia de Costa Rica?*, 30–31.

31 CECODERS and Cáritas, *¿La historia de Costa Rica?*, 33.

32 Aixa Saborío, "Folleto ocasiona pugna en Iglesia," *La Nación*, March 13, 1987, 6A.

33 Miguel Picado, *La Iglesia costarricense entre el pueblo y el estado (de 1949 a nuestros días)* (San José, CR: Ediciones Guayacán, 1989), 172. Many of the most important of these articles have been gathered and reprinted in Pablo Richard, ed., *La pastoral social en Costa Rica: Documentos y comentarios acerca de la polémica entre la Iglesia católica y el periódico La Nación* (San José, CR: DEI, 1987). Subsequent references to documents in this collection are to *La pastoral social en Costa Rica*.

34 Julio Rodríguez, "Los mercaderes," *La Nación*, March 17, 1987, 15A, and "La cuestión de fondo," *La Nación*, March 20, 1987, 14A.

35 "Obispos y sacerdotes preocupa influencia marxista en Iglesia," *La Nación*, March 14, 1987, 6A; and "La cuestión," 14A.

36 Saborío, "Folleto," 6A; and "La infiltración en la Iglesia," *La Nación*, March 15, 1987, 14A.

37 Mons. Arrieta, "Una respuesta a *La Nación*," in *La pastoral social en Costa Rica*, 25.

38 Mons. Arrieta, "Otra respuesta a *La Nación*," *La Nación*, March 23, 1987, 18A, and his "Que la Santa Sede decida," *La Nación*, March 31, 1987, 16A.

39 Mons. Arrieta, "Que la Santa Sede," 16A.

40 José Rafael Barquero A., Ignacio Trejos P., Héctor Morera, et al., "Nos impulsa el Evangelio," *La Nación*, March 25, 1987, 16A.

41 Mons. Arrieta, "Una respuesta," 25-26.

42 Saborío, "Folleto," 6A.

43 Orlando Navarro, "Carta del Padre Orlando Navarro, Director de CECODERS, a Mons. Román Arrieta Villalobos, sobre la labor que este centro realiza," *Mensajero del Clero*, no. 21 (May 1987): 26.

44 Navarro, "Carta," 26-27.

45 See, for example, Arnoldo Mora, "Doctrina social de la Iglesia y lucha de clases," in Richard, ed., *La Pastoral social en Costa Rica*, 63-65; and Arnoldo Mora, "Magisterio eclesiastico, Iglesia de los pobres y teología de liberación," in *La pastoral social en Costa Rica*, 67-68.

46 See "¿Pugna en la Iglesia o pugna de 'La Nación' contra la Iglesia?" in *La pastoral social de Costa Rica*, 73-80; and Jorge Arturo Chavez, "Los 'pseudo-teologos de La Nación,' y el peligro de un 'magisterio paralelo,'" *Eco Católico*, April 5, 1987, 8.

47 CECODERS, "La Rerum Novarum y el estado," *Eco Católico*, February 4, 1990, 12.

48 CECODERS, "La espiritualidad en la Populorum Progressio," *Eco Católico*, March 6, 1988, 3.

49 CECODERS, "Bien común y solidaridad en el magisterio de la Iglesia: Doctrina Social postconciliar," *Eco Católico*, June 16, 1991, 12.

50 See, for example, CECODERS, "Algunos aspectos fundamentales de la encíclica Rerum Novarum," *Eco Católico*, January 21, 1990, 12.

51 See, for example, the summary of John Paul II's *Sollicitudo Rei Socialis* in CECODERS, "La preocupación social de la Iglesia," *Eco Católico*, February 28, 1988, 10.

52 CECODERS, "Centenario de la encíclica Rerum Novarum: En el año de la Doctrina Social de la Iglesia," *Eco Católico*, February 10, 1991, 9, and "Centenario de la encíclica Rerum Novarum," *Eco Católico*, February 17, 1991, 16.

53 CECODERS, "La encíclica Rerum Novarum y la Doctrina Social," *Eco Católico*, January 14, 1990, 12, and "Algunos aspectos fundamentales de la encíclica Rerum Novarum," 12.

54 Orlando Navarro R., and Yadira Bonilla O., "La Iglesia y el avance de la Doctrina Social," in Franz J. Hinkelhammert, Arnoldo Mora, and Carmelo Alvarez et al., *El pensamiento social de Juan Pablo II: Documentos y comentarios* (San José, CR: DEI, 1988), 129.

55 CECODERS, "De la encíclica 'Populorum Progressio' a la encíclica 'Sollicitudo Rei Socialis': Década de los setenta," *Eco Católico*, March 20, 1988, 13.

56 CECODERS, "Derechos de los trabajadores a la luz de la Doctrina Social," *Eco Católico*, August 20, 1989, 11; and Navarro and Bonilla, "La Iglesia e el avance de la Doctrina Social," 128 and 130.

57 CECODERS, "La Iglesia y los acontecimientos de los años 80," *Eco Católico*, April 10, 1988, 3; and Orlando Navarro Rojas, "El pensamiento actual en la Doctrina Social de la Iglesia," *Senderos*, no. 39 (July 1991): 75-77.

58 Navarro, "El pensamiento actual en la Doctrina Social," 77.

59 CECODERS, "La cuestión social y el reajuste estructural," *Eco Católico*, July 16, 1989, 7.

60 CECODERS, "Los efectos económicos y sociales de la crisis Latinoamericana (una iluminación desde la Populorum Progressio y la Sollicitudo Rei Socialis)," *Eco Católico*, August 6, 1989, 16.

61 CECODERS, "De la encíclica 'Populorum Progressio' a la encíclica 'Sollicitudo Rei Socialis,'" 13.

62 CECODERS, "La deuda externa a la luz de la 'Populorum Progressio' y la 'Sollicitudo Rei Socialis,'" *Eco Católico*, July 23, 1989, 7.

63 CECODERS, "Pobres, solidaridad, y liberación," *Eco Católico*, December 23, 1990, 14.

64 Gustavo Blanco and Orlando Navarro, *El solidarismo: Pensamiento y dinámica social de un movimiento obrero patronal* (San José, CR: Editorial Costa Rica, 1984).

65 Gustavo Leonel Blanco B., co-founder of ASEPROLA and sociologist, interview by Dana Sawchuk, San José, Costa Rica, June 19, 1997.

66 Blanco interview.

67 Hernán Hermosilla Barrientos, coodinator of the Christian Program, ASEPROLA, Dana Sawchuk interview, San José, Costa Rica, June 3, 1997; and Navarro interview.

68 Blanco interview.

69 CECODERS, "El mundo obrero y la Iglesia," *Eco Católico*, November 12, 1989, 12; and CECODERS, "Las organizaciones sociales en la década de los ochenta," *Eco Católico*, October 22, 1989, 12.

70 Navarro himself, when asked directly about *solidarismo*, is critical but diplomatic. He maintains that, while there may be some important elements in *solidarismo*, the solidarity movement has goals that serve the neo-liberal agenda and that therefore are fundamentally different from the goals of the union movement (Navarro interview).

71 Hermosilla interview.

72 CECODERS, "Las relaciones entre las naciones y su influencia en el trabajo," *Eco Católico*, August 27, 1989, 12; and Navarro, "El pensamiento actual en la Doctrina Social," 69.

73 Víctor Fernández Castillo, "Honrar a nuestros trabajadores con salario justo," *Eco Católico*, May 2, 1993, 17.

74 Navarro and Bonilla, "La Iglesia e el avance de la Doctrina Social," 129; and Navarro interview.

75 Navarro and Bonilla, "La Iglesia e el avance de la Doctrina Social," 129.

76 Navarro, "El pensamiento actual en la Doctrina Social," 69.

77 Leo XIII, Rerum Novarum, no. 31 (as cited in CECODERS, "Las huelgas de 1934 y sus repercusiones sociales," *Eco Católico*, September 9, 1990, 18).

78 CECODERS, "Las huelgas de 1934," 18; CECODERS, "Las huelgas en Costa Rica en el movimiento artesanal obrero," *Eco Católico*, August 12, 1990, 13; and CECODERS, "La huelga bananera de 1934," *Eco Católico*, September 16, 1990, 16.

79 CECODERS, "Las huelgas de 1934," 18.

80 Solis interview.

81 CECODERS and sacerdotes de diversa diócesis de Costa Rica, "Fax sobre la huelga del Magisterio [1995]," (CECODERS archives, photocopy).

82 Second Vatican Council, Gaudium et Spes, no. 68 (as cited in CECODERS and sacerdotes de diversa diócesis de Costa Rica, "Fax").

83 Navarro interview.

84 Orlando Navarro, "La Iglesia católica frente al Proyecto de la Reforma de Salud" (CECODERS archives, photocopy); and CECODERS, "Situación en que se encuentra el sector salud en Costa Rica" (CECODERS archives, photocopy).

85 The workers of the CCSS alone, for example, belong to forty-three separate unions (Solis interview).

86 CECODERS, "Plan de trabajo del Frente de Organizaciones Sindicales del Sector Salud [1995]," (CECODERS archives, photocopy).

87 CECODERS, "Encuentro sacerdotes y organizaciones sindicales," (CECODERS archives, photocopy), 1.

88 CECODERS, "Encuentro sacerdotes," 2.

89 CECODERS, "Tercer encuentro de sacerdotes y organizaciones sindicales [1996]," (CECODERS archives, photocopy).

90 CECODERS, "Tercer encuentro," 4.

91 Juan Luis Segundo, *The Liberation of Theology*, trans. John Drury (Maryknoll, NY: Orbis Books, 1976), 7–9.

92 This application is legitimate not only because scripture and tradition are accorded equivalent status in the eyes of the Catholic Church but because, as Segundo also points out, a hermeneutic of suspicion is necessary vis-à-vis any type of tradition (Segundo, *The Liberation of Theology*, 35–36, n. 22).

Notes to Chapter 7 : Limón Province

1 Hernán Hermosilla and Tania Palencia, *Creación de una instancia coordinadora para detener el impacto de la expansión bananera incontrolada: Costa Rica* (San José, CR: Fundación Arias para la Paz y el Progreso Humano, 1997), 16. For detailed statistics that illustrate the importance of banana production to the Costa Rican economy, see Juan Miguel Goluboay Montoya and Herbert Vega Rodríguez, "La actividad bananera en Costa Rica," in *Cambio y continuidad en la economía bananera*, ed. FLASCO and CEDAL (San José, CR: Ediciones FLASCO/CEDAL/FES, 1988), 145–59. Subsequent documents in this collection are cited as in *Cambio y continuidad*.

2 Jorge Arturo Chaves, *Magisterio social y pastoral de los trabajadores* (San José, CR: ASEPROLA, Editorial Fundación UNA, and Pastoral Social Diócesis de Limón, 1996), 11.

3 See the census data and other statistics cited in Hernán Hermosilla Barrientos, "Transformación de practicas eclesiales en el Vicariato Apostólico de Limón (1980–1991)," M.Sc. Thesis, Ciudad Universitaria "Rodrigo Facio," Costa Rica (1991), 8–29.

4 Christopher P. Baker, *Costa Rica Handbook*, 2nd ed. (Chico, CA: Moon Publications, 1996), 424.

5 For a brief history of the development of these industries in Costa Rica from the 1880s to the 1980s, see Goluboay and Vega, "La actividad bananera," 131–61.

6 For a detailed analysis of the complexities of ethnicity on banana plantations in the Atlantic region of Costa Rica (and Panama), see Philippe I. Bourgois, *Ethnicity at Work: Divided Labor on a Central American Banana Plantation* (Baltimore, MD: Johns Hopkins University Press, 1989).

7 For an account of the popular perception of *los negros* and life in Limón during the early and mid-1900s, see Chaves, *Magisterio social*, 11–12.

8 Chaves reports that as late as twenty years ago, government functionaries still thought of a posting in the Atlantic zone as a punishment or a demotion (*Magisterio social*, 12).

9 The account of the earthquake and its effects is adapted from Baker, *Costa Rica Handbook*, 7.

10 José Enrique Sibaja, "Acción inmediata de la Iglesia," *Eco Católico*, March 3, 1996, 19.

11 Goluboay and Vega, "La actividad bananera," 144–45.

12 Leonardo Garnier, Gladys Gonzáles, and Jorge Cornick, "Costa Rica: Las vicisitudes de una política bananera nacional," in *Cambio y continuidad,"* 122–25; and Goluboay and Vega, "La actividad bananera," 145.

13 Hermosilla and Palencia, *Creación de una instancia coordinadora*, 12.

14 Foro Emaús, *Bananos para el mundo ¿Y el daño para Costa Rica? Los impactos sociales y ambientales de la producción bananera en Costa Rica* (San José, CR: Comité Coordinador de Foro Emaús, 1997), 19–20.

15 Hermosilla and Palencia, *Creación de una instancia coordinadora*, 9 and 12.

16 Costa Rica has the highest rate of agricultural chemical use per hectare in the world. In addition, it has been estimated that 2.5 kilograms of waste is left behind for every kilogram of bananas exported: Gilberth Bermúdez, member of the Coordinadora de Sindicatos Bananeros and of the coordinating committee of Foro Emaús, interview by Dana Sawchuk, San José, Costa Rica, July 2, 1997; and Hermosilla and Palencia, *Creación de una instancia coordinadora*, 13.

17 Bermúdez interview.

18 Bermúdez interview; Foro Emaús, *Bananos para el mundo*, 13; and Hermosilla and Palencia, *Creación de una instancia coordinadora*, 15.

19 To put things into perspective, consider that, in Costa Rica, transnational companies annually use an average of 40 kilograms of agricultural chemicals per worker, the Central American average is 16 kilograms, and in the industrialized countries that import Costa Rican bananas, pesticide use in agricultural production is limited to 4 kilograms per person annually (Hermosilla and Palencia, *Creación de una instancia coordinadora*, 12).

20 Bermúdez interview.

21 A detailed and well-documented account of the health hazards of chemical use on banana plantations is Jorge Norman Jiménez Céspedes, *Plaguicidas y salud en las bananeras de Costa Rica* (San José, CR: ASEPROLA, 1995).

22 Foreign workers are typically assigned the most physically demanding jobs on plantations (e.g., cutting the bamboo stalks that are used to hold the leaves of the banana plants upright). Women are particularly affected in terms of discrimination in hiring, sexual harassment and assaults, lower wages, and lack of adequate provisions for pregnant workers and for women who need maternity leave. In the case of pesticides, women are exposed to them not only during their paid labour but also when they wash by hand the chemical-laden clothes of their male relatives. See Foro Emaús, *Bananos para el mundo*, 22–23.

23 Mons. Alfonso Coto Monge, former bishop of Limón, interview by Dana Sawchuk, San José, Costa Rica, June 25, 1997; and "El Vicariato Apostólico de Limón: Un camino particular, II parte," *Eco Católico*, March 12, 1989, 7.

24 Miguel Picado, *La Iglesia costarricense entre el pueblo y el estado (de 1949 a nuestros días)* (San José, CR: Ediciones Guayacán, 1989), 256.

25 Padre Eduardo Ramírez, priest in the parish of Puerto Limón, interview by Erick Solera, Puerto Limón, Costa Rica, May 1, 1997 (personal archives of Erick Solera, photocopy).

26 Mons. Coto interview.

27 Ramírez interview by Solera.

28 Mons. Alfonso Coto, "Limón va adelante con buen plan pastoral," interview by Gonzalo Muñoz, *Eco Católico*, January 22, 1995, 6.

29 Ramírez interview by Solera.

30 Padre Eduardo Ramírez, priest in the parish of Puerto Limón, interview by Dana Sawchuk and Erick Solera, Puerto Limón, Costa Rica, July 10, 1997; and Ramírez interview by Solera.

31 The two-week strike, which involved ten thousand workers in a conflict against the United Fruit Company in Limón, was one of the largest Latin American strikes against a North American company in history. See Carlos Luis Fallas, "The Great Atlantic Banana Plantation Strike of 1934," in *The Costa Rica Reader*, ed. Marc Edelman and Joanne Kenen (New York: Grove Weidenfeld, 1989), 76–82.

32 David Smith and Rolando Rivera, "Organización, movilización popular y desarrollo regional en el Atlántico costarricense," *Revista de Ciencias Sociales* nos. 37–38 (1987): 52.

33 Smith and Rivera, "Organización, movilización popular," 50 and 52.

34 "Huelga bananera cumple 35 días: Aumento de salarios y jornada de trabajo mantienen en suspenso negociaciones," *Libertad*, January 15–21, 1982, 3.

35 Burbach and Flynn point out that: "Bananas are a highly perishable commodity, and time is critical in the marketing process. A plantation or port work stoppage of even a day can mean the loss of hundreds of thousands of dollars in overripe bananas … The whole process must be regulated like clockwork, and delays avoided at any cost" (Roger Burbach and Patricia Flynn, "A New 'Banana Republic': Del Monte in Guatemala" in *Revolution in Central America*, ed. Stanford Central American Action Network (Boulder, CO: Westview Press, 1983), 181–82).

36 Mons. Francisco Ulloa Rojas, bishop of Limón, interview by Dana Sawchuk and Erick Solera, Puerto Limón, Costa Rica, July 10, 1997; and Mons. Coto interview.

37 Mons. Coto has stated that: "People were not 'convinced' communists; they were not communist for the ideology, but out of necessity" (Mons. Coto interview).

38 Mons. Coto interview; "Iglesias piden investigar caos en Limón," *La Prensa Libre*, February 19, 1996, 7; José Enrique Sibaja, "Iglesias limonenses: Defienden derechos de muelleros," *Eco Católico*, March 3, 1996, 6; and Mons. Ulloa interview by Sawchuk and Solera.

39 Javier Robles Monge and Héctor Fallas, "Las sectas: Esas grandes desconocidas (I parte)," *Eco Católico*, May 8, 1988, 8; and Jaime Valverde, *Las sectas en Costa Rica: Pentecostalismo y conflicto social* (San José, CR: DEI, 1990), 89–90.

40 Mons. Coto interview; Ramírez interview by Solera; and Vicariato Apostólico de Limón, *Plan pastoral del Vicariato Apostólico de Limón* (San José, CR: Varitec, 1990), 23. While many Church officials attribute the presence and growth of the *sectas* in Limón to "religious ignorance" and to the precarious socio-economic situation that leads people to view the *sectas* as a means to evade reality, some also acknowledge that pastoral shortcomings (e.g., in the area of Catholic spirituality) may also be responsible for the Church's loss of constituents to the Pentecostal churches: Mons. Ulloa interview by Sawchuk and Solera; and Diócesis de Limón, *Limón: Plan diocesano de pastoral. "Un nuevo modo de ser Iglesia": 1996-2000* (Limón, CR: n.p., 1995), 59–60.

41 Pastor Ronaldo Vargas, minister in the Assemblies of God, interview by Dana Sawchuk, San José, Costa Rica, July 29, 1997.

42 Jaime Valverde, "Efectos sociales e ideologicos de las sectas de origen Protestante en Costa Rica," in *Protestantismo y procesos sociales en Centroamérica*, ed. Luis E. Samandú (San José, CR: Editorial Universitaria Centroamericana, 1990), 251–54.

43 Valverde, "Efectos sociales," 251–55.

44 R. Vargas interview. Consistent with this assertion, Steigenga has also reported that, compared to other religious groups, Pentecostals in Costa Rica are rela-

tively likely to agree that the government should be obeyed in all circumstances. They are also relatively reluctant to criticize public officials. See Timothy J. Steigenga, *The Politics of the Spirit: The Political Implications of Pentecostalized Religion in Costa Rica and Guatemala* (Lanham, MD: Lexington Books, 2001), 116–20.

45 R. Vargas interview.

46 Valverde, "Efectos sociales," 253.

Notes to Chapter 8 : The ESJ23

1 Mons. Carlos Humberto Rodríguez Quiros, "[Decreto]," *El Mensajero del Clero* (March 1963), 57–61 (as quoted in James Backer, *La Iglesia y el sindicalismo en Costa Rica*, 3rd ed. (San José, CR: Editorial Costa Rica, 1978), 191).

2 Details of the early years of the ESJ23 can be found in Backer, *La Iglesia*, 191–94; and "La Escuela Social Juan XXIII ayer y hoy," *Eco Católico* (*Suplemento Campesino*), October 12, 1980, 4.

3 Claudio Maria Solano Cerdas, "Curriculo" (ESJ23 archives, photocopy), 1–2.

4 Escuela Social Juan XXIII (ESJ23), *Solidarismo y democracia* (Curridabat, CR: Escuela Social Juan XXIII, 1994), 19.

5 ESJ23, *Escuela Social Juan XXIII: Su origen, sus objetivos, sus actividades, su cobertura* (Curridabat, CR: Escuela Social Juan XXIII, 1992), 1; and *Manual para el estudio de la Doctrina Social de la Iglesia* (Curridabat, CR: Escuela Social Juan XXIII, [1973]), 4.

6 Padre Claudio Maria Solano Cerdas, director of the ESJ23, interview by Dana Sawchuk, Curridabat, Costa Rica, July 9, 1996; Eugenio Trejos, legal advisor to the ESJ23, interview by Dana Sawchuk, Curridabat, Costa Rica, July 9, 1996; and Roberto Vásquez, assistant to Padre Solano, interview by Dana Sawchuk, Curridabat, Costa Rica, July 9, 1996.

7 Trejos interview.

8 ESJ23, *Solidarismo y democracia*, p. 23; ESJ23, *Escuela Social Juan XXIII* (Curridabat, CR: Escuela Social Juan XXIII, n.d.); Carlos Villalta, director of education at the ESJ23 Centro Nacional de Capacitación, interview by Dana Sawchuk, Tres Ríos, Costa Rica, July 11, 1996.

9 Villalta interview.

10 ESJ23, ed., *Ley de asociaciones solidaristas*, 13, and *Solidarismo, solidarismo* (Curridabat, CR: Escuela Social Juan XXIII, n.d.); Solano interview; Villalta interview; and José Mairena, "Gigante de ₡50 mil millones," *Rumbo*, June 3, 1996, 15 and 17.

11 Claudio M. Solano, "Hemos transformado la zona Atlántica," *La Nación*, January 21, 1990, 16A; ESJ23, *Solidarismo y democracia*, 15; Miguel Vargas Solano, *solidarista* promoter, interview by Dana Sawchuk, Guapiles, Costa Rica, July 29, 1996.

12 Curtin Winsor, Jr., "The Solidarista Movement: Labor Economics for Democracy," *Washington Quarterly* 9, 4 (Fall 1986): 181; Bernal Masís Vega, director of administration at the ESJ23 Centro Nacional de Capacitación, interview by Dana Sawchuk, Tres Ríos, Costa Rica, July 11, 1996; Trejos interview; ESJ23, *Ventajas del solidarismo* (Curridabat, CR: Escuela Social Juan XXIII, n.d.).

13 ESJ23, ed., *Ley de asociaciones solidaristas*, 13.

14 M. Vargas interview.

15 ESJ23, *Manual*; ESJ23, *Solidarismo: Aspectos doctrinales* (San José, CR: Editorial Ministerio de Educación Pública, 1985); Solano interview.

16 See, for example, ESJ23, "Concepto cristiano de la empresa," *Eco Católico*, June 9, 1974, 14; and its *Manual*.

17 ESJ23, *Manual*, 47–50.

18 ESJ23, "La huelga es arma extrema," *Eco Católico*, August 25, 1974, 3.

19 ESJ23, *La Doctrina Social de la Iglesia (introducción a su estudio)* (San José, CR: Editorial Ministerio de Educación Pública, 1985), 76–82; and "El fruto incierto de las huelgas," *Eco Católico*, July 14, 1974, 3.

20 Pope Leo XIII, *Rerum Novarum*, nos. 1–3 and 14–16; and Pope Pius XI, *Quadragesimo Anno*, nos. 111–25, both in *Catholic Social Thought: The Documentary Heritage*, ed. David J. O'Brien and Thomas A. Shannon (Maryknoll, NY: Orbis Books, 1992).

21 ESJ23, *La Doctrina Social*, 3–90 passim.

22 ESJ23, *La Doctrina Social*, 91.

23 ESJ23, *La Doctrina Social*, 92–94.

24 ESJ23, *Solidarismo: Aspectos doctrinales*, 5.

25 ESJ23, *Solidarismo: Aspectos doctrinales*, 5–8.

26 ESJ23, *Solidarismo: Aspectos doctrinales*, 6.

27 See, for example, ESJ23, *Manual*, 58, and *Solidarismo: Aspectos doctrinales*, 17.

28 Pope Pius XII, *Summi Pontificatus: Encyclical Letter Exhorting Unity in Opposing World Evils* (New York: Paulist Press, 1939), nos. 28–30 (as cited in *Solidarismo: Aspectos doctrinales*, 7–8).

29 ESJ23, *La solidaridad y el solidarismo en la empresa* (Curridabat, CR: Escuela Social Juan XXIII, n.d.), 4 and 5–6; and Claudio Solano, "Solidarismo: Un movimiento integral y solidario," paper presented at the *Primera Conferencia Internacional Solidarista*, San José, CR, June 1995, 1–5.

30 ESJ23, *La Doctrina Social*, 53.

31 Solano, "Hemos transformado," 16A.

32 ESJ23, "El fruto incierto," 3, *La Doctrina Social*, 81, and "La huelga," 3.

33 Lawrence Kent, "The Social Pastoral Work of the Catholic Church in Costa Rica," *Michigan Journal of Political Science* 6 (1985), 22; and Víctor Vega, "La ideología solidarista," in *El problema solidarista y la respuesta sindical en Centroamérica*, ed. CEDAL and ASEPROLA (Heredia, CR: CEDAL, 1989), 39.

34 See, for example, Pope John Paul II, *Centesimus Annus*, no. 10 (as quoted in Claudio Solano, "El solidarismo en los albores del siglo XXI," paper presented at the BANDECO Managerial Seminar, San José, CR, 1997, 2); *Laborem Exercens*, no. 8 (as quoted in ESJ23, *Solidarismo: Aspectos doctrinales*, 10); *Sollicitudo Rei Socialis*, no. 38 (as quoted in ESJ23, *La solidaridad*, 2–3). Original documents are in *Catholic Social Thought: The Documentary Heritage*, ed. David J. O'Brien and Thomas A. Shannon (Maryknoll, NY: Orbis Books, 1992).

35 See, for example, Pope John Paul II, *Centesimus Annus*, no. 60 (as quoted in ESJ23, *Solidarismo y democracia*, 26), and *Sollicitudo Rei Socialis*, no. 32 (as quoted in Solano, "El solidarismo," 5).

36 ESJ23, *Manual*, 9–10.

37 Pope Paul VI, *Populorum Progressio*, in *Catholic Social Thought: The Documentary Heritage*, ed. David J. O'Brien and Thomas A. Shannon (Maryknoll, NY: Orbis Books, 1992), no. 43 (as cited in Solano Cerdas, "El solidarismo," 6).

38 Claudio Solano, comments in round table on "Expresión de los problemas políticos en el clero," as quoted in *Iglesia Solidaria*, 3, 27 (October 1987): 19 (as cited in Alvaro Fernández, *Iglesia católica y conflicto social en Costa Rica, 1979-1989: Transformaciones político-ideológicas en una fase de ajuste estructural* (San José, CR: Instituto de Investigaciones Sociales, Universidad de Costa Rica, 1990), 38).

39 Claudio Solano, "Iglesia: Promotora del diálogo," *Al Día*, September 25, 1994, 16.

40 This is the position that was presented to me, for example, by Hernán Hermosilla Barrientos, coodinator of the Christian Program, ASEPROLA, interview by Dana Sawchuk, San José, Costa Rica, June 3, 1997.

41 Kent, "Social Pastoral Work," 21.

42 Gustavo Blanco B., "La paz del silencio obrero," *Revista Aportes* 7, 32–33 (Jan.–Apr. 1987): 21; and Juan José Flores Madrigal, *El solidarismo desde adentro: Testimonio de Juan José Flores* (San José, CR: ASEPROLA, 1989), 65.

43 ASEPROLA, *Solidarismo* (Archives of Padre Eduardo Ramírez, photocopy), 3 and 5–6.

44 It should be also noted that, while it is extremely difficult to get company or school officials to admit to the existence of the *lista negra* on the *fincas*, it is frequently commented that, among workers, "everybody knows" about the practice of blacklisting. Hence, regardless of such factors as the actual contents of the list or the number of workers themselves named on it, the widespread perception that the list exists has the very real consequence of helping to silence workers' complaints. See Padre Jesús Doncel, parish priest in Río Frío, interview by Dana Sawchuk, Río Frío, Costa Rica, August 17, 1996; Flores, *El solidarismo desde adentro*, 65–66; and Kent, "Social Pastoral Work," 18–19.

45 ASEPROLA, "Solidarismo," 5; and Kent, "Social Pastoral Work," 19.

46 Flores, *El solidarismo desde adentro*, 66–67.

47 Solano interview.

48 Solano, "Hemos transformado," 16A.

49 Masís interview.

50 Gustavo Blanco and Orlando Navarro, *El solidarismo: Pensamiento y dinámica social de un movimiento obrero patronal* (San José, CR: Editorial Costa Rica, 1984), 179 and 358–65.

51 Blanco and Navarro, *El solidarismo*, 181; and "Fijan donación para Escuela Juan XXIII," *La Nación*, January 10, 1987, 2A.

52 Blanco and Navarro, *El solidarismo*, 180; Villalta interview.

53 ASEPROLA, "Solidarismo," 2 and 5; Gustavo Leonel Blanco B., co-founder of ASEPROLA and sociologist, interview by Dana Sawchuk, San José, Costa Rica, June 19, 1997.

54 Masís interview.

55 Blanco and Navarro, *El solidarismo*, 291–93.

56 Solano, "Curriculo," 2–3.

57 Masís interview.

58 See, for example, "Palabras pronunciadas por el Señor Ministro de Trabajo, Licenciado German Serrano Pinto, en la inauguración de las nuevas edificaciones de la Escuela Social Juan XXIII," *Eco Católico* (*Suplemento Campesino*), October 26, 1980, 2.

59 "Solidarismo, orgullo nacional," *El Diario Extra*, January 22, 1990, 14–15.

60 Flores, *El solidarismo desde adentro*, 114–15.

61 Gustavo Leonel Blanco B. "Iglesia católica y pastoral social," Master's Thesis, Ciudad Universitaria "Rodrigo Facio," Costa Rica, 1987, 142; Blanco and Navarro, *El solidarismo*, 180; and Flores, *El solidarismo desde adentro*, 131.

62 Solano, "Curriculo," 3.

63 Jaime Valverde, *"Pragmatismo" de los trabajadores y coexistencia solidarismo-sindicalismo en el sector público de Costa Rica* (San José, CR: Fundación Ebert, 1993), 38–39.

64 See ESJ23, *Solidarismo y democracia*, 7. Both *solidarismo* Law No. 6970 and the supplementary regulations (approved through Executive Decree No. 2068-TSS) can be found in ESJ23, ed., *Ley de asociaciones solidaristas*, 17–35 and 43–49, respectively.

65 I have discussed (chap. 1 and chap. 5) the broader significance of the legislative enshrinement of Catholicism in Costa Rica. In fact, almost every school document and public statement by Solano contains some reference to these juridical facts. See, for example, ESJ23, *Solidarismo, solidarismo*; Solano, *El solidarismo en los albores*, 2–3; and Solano interview.

66 Villalta interview.

67 Mons. Arrieta, "Trigésimo aniversario de la Escuela Social Juan XXIII," *Eco Católico*, February 7, 1993, 4.

68 "Solidarismo, orgullo nacional," 14; and Mons. Arrieta, archbishop of San José, interview by Dana Sawchuk, San José, Costa Rica, July 4, 1997.

69 Mons. Arrieta, "Vigésimo sétimo aniversario de la Escuela Social Juan XXIII," *Eco Católico*, January 28, 1990, 3.

70 "Fijan donación," 2A.

71 Mons. Alfonso Coto Monge, former bishop of Limón, interview by Dana Sawchuk, San José, Costa Rica, June 25, 1997; Padre Eduardo Ramírez, priest in the parish of Puerto Limón, interview by Dana Sawchuk and Erick Solera, Puerto Limón, Costa Rica, July 10, 1997; and Padre Gerardo Vargas, priest and coordinator of the Comisión Diocesana de Pastoral Social in Limón, interview by Dana Sawchuk and Erick Solera, Siquirres, Costa Rica, July 11, 1997.

72 Solano interview.

73 ASEPROLA, "Solidarismo," 2.

74 See Philip J. Williams, *The Catholic Church and Politics in Nicaragua and Costa Rica* (London: Macmillan, with St. Anthony's College, Oxford, 1989), 162.

Notes to Chapter 9 : The Official Church in Limón

1 Padre Eduardo Ramírez, priest in the parish of Puerto Limón, interview by Erick Solera, Puerto Limón, Costa Rica, May 1, 1997 (personal archives of Erick Solera, photocopy).

2 Hernán Hermosilla Barrientos, "Transformación de practicas eclesiales en el Vicariato Apostólico de Limón (1980–1991)," M.Sc. Thesis, Ciudad Universitaria "Rodrigo Facio," Costa Rica (1991), 8–29, 36.

3 Mons. Alfonso Coto Monge, "Con inmenso gozo," *Documentos de pastoral del Vicariato Apostólico de Limón*, no. 1, September 1980 (personal archives of Eduardo Ramírez, photocopy).

4 Mons. Coto, "Con inmenso gozo," no. 1.1.

5 Mons. Coto, "Con inmenso gozo," nos. 3.1–3.3.

6 Mons. Alfonso Coto, et al., "Somos solidarios con quienes sufren no con los que se aprovechan de ese dolor," *Eco Católico*, September 28, 1980, 8.

7 Vicariato Apostólico de Limón, "Opciones pastorales: Documento conclusivo de la semana de pastoral para el Vicariato Apostólico-Limón," *Cuaderno de pastoral*, no. 3, February 1981 (personal archives de Eduardo Ramírez, photocopy), 6.

8 Eduardo Ramírez, "El Vicariato dio forma a su experiencia pastoral con un plan global de acción, III parte," *Eco Católico*, April 2, 1989, 11.

9 Hermosilla, "Transformación de practicas," 57–59; and Padre Gerardo Vargas, priest and coordinator of the Comisión Diocesana de Pastoral Social in Limón, interview by Dana Sawchuk and Erick Solera, Siquirres, Costa Rica, July 11, 1997.

10 Hermosilla, "Transformación de practicas," 58.

11 G. Vargas interview by Sawchuk and Solera.

12 Mons. Coto's personal attitude toward such democracy within the institution is revealed by his position on criticism from the clergy and laity, which he actively solicited: "one is not perfect, they are not going to believe that the episcopate receives a monopoly on the Holy Spirit and on the absolute truth" (Mons. Alfonso

Coto, "Limón va adelante con buen plan pastoral," interview by Gonzalo Muñoz, *Eco Católico*, January 22, 1995, 6). Compare this attitude with that of the representatives of the conservative wing in the Church who tend to emphasize obedience to the magisterium.

13 Vicariato Apostólico de Limón, *Plan pastoral del Vicariato Apostólico de Limón* (San José, CR: Varitec, 1990).

14 Vicariato Apostólico de Limón, *Plan pastoral*, 11.

15 See, for example, Vicariato Apostólico de Limón, *Plan pastoral*, 91 and 93.

16 Vicariato Apostólico de Limón, *Plan pastoral*, 33–35.

17 Vicariato Apostólico de Limón, *Plan pastoral*, 23.

18 Vicariato Apostólico de Limón, *Plan pastoral*, 22 and 42.

19 Vicariato Apostólico de Limón, *Plan pastoral*, 87–89.

20 Vicariato Apostólico de Limón, *Plan pastoral*, 100–102.

21 Obispo y presbíteros del Vicariato Apostólico de Limón, *Carta pastoral*, December 25, 1989, photocopy.

22 Arnoldo Mora R., "Una carta pastoral histórica," *La Nación* January 19, 1990, 16A.

23 Padre Eduardo Ramírez, priest in the parish of Puerto Limón, interview by Dana Sawchuk and Erick Solera, Puerto Limón, Costa Rica, July 10, 1997.

24 Ramírez interview by Sawchuk and Solera; and Efrén Romero, "¿Cómo nació la carta pastoral?" in *Foro Iglesia-sindicalismo*, ed. FES, Proyecto CAAS, ASPEROLA, and CPT (n.p., 1990), 28–29.

25 Obispo y presbíteros del Vicariato Apostólico de Limón, *Carta pastoral*, no. 8.

26 Obispo y presbíteros del Vicariato Apostólico de Limón, *Carta pastoral*, no. 11.

27 Obispo y presbíteros del Vicariato Apostólico de Limón, *Carta pastoral*, no. 14.

28 Obispo y presbíteros del Vicariato Apostólico de Limón, *Carta pastoral*, no. 18.

29 Obispo y presbíteros del Vicariato Apostólico de Limón, *Carta pastoral*, no. 31.

30 Obispo y presbíteros del Vicariato Apostólico de Limón, *Carta pastoral*, nos. 22–24.

31 Obispo y presbíteros del Vicariato Apostólico de Limón, *Carta pastoral*, no. 23.

32 Obispo y presbíteros del Vicariato Apostólico de Limón, *Carta pastoral*, no. 25.

33 Obispo y presbíteros del Vicariato Apostólico de Limón, *Carta pastoral*, nos. 37 and 42.

34 Obispo y presbíteros del Vicariato Apostólico de Limón, *Carta pastoral*, nos. 35, 36, 38, and 41.

35 Obispo y presbíteros del Vicariato Apostólico de Limón, *Una versión popular de la carta pastoral: La expansión bananera incontrolada*, July 1990, photocopy. Compare the title of this letter with the innocuous-sounding names of such CECOR documents as "United in Hope," "Mother Earth," and "The Church and the Current Moment."

36 See, for example, Carlos Arguedas C., "Afirman que bananeras crean muchos beneficios," *La Nación*, February 19, 1990, 5A; Oscar Bejarano, "La carta pastoral de Limón," *La Nación*, January 19, 1990, 15A; and Juan Gabriel Nuñez B., "La pastoral de Limón," *La Nación*, February 21, 1990, 16A.

37 Armando Alfaro, "La carta pastoral del obispo y sacerdotes de Limón," *Eco Católico*, January 21, 1990, 2; Alvaro Montero V. "Apoyo a Mons. Coto," *La Nación*, January 20, 1990, 16A; and Mora, "Una carta pastoral histórica," 16A.

38 Obispo y presbíteros del Vicariato Apostólico de Limón, "A la opinión pública," *Eco Católico*, January 28, 1990, 5.

39 Sacerdotes del Presbiterio de la Diócesis de Tilarán, "Al obispo, sacerdotes y comunidades cristianas del Vicariato Apostólico de Limón," *Eco Católico*, February 25, 1990, 15.

40 Ramírez interview by Sawchuk and Solera.

41 Ramírez interview by Sawchuk and Solera.

42 Mons. Alfonso Coto Monge, former bishop of Limón, interview by Dana Sawchuk, San José, Costa Rica, June 25, 1997.

43 Mons. Coto interview; and Ramírez interview by Sawchuk and Solera.

44 G. Vargas interview by Sawchuk and Solera.

45 Consejo Permanente de los Trabajadores, *A los trabajadores costarricenses, a los trabajadores bananeros, al clero y obispo de Limón, a la Iglesia católica y ciudadania en general* (personal archives of Eduardo Ramírez, photocopy).

46 See FES, Proyecto CAAS, ASPEROLA, and CPT, ed. *Foro Iglesia-sindicalismo* (n.p., 1990).

47 Gilberth Bermúdez, member of the Coordinadora de Sindicatos Bananeros and of the coordinating committee of Foro Emaús, interview by Dana Sawchuk, San José, Costa Rica, July 2, 1997.

48 G. Vargas interview by Sawchuk and Solera.

49 Ramón Barrantes, "Introductory Remarks," launch of Jorge Arturo Chaves, *Magisterio social y pastoral de los trabajadores* (San José, CR: ASEPROLA, Editorial Fundación UNA, and Pastoral Social Diócesis de Limón, 1996) at the Instituto Teológico de América Central, San José, Costa Rica, May 28, 1997.

50 Mons. Coto interview; and Mons. Francisco Ulloa Rojas, bishop of Limón, interview by Dana Sawchuk and Erick Solera, Puerto Limón, Costa Rica, July 10, 1997.

51 Mons. Coto interview.

52 G. Vargas interview by Sawchuk and Solera.

53 G. Vargas interview by Sawchuk and Solera.

54 A history of Foro Emaús can be found in Hernán Hermosilla and Tania Palencia, *Creación de una instancia coordinadora para detener el impacto de la expansión bananera incontrolada: Costa Rica* (San José, CR: Fundación Arias para la Paz y el Progreso Humano, 1997); and Roy H. May, *"La tierra no cae del cielo, hay que luchar por ella": La pastoral de la tierra en la Diócesis de Limón* (n.p.: ASEPROLA, 1996): 20–21. Two dozen of the coalition's members are listed in Foro Emaús, *Bananos para el mundo ¿Y el daño para Costa Rica? Los impactos sociales y ambientales de la producción bananera en Costa Rica* (San José, CR: Comité Coordinador de Foro Emaús, 1997), 47, n. 57.

55 Mons. Coto was named secretary of CECOR in May 1995 and has since retired from that post as well.

56 Ronald Matute and Marvin Barquero, "Sacerdotes de Limón prevén un gran reto," *La Nación*, January 1, 1995, 16A.

57 Mons. Francisco Ulloa, "Servicio y diálogo base de mi episcopado," interview by Gonzalo Muñoz A., *Eco Católico*, January 8, 1995, 6; and Víctor Fernández Castillo, "Primeros pasos en la nueva diócesis," *Eco Católico*, April 16, 1995, 14.

58 Fernández, "Primeros pasos," 14.

59 Asociación Ministerial de Limón, "Comunicado pastoral a Señor Ingeniero José María Figueres Olson [February 19, 1996]" (Archives of the Department of Social Communications, Conferencia Episcopal de Costa Rica, photocopy); Mons. Ulloa interview by Sawchuk and Solera; and Gilberto Valencia Navarro, "Iglesias censuran trato a muelleros," *El Heraldo*, February 20, 1996, 4.

60 G. Vargas interview by Sawchuk and Solera.

61 Mons. Ulloa interview by Sawchuk and Solera.

62 "Líneas pastorales que aplicará Mons. Ulloa Rojas," *Eco Católico*, February 19, 1995, 6; and G. Vargas interview by Sawchuk and Solera.

63 Diócesis de Limón, *Limón: Plan diocesano de pastoral. "Un nuevo modo de ser Iglesia": 1996-2000* (Limón, CR: n.p., 1995).

64 Mons. Ulloa interview by Sawchuk and Solera; and G. Vargas interview by Sawchuk and Solera.

65 Diócesis de Limón, *Plan diocesano*, 140–75.

66 G. Vargas interview by Sawchuk and Solera; and Gerardo Vargas Varela, "Limón con segundo plan pastoral," *Eco Católico*, December 15, 1996, 19.

67 Mons. Ulloa interview by Sawchuk and Solera.

68 Vargas, "Limón con segundo plan pastoral," 19.

69 "Líneas pastorales," 6.

70 Ramírez interview by Solera; and G. Vargas interview by Sawchuk and Solera.

71 Vicariato Apostólico de Limón, *Plan pastoral*, 85, see also 101-102.

72 Diócesis de Limón, *Plan diocesano*, 133.

73 Diócesis de Limón, *Plan diocesano*, 158-59.

74 Chaves, *Magisterio social*, 7.

75 Chaves, *Magisterio social*, 18-26.

76 Chaves, *Magisterio social*, 99-112.

77 Chaves, *Magisterio social*, 6-7, 25, and 118.

78 Chaves, *Magisterio social*, 116-17 and 32-33.

79 Chaves, *Magisterio social*, 31.

80 Hernán Hermosilla, co-ordinator of the Christian Program, ASEPROLA, interview by Dana Sawchuk, San José, Costa Rica, June 3, 1997.

81 Chaves, *Magisterio social*, 116.

82 Hermosilla interview.

83 Alfredo Fierro, *The Militant Gospel: A Critical Introduction to Political Theologies*, trans. John Drury (Maryknoll, NY: Orbis Books, 1977), 105-106. While in the original quotation Fierro refers to interpretation and evaluation in terms of the gospel, the concept of historical or political mediation can just as well refer to Catholic social teaching.

84 Fierro, *The Militant Gospel*, 74.

85 Obispo y presbíteros del Vicariato Apostólico de Limón, *Carta pastoral*, no. 15.

86 Obispo y presbíteros del Vicariato Apostólico de Limón, *Carta pastoral*, no. 24, and *Una versión popular*, no. 5.

87 Obispo y presbíteros del Vicariato Apostólico de Limón, *Carta pastoral*, no. 25, and *Una versión popular*, no. 5.

88 Obispo y presbíteros del Vicariato Apostólico de Limón, *Carta pastoral*, no. 39, and *Una versión popular*, no. 8. Note that the *carta pastoral* incorrectly quotes the CELAM text by using the term "ministries"; the Puebla document refers to parallel "magisteria" (III Conferencia General del Episcopado Latinoamericano, *Puebla: La evangelización en el presente y en el futuro de América Latina* (Bogotá, Colombia: Secretariado General del Consejo Episcopal Latinoamericano, 1990), no. 687).

89 Obispo y presbíteros del Vicariato Apostólico de Limón, *Carta pastoral*, nos. 37 and 42, and *Una versión popular*, no. 8.

90 Chaves, *Magisterio social*, 29 and 40-42.

91 Chaves, *Magisterio social*, 2 and 32.

92 Chaves, *Magisterio social*, 29-30.

93 Chaves, *Magisterio social*, 30.

94 Chaves, *Magisterio social*, 58 and 99.

95 Chaves, *Magisterio social*, 7-8.

96 Chaves, *Magisterio social*, 2.

97 See, for example, his detailed responses to a variety of criticisms aimed at the letter in Jorge Arturo Chaves, "Los ataques al pastor," *Eco Católico*, March 4, 1990, 15, and Jorge Arturo Chaves, "Los ataques al pastor, parte 2a: ¿Desconocimiento de la economía?," *Eco Católico*, March 11, 1990, 11.

98   Mons. Alfonso Coto Monge, "15 preguntas," interview by José Enrique Sibaja, *Eco Católico*, November 19, 1996, 14.
99   "Líneas pastorales," 6.
100 Mons. Ulloa interview by Sawchuk and Solera.

Notes to Chapter 10 : Liberationist and Conservative Catholicisms in Costa Rica and Beyond

1   Hugo Villela, "The Church and the Process of Democratization in Latin America," *Social Compass* 26, 2–3 (1979): 254.
2   See Antonio Gramsci, *Selections from the Prison Notebooks of Antonio Gramsci*, ed. and trans. Quintin Hoare and Geoffrey Nowell Smith (London, UK: Lawrence and Wishart, 1971), 420.
3   This is the process illustrated by the essays collected in Scott Mainwaring and Alexander Wilde, ed., *The Progressive Church in Latin America* (Notre Dame, IN: University of Notre Dame Press, 1989). Subsequent essays from this collection are cited as in *The Progressive Church*.
4   See the expression of this hypothesis in Scott Mainwaring and Alexander Wilde, "The Progressive Church in Latin America: An Interpretation," in *The Progressive Church*, 14.
5   See the comments in Warren Edward Hewitt, "Introduction: The Legacy of the Progressive Church in Latin America," in *The Church at the Grassroots in Latin America: Perspectives on Thirty Years of Activism*, ed. John Burdick and Warren Edward Hewitt (Westport, CT, and London, UK: Praeger, 2000), viii; and Iain S. Maclean, *Opting for Democracy? Liberation Theology and the Struggle for Democracy in Brazil* (New York: Peter Lang, 1999), 221.
6   Atilio A. Boron, *State, Capitalism, and Democracy in Latin America* (Boulder, CO: Lynne Rienner, 1995).
7   Otto Maduro, *Religion and Social Conflicts*, trans. Robert R. Barr (Maryknoll, NY: Orbis Books, 1982), 134.
8   Mainwaring and Wilde, "The Progressive Church in Latin America," 16.
9   Proyecto Estado de la Nación, *Estado de la nación en desarrollo humano sostenible: Un análisis amplio y objetivo sobre la Costa Rica que tenemos a partir de los indicadores más actuales* (San José, CR: Impr. Lara Segura, 1996), 141.
10 Among those who have indicated that a bishop's favour or disfavour can have a significant effect on the nature and persistence of CEB activism or progressive Church innovation are Thomas C. Bruneau, *The Church in Brazil: The Politics of Religion* (Austin: University of Texas, 1982), 109–111; Warren Edward Hewitt, *Base Christian Communities and Social Change in Brazil* (Lincoln, NB and London: University of Nebraska Press, 1991), 53–56; and Mainwaring and Wilde, "The Progressive Church in Latin America," 15–16.
11 For details of the Vatican's campaign against progressive bishops in Latin America, see John L. Allen, Jr., "These Paths Lead to Rome," *National Catholic Reporter*, June 2, 2000, 13–16; Madeleine Cousineau, "Innovation and Retrenchment in the Brazilian Catholic Church: Consequences for the Base Communities," *Social Compass* 44, 4 (December 1997): 573–74; Hewitt, *Base Christian Communities*, 100–101; and Anna L. Peterson and Manuel A. Vásquez, "The New Evangelization in Latin American Perspective," *Cross Currents* 48, 3 (Fall 1998): 329, n. 30.
12 Tom Fox, "John Paul Reflection: Liberating the Poor," *National Catholic Reporter*, February 23, 1996, 2.
13 For descriptions of the some of the most recent cases, see Jean François Nothomb, "Does the Papacy Have a Future?" *Cross Currents* 49, 1 (Spring 1999): 102.

14 Pope John Paul II, "On Bishops and Bishops' Conferences (July 23, 1998)," *The Pope Speaks* 44, 2 (1999): 102–14.
15 Pope John Paul II, "To Defend the Faith (May 28, 1998)," *The Pope Speaks* 46, 6 (1998): 327–30.
16 Michael L. Budde, *The Two Churches: Catholicism and Capitalism in the World-System* (Durham, NC: Duke University Press, 1992), 19.

Bibliography

Contrary to popular convention, each separate newspaper article cited in this work has also been listed as either a primary or secondary source document below. This is because most of the articles cited are not merely news items, but are often either editorial pieces written by or about key Costa Rican Church figures, or are reproductions of official Church documents.

Interviews

Aguilar, Rodrigo. Secretary of the Confederación de Trabajadores Rerum Novarum. Interview by Dana Sawchuk. San José, Costa Rica, July 16, 1997.

Arrieta Villalobos, Mons. Román. Archbishop of San José. Interview by Dana Sawchuk. San José, Costa Rica, July 4, 1997.

Bermúdez, Gilberth. Member of the Coordinadora de Sindicatos Bananeros and of the coordinating committee of Foro Emaús. Interview by Dana Sawchuk. San José, Costa Rica, July 2, 1997.

Blanco B., Gustavo Leonel. ASEPROLA co-founder and sociologist. Interview by Dana Sawchuk. San José, Costa Rica, June 19, 1997.

Bonilla, Yadira. Assistant director of CECODERS. Interview by Dana Sawchuk. San José, Costa Rica, July 26, 1997.

Coto Monge, Mons. Alfonso. Former bishop of Limón. Interview by Dana Sawchuk. San José, Costa Rica, June 25, 1997.

Doncel, Padre Jesús. Parish priest in Río Frío. Interview by Dana Sawchuk. Río Frío, Costa Rica, August 17, 1996.

Hermosilla Barrientos, Hernán. Coordinator of the Christian Program, ASEPROLA. Interview by Dana Sawchuk. San José, Costa Rica, June 3, 1997.

Masís Vega, Bernal. Director of administration at the ESJ23 Centro Nacional de Capacitación. Interview by Dana Sawchuk. Tres Ríos, Costa Rica, July 11, 1996.

Navarro Rojas, Padre Orlando. Director of CECODERS. Interview by Dana Sawchuk. San José, Costa Rica, July 18, 1996.

Ramírez, Padre Eduardo. Priest in the parish of Puerto Limón. Interview by Erick Solera. Puerto Limón, Costa Rica, May 10, 1997. Personal archives of Erick Solera, photocopy.

Ramírez, Padre Eduardo. Priest in the parish of Puerto Limón. Interview by Dana Sawchuk and Erick Solera. Puerto Limón, Costa Rica, July 10, 1997.

Solano Cerdas, Padre Claudio Maria. Director of the ESJ23. Interview by Dana Sawchuk. Curridabat, Costa Rica, July 9, 1996.

Solis, Mario. CECODERS theologian. Interview by Dana Sawchuk. San José, Costa Rica, July 24, 1996.

Trejos, Eugenio. Legal advisor to the ESJ23. Interview by Dana Sawchuk. Curridabat, Costa Rica, July 9, 1996.

Ulloa Rojas, Mons. Francisco. Bishop of Limón. Interview by Dana Sawchuk and
Erick Solera. Puerto Limón, Costa Rica, July 10, 1997.

Vargas, Padre Gerardo. Priest and coordinator of the Comisión Diocesana de Pastoral Social in Limón. Interview by Dana Sawchuk and Erick Solera. Siquirres, Costa Rica, July 11, 1997.

Vargas, Pastor Ronaldo. Minister in the Assemblies of God. Interview by Dana
Sawchuk. San José, Costa Rica. July 29, 1997.

Vargas Solano, Miguel. Solidarista promoter. Interview by Dana Sawchuk. Guapiles,
Costa Rica, July 29, 1996.

Vásquez, Roberto. Assistant to Padre Claudio Solano of the ESJ23. Interview by
Dana Sawchuk. Curridabat, Costa Rica, July 9, 1996.

Villalta, Carlos. Director of education at the ESJ23 Centro Nacional de Capacitación. Interview by Dana Sawchuk. Tres Ríos, Costa Rica, July 11, 1996.

Primary Sources

♦ Official Church Documents, Statements, and Editorials by Church Representatives

II Conferencia General del Episcopado Latinoamericano. "Catequesis." In *Medellín
conclusiones: La Iglesia en la actual transformación de América Latina a la
luz del Concilio*. Bogotá, Colombia: Secretariado General del CELAM, 1990.

———. "Educación." In *Medellín conclusiones: La Iglesia en la actual transformación de América Latina a la luz del Concilio*. Bogotá, Colombia: Secretariado General del CELAM, 1990.

———. "Formación del clero." In *Medellín conclusiones: La Iglesia en la actual
transformación de América Latina a la luz del Concilio*. Bogotá, Colombia: Secretariado General del CELAM, 1990.

———. "Justicia." In *Medellín conclusiones: La Iglesia en la actual transformación
de América Latina a la luz del Concilio*. Bogotá, Colombia: Secretariado
General del CELAM, 1990.

———. "Juventud." In *Medellín conclusiones: La Iglesia en la actual transformación de América Latina a la luz del Concilio*. Bogotá, Colombia: Secretariado General del CELAM, 1990.

———. *Medellín conclusiones: La Iglesia en la actual transformación de América
Latina a la luz del Concilio*. Bogotá, Colombia: Secretariado General del
CELAM, 1990.

———. "Medios de comunicación social." In *Medellín conclusiones: La Iglesia en
la actual transformación de América Latina a la luz del Concilio*. Bogotá,
Colombia: Secretariado General del CELAM, 1990.

———. "Movimientos de laicos." In *Medellín conclusiones: La Iglesia en la actual
transformación de América Latina a la luz del Concilio*. Bogotá, Colombia: Secretariado General del CELAM, 1990.

———. "Pastoral de conjunto." In *Medellín conclusiones: La Iglesia en la actual
transformación de América Latina a la luz del Concilio*. Bogotá, Colombia: Secretariado General del CELAM, 1990.

————. "Pastoral de élites." In *Medellín conclusiones: La Iglesia en la actual transformación de América Latina a la luz del Concilio*. Bogotá, Colombia: Secretariado General del CELAM, 1990.

————. "Paz." In *Medellín conclusiones: La Iglesia en la actual transformación de América Latina a la luz del Concilio*. Bogotá, Colombia: Secretariado General del CELAM, 1990.

————. "Religiosos." In *Medellín conclusiones: La Iglesia en la actual transformación de América Latina a la luz del Concilio*. Bogotá, Colombia: Secretariado General del CELAM, 1990.

III Conferencia General del Episcopado Latinoamericano. *Puebla: La evangelización en el presente y en el futuro de América Latina*. Bogotá, Colombia: Secretariado General del CELAM, 1990.

IV Conferencia General del Episcopado Latinoamericano. *Santo Domingo conclusiones: Nueva evangelización, promoción humana, cultura cristiana*. Santafé de Bogotá, Colombia: CELAM, 1992.

V Sínodo Arquidiocesano. *Decretos sinodales*. Curridabat, CR: Ludovico, 1985.

Arrieta Villalobos, Mons. Román. "Alocución de Mons. Román Arrieta en el desayuno de amistad cristiana." *El Mensajero del Clero* 4 (August 1981): 12.

————. "Alocución de Mons. Román Arrieta Villalobos, Arzobispo de San José, con motivo de la elección de don Luis Alberto Monge, como Presidente de la República." *El Mensajero del Clero* 8 (December 1982): 4–5.

————. "Como debe ser la liberación cristiana." *Eco Católico*. May 19, 1996, 4.

————. "Comunicado del Arzobispo de San José sobre un editorial del Eco Católico." *Eco Católico (Suplemento Campesino)*. April 11, 1982, 1.

————. "Las conquistas del Código del Trabajo son derechos del trabajador, no dádivas." *Eco Católico*. October 3, 1993, 4.

————. "En los cuarenta años de la promulgción del Código de Trabajo." *El Mensajero del Clero* 14 (June 1984): 18–19.

————. "Decálogo de la austeridad." *Eco Católico*. January 15, 1984, 3.

————. "Decálogo de los derechos de los trabajadores." *Eco Católico*. September 26, 1993, 4.

————. "Declaración sobre la Instrucción de la Sagrada Congregación para la Doctrina de la Fe, con relación a algunas aspectos de la teología de la liberación." *El Mensajero del Clero* 15 (September 1984): 29–30.

————. "Dios nos llama a la vigencia y la práctica de la justicia." *Gente*. April 20, 1987, 6.

————. "Discurso de Mons. Román Arrieta a los trabajadores el primero de mayo." *Eco Católico*. May 11, 1986, 2.

————. "Festividad de Nuesta Señora de los Angeles–Cartago, 2 de agosto de 1984: Homilía." *El Mensajero del Clero* 15 (September 1984): 17–19.

————. "Fiesta de San José Obrero: Homilía (1996)." CECOR archives. Photocopy.

————. "Homilía de Mons. Román Arrieta Villalobos, Arzobispo de San José, en la fiesta de María Reina de Los Angeles." *Eco Católico*. August 12, 1990, 2.

————. "La Iglesia de Cristo siempre se ha preocupado por los pobres." *Eco Católico*. November 22, 1981, 2.

————. "Iglesia sí intervino por solución a huelga." *Eco Católico*. September 10, 1995, 4.

———. "La Iglesia tiene un compromiso con los más pobres." *Eco Católico.* April 8, 1990, 3.

———. "Liberación cristiana: Características que la distinguen." *Eco Católico.* June 17, 1990, 3.

———. "Liberación cristiana opta sólo por Cristo." *Eco Católico.* September 28, 1980, 2.

———. "Misa de acción de gracias por el Acuerdo de Paz." *El Mensajero del Clero* 23 (November 1987): 20–21.

———. *Nueva evangelización y promoción humana.* Curridabat, CR: Escuela Social Juan XXIII, 1993.

———. "Otra respuesta a La Nación." *La Nación.* March 23, 1987, 18A.

———. "Pacíficos, trabajadores, y honrados por la Patria." *Eco Católico.* September 15, 1991, 4.

———. "La penetración protestante." *Eco Católico.* December 18, 1988, 3.

———. "El 1º de mayo." *Eco Católico.* May 8, 1988, 5.

———. "Que la Santa Sede decida." *La Nación.* March 31, 1987, 16A.

———. "Reacción del Arzobispo de San José frente a declaraciones del comandante Daniel Ortega." *Eco Católico.* July 29, 1994, 2.

———. "Reflexión de Mons. Román Arrieta en la Asamblea Legislativa, sobre la Rerum Novarum." *Eco Católico.* June 23, 1991, 2.

———. "Reflexiones de Año Nuevo." *Eco Católico.* January 13, 1991, 3.

———. "Una respuesta a La Nación." In *La pastoral social en Costa Rica: Documentos y comentarios acerca de la polémica entre la Iglesia católica y el periódico La Nación*, ed. Pablo Richard. San José, CR: DEI, 1987.

———. "Segundo aniversario de la proclama de neutralidad." *Eco Católico.* November 24, 1985, 2.

———. "Sobre sectas protestantes." *Eco Católico.* April 14, 1991, 4.

———. "Solemnidad de nuestra Señora de los Angeles." *Eco Católico.* August 9, 1987, 2.

———. "Solemnidad de nuestra Señora de los Angeles, Cartago, agosto 2 de 1996: Homilía." CECOR archives. Photocopy.

———. "Los trabajadores, con el auxilio divino, son los artifices de la justicia, la paz y el amor en el mundo." *Eco Católico.* May 10, 1992, 4.

———. "Trigésimo aniversario de la Escuela Social Juan XXIII." *Eco Católico.* February 7, 1993, 4.

———. "Unidad para solucionar problemas del país." *Eco Católico.* August 6, 1995, 4.

———. "Vigésimo sétimo aniversario de la Escuela Social Juan XXIII." *Eco Católico.* January 28, 1990, 3.

Asociación Ministerial de Limón. "Comunicado pastoral a Señor Ingeniero José María Figueres Olson [February 19, 1996]." Archives of the Department of Social Communications, CECOR. Photocopy.

Barquero A., José, Ignacio Trejos P., Héctor Morera, et al. "Nos impulsa el Evangelio." *La Nación.* March 25, 1987, 16A.

Centro Coordinador de Evangelización y Realidad Social (CECODERS). "Algunos aspectos fundamentales de la encíclica Rerum Novarum." *Eco Católico.* January 21, 1990, 12.

———. "Bien común y solidaridad en el magisterio de la Iglesia: Doctrina Social postconciliar." *Eco Católico.* June 16, 1991, 12.

————. *Censo parroquial familiar.* San José, CR: CECODERS, n.d.

————. "Centenario de la encíclica Rerum Novarum." *Eco Católico.* February 17, 1991, 16.

————. "Centenario de la encíclica Rerum Novarum: En el año de la Doctrina Social de la Iglesia." *Eco Católico.* February 10, 1991, 9.

————. "La cuestión social y el reajuste estructural." *Eco Católico.* July 16, 1989, 7.

————. "Derechos de los trabajadores a la luz de la Doctrina Social." *Eco Católico.* August 20, 1989, 11.

————. "La deuda externa a la luz de la 'Populorum Progressio' y la 'Sollicitudo Rei Socialis.'" *Eco Católico.* July 23, 1989, 7.

————. "Los efectos económicos y sociales de la crisis Latinoamericana (una iluminación desde la Populorum Progressio y la Sollicitudo Rei Socialis)." *Eco Católico.* August 6, 1989, 16.

————. "De la encíclica 'Populorum Progressio' a la encíclica 'Sollicitudo Rei Socialis': Década de los setenta." *Eco Católico.* March 20, 1988, 13.

————. "La encíclica Rerum Novarum y la Doctrina Social." *Eco Católico.* January 14, 1990, 12.

————. "Encuentro sacerdotes y organizaciones sindicales." CECODERS archives. Photocopy.

————. "La espiritualidad en la Populorum Progressio." *Eco Católico.* March 6, 1988, 3.

————. "La huelga bananera de 1934." *Eco Católico.* September 16, 1990, 16.

————. "Las huelgas de 1934 y sus repercusiones sociales." *Eco Católico.* September 9, 1990, 18.

————. "Las huelgas en Costa Rica en el movimiento artesanal obrero." *Eco Católico.* August 12, 1990, 13.

————. "La Iglesia y los acontecimientos de los años 80." *Eco Católico.* April 10, 1988, 3.

————. "El mundo obrero y la Iglesia." *Eco Católico.* November 12, 1989, 12.

————. "Las organizaciones sociales en la década de los ochenta." *Eco Católico.* October 22, 1989, 12.

————. "Plan de trabajo del Frente de Organizaciones Sindicales del Sector Salud [1995]." CECODERS archives. Photocopy.

————. "Pobres, solidaridad, y liberación." *Eco Católico.* December 23,1990, 14.

————. "La preocupación social de la Iglesia." *Eco Católico.* February 28, 1988, 10.

————. "Las relaciones entre las naciones y su influencia en el trabajo." *Eco Católico.* August 27, 1989, 12.

————. "La Rerum Novarum y el estado." *Eco Católico.* February 4, 1990, 12.

————. "Situación en que se encuentra el sector salud en Costa Rica." CECODERS archives. Photocopy.

————. "Tercer encuentro de sacerdotes y organizaciones sindicales [1996]." CECODERS archives. Photocopy.

CECODERS and Cáritas. *¡La historia de Costa Rica? Y la de nuestra comunidad!!!* Cuadernos para la pastoral social no. 1. San José, CR: CECODERS–Cáritas, 1986.

CECODERS and Sacerdotes de diversa diócesis de Costa Rica. "Fax sobre la huelga de Magisterio [1995]." CECODERS archives. Photocopy.

Chaves, Jorge Arturo. *Magisterio social y pastoral de los trabajadores*. San José, CR: ASEPROLA, Editorial Fundación UNA, and Pastoral Social Diócesis de Limón, 1996.

Comisión Nacional Episcopal de Laicos. *Las comunidades eclesiales de base en la Iglesia costarricense*. San José, CR: Ediciones CECOR[?], 1995.

Conferencia Episcopal de Costa Rica (CECOR). "Acuerdos importantes tomados por la CECOR, en su primera reunión extraordinaria de 1986." *El Mensajero del Clero* 19 (October 1986): 5-6.

————. *Bendito el que viene en el nombre del Señor: Exhortación de los obispos de Costa Rica ante la próxima venida de S.S. Juan Pablo II*. San José, CR: Ediciones CECOR, 1983.

————. "Carta circular de la conferencia episcopal." *Eco Católico*, August 26, 1979, 3.

————. "Comentarios sobre el Proyecto de Nuevo Código de Trabajo." In *Iglesia Católica, crisis y democratización en Centro América (Documentos seleccionados de las conferencias episcopales y del SEDAC, 1979-1990)*, ed. Instituto Centroamericano de Estudios Políticos. Guatemala City: INCEP, 1990.

————. "Evangelización y realidad social de Costa Rica: Carta pastoral colectiva." In *La palabra social de los obispos costarricenses: Selección de documentos de la Iglesia Católica costarricense 1893-1981*, ed. Miguel Picado. San José, CR: DEI, n.d.

————. "La Iglesia ante el proceso electoral: Exhortación pastoral de la Conferencia Episcopal de Costa Rica." *Eco Católico*. September 15, 1985: 2-3.

————. "Iglesia y momento actual: Carta pastoral del episcopado costarricense sobre la actual situación del país y la campaña electoral (1981)." In *La palabra social de los obispos costarricenses: Selección de documentos de la Iglesia Católica costarricense 1893-1981*, ed. Miguel Picado. San José, CR: DEI, n.d.

————. *Una llamada de los obispos de Costa Rica a la conciencia del país*. San José, CR: Ediciones CECOR[?], 1988.

————. *Madre Tierra: Mensaje de los obispos de Costa Rica sobre la situación de los campesinos y los indígenas*. San José, CR: Ediciones CECOR[?], 1994.

————. "Navidad 1981—Unidos en la esperanza: carta pastoral del episcopado sobre la crítica situación que vive el país." In *La palabra social de los obispos costarricenses: Selección de documentos de la Iglesia Católica costarricense 1893-1981*, ed. Miguel Picado. San José, CR: DEI, n.d.

Coto Monge, Mons. Alfonso. "15 preguntas ...." Interview by José Enrique Sibaja. *Eco Católico*. November 19, 1996, 14.

————. *Con inmenso gozo*. Documentos de pastoral del Vicariato Apostólico de Limón. No. 1. September 1980. Personal archives of Eduardo Ramírez. Photocopy.

————. "Limón va adelante con buen plan pastoral." Interview by Gonzalo Muñoz. *Eco Católico*. January 22, 1995, 6.

Coto Monge, Mons. Alfonso, et al. "Somos solidarios con quienes sufren no con los que se aprovechan de ese dolor." *Eco Católico*. September 28, 1980, 8.

Diócesis de Limón. *Limón: Plan diocesano de pastoral. "Un nuevo modo de ser Iglesia": 1996-2000*. Limón, CR: n.p., 1995.

Escuela Social Juan XXIII (ESJ23). "Concepto cristiano de la empresa." *Eco Católico*. June 9, 1974, 14.

———. *La Doctrina Social de la Iglesia (introducción a su estudio)*. San José, CR: Editorial Ministerio de Educación Pública, 1985.

———. *Escuela Social Juan XXIII*. Curridabat, CR: Escuela Social Juan XXIII, n.d.

———. *Escuela Social Juan XXIII: Su origen, sus objetivos, sus actividades, su cobertura*. Curridabat, CR: Escuela Social Juan XXIII, 1992.

———. "El fruto incierto de las huelgas." *Eco Católico*. July 14, 1974, 3.

———. "La huelga es arma extrema." *Eco Católico*. August 25, 1974, 3.

———. *Manual para el estudio de la Doctrina Social de la Iglesia*. Curridabat, CR: Escuela Social Juan XXIII, [1973].

———. *La solidaridad y el solidarismo en la empresa*. Curridabat, CR: Escuela Social Juan XXIII, n.d.

———. *Solidarismo: Aspectos doctrinales*. San José, CR: Editorial Ministerio de Educación Pública, 1985.

———. *Solidarismo, solidarismo*. Currudabat, CR: Escuela Social Juan XXIII, n.d.

———. *Solidarismo y democracia*. Curridabat, CR: Escuela Social Juan XXIII, 1994.

———. *Ventajas del solidarismo*. Curridabat, CR: Escuela Social Juan XXIII, n.d.

Escuela Social Juan XXIII (ESJ23), ed. *Ley de asociaciones solidaristas: Su reglamento y otros documentos afines*. 4th ed. Curridabat, CR: ESJ23, 1993.

John XXIII, Pope. *Humanae Salutis, The Encyclicals and Other Messages of John XXIII*, ed. The staff of *The Pope Speaks*. Washington, DC: The Pope Speaks Press, 1964.

———. "Mater et Magistra." In *Catholic Social Thought: The Documentary Heritage*, ed. David J. O'Brien and Thomas A. Shannon. Maryknoll, NY: Orbis Books, 1992.

———. "Pacem in Terris." In *Catholic Social Thought: The Documentary Heritage*, ed. David J. O'Brien and Thomas A. Shannon. Maryknoll, NY: Orbis Books, 1992.

John Paul II, Pope. "Centesimus Annus." In *Catholic Social Thought: The Documentary Heritage*, ed. David J. O'Brien and Thomas A. Shannon. Maryknoll, NY: Orbis Books, 1992.

———. "Laborem Exercens." In *Catholic Social Thought: The Documentary Heritage*, ed. David J. O'Brien and Thomas A. Shannon. Maryknoll, NY: Orbis Books, 1992.

———. "On Bishops and Bishops' Conferences (July 23, 1998)." *The Pope Speaks* 44, 2 (1999): 102–14.

———. "Preferential Option for the Poor Must Be Gospel-Based." *The Pope Speaks* 32 (1987): 236–42.

———. *Reconciliatio et Paenitentia: Post-Synodal Apostolic Exhortation of John Paul II to the Bishops, Clergy and Faithful on Reconciliation and Penance in the Mission of the Church Today*. Ottawa, ON: Canadian Conference of Catholic Bishops, 1985.

———. *Redemptoris Missio: Encyclical Letter of Pontiff John Paul II on the Permanent Validity of the Church's Missionary Mandate*. Sherbrooke, QC: Editions Paulines, 1991.

——. "Sollicitudo Rei Socialis." In *Catholic Social Thought: The Documentary Heritage*, ed. David J. O'Brien and Thomas A. Shannon. Maryknoll, NY: Orbis Books, 1992.

——. "To Defend the Faith (May 28, 1998)." *The Pope Speaks* 46, 6 (1998): 327–30.

——. "Unity of the Church." *The Pope Speaks* 28, 3 (1983): 206–10.

——. "Veritatis Splendor: The Splendor of Truth." *The Pope Speaks* 39, 1 (1993): 6–63.

Leo XIII, Pope. "Rerum Novarum." In *Catholic Social Thought: The Documentary Heritage*, ed. David J. O'Brien and Thomas A. Shannon. Maryknoll, NY: Orbis Books, 1992.

Navarro Rojas, Orlando. "Carta del Padre Orlando Navarro, Director de CECODERS, a Mons. Román Arrieta Villalobos, sobre la labor que este centro realiza." *El Mensajero del Clero* 21 (May 1987): 26–27.

——. "La Iglesia católica frente al Proyecto de la Reforma de Salud." CECODERS archives. Photocopy.

——. "El pensamiento actual en la Doctrina Social de la Iglesia." *Senderos*, no. 39 (July 1991): 65–81.

Navarro Rojas, Orlando, and Yadira Bonilla O. "La Iglesia y el avance de la Doctrina Social." In *El pensamiento social de Juan Pablo II: Documentos y comentarios*, ed. Franz J. Hinkelhammert, Arnoldo Mora, and Carmelo Alvarez et al. San José, CR: DEI, 1988.

Obispo y presbíteros del Vicariato Apostólico de Limón. "A la opinion pública." *Eco Católico*. January 28, 1990, 5.

——. *Carta pastoral*. December 25, 1989. Photocopy.

——. *Una versión popular de la carta pastoral: La expansión bananera incontrolada*. July 1990. Photocopy.

O'Brien, David J., and Thomas A. Shannon, ed., *Catholic Social Thought: The Documentary Heritage*. Maryknoll, NY: Orbis Books, 1992.

Pastoral de la Esperanza–CECODERS. *SIDA y VIDA*. Curridabat, CR: Ludovico, n.d.

Paul VI, Pope. "Changing Social Structures: A Time of Crisis." Address in Bogotá, Colombia, August 23, 1968. *The Pope Speaks* 13, 3 (1968): 237–43.

——. "Discurso de S.S. Pablo VI en la apertura de la segunda conferencia (1968)." In *Medellín conclusiones: La Iglesia en la actual transformación de América Latina a la luz del Concilio a la luz del Concilio*. Bogotá, Colombia: Secretariado General del CELAM, 1990.

——. "Evangelii Nuntiandi." In *Catholic Social Thought: The Documentary Heritage*, ed. David J. O'Brien and Thomas A. Shannon. Maryknoll, NY: Orbis Books, 1992.

——. "Honoring Christ in His Poor." Address in San José, Colombia. August 23, 1968. *The Pope Speaks* 13, 3 (1968): 232–37.

——. "Octogesima Adveniens." In *Catholic Social Thought: The Documentary Heritage*, ed. David J. O'Brien and Thomas A. Shannon. Maryknoll, NY: Orbis Books, 1992.

——. "Populorum Progressio." In *Catholic Social Thought: The Documentary Heritage*, ed. David J. O'Brien and Thomas A. Shannon. Maryknoll, NY: Orbis Books, 1992.

Picado, Miguel, ed. *La palabra social de los obispos costarricenses: Selección de documentos de la Iglesia Católica costarricense 1893–1981.* San José, CR: DEI, n.d.

Pius XI, Pope. "Quadragesimo Anno." In *Catholic Social Thought: The Documentary Heritage*, ed. David J. O'Brien and Thomas A. Shannon. Maryknoll, NY: Orbis Books, 1992.

Pius XII, Pope. *Summi Pontificatus: Encyclical Letter Exhorting Unity in Opposing World Evils.* New York: Paulist Press, 1939.

Rodríguez Quíros, Mons. Carlos Humberto. "[Decreto]." *El Mensajero del Clero* (March 1963): 57–61.

Sacerdotes del presbiterio de la Diócesis de Tilarán. "Al obispo, sacerdotes y comunidades cristianas del Vicariato Apostólico de Limón." *Eco Católico.* February 25, 1990, 15.

Sacred Congregation for the Doctrine of the Faith. *Instruction on Certain Aspects of the "Theology of Liberation."* Washington, DC: United States Catholic Conference, 1984.

———. *Instruction on Christian Freedom and Liberation.* Washington, DC: United States Catholic Conference, 1986.

Second Vatican Council. "Gaudium et Spes." In *Catholic Social Thought: The Documentary Heritage*, ed. David J. O'Brien and Thomas A. Shannon. Maryknoll, NY: Orbis Books, 1992.

———. "Lumen Gentium." In *Vatican Council II: The Conciliar and Post Conciliar Documents*, ed. Austin Flannery. Northport, NY: Costello Publishing, 1987.

Solano Cerdas, Claudio Maria. Comments. Round table on "Expresión de los problemas políticos en el clero." *Iglesia Solidaria*, 3, 27 (October 1987): 19.

———. "Curriculo." ESJ23 archives. Photocopy.

———. "Hemos transformado la zona Atlántica." *La Nación.* January 21, 1990, 16A.

———. "Iglesia: Promotora del diálogo." *Al Día.* September 25, 1994, 16.

———. "El solidarismo en los albores del siglo XXI." Paper presented at the BANDECO Managerial Seminar, San José, CR, 1997.

———. "Solidarismo: Un movimiento integral y solidario." Paper presented at the Primera Conferencia Internacional Solidarista, San José, CR, June 1995.

Thiel, Mons. Bernardo Augusto. "Trigésima carta pastoral sobre el justo salario." In *La palabra social de los obispos costarricenses: Selección de documentos de la Iglesia Católica costarricense 1893–1981*, ed. Miguel Picado. San José, CR: DEI, n.d.

Ulloa Rojas, Mons. Francisco. "Servicio y diálogo base de mi episcopado." Interview by Gonzalo Muñoz. *Eco Católico.* January 8, 1995, 6.

Vicariato Apostólico de Limón. "Opciones pastorales: Documento conclusivo de la semana de pastoral para el Vicariato Apostólico–Limón." Cuaderno de pastoral, no. 3. February 1981. Photocopy.

———. *Plan pastoral de Vicariato Apostólico de Limón.* San José, CR: Varitec, 1990.

Government Documents

Administración Figueres Olsen. *Plan nacional de combate a la pobreza: Hacia una Costa Rica integrada de oportunidades*. San José, CR: Consejo Social, Segunda Vicepresidencia de la República, 1996.

Costa Rica. *Código de trabajo* [Labour Code]. 12th ed. San José, CR: Editorial Porvenir, 1997.

———. *Constitución política de la República de Costa Rica (7 de noviembre de 1949)*. Updated by Marco Castillo Rojas. Cartago, CR: Uruk Ediciones, 1996.

———. *Ley de asociaciones solidaristas* [Law on solidarity associations]. In *Ley de asociaciones solidaristas: Su reglamento y otros documentos afines*. Asamblea Legislativa de la República de Costa Rica. 4th ed., ed. ESJ23. Curridabat, CR: ESJ23, 1993.

Díaz Alemán, Eduardo. *Sindicatos: Naturaleza, características, problemática y cifras, setiembre 1993*. San José, CR: Ministerio de Trabajo y Seguridad Social, Dirección General de Planificación, 1995.

Secondary Sources: Books, Articles, and Other Documents

Adriance, Madeleine [Cousineau.] "Opting for the Poor: A Social-Historical Analysis of the Changing Brazilian Catholic Church." *Sociological Analysis* 46, 2 (1985): 131–46.

———. *Opting for the Poor: Brazilian Catholicism in Transition*. Kansas City, MS: Sheed and Ward, 1986.

———. *Promised Land: Base Christian Communities and the Struggle for the Amazon*. Albany, NY: State University of New York Press, 1995.

"Agrupación internacional condena solidarismo tico." *La Nación*. June 19, 1989, 4A.

Aguilar, Marielos. *Clase trabajadora y organización sindical en Costa Rica, 1943–1971*. San José, CR: Editorial Porvenir, FLASCO, and ICES, 1989.

Aguilar, Marielos, and Victoria Ramírez. "Crisis económica y acción sindical en Costa Rica (1980–1987)." *Revista de Ciencias Sociales* 44 (June 1989): 49–68.

Aguilar Arce, Rodrigo. *Actualidad del movimiento sindical en Costa Rica*. San José, CR: Fundación Friedrich Ebert, 1993.

Aguilar Bulgarelli, Oscar. *Costa Rica y sus hechos políticos de 1948: Problemática de una década*. 2nd ed. San José, CR: EDUCA, 1974.

Alfaro, Armando. "La carta pastoral del obispo y sacerdotes de Limón." *Eco Católico*. January 21, 1990, 2.

Allen, John L., Jr. "These Paths Lead to Rome." *National Catholic Reporter*. June 2, 2000, 13–16.

Arguedas C., Carlos. "Afirman que bananeras crean muchos beneficios." *La Nación*. February 19, 1990, 5A.

———. "Gobierno acepta críticas de obispos." *Al Día*. August 19, 1994, 4.

Asociación Servicios de Promoción Laboral (ASEPROLA). *Solidarismo*. Archives of Padre Eduardo Ramírez. Photocopy.

Backer, James. *La Iglesia y el sindicalismo en Costa Rica*. 3rd ed. San José, CR: Editorial Costa Rica, 1978.

Baker, Christopher P. *Costa Rica Handbook*. 2nd ed. Chico, CA: Moon Publications, 1996.

Barrantes, Ramón. "Introductory remarks." Launch of Jorge Arturo Chaves, *Magisterio social y pastoral de los trabajadores*, at Instituto Teológico de América Central, San José, Costa Rica, May 28, 1997.

Baum, Gregory. *The Priority of Labor: A Commentary on Laborem Exercens, Encyclical Letter of Pope John Paul II*. New York: Paulist Press, 1982.

Bejarano, Oscar. "La carta pastoral de Limón." *La Nación*. January 19, 1990, 15A.

Bell, John Patrick. *Crisis in Costa Rica: The 1948 Revolution*. Austin: University of Texas Press, 1971.

Berryman, Phillip. *The Religious Roots of Rebellion: Christians in Central American Revolutions*. Maryknoll, NY: Orbis Books, 1984.

———. *Stubborn Hope: Religion, Politics, and Revolution in Central America*. New York: New Press, and Maryknoll, NY: Orbis Books, 1994.

Blachman, Morris J., and Ronald G. Hellman. "Costa Rica." In *Confronting Revolution: Security through Diplomacy in Central America*, ed. Morris J. Blachman, William M. Leogrande, Kenneth Sharpe. New York: Pantheon Books, 1986.

Blanco B., Gustavo Leonel. "Iglesia católica y pastoral social." Master's thesis, Ciudad Universitaria "Rodrigo Facio," Costa Rica, 1987.

———. "La paz del silencio obrero." *Revista Aportes* 7, 32–33 (January to April 1987): 20–22.

Blanco, Gustavo, and Orlando Navarro. *El solidarismo: Pensamiento y dinámica social de un movimiento obrero patronal*. San José, CR: Editorial Costa Rica, 1984.

Boff, Leonardo. *Church: Charism and Power. Liberation Theology and the Institutional Church*. trans. John W. Diercksmeier. New York: Crossroad, 1985.

———. *Ecclesiogenesis: The Base Communities Reinvent the Church*. trans. Robert R. Barr. Maryknoll, NY: Orbis Books, 1986.

Booth, John A. *Costa Rica: Quest for Democracy*. Boulder, CO: Westview Press, 1998.

Boron, Atilio A. *State, Capitalism, and Democracy in Latin America*. Boulder, CO: Lynne Rienner, 1995.

Botero Restrepo, Juan. *El CELAM: Elementos para su historia*. Medellín, Colombia: CELAM, 1982.

Bourgois, Philippe I. *Banano, etnia y lucha social en Centro América*. San José, CR: DEI, 1994.

———. *Ethnicity at Work: Divided Labor on a Central American Banana Plantation*. Baltimore, MD: Johns Hopkins University Press, 1989.

Brenes Leiva, Víctor Hugo. *40 años de la muerte de Monseñor Sanabria*. San José, CR: Ediciones CECOR, 1992.

Brenes S., Rosa. "Alejandro Soto: Pastoral confirma nuestra tesis." *La Prensa Libre*, November 23, 1993, 11.

Brett, Edward T. "The Impact of Religion in Central America: A Bibliographical Essay." *The Americas* 49, 3 (January 1993): 297–341.

Briceño, José Alberto. "Calderón rechaza críticas de Arzobispo." *La República*. November 19, 1993, 5A.

Bruneau, Thomas C. *The Church in Brazil: The Politics of Religion*. Austin, TX: University of Texas Press, 1982.

———. *The Political Transformation of the Brazilian Catholic Church*. London: Cambridge University Press, 1974.

Budde, Michael L. *The Two Churches: Catholicism and Capitalism in the World System*. Durham, NC: Duke University Press, 1992.

Burbach, Roger, and Patricia Flynn. "A New 'Banana Republic': Del Monte in Guatemala." In *Revolution in Central America*, ed. the Stanford Central American Action Network. Boulder, CO: Westview Press, 1983.

Burdick, John. "The Progressive Church in Latin America: Giving Voice or Listening to Voices?" *Latin American Research Review* 29, 1 (1994): 184–97.

Caceres, Mario. "Gramsci, la religion et les systèmes socio-économiques." *Social Compass* 35, 2–3 (1988): 279–96.

Calvez, Jean-Yves, and Jacques Perrin. *The Church and Social Justice: The Social Teaching of the Popes from Leo XIII to Pius XII (1878-1958)*. Chicago: Henry Regnery Company, 1961.

Campos, Marielos. "Gobierno intenta frenar huelgas." *Al Día*. July 27, 1993, 4.

Campos, Marielos, and Fernando Lopez G. "Ministros alegan desconocimiento de Arzobispo." *Al Día*. November 24, 1993, 6.

Cardenal, Rodolfo. "The Rise and Fall of Social Catholicism in Costa Rica." In *Church and Politics in Latin America*, ed. Dermot Keogh. London: Macmillan, 1990.

Cartín S., Luis. "Monseñor debe buscar mejor información." *La Prensa Libre*. November 22, 1993, 6.

Cartín, Sandra, and Isabel Román. *Echando raices: La lucha por la tierra en Costa Rica*. San José, CR: CEPAS, 1991.

Castro Calzada, Carlos. "Las comunidades eclesiales de base: ¿Una opción pastoral de la Arquidiocesis de San José?" *Senderos* 52 (January–April 1996): 111–40.

Centro de Estudios para la Acción Social. *Costa Rica en el umbral de los años 90: deterioro y auge de lo social en el marco del ajuste*. San José, CR: CEPAS, 1992.

Centro Nacional de Trabajadores. *Denuncia sindical sobre el solidarismo en Costa Rica*. San José, CR: Asociación Servicios de Promoción Laboral, 1989.

Cerdas Cruz, Rodolfo. "Costa Rica since 1930." Trans. Elizabeth Ladd. In *Central America since Independence*, ed. Leslie Bethell. Cambridge University Press, 1991.

Chacon V., Alfredo. "Socialcristianos critican a Monseñor." *La Prensa Libre*. August 3, 1990, 6.

Chavez, Jorge Arturo. "Los ataques al pastor." *Eco Católico*. March 4, 1990, 15.

———. "Los ataques al pastor, parte 2A: ¿Desconocimiento de la economía?" *Eco Católico*. March 11, 1990, 11.

———. *Magisterio social y pastoral de los trabajadores*. San José, CR: ASEPROLA, Editorial Fundación UNA, and Pastoral Social Diócesis de Limón, 1996.

———. "Los 'pseudo–teologos de La Nación' y el peligro de un 'magisterio paralelo.'" *Eco Católico*. April 5, 1987, 8.

CIOSL, ORIT, CATD, CCTD, and CNT. "Fallo de la OIT favorece al movimiento sindical." Paid advertisement. In *Eco Católico*. June 16, 1991, 13.

Cleary, Edward L. "The Journey to Santo Domingo." In *Santo Domingo and Beyond: Documents and Commentaries from the Fourth General Conference of Latin American Bishops*, ed. Alfred T. Hennelly. Maryknoll, NY: Orbis Books, 1993.

Coleman, John. "Development of Church Social Teaching." In *Official Catholic Social Teaching*. Readings in Moral Theology, no. 5, ed. Charles E. Curran and Richard A. McCormick. New York: Paulist Press, 1986.

Consejo Permanente de los Trabajadores. *A los trabajadores costarricenses, a los trabajadores bananeros, al clero y obispo de Limón, a la Iglesia católica y ciudadania en general*. Archives of Padre Eduardo Ramírez. Photocopy.

Cousineau [Adriance], Madeleine. "Innovation and Retrenchment in the Brazilian Catholic Church: Consequences for Base Communities." *Social Compass* 44, 4 (December 1997): 567-77.

Cox, Harvey. *The Silencing of Leonardo Boff: The Vatican and the Future of World Christianity*. London: Collins, 1989.

"La cuestión de fondo." *La Nación*. March 20, 1987, 14A.

"Curriculum vitae de Mons. Román Arrieta Villalobos, Arzobispo de San José." *Eco Católico*. September 21, 1986, 5.

de Kadt, Emanuel. *Catholic Radicals in Brazil*. London and New York: Oxford University Press.

de la Cruz, Vladimir. "Características y rasgos históricos del movimiento sindical en Costa Rica." In *El sindicalismo frente al cambio: Entre la pasividad y el protagonismo*, ed. Jorge Nowalski. San José, CR: DEI and Fundación Friedrich Ebert, 1997.

de Lora Soria, Cecilio. "History, Structure, and Present Activities of CELAM." In *The Church and Social Change in Latin America*, ed. Henry A. Landsberger. Notre Dame, IN: University of Notre Dame Press, 1970.

Donahue, Thomas R. "From Rerum Novarum to Laborem Exercens: A United States Labor Perspective." In *Official Catholic Social Teaching*. Readings in Moral Theology, no.5, ed. Charles E. Curran and Richard A. McCormick. New York: Paulist Press, 1986.

Donato Monge, Elisa, and Manuel Rojas Bolaños. *Sindicatos, política y economía: 1972-1986*. San José, CR: Editorial Alma Mater, 1987.

Dorr, Donal. *Option for the Poor: A Hundred Years of Vatican Social Teaching*. Maryknoll, NY: Orbis Books, 1983; rev. ed., 1992.

Dunkerley, James. "Costa Rica: Stability at a Price." In *Power in the Isthmus: A Political History of Modern Central America*. London: Verso, 1988.

Edelman, Marc. "Back from the Brink." *NACLA Report on the Americas* 19, 6 (1985): 37-48.

———. *Peasants against Globalization: Rural Social Movements in Costa Rica*. Stanford, CA: Stanford University Press, 1999.

Edelman, Marc, and Jayne Hutchcroft, "Costa Rica: Resisting Austerity." *NACLA Report on the Americas* 18, 1 (1984): 37-40.

Edelman, Marc, and Joanne Kenen. "The 1980s Economic Crisis: Editors' Introduction." In *The Costa Rica Reader*, ed. Marc Edelman and Joanne Kenen. New York: Grove Weidenfeld, 1989.

————. "Costa Rica and the Nicaraguan Revolution: Editors' Introduction." In *The Costa Rica Reader*, ed. Marc Edelman and Joanne Kenen. New York: Grove Weidenfeld, 1989.

————. "The Origins of Costa Rican Exceptionalism—Colonial Period and the Nineteenth Century: Editors' Introduction." In *The Costa Rica Reader*, ed. Marc Edelman and Joanne Kenen. New York: Grove Weidenfeld, 1989.

Engels, Friedrich. "Engels to Bloch. Letter. September 21-22, 1890." In Karl Marx and Friedrich Engels, *On Religion*. 2nd impr. Moscow: Foreign Languages Publishing House, 1964.

"La Escuela Social Juan XXIII ayer y hoy." *Eco Católico (Suplemento Campesino)*, October 12, 1980, 4.

Fallas, Carlos Luis. "The Great Atlantic Banana Plantation Strike of 1934." In *The Costa Rica Reader*, ed. Marc Edelman and Joanne Kenen. New York: Grove Weidenfeld, 1989.

Fernández Castillo, Víctor. "Honrar a nuestros trabajadores con salario justo." *Eco Católico*. May 2, 1993, 17.

————. "Primeros pasos en la nueva diócesis." *Eco Católico*. April 16, 1995, 14.

Fernández González, Alvaro. "Iglesia católica y ajuste estructural: Dilemas y conflictos." *Ciencias Sociales* 61 (September 1993): 87-95.

————. "Iglesia católica y conflicto social en Costa Rica, 1979-1989." *Cristianismo y Sociedad* 103 (1990): 59-86.

————. *Iglesia católica y conflicto social en Costa Rica, 1979-1989: Transformaciones político-ideológicas en una fase de ajuste estructural.* San José, CR: Instituto de Investigaciones Sociales, Universidad de Costa Rica, 1990.

FES, Proyecto CAAS, ASEPROLA, and CPT, ed. *Foro Iglesia-sindicalismo.* n.p., 1990.

Fierro, Alfredo. *The Militant Gospel: A Critical Introduction to Political Theologies.* Trans. John Drury. Maryknoll, NY: Orbis Books, 1977.

"Fijan donación para Escuela Juan XXIII." *La Nación*, 10 January 1987, 2A.

Fleet, Michael, and Brian H. Smith. *The Catholic Church and Democracy in Chile and Peru.* Notre Dame, IN: University of Notre Dame Press, 1997.

Flores Madrigal, Juan José. *El solidarismo desde adentro: Testimonio de Juan José Flores.* San José, CR: ASEPROLA, 1989.

Foro Emaús. *Bananas para el mundo ¿Y el daño para Costa Rica? Los impactos sociales y ambientales de la producción bananera en Costa Rica.* San José, CR: Comité Coordinador de Foro Emaús, 1997.

Fox, Tom. "John Paul Reflection: Liberating the Poor." *National Catholic Reporter.* February 23, 1996, 2.

Freire, Paulo. *Pedagogy of the Oppressed.* Trans. Myra Bergman Ramos. New York: Seabury Press, 1970.

García-Huidobro, Guillermo. *Política económica de ajuste y mercado de trabajo: el caso de Costa Rica, 1982-86.* Santiago, Chile: OIT-PREALC, 1987.

Garnier, Leonardo, Gladys Gonzáles, and Jorge Cornick. "Costa Rica: Las vicisitudes de una política bananera nacional." In *Cambio y continuidad en la economía bananera*, ed. FLASCO and CEDAL. San José, CR: Ediciones FLASCO/CEDAL/FES, 1988.

Giblin, Marie J. "Corporatism." In *The New Dictionary of Catholic Social Thought*, ed. Judith A. Dwyer. Collegeville, MN: Liturgical Press, 1994.

Golden, Tim. "After the Bitter Pill, Costa Rica Improves." In *The Costa Rica Reader*, ed. Marc Edelman and Joanne Kenen. New York: Grove Weidenfeld, 1989.

Goluboay Montoya, Juan Miguel, and Herbert Vega Rodríguez. "La actividad bananera en Costa Rica." In *Cambio y continuidad en la economía bananera*, ed. FLASCO and CEDAL. San José, CR: Ediciones FLASCO/CEDAL/FES, 1988.

Gramsci, Antonio. *Selections from the Prison Notebooks of Antonio Gramsci*. Ed. and trans. Quintin Hoare and Geoffrey Nowell Smith. London: Lawrence and Wishart, 1971.

Gudmundson, Lowell. "Costa Rica before Coffee: The Village Economy of the Late 1840s." In *The Costa Rica Reader*, ed. Marc Edelman and Joanne Kenen. New York: Grove Weidenfeld, 1989.

Guevara, José David. "Arduas negociaciones en Limón." *La Nación*. September 3, 1996, 8A.

———. "Brote de violencia en Limón." *La Nación*. August 16, 1996, 4A.

Guevara, José David, and Marvin Barquero. "Comité declara huelga en Limón." *La Nación*. August 23, 1996, 4A.

———. "Pulso entre gobierno y muelleros." *La Nación*. August 15, 1996, 4A.

Guevara, José David, and Carlos Villalobos. "Paralizan muelles de Limón." *La Nación*. August 14, 1996, 4A.

Gutiérrez, Gustavo. *A Theology of Liberation: History, Politics and Salvation*. Trans. and ed. Sister Caridad Inda and John Eagleson. Maryknoll, NY: Orbis Books, 1973.

Harpelle, Ronald N. "West Indians in Costa Rica: Racism, Class and Ethnicity in the Transformation of a Community." Ph.D. diss. University of Toronto, 1992.

Hebblethwaite, Peter. "The Popes and Politics: Shifting Patterns in Catholic Social Doctrine." In *Official Catholic Social Teaching*. Readings in Moral Theology, no. 5, ed. Charles E. Curran and Richard A. McCormick. New York: Paulist Press, 1986.

Hermosilla Barrientos, Hernán. "Transformación de practicas eclesiales en el Vicariato Apostólico de Limón (1980–1991)." M.Sc. thesis, Ciudad Universitaria "Rodrigo Facio," Costa Rica, 1991.

Hermosilla, Hernán, and Tania Palencia. *Creación de una instancia coordinadora para detener el impacto de la expansión bananera incontrolada: Costa Rica*. San José, CR: Fundación Arias para la Paz y el Progreso Humano, 1997.

Hernández, Gabriela. "Bananeros denuncian arreglos directos con La Standard." *Revista Aportes* 7, 37 (September 1987): 14–15.

Hernández Naranjo, Gerardo. "El discurso del pacto Figueres-Calderón." *Revista de Ciencias Sociales* 72 (June 1996): 29–43.

Hewitt, Marsha. *From Theology to Social Theory: Juan Luis Segundo and the Theology of Liberation*. New York: Peter Lang, 1990.

Hewitt, Warren Edward. *Base Christian Communities and Social Change in Brazil*. Lincoln, NB: University of Nebraska Press, 1991.

———. "Introduction: The Legacy of the Progressive Church in Latin America." In *The Church at the Grassroots in Latin America: Perspectives on Thirty Years of Activism*, ed. John Burdick and Warren Edward Hewitt. Westport, CT: Praeger, 2000.

———. "Liberation Theology as Social Science: Contributions and Limitations." In *Sociological Studies in Roman Catholicism: Historical and Contemporary Perspectives*. ed. Roger O'Toole. Studies in Religion and Society, vol. 24. Lewiston, NY: Edwin Mellen Press, 1989.

Hill, Christopher. *Change and Continuity in Seventeenth-Century England*. London: Weidenfeld and Nicolson, 1974.

Himes, Kenneth R. "War." In *The New Dictionary of Catholic Social Thought*, ed. Judith A. Dwyer. Collegeville, MN: Liturgical Press, 1994.

Hobgood, Mary E. "Conflicting Paradigms in Social Analysis." In *The Logic of Solidarity: Commentaries on Pope John Paul II's Encyclical on Social Concern*, ed. Gregory Baum and Robert Ellsberg. Maryknoll, NY: Orbis Books, 1989.

"Honduras critica 'militarismo' costarricense." *La Nación*. October 7, 1996, 24A.

Hopfensperger, Jean. "Costa Rica's Right-Wing Paramilitary Groups." In *The Costa Rica Reader*, ed. Marc Edelman and Joanne Kenen. New York: Grove Weidenfeld, 1989.

Houtart, François. "L'histoire du CELAM ou l'oubli des origines." *Archives de Sciences Sociales des Religions* 62, 1 (July–September 1986): 93–105.

"Huelga bananera cumple 35 días: Aumento de salarios y jornada de trabajo mantienen en suspenso negociaciones." *Libertad*. January 15–21, 1982, 3.

"Iglesias piden investigar caos en Limón." *La Prensa Libre*. February 9, 1996, 7.

"La infiltración en la Iglesia." *La Nación*. March 15, 1987, 14A.

Itzigsohn, José. *Developing Poverty: The State, Labor Market Deregulation, and the Informal Economy in Costa Rica and the Dominican Republic*. University Park, PA: Pennsylvania State University Press, 2000.

Ireland, Rowan. *Kingdoms Come: Religion and Politics in Brazil*. Pittsburgh, PA: University of Pittsburgh Press, 1991.

Jiménez Céspedes, Jorge Norman. *Plaguicidas y salud en las bananeras de Costa Rica*. San José, CR: ASEPROLA, 1995.

Kent, Lawrence. "The Social Pastoral Work of the Catholic Church in Costa Rica." *Michigan Journal of Political Science* 6 (1985): 8–37.

Korten, Alicia. *Ajuste estructural en Costa Rica: Una medicina amarga*. San José, CR: DEI, 1997.

Leandro, Marco. "Gobierno asegura que ya cumplió con Limón." *El Diario Extra*. February 15, 1997, 2.

Lenin, V.I. "The Attitude of the Workers' Party towards Religion." In *On Socialist Ideology and Culture*. 2nd ed. Moscow: Foreign Languages Publishing House, 1962.

———. "Socialism and Religion." In *On Socialist Ideology and Culture*. 2nd ed. Moscow: Foreign Languages Publishing House, 1962.

Levine, Daniel H. "Colombia: The Institutional Church and the Popular." In *Religion and Political Conflict in Latin America*, ed. Daniel H. Levine. Chapel Hill, NC: University of North Carolina Press, 1986.

———. "Conflict and Renewal." In *Religion and Political Conflict in Latin America*, ed. Daniel H. Levine. Chapel Hill, NC: University of North Carolina Press, 1986.

———. "Continuities in Colombia." *Journal of Latin American Studies* 17, Pt. II (1985): 295–317.

———. *Popular Voices in Latin American Catholicism*. Princeton, NJ: Princeton University Press, 1992.

———. *Religion and Politics in Latin America: The Catholic Church in Venezuela and Colombia*. Princeton, NJ: Princeton University Press, 1981.

———. "Religion, the Poor, and Politics in Latin America Today." In *Religion and Political Conflict in Latin America*, ed. Daniel H. Levine. Chapel Hill, NC: University of North Carolina Press, 1986.

"Líneas pastorales que aplicará Mons. Ulloa Rojas." *Eco Católico*. February 19, 1995, 6.

Maduro, Otto. "Marxist Analysis and the Sociology of Religion: An Introduction." *Social Compass* 22, 3–4 (1975): 305–22.

———. "New Marxist Approaches to the Relative Autonomy of Religion." *Sociological Analysis* 38, 4 (1977): 359–67.

———. *Religion and Social Conflicts*. Trans. Robert R. Barr. Maryknoll, NY: Orbis Books, 1982.

Mainwaring, Scott. *The Catholic Church and Politics in Brazil, 1916–1985*. Stanford, CA: Stanford University Press, 1986.

Mainwaring, Scott, and Alexander Wilde. "The Progressive Church in Latin America: an Interpretation." In *The Progressive Church in Latin America*, ed. Scott Mainwaring and Alexander Wilde. Notre Dame, IN: University of Notre Dame Press, 1989.

Mainwaring, Scott, and Alexander Wilde, ed. *The Progressive Church in Latin America*. Notre Dame, IN: University of Notre Dame Press, 1989.

Mairena, José. "Gigante de ₡ 50 mil millones." *Rumbo*. June 3, 1996, 14–19.

Martínez, Laura. "Solo 22 huelgas legales en los últimos 50 años." *La Nación*. October 15, 1993, 4A.

Marx, Karl. "Contribution to the Critique of Hegel's Philosophy of Right." In Karl Marx and Friedrich Engels, *On Religion*. 2nd impr. Moscow: Foreign Languages Publishing House, 1964.

———. *Theories of Surplus Value*. Vol. 1. Moscow: Progress Publishers, 1963.

Matute, Ronald, and Marvin Barquero. "Sacerdotes de Limón prevén un gran reto." *La Nación*. January 1, 1995, 16A.

May, Roy H. *La tierra no cae del cielo, hay que luchar por ella: La Pastoral de la Tierra en la Diócesis de Limón*. n.p.: ASEPROLA and Pastoral Social, Diócesis de Limón, 1996.

Mayorga, Armando. "Conferencia Episcopal de Costa Rica: Desautorizado folleto de 'iglesia popular.'" *La Nación*. November 30, 1988, 12A.

McCormick, Richard A. "Laborem Exercens and Social Morality." In *Official Catholic Social Teaching*. Readings in Moral Theology, no. 5, ed. Charles E. Curran and Richard A. McCormick. New York: Paulist Press, 1986.

———. "The Teaching Office as a Guarantor of Unity in Morality." In *Christian Ethics: Uniformity, Universality, Pluralism. Concilium* no. 150, ed. Jacques Pohier and Dietmar Mieth. New York: Seabury Press, 1981.

McGovern, Arthur F. *Liberation Theology and Its Critics: Toward an Assessment*. Maryknoll, NY: Orbis Books, 1989.

———. *Marxism: An American Christian Perspective*. Maryknoll, NY: Orbis Books, 1980.

Maclean, Iain S. *Opting for Democracy? Liberation Theology and the Struggle for Democracy in Brazil*. New York: Peter Lang, 1999.

Mecham, J. Lloyd. *Church and State in Latin America: A History of Politico-Ecclesiastical Relations*. Rev. ed. Chapel Hill, NC: University of North Carolina Press, 1966.

Meléndez Chaverri, Carlos. "Land Tenure in Colonial Costa Rica." In *The Costa Rica Reader*, ed. Marc Edelman and Joanne Kenen. New York: Grove Weidenfeld, 1989.

Mendez, William. "Despenalizan participación en huelgas." *La Nación*, June 16, 1993, 6A.

Miller, Eugene D. *A Holy Alliance? The Church and the Left in Costa Rica, 1932–1948*. Armonk, NY: M.E. Sharp, 1996.

Miranda, José Porfirio. *Marx against the Marxists: The Christian Humanism of Karl Marx*. Trans. John Drury. Maryknoll, NY: Orbis Books, 1980.

Minsky Acosta, Larissa. "¿Somos lo que creemos?" *La Nación (Revista Dominical)*. March 17, 1997, 8–12.

Monge, Luis Alberto. "Necesito solidaridad entre los costarricenses." *Betania*. May 9, 1982, 2.

Monge Alfaro, Carlos. "The Development of the Central Valley." In *The Costa Rica Reader*, ed. Marc Edelman and Joanne Kenen. New York: Grove Weidenfeld, 1989.

Montero V., Alvaro. "Apoyo a Mons. Coto." *La Nación*. January 20, 1990, 16A.

Mora R., Arnoldo. "Una carta pastoral histórica." *La Nación*. January 19, 1990, 16A.

———. "Doctrina Social de la Iglesia y lucha de clases." In *La pastoral social en Costa Rica: Documentos y comentarios acerca de la polémica entre la Iglesia católica y el periódico La Nación*, ed. Pablo Richard. San José, CR: DEI, 1987.

———. *Las fuentes del cristianismo social en Costa Rica*. San José, CR: DEI, 1989.

———. "Magisterio eclesiastico, Iglesia de los pobres y teología de liberación." In *La pastoral social en Costa Rica: Documentos y comentarios acerca de la polémica entre la Iglesia católica y el periódico La Nación*, ed. Pablo Richard. San José, CR: DEI, 1987.

Morgan, Lynn M. "Health Effects of the Costa Rican Economic Crisis." In *The Costa Rica Reader*, ed. Marc Edelman and Joanne Kenen. New York: Grove Weidenfeld, 1989.

Nothomb, Jean François. "Does the Papacy Have a Future?" *Cross Currents* 49, 1 (Spring 1999): 96–103.

Nowalski, Jorge. "El sindicalismo: ¿Actor pasivo en el proceso de desarrollo de Costa Rica?" In *El sindicalismo frente al cambio: Entre la pasividad y el protagonismo*, ed. Jorge Nowalski. San José, CR: DEI and Fundación Friedrich Ebert, 1997.

Nuñez B., Juan Gabriel. "La pastoral de Limón." *La Nación*. February 21, 1990, 16A.

"Obispos y sacerdotes preocupa influencia marxista en Iglesia." *La Nación*. March 14, 1987, 6A.

Opazo Bernales, Andrés. *Costa Rica: La Iglesia católica y el orden social*. San José, CR: DEI, 1987.

———. "La fonction de l'Eglise dans la lutte pour l'hégémonie." *Social Compass* 26, 2–3 (1979): 237–60.

Orozco, Angela. "Limón es un infierno." *La República*. August 28, 1996, 4A.

————. "Negociaciones de Limón en punto muerto." *La República*. August 25, 1996, 4A.

————. "Tambores de guerra en Limón." *La República*. February 15, 1997, 5A.

O'Toole, Roger. "Introduction." In *Sociological Studies in Roman Catholicism: Historical and Contemporary Perspectives*, ed. Roger O'Toole. Studies in Religion and Society, Volume 24. Lewiston, Lampeter, Queenston, NY: Edwin Mellen Press, 1989.

————. *Religion: Classic Sociological Approaches*. Toronto, ON: McGraw–Hill Ryerson, 1984.

"Palabras pronunciadas por el Señor Minstro de Trabajo, Licenciado German Serrano Pinto, en la inauguración de las nuevas edificaciones de la Escuela Social Juan XXIII." *Eco Católico (Suplemento Campesino)*. October 26, 1980, 2.

Palma, Diego. "The State and Social Co-optation in Costa Rica." In *The Costa Rica Reader*, ed. Marc Edelman and Joanne Kenen. New York: Grove Weidenfeld, 1989.

Peerman, Dean. "CELAM III: Measured Steps Forward." *The Christian Century* 96, 12 (April 1979): 373–78.

Peterson, Anna L., and Manuel A. Vásquez. "The New Evangelization in Latin American Perspective." *Cross Currents* 48, 3 (Fall 1998): 311–29.

Picado G., Miguel. "La Iglesia Católica costarricense en la crisis centroamericana." *Cristianismo y Sociedad* 89 (1986): 81–89.

————. *La Iglesia costarricense: Entre Dios y el César*. 2nd ed. San José, CR: DEI, 1983.

————. *La Iglesia costarricense entre el pueblo y el estado (de 1949 a nuestros días)*. San José, CR: Ediciones Guayacán, 1989.

"El Plan Reagan: Una trampa moral." *Eco Católico*. March 21, 1982, 2.

"Popularidad que es aceptación." *El Mensajero del Clero* 23 (November 1987): 16.

Proyecto Estado de la Nación. *Estado de la nación en desarrollo humano sostenible: Un análisis amplio y objetivo sobre la Costa Rica que tenemos a partir de los indicadores más actuales*. San José, CR: Impr. Lara Segura, 1996.

"¿Pugna en la Iglesia o pugna de 'La Nación' contra la Iglesia?" In *La pastoral social en Costa Rica: Documentos y comentarios acerca de la polémica entre la Iglesia católica y el periódico La Nación*, ed. Pablo Richard. San José, CR: DEI, 1987.

Ramírez, Eduardo. "El Vicariato dio forma a su experiencia pastoral con un plan global de acción, III parte." *Eco Católico*. April 2, 1989, 11.

Revista Aportes. "Electricity Rates: From Discontent to Organized Resistance." In *The Costa Rica Reader*, ed. Marc Edelman and Joanne Kenen. New York: Grove Weidenfeld, 1989.

Richard, Pablo. "The Latin American Church: 1959–1978." *Cross Currents* 28, 1 (Spring 1978): 34–46.

————. "Puebla: Hope of the Poor." Trans. Robert Lazear. *Missiology: An International Review* 7, 3 (July 1979): 287–93.

Richard, Pablo, ed. *La pastoral social en Costa Rica: Documentos y comentarios acerca de la polémica entre la Iglesia católica y el periódico La Nación*. San José, CR: DEI, 1987.

Richard, Pablo, and Guillermo Meléndez. "La Iglesia de los pobres in Costa Rica." In *La Iglesia de los pobres en América Central: Un análisis socio-político y teológico de la Iglesia centroamericana (1960–1982)*, ed. Pablo Richard and Guillermo Meléndez. San José, CR: DEI, 1982.

Rivera Chang, Sileny. "'Limón en Lucha'... interna." *Al Día*. August 20, 1996, 4.

Robles Monge, Javier, and Héctor Fallas. "Las sectas: Esas grandes desconocidas (I parte)." *Eco Católico*. May 8, 1988, 8.

Robles Robles, J. Amando. "Movimientos eclesiales de la Iglesia católica en Costa Rica." *El Mensajero del Clero*, extr. iss. (September 1983).

Rodríguez, José Miguel. "Política y religión: La función política de la Iglesia Católica en Costa Rica." *Revista de Ciencias Sociales* 13 (April 1977): 77–101.

Rodríguez, Julio. "La cuestión de fondo." *La Nación*. March 20, 1987, 14A.

———. "Los mercaderes." *La Nación*. March 17, 1987, 15A.

Rojas Bolaños, Manuel. *Los años ochenta y el futuro incierto*. Nuestra Historia Series, no. 20. San José, CR: EUNED, 1992.

———. *Luchas sociales y guerra civil en Costa Rica, 1940–1948*. 4th ed. San José, CR: Editorial Porvenir, 1989.

———. "El movimiento obrero y popular en los años setenta." *Anuario de Estudios Centroamericanos* 6 (1980): 75–81.

Romero, Efrén. "¿Cómo nació la carta pastoral?" In *Foro Iglesia-sindicalismo*, ed. FES, Proyecto CAAS, ASEPROLA, and CPT. n.p., 1990.

Saborío, Aixa. "Folleto ocasiona pugna en Iglesia." *La Nación*. March 13, 1987, 6A.

Salazar Mora, Jorge Mario. *La Iglesia rebelde en América Latina: El caso de Costa Rica*. San José, CR: Universidad de Costa Rica, 1978.

Sanabria Martínez, Víctor. *Anselmo Llorente y Lafuente, primer obispo de Costa Rica: Apuntamientos históricos*. San José, CR: Editorial Costa Rica, 1972.

———. *Bernardo Augusto Thiel, segundo obispo de Costa Rica: Apuntamientos históricos y primeros*. San José, CR: Editorial Costa Rica, 1982.

———. *La primera vacante de la diócesis de San José, 1871–1880*. San José, CR: Editorial Costa Rica, 1973.

———. *Reseña histórica de la Iglesia en Costa Rica desde 1502 hasta 1850*. San José, CR: DEI, 1984.

Sawchuk, Dana. "The Catholic Church in the Nicaraguan Revolution: A Gramscian Analysis." *Sociology of Religion* 58, 1 (Spring 1997): 39–51.

Schubeck, Thomas L. *Liberation Ethics: Sources, Models, and Norms*. Minneapolis, MN: Fortress Press, 1993.

Schuck, Michael. *That They Be One: The Social Teaching of the Papal Encyclicals, 1740–1989*. Washington, DC: Georgetown University Press, 1991.

Segundo, Juan Luis. *The Liberation of Theology*. Trans. John Drury. Maryknoll, NY: Orbis Books, 1976.

———. *Theology and the Church: A Response to Cardinal Ratzinger and a Warning to the Whole Church*. Revised edition. Trans. John W. Diercksmeier. San Francisco: Harper and Row, 1987.

Seligson, Mitchell A. "Agrarian Reform in Costa Rica." In *The Costa Rica Reader*, ed. Marc Edelman and Joanne Kenen. New York: Grove Weidenfeld, 1989.

Sibaja, José Enrique. "Acción inmediata de la Iglesia. "*Eco Católico*. March 3, 1996, 19.

———. "Iglesias limonenses: Defienden derechos de muelleros." *Eco Católico*. May 8, 1988, 8.

Smith, Brian H. *The Church and Politics in Chile: Challenges to Modern Catholicism*. Princeton, NJ: Princeton University Press, 1982.

Smith, David, and Rolando Rivera. "Organización, movilización popular y desarrollo regional." *Revista de Ciencias Sociales* 37–38 (1987): 43–59.

Sobrino, Jon. "Bearing with One Another in Faith." In *Theology of Christian Solidarity*, Trans. Phillip Berryman. Maryknoll, NY: Orbis Books, 1985.

"Solidarismo, orgullo nacional." *El Diario Extra*. January 22, 1990, 14–15.

Solís, Javier. *La herencia de Sanabria: Análisis político de la Iglesia costarricense*. San José, CR: DEI, 1983.

Starcevic, Dino. "Arzobispo condena a Ministro." *La República*. August 6, 1990, 2A.

Steigenga, Timothy J. *The Politics of the Spirit: The Political Implications of Pentecostalized Religion in Costa Rica and Guatemala*. Lanham, MD: Lexington Books, 2001.

Stone, Samuel Z. "Aspects of Power Distribution in Costa Rica." In *The Costa Rica Reader*, ed. Marc Edelman and Joanne Kenen. New York: Grove Weidenfeld, 1989.

Torres, Carlos Alberto. *The Church, Society, and Hegemony: A Critical Sociology of Religion in Latin America*. Trans. Richard A. Young. Westport, CT: Praeger, 1992.

Torres, Sergio. *Puebla 1979: The III Conference of the Latin American Bishops*. Theology in the Americas Documentation Series, no. 7. New York: Theology in the Americas, 1979.

Trejos S., Juan Diego. *Costa Rica: Economic Crisis and Public Policy, 1978–1984*. Latin American and Caribbean Center. Occasional Paper Series, no. 11. Miami: Florida International University, 1985.

Turner, Frederick C. *Catholicism and Political Development in Latin America*. Chapel Hill, NC: University of North Carolina Press, 1971.

Tyson, Brady. "Brazil: End of an Era?" *Christianity and Crisis*. June 12, 1989, 193–94.

Valencia Navarro, Gilberto. "Iglesias censuran trato a muelleros." *El Heraldo*. February 20, 1996, 4.

Vallier, Ivan. *Catholicism, Social Control, and Modernization in Latin America*. Englewood Cliffs, NJ: Prentice-Hall, 1970.

———. "Extraction, Insulation, and Re-Entry: Toward a Theory of Religious Change." In *The Church and Social Change in Latin America*, ed. Henry A. Landsberger. Notre Dame, IN: University of Notre Dame Press, 1970.

Valverde R., José Manuel. *Proceso de privatización en Costa Rica...¿Y la respuesta sindical?* 2nd ed. San José, CR: ASEPROLA, 1994.

Valverde Rojas, Jaime. "Efectos sociales e ideologicos de las sectas de origen Protestante en Costa Rica." In *Protestantismo y procesos sociales en Centroamérica*, ed. Luis E. Samandú. San José, CR: Editorial Universitaria Centroamericana, 1990.

———. *Pragmatismo de los trabajadores y coexistencia solidarismo-sindicalismo en el sector público de Costa Rica*. San José, CR: Fundación Ebert, 1993.

———. *Las sectas en Costa Rica: Pentecostalismo y conflicto social*. San José, CR: DEI, 1990.

Vargas Varela, Gerardo. "Limón con segundo plan pastoral." *Eco Católico*. December 15, 1996, 19.

Vásquez, Manuel A. *The Brazilian Popular Church and the Crisis of Modernity*. Cambridge Studies in Ideology and Religion. Cambridge, UK: Cambridge University Press, 1998.

Vega, Mylena. "CODESA, Autonomous Institutions, and the Growth of the Public Sector." In *The Costa Rica Reader*, ed. Marc Edelman and Joanne Kenen. New York: Grove Weidenfeld, 1989.

Vega, Víctor. "La ideología solidarista." In *El problema solidarista y la respuesta sindical en Centroamérica*, ed. CEDAL and ASEPROLA. Heredia, CR: CEDAL, 1989.

"El Vicariato Apostólico de Limón: Un camino particular, II parte." *Eco Católico*. March 12, 1989, 7.

Villasuso Etomba, Juan Manuel. "The Impact of the Economic Crisis on Income Distribution." In *The Costa Rica Reader*, ed. Marc Edelman and Joanne Kenen. New York: Grove Weidenfeld, 1989.

Villela, Hugo. "The Church and the Process of Democratization in Latin America." *Social Compass* 26, 2–3 (1979): 261–83.

Williams, Philip J. *The Catholic Church and Politics in Nicaragua and Costa Rica*. London: Macmillan, in association with St. Anthony's College, Oxford, 1989.

Wilson, Bruce M. "Leftist Parties, Neoliberal Policies, and Re-election Strategies: The Case of the PLN in Costa Rica." *Comparative Political Studies* 32 (September 1999): 752–79.

Winson, Anthony. *Coffee and Democracy in Modern Costa Rica*. Toronto, ON: Between the Lines, 1989.

Winsor, Curtin, Jr. "The Solidarista Movement: Labor Economics for Democracy." *Washington Quarterly* 9, 4 (Fall 1986): 177–88.

Wirpsa, Leslie. "Vatican Clampdown on CLAR Continues." *National Catholic Reporter*. May 24, 1991, 9.

Wojtyla, Karol. "The Self and the Act." In *Karol Wojtyla (Pope John Paul II): An Anthology*, ed. Alfred Bloch and George T. Czuczka. New York: Crossroad, 1981.

Zeitlin, Irving M. *Ideology and the Development of Sociological Theory*, 3rd ed. Englewood Cliffs, NJ: Prentice-Hall, 1987.

Costa Rican Newspapers

Al Día (San José)
El Diario Extra (San José)
Eco Católico (San José)
El Heraldo (San José)
Libertad (San José)
La Nación (San José)
La Prensa Libre (San José)
La República (San José)

Index

Series Published by Wilfrid Laurier University Press for the Canadian Corporation for Studies in Religion / Corporation Canadienne des Sciences Religieuses

Series numbers not mentioned are out of print.

10 *Parables of War: Reading John's Jewish Apocalypse*
    by John W. Marshall / 2001 / viii + 262 pp.
11 *Mishnah and the Social Formation of the Early Rabbinic Guild:
    A Socio-Rhetorical Approach*
    by Jack N. Lightstone / 2002 / xii + 240 pp.
12 *The Social Setting of the Ministry as Reflected in the Writings of Hermas,
    Clement and Ignatius*
    Harry O. Maier / 1991, second impression 2002 / x + 234 pp.
13 *Playing a Jewish Game: Gentile Christian Judaizing in the First and
    Second Centuries CE*
    Michele Murray / 2004 / xii + 228 pp.

The Study of Religion in Canada /
Series
no. # Sciences Religieuses au Canada

1 *Religious Studies in Alberta: A State-of-the-Art Review*
   Ronald W. Neufeldt / 1983 / xiv + 145 pp.
2 *Les sciences religieuses au Québec depuis 1972*
   Louis Rousseau et Michel Despland / 1988 / 158 p.
3 *Religious Studies in Ontario: A State-of-the-Art Review*
   Harold Remus, William Closson James and Daniel Fraikin / 1992 / xviii + 422 pp.
4 *Religious Studies in Manitoba and Saskatchewan: A State-of-the-Art Review*
   John M. Badertscher, Gordon Harland and Roland E. Miller / 1993 / vi + 166 pp.
5 *The Study of Religion in British Columbia: A State-of-the-Art Review*
   Brian J. Fraser / 1995 / x + 127 pp.
6 *Religious Studies in Atlantic Canada: A State-of-the-Art Review*
   Paul W. R. Bowlby with Tom Faulkner / 2001 / xii + 208 pp.

Studies in Women and Religion /
Series
no. # Études sur les femmes et la religion

1 *Femmes et religions**
   Sous la direction de Denise Veillette / 1995 / xviii + 466 p.
2 *The Work of Their Hands: Mennonite Women's Societies in Canada*
   Gloria Neufeld Redekop / 1996 / xvi + 172 pp.
3 *Profiles of Anabaptist Women: Sixteenth-Century Reforming Pioneers*
   Edited by C. Arnold Snyder and Linda A. Huebert Hecht / 1996 / xxii + 438 pp.
4 *Voices and Echoes: Canadian Women's Spirituality*
   Edited by Jo-Anne Elder and Colin O'Connell / 1997 / xxviii + 237 pp.
5 *Obedience, Suspicion and the Gospel of Mark: A Mennonite-Feminist
   Exploration of Biblical Authority*
   Lydia Neufeld Harder / 1998 / xiv + 168 pp.
6 *Clothed in Integrity: Weaving Just Cultural Relations and the Garment Industry*
   Barbara Paleczny / 2000 / xxxiv + 352 pp.
7 *Women in God's Army: Gender and Equality in the Early Salvation Army*
   Andrew Mark Eason / 2003 / xiv + 246 pp.
8 *Pour libérer la théologie.* Variations autour de la pensée féministe d'Ivone
   Gebara Pierrette Daviau, dir. / 2002 / 212 pp.
9 *Linking Sexuality & Gender: Naming Violence against Women in The United
   Church of Canada*
   Tracy J. Trothen / 2003 / x + 166 pp.

*Only available from Les Presses de l'Université Laval

^{Series}
_{no.} **SR Supplements**

9 *Developments in Buddhist Thought: Canadian Contributions to Buddhist Studies*
 Edited by Roy C. Amore / 1979 / iv + 196 pp.

11 *Political Theology in the Canadian Context*
 Edited by Benjamin G. Smillie / 1982 / xii + 260 pp.

14 *The Moral Mystic*
 James R. Horne / 1983 / x + 134 pp.

16 *Studies in the Book of Job*
 Edited by Walter E. Aufrecht / 1985 / xii + 76 pp.

17 *Christ and Modernity: Christian Self-Understanding in a Technological Age*
 David J. Hawkin / 1985 / x + 181 pp.

19 *Modernity and Religion*
 Edited by William Nicholls / 1987 / vi + 191 pp.

Series discontinued

Available from:

Wilfrid Laurier University Press

Waterloo, Ontario, Canada N2L 3C5

Telephone: (519) 884-0710, ext. 6124

Fax: (519) 725-1399

E-mail: press@wlu.ca

World Wide Web: http://www.wlupress.wlu.ca